Biography Today

Profiles of People of Interest to Young Readers

Volume 20—2011
Annual Cumulation

Cherie D. Abbey
Managing Editor

Omnigraphics

155 West Congress
Suite 200
Detroit, MI 48226

Cherie D. Abbey, *Managing Editor*

Peggy Daniels Becker, Laurie DiMauro, Joan Goldsworthy, Jeff Hill,
Kevin Hillstrom, Laurie Collier Hillstrom, Justin Karr, Leslie Karr,
Meredith Mayberry, and Diane Telgen, *Sketch Writers*

Allison A. Beckett and Mary Butler, *Research Staff*

* * *

Peter E. Ruffner, *Publisher*
Matthew P. Barbour, *Senior Vice President*

* * *

Elizabeth Collins, *Research and Permissions Coordinator*
Kevin M. Hayes, *Operations Manager*
Cherry Edwards, *Permissions Assistant*

Shirley Amore, Joseph Harris, Martha Johns, and Kirk Kauffmann, *Administrative Staff*

Special thanks to Frederick G. Ruffner for creating this series.

ISSN 1058-2347 • ISBN 978-0-7808-1182-9

Library of Congress Cataloging-in-Publication Data

∞

This book is printed on acid-free paper meeting the ANSI Z39.48 Standard. The infinity symbol that appears above indicates that the paper in this book meets that standard.

Printed in the United States

Contents

Preface

Biography Today is a magazine designed and written for the young reader—ages 9 and above—and covers individuals that librarians and teachers tell us that young people want to know about most: entertainers, athletes, writers, illustrators, cartoonists, and political leaders.

The Plan of the Work

The publication was especially created to appeal to young readers in a format they can enjoy reading and readily understand. Each issue contains approximately 10 sketches arranged alphabetically. Each entry provides at least one picture of the individual profiled, and bold-faced rubrics lead the reader to information on birth, youth, early memories, education, first jobs, marriage and family, career highlights, memorable experiences, hobbies, and honors and awards. Each of the entries ends with a list of easily accessible sources designed to lead the student to further reading on the individual and a current address. Retrospective entries are also included, written to provide a perspective on the individual's entire career.

Biographies are prepared by Omnigraphics editors after extensive research, utilizing the most current materials available. Those sources that are generally available to students appear in the list of further reading at the end of the sketch.

Indexes

Cumulative indexes are an important component of *Biography Today*. Each issue of the *Biography Today* General Series includes a Cumulative Names Index, which comprises all individuals profiled in *Biography Today* since the series began in 1992. In addition, we compile three other indexes: the Cumulative General Index, Places of Birth Index, and Birthday Index. See our web site, www.biographytoday.com, for these three indexes, along with the Names Index. All *Biography Today* indexes are cumulative, including all individuals profiled in both the General Series and the Subject Series.

Our Advisors

This series was reviewed by an Advisory Board comprising librarians, children's literature specialists, and reading instructors to ensure that the concept of this publication—to provide a readable and accessible biographical magazine for young readers—was on target. They evaluated the title as it developed, and their suggestions have proved invaluable. Any errors, however, are ours alone. We'd like to list the Advisory Board members, and to thank them for their efforts.

Gail Beaver
Adjunct Lecturer
University of Michigan
Ann Arbor, MI

Cindy Cares
Youth Services Librarian
Southfield Public Library
Southfield, MI

Carol A. Doll
School of Information Science and Policy
University of Albany, SUNY
Albany, NY

Kathleen Hayes-Parvin
Language Arts Teacher
Birney Middle School
Southfield, MI

Karen Imarisio
Assistant Head of Adult Services
Bloomfield Twp. Public Library
Bloomfield Hills, MI

Rosemary Orlando
Director
St. Clair Shores Public Library
St. Clair Shores, MI

Our Advisory Board stressed to us that we should not shy away from controversial or unconventional people in our profiles, and we have tried to follow their advice. The Advisory Board also mentioned that the sketches might be useful in reluctant reader and adult literacy programs, and we would value any comments librarians might have about the suitability of our magazine for those purposes.

Your Comments Are Welcome

Our goal is to be accurate and up to date, to give young readers information they can learn from and enjoy. Now we want to know what you think. Take a look at this issue of *Biography Today*, on approval. Contact me with your comments. We want to provide an excellent source of biographical information for young people. Let us know how you think we're doing.

Cherie Abbey
Managing Editor, *Biography Today*
Omnigraphics, Inc.
155 West Congress
Suite 200
Detroit, MI 48226
www.omnigraphics.com
editorial@omnigraphics.com

Congratulations!

Congratulations to the following individuals and libraries who are receiving a free copy of *Biography Today* for suggesting people who appear in this volume.

Carol Arnold, Hoopeston Public Library, Hoopeston, IL

Lynn Baroun, Reedsville Public Library, Cato, WI

Annie Curtis and Sharon Thackston, Gallatin Public Library, Gallatin, TN

Sean Fallon, West Avenue School, Bridgeton, NJ

Amie Flora, Knox Middle School, Knox, TN

Kathleen Grober, Liverpool Middle School, Liverpool. NY

Jasmine Johnson, Longfellow School, Wheaton, IL

Randalle Lewis, Coram, NY

Darius Maclin, Romulus, NY

Mikayla

Mimy Poon, San Lorenzo, CA

Jessica Sanchez, William R. Peck Middle School, Holyoke, MA

Owen V., McKenna Elementary School, Massapequa, NY

Matthew White, Park Falls Public Library, Park Falls, WI

Usain Bolt 1986-

Jamaican Track Sprinter

Winner of Three Gold Medals at the 2008 Olympic Games

World Record Holder in the 100 Meters and 200 Meters

BIRTH

Usain St. Leo Bolt was born on August 21, 1986, in Trelawny Parish, a rural area located on the north coast of the Caribbean island nation of Jamaica. His father, Wellesley Bolt, runs a small, local grocery store. His mother, Jennifer Bolt, is a dress-maker. Usain has one brother and one sister. Jennifer Bolt chose her son's unusual first name during her pregnancy, when a little boy approached her on the street and suggested it. "I loved the name, so I called him Usain," she recalled. "I've never met anyone else by that name."

YOUTH

Usain grew up in the small village of Sherwood Content in Trelawny Parish. The village was surrounded by farms that grew yams, sugar cane, coffee beans, and bananas. The Bolt family lived in a pink bungalow with a big front porch. Since the house had no running water, Usain's father made him carry buckets of water for the family to use. "Those were my weights," he explained. "In the country, you always find something to do. Go through the bushes, ride your bicycle, go walking. So you work your muscles when you're young."

Usain was an active boy who spent much of his spare time playing sports. "When I was young, I didn't really think about anything other than sports," he remembered. He especially loved cricket, a British game that is similar to baseball. Like many other Jamaican children, however, Usain also competed in running races. Jamaica is a relatively small country, with a population of 2.8 million, about the same as the city of Chicago. Despite its small size, Jamaica has produced numerous world-class runners over the years. Track and field is a national obsession in Jamaica, and people there honor sprint champions the way Americans honor football or basketball stars. Many Jamaican children dream of running in the Olympics someday. "People see this as a way out of tough challenges and living conditions," said Grace Jackson, a Jamaican track official and Olympic sprint medalist.

EDUCATION

Bolt received his early education at Waldensia Primary and All-Age School. While there, he often ran in races against his classmates. They competed on a grass track, and the lines marking the lanes were burned into the turf. Most of the children ran without shoes. "When you're growing up, you can't afford spikes," Bolt explained. "I got my first pair of spikes when I was 13." Despite the difficult conditions, it became clear early on that Bolt was exceptionally fast. As his physical education teacher Dwight Barnett remembered, "Sometimes I'd look at that stopwatch and think, 'There's something wrong with this watch. No kid can run that quickly.'"

When Bolt moved on to attend William Knibb Memorial High School, his cricket coach noticed his speed and urged him to try track and field. At first Bolt had trouble deciding which events to enter, because he was good at all of them. He eventually settled on the sprint distances of 200 meters (halfway around a standard track) and 400 meters (one lap around a standard track). In 2001 Bolt competed in the Jamaican High School Championships, a prestigious event held annually since 1910 that attracts 30,000 spectators. He won a silver medal in the 200 meters with a time of 22.04 seconds.

During his high school years, Bolt also competed in international track and field meets at the junior level. In July 2002 the World Junior Championships were held in Kingston, Jamaica's capital city. Boosted by the home crowd, the 15-year-old Bolt won the 200 meters in a personal-best time of 20.61 seconds. He thus became the youngest person ever to win a gold medal in the World Junior Championships. The following year he earned another gold medal at the International Association of Athletics Federations (IAAF) World Youth Championships, winning the 200 meters in a time of 20.40 seconds. In honor of his impressive performances, the IAAF presented him with its Rising Star Award for both 2002 and 2003.

> *When Bolt was young, his house had no running water, so he had to carry buckets of water for the family to use. "Those were my weights," he explained. "In the country, you always find something to do. Go through the bushes, ride your bicycle, go walking. So you work your muscles when you're young."*

By the time he competed in his final high school championship meet in 2003, Bolt had established himself as one of the best young runners in the world. He set new Jamaican high school records in both the 200 meters (with a time of 20.25 seconds) and the 400 meters (with a time of 45.30 seconds). His performances earned him the nickname "Lightning" Bolt. Upon graduating that year, Bolt received a number of athletic scholarship offers from American colleges. Many other top Jamaican runners had left home to take advantage of opportunities to study and train abroad. But Bolt decided to remain in Jamaica. He accepted an offer from the government to train with the Jamaican Amateur Athletic Association (JAAA) at the University of Technology in Kingston.

CAREER HIGHLIGHTS

Turning Pro

In 2004, at the age of 17, Bolt decided to turn professional. His decision meant that he could earn appearance fees, prize money, and endorsements

Bolt reacts after winning the 200 meters at the 2002 World Junior Championships in front of a hometown crowd in Jamaica.

as a track and field athlete. A short time later Bolt competed in the Caribbean Regional Championships (CARIFTA Games) in Bermuda. When he won the 200 meters in a time of 19.93 seconds, he became the first athlete under the age of 20 to break the 20-second barrier. He also earned an opportunity to represent Jamaica at the 2004 Olympic Games in Athens, Greece. Bolt struggled with injuries in the weeks leading up to the Games, however, and was eliminated during the first-round qualifying heats for the 200 meters with a disappointing time of 21.05 seconds.

Around this time, Bolt began to gain a reputation as an athlete with tremendous potential who did not take his training or preparation very seriously. "I was really lazy," he admitted. "I was coming out of high school doing absolutely nothing." Once Bolt arrived in Kingston, he became distracted by city life and lost his focus on running. He ate lots of fast food, played countless games of street basketball, and stayed out late at dance clubs. After a while, though, Bolt realized that he could not expect to reach the top of the track world with natural ability alone. "You grow up and see the bigger picture," he explained. "It takes a lot of hard work and dedication. I decided it was time to change."

In 2005 Bolt began working with a new coach, Glen Mills, who demanded self-discipline and hard work. As Bolt improved his attitude, work ethic, and technique, his times improved as well. He hoped to make a strong showing at the 2005 World Championships in Helsinki, Finland. "I really want to make up for what happened in Athens," he said. "Hopefully, everything will fall into place." Unfortunately, Bolt pulled up with an injury during the final of the 200 meters and finished last.

Changing Focus

Bolt continued to struggle with injuries during the 2006 season. Although he managed to set a new personal-best time of 19.88 seconds in the 200 meters at a meet in Switzerland, he was not pleased with his overall results. Mills and other Jamaican coaches tried to convince him to switch to longer races, like the 400 meters. They felt that his height—at six feet, five inches—made him better suited to longer distances. Most world-class sprinters are shorter and more compact than Bolt. Men with this build do not take as long to straighten up, so they can explode out of the blocks more quickly than taller men. They can also churn their legs with greater frequency (known as the turnover rate) because it requires less work to lift shorter limbs. These physical advantages are neutralized over longer distances by the greater stride length of taller athletes.

Bolt understood the physics of running, but he still disagreed with his coaches. "He didn't have any interest in doing the work for the 400," Mills acknowledged. Instead of moving up from the 200 meters to compete at longer distances, Bolt wanted to challenge himself by racing track and field's shortest sprint race—the 100 meters. The 100 meters is considered the purest test of raw speed in running. The world record holder in the 100 meters is widely hailed as "the fastest man in the world." Bolt was determined to put his speed to the ultimate test, and he worked hard to convince his coaches to let him try the 100 meters. He lifted weights to increase his strength and explosiveness, and his times improved as a result. "He got bigger and stronger. He trained more diligently in practice," Mills noted. "When he began running, the times were no surprise."

Impressed with Bolt's new focus, Mills offered the young runner a deal at the start of the 2007 season. If Bolt beat the Jamaican national record of 19.86 seconds in the 200 meters—a mark set by Don Quarrie that had stood for 36 years—Mills would allow him to try the 100 meters in competition. Bolt immediately went out and ran a 19.75 in the Jamaican Championships. In July 2007 the coach made good on his end of the bargain by entering Bolt in his first professional 100 meter race at a meet in Crete. Bolt responded with an astonishing time of 10.03 seconds, less than two-tenths of a second slower than the fastest 100 meters ever run up to that time.

Setting World Records

Bolt did not compete in the 100 meters at the 2007 World Championships in Osaka, Japan. He still made a strong showing, though, earning silver medals in both the 200 meters and the 4x100 meter relay. During the off-season, he went home to Jamaica and spent the winter training specifically for the 100 meters. Taking notice of his enthusiasm, his coach finally gave up trying to convince him to run the 400 meters. "We've had our differences and we've had our ups and downs," said Mills. "But I can say for him he never lost sight of what the big picture is."

Bolt's training paid off in the spring of 2008, when he joined the ranks of the world's top 100-meter sprinters. On May 3, at the Jamaica Invitational in Kingston, he turned in an amazing time of 9.76 seconds. The mark was only two-hundredths of a second behind the world record of 9.74 seconds set by fellow Jamaican sprinter Asafa Powell the previous year. Afterward, when Bolt was asked whether he thought he might eventually beat Powell's record, he replied, "I am not worried about that right now. I really don't know how fast I can run the 100."

As it turned out, Bolt set a new world record less than a month later. He ran the 100 meters in a blistering 9.72 seconds on May 31 at the Reebok

In his fifth time competing in the 100 meters,
Bolt completed the event in a blistering 9.72 at the 2008 Reebok Grand Prix,
earning the coveted title "world's fastest man."

Grand Prix in New York City. He thus earned the coveted title of "world's fastest man" in only his fifth time competing in a 100-meter final. American sprinter Tyson Gay, who finished second in 9.85 seconds, noted that "We were on the same rhythm. But his stride pattern is a whole lot bigger than mine.... It looked like his knees were going past my face." Although Bolt was pleased to achieve his first world record, he chose to focus on the upcoming 2008 Olympic Games in Beijing, China. "I'm just happy right now, but I'm not overexcited," he declared. "The gold medal is more important to me. Somebody's got to wait four years to beat you. Someone can take the world record from you any time."

Winning Gold Medals

The Olympic track and field events got underway in August 2008. First up for Bolt was the 100 meters. He sailed through the two qualifying heats with times of 9.92 and 9.85 seconds to reach the final. As Bolt entered the Beijing stadium known as the Bird's Nest for the final heat on August 16, he appeared relaxed and confident. During warm-ups, he delighted the 91,000 fans in the stadium—and millions more watching on television—with a series of comical gestures. He danced around, pointed to the word "Jamaica" on his jersey, and fired imaginary pistols into the air.

The outcome of the race became clear almost as soon as Bolt and his competitors left the starting blocks. Bolt took the lead within the first 30 meters and extended it with each of his long strides. He won the gold medal so easily that he began celebrating before he even reached the finish line, spreading his arms wide and then pounding on his chest. Even though he did not push himself all the way to the finish, Bolt still broke his own world record with an incredible time of 9.69 seconds.

Bolt continued celebrating his gold medal performance with an exuberant victory lap. He high-fived the crowd, waved a Jamaican flag, showed off his dance moves, and adopted a pose that became known as "To the World" (one arm pointing upward and the other cocked behind him as if he were firing an arrow into the sky). Afterward, some critics complained that Bolt's victory celebration was excessive. Four-time Olympic medalist and TV analyst Ato Bolton described it as "Good TV, bad sportsmanship. A little bit too much of 'You can't run with me.'" Jacques Rogge, president of the International Olympic Committee, said that Bolt "should show more respect for his competitors." But many other people appreciated his expression of joy and felt that his behavior was appropriate under the circumstances. "I talked to other athletes and they're OK with it," he stated. "I'm just enjoying myself. I'm just showing the fans my personality. I try to enjoy myself at all times."

At the 2008 Olympics, Bolt celebrates winning the gold medal in the 200 meters—and breaking the world record.

A few days later Bolt competed in the final of the 200 meters. He was a heavy favorite to win the gold medal, but most observers felt that the world record in the event—19.32 seconds, set by American Michael Johnson at the 1996 Olympic Games—was out of reach. Once again, Bolt sprinted out to an early lead in the race. This time, though, he pushed himself all the way to the end and even leaned across the finish line for the gold medal. His extra effort enabled him to break Johnson's record with a remarkable time of 19.30 seconds."I saw that I could get the record in the 200 meters. I told myself I was going to leave everything on the track, and I did just that," he explained. "I blew my mind and blew the world's mind."Bolt became the first person to break world records in both the 100 meters and 200 meters at the same Olympics, and the first person to hold both records at the same time since the introduction of electronic timing to international track meets in 1977. As Bolt took his victory lap, the loudspeakers played "Happy Birthday" in honor of the fact that he would turn 22 the following day.

With two hard-earned gold medals to his credit, Bolt felt ready to sit back and relax."I just want to chill out. I just want to sleep," he said."I wish I was in sandals right now, just taking a weekend off and then go to a club or something." But he knew that he had to represent Jamaica in one more race, the 4x100 relay."I know the guys are looking forward to it," he said of teammates Nesta Carter, Michael Frater, and Asafa Powell. "So I'm just really trying to refocus again to get one more gold medal."The Jamaican men not only claimed the gold medal in the race, but also set yet another world record with a time of 37.10 seconds. In recognition of his Olympic successes, Bolt received Athlete of the Year awards from the IAAF and the International Sports Press Association.

Going Even Faster

When Bolt returned to Jamaica with his three gold medals, he was greeted as a national hero. As part of a whirlwind of parades, public appearances, interviews, and photo shoots, the prime minister of Jamaica presented him with the nation's highest honor, the Order of Distinction. Bolt also signed lucrative endorsement contracts with Puma and Gatorade, and he made arrangements with HarperCollins to publish his autobiography. But he promised that he would not allow his newfound fame to distract him. "It may change my life, but I won't change," he stated. "I'll still train hard and work hard to stay on top."

Bolt's hard work paid off during the 2009 season. At the IAAF World Championships in Berlin, Germany, he broke his own world record in the 100 meters with a time of 9.58 seconds—an amazing .11 seconds faster than he had run in Beijing the year before. Some analysts noted that he might have posted a similar time at the Olympics if he had not celebrated before reaching the finish line. A few days later he struck again, breaking his own world record in the 200 meters with a time of 19.19 seconds. This time also marked an improvement of .11 seconds over Beijing, but it was even more impressive because Bolt had expended maximum effort during the Olympic 200 meters. Once again, he rounded out the meet by helping the Jamaican team claim a gold medal in the 4x100 relay, although their time of 37.31 seconds fell short of the world record.

As the 2010 season got underway, Bolt struggled with injuries to his back and Achilles tendon that forced him to withdraw from a few early meets. Upon returning to action in Sweden in August, he suffered a shocking defeat in the 100 meters at the hands of Tyson Gay. Afterward, Bolt announced plans to take the rest of the season off to recuperate. By early 2011, he claimed that he had recovered from his injuries and was training again. His performance at the 2011 world championships in Daegu, South Korea, bolstered that claim. He opened with a false start in the 100-meter finals and was disqualified, but he soon came back. In the 200, he clocked in at 19.4 and won the gold. In his closing race, Bolt anchored Jamaica's team in the 4x100 meter relay, winning gold with a world record time of 37.04 seconds. He followed that up with another win at the Van Damme Memorial in Brussels, Belgium, where he posted the season's fastest time in the 100 meters at 9.76 seconds. But his run was upstaged by fellow Jamaican Yohan Blake, who ran the 200 meters in 19.26 seconds, the second fastest 200 in history.

Bolt is looking forward to defending his gold medals at the 2012 Olympic Games in London, England—a city that boasts a large Jamaican population. "2012 is one thing I'm thinking about always," he stated. "It's not even the fact that it's the Olympics—it's the crowd. The crowd is going to be just wonderful and I think it'll probably be one of the best Olympics ever."

Revolutionizing His Sport

With his remarkable string of gold medals and world records—as well as his youthful exuberance—Bolt has rejuvenated public interest in track and field. "Bolt has shaken the historical moorings of his sport, dragging it to a distant, unimaginable place," Tim Layden wrote in *Sports Illustrated.* "A decade's worth of championship gold medals appear inaccessible to anyone but Bolt—provided he stays healthy and motivated. He carries the sport on his shoulders."

"My main goal is to be a legend in my sport," Bolt declared. "I'll keep trying to break barriers and make the world happy."

”

Bolt has lowered world records at such an amazing pace that some analysts believe he is pushing the limits of human performance. He reduced the world record in the 100 meters by .16 seconds in less than 15 months, for instance, while the previous reduction of .16 seconds took other athletes more than 15 years to achieve. Track analysts argue that he has revolutionized the science of sprinting. He somehow manages to match the turnover rate of shorter runners while also taking much longer strides. Bolt typically requires only 41 strides to complete a 100-meter race, while most of his competitors take at least 45. "You have people who are exceptions," said running coach Stephen Francis. "You have Einstein. You have Isaac Newton. You have Beethoven. You have Usain Bolt. It's not explainable how and what they do."

Bolt's achievements are so remarkable that some critics believe they would not be possible without the help of performance-enhancing drugs. Nine-

Bolt continues to push his training, hoping to lower his world record time in the 100 meters from 9.58 seconds to 9.4 seconds.

time Olympic medalist Carl Lewis is among those who have questioned whether Bolt might be cheating: "When people ask me about Bolt, I say he could be the greatest athlete of all time, but for someone to run 10.03 one year and 9.69 the next, if you don't question that … you're a fool. Period." Over the years, a number of world-class track and field athletes have tested positive for steroids, including three of the five Olympic 100-meter champions before Bolt. "The sport has been humiliated," Bolt acknowledged. "People believe that anyone who runs fast is taking drugs. When people say that to me, I understand."

Bolt insists that he has never taken drugs, however, and he submits to frequent drug tests in an effort to prove it. "We will test any time, any day, any part of the body," said Mills. "Usain doesn't even like to take vitamins." Bolt feels that he has a responsibility to stay clean in order to set a good example for his fans in Jamaica. "One thing in Jamaica, we take our sports very, very seriously," he noted. "One person who got caught years ago had to leave the country because we don't like to be disgraced." He believes that if he continues running fast and breaking records for a number of years, the questions will eventually fade away. "My main goal is to be a legend in my sport," he declared. "I'll keep trying to break barriers and make the world happy."

Future Plans

In 2010, Bolt said that he believed he has four years left in track and field. During that time, he hopes to lower his world record in the 100 meters from his best time of 9.58 seconds to 9.4 seconds. In a comment that surprised many observers, Bolt also said that he hopes to try playing professional soccer (called football throughout much of the world). "I have four more good years in me if I train hard," he told an interviewer. "When I finish I'd like to play football for two years. I always watch those guys and I think I could be a professional footballer."

HOME AND FAMILY

Bolt, who is single, lives in a luxury condominium in Kingston, Jamaica, on a hilltop overlooking the track complex where he trains. He remains close to his family and enjoys making visits to the small village where he grew up. Although Bolt could easily afford to fund his parents' retirement with his estimated $4 million in annual earnings, his father insists on continuing to run his grocery store. "I told him, 'Yo, Dad, stop working, I can take care of you guys,'" Bolt related. "He's like, 'Nah.' He wants something to do. He's a guy who likes to be independent."

HOBBIES AND OTHER INTERESTS

In his spare time, Bolt enjoys playing basketball and watching cricket and tennis matches. His favorite pastime, however, is dancing. He loves dance-hall, a style of music that is popular in Jamaica. It features a combination of pulsating hip-hop beats and Caribbean themes. Bolt occasionally unwinds by showing off his moves in Kingston dance clubs. "I'm still young. I'm going to go out and enjoy myself," he noted. "I used to party three times a month but now it is maybe five times a year."

HONORS AND AWARDS

IAAF Rising Star Award: 2002, 2003
Athlete of the Year (International Sports Press Association): 2008
Male Athlete of the Year (International Association of Athletics Federations): 2008
Olympic Games, Men's 100 Meters: gold medal, 2008
Olympic Games, Men's 200 Meters: gold medal, 2008
Olympic Games, Men's 4x100 Relay: gold medal, 2008
Order of Distinction (Government of Jamaica): 2008
Laureus World Sportsman of the Year: 2009

FURTHER READING

Book

Bolt, Usain. *9.58*, 2010 (autobiography)

Periodicals

Black Sports The Magazine (BSTM), Mar. 2009, p.36
Boston Globe, June 1, 2008, p.C5
Current Biography Yearbook, 2009
Maclean's, Sep. 7, 2009, p.38
New York Times, Aug. 17, 2009, p.D1; Aug. 25, 2011; Sep. 3, 2011
Sports Illustrated, June 9, 2008, p.64; July 28, 2008, p.98; Aug. 25, 2008, p.58; Sep. 1, 2008, p.160; Oct. 20, 2008, p.48; Aug. 31, 2009, p.36
Time, Dec. 28, 2009, p.125
USA Today, Aug. 21, 2008, p.D3; Aug. 12, 2009, p.C1
Washington Post, Aug. 1, 2008, p.E1

Online Articles

http://www.jamaica-gleaner.com/gleaner/20080603/sports/sports9.html
(Jamaica Gleaner Online, "Usain Bolt and Glen Mills," June 3, 2008)
http://topics.nytimes.com
(New York Times, "Usain Bolt," multiple articles, various dates)

ADDRESS

Usain Bolt
Jamaica Olympic Association
9 Cunningham Ave.
Kingston 6, Jamaica

WORLD WIDE WEB SITES

http://www.usainbolt.com
http://www.iaaf.org
http://www.jamolympic.org

Chris Bosh 1984-

American Professional Basketball Player for the Miami Heat
Six-Time NBA All Star

BIRTH

Christopher Wesson Bosh was born on March 24, 1984, in Dallas, Texas. He grew up in Hutchins, a working-class suburb of Dallas. His father, Noel Bosh, was a plumbing engineer and a volunteer youth minister. His mother, Freida Bosh, worked as a systems analyst for a small computer company. Chris has one younger brother, Joel.

YOUTH AND EDUCATION

Bosh grew up in a close-knit, supportive family. His parents raised him to be respectful, to work hard, and to value education. He enjoyed both watching and playing sports during his childhood. His earliest basketball memory involved bouncing a ball in the gym while his father competed in pick-up games. "I was the little dude—about four—trying to dribble on the sidelines," Bosh remembered. He joined his first basketball team in fourth grade. He also played first base for a youth baseball team until he got to high school. Aside from sports, his biggest childhood interest was computers. His mother brought a computer home from work and allowed him to tinker around with it. "That got me hooked," he explained.

Bosh attended Lincoln High School in Dallas, where he was an honors student. His parents made sure that he kept his grades up. "Schoolwork came kind of natural to me," he recalled, "but when I brought home a grade that wasn't up to par, my parents let me know it." This emphasis on education paid off when Bosh was elected to the National Honor Society in high school.

> *When Bosh was young, his family emphasized sports and school. "Schoolwork came kind of natural to me," he recalled, "but when I brought home a grade that wasn't up to par, my parents let me know it."*

Blessed with above-average height and athleticism, Bosh made the varsity basketball team as a freshman at Lincoln. During his sophomore year in 1999, the school hired a new head coach, Leonard Bishop. Bishop prepared weekly handouts for each of his players, evaluating their performance in practices and games and providing suggestions for improvement. Bosh took the coach's advice seriously and focused his training to develop his skills. That year, Lincoln advanced to the regional finals in the state tournament. The following year Bosh and his teammates made it to the state semifinals. During his senior year, Bosh led his team to a perfect 40-0 record, a number-one ranking in the *USA Today* national poll, and the Class 4A Texas state championship. He scored 23 points, grabbed 17 rebounds, and blocked 9 shots in the title game.

Bosh concluded his high school basketball career with impressive averages of 21 points and 11 rebounds per game. At the end of his senior season, he was named Mr. Basketball for the state of Texas and a McDonald's High School All-American. Upon graduating from Lincoln in 2002, Bosh consid-

Bosh (Georgia Tech, #4) demonstrating his dunking skills in a game against Wake Forest, 2003.

ered turning professional and entering the National Basketball Association (NBA) draft. But his parents convinced him to accept one of the many athletic scholarship offers he received and go to college instead. Bosh decided to attend the Georgia Institute of Technology (better known as Georgia Tech) in Atlanta. He liked the fast-paced, transition offense that the Yellow

Jackets ran under Coach Paul Hewitt. He also relished the opportunity to compete in the Atlantic Coast Conference (ACC), which was widely considered one of college basketball's powerhouse leagues.

College—Georgia Tech Yellow Jackets

After making the starting lineup as a freshman at Georgia Tech, Bosh immediately established himself as one of the best players in the conference. In his very first game with the Yellow Jackets, he scored 26 points and pulled down 14 rebounds."Going into every game people realized that in order to beat Georgia Tech you had to stop Chris Bosh,"Hewitt noted."He did a great job for us."Bosh went on to post averages of 15.6 points, 9 rebounds, and 2.2 blocks for his freshman season. He made 56 percent of his shots from the field to lead the ACC in field goal percentage. He also led the conference with 67 blocked shots and was the second-leading rebounder with 278. His strong performance helped Georgia Tech earn a berth in the 2003 National Invitational Tournament (NIT), but the Yellow Jackets lost in the quarterfinals to Texas Tech.

At the conclusion of his freshman year, Bosh was named ACC Rookie of the Year and selected for the Freshman All-America Team by the U.S. Basketball Writers Association. His exceptional basketball talents and 6-foot, 11-inch frame attracted a great deal of attention from NBA scouts. In fact, many analysts predicted that Bosh would be a first-round draft pick if he chose to turn pro. After discussing his options with his parents, Bosh decided to leave college early and declare himself eligible for the NBA draft. But he promised his mother that he would go back to school someday to complete the degree in business management that he had started at Georgia Tech.

CAREER HIGHLIGHTS

NBA—Toronto Raptors

Bosh's decision to go pro paid off when he was selected fourth overall in the 2003 NBA draft by the Toronto Raptors. He signed a contract that paid him an estimated $9.3 million over three years. Bosh was part of an exceptionally strong draft class that included future stars LeBron James, Dwyane Wade, and Carmelo Anthony. Although he did not get as much attention as these other high-profile rookies, Bosh quickly established himself as one of the most talented young players in the league. He impressed his coaches and teammates alike with his intelligence, dedication, focus, and composure. "Chris asks questions, accepts criticism, and takes advice," said Raptors star Vince Carter. "All that, and he can really play. There aren't many rookies like that, and I'm glad we've got one of them."

Bosh started 63 games during his rookie season and averaged 11.5 points, 7.4 rebounds, and 1.4 blocks per game. He also set a new team record for rebounds by a first-year player by grabbing a total of 557. Remarkably, he posted these solid numbers even though he spent most of the season playing the center position, rather than his natural position of power forward. Most NBA centers were much larger than Bosh—he gave up 5 inches and over 100 pounds to Shaquille O'Neal, for instance—but the lanky rookie valiantly battled the big men under the boards night after night. "The thing you were impressed with was he took a beating in his rookie year but he played every game," recalled Raptors Coach Sam Mitchell. "He played hurt, tired, he kept dragging himself out and that told you right there he had heart."

The Raptors posted a disappointing 33-49 record in 2003-04 to finish sixth in the Central Division of the Eastern Conference. Despite his team's failure to make the playoffs, Bosh received recognition for his spirited play. He was named to the NBA All-Rookie Team, and *Sports Illustrated* writer Jack McCallum gave him credit for elevating the Raptors "from virtually unwatchable to downright entertaining." Fellow players, coaches, and analysts all predicted that Bosh would continue to improve and become an NBA star. "He's a very unselfish player, he's a very smart player, and I think he's going to just keep getting better," said his college coach, Paul Hewitt.

> *Bosh expressed delight at being picked for the NBA All-Star Game in only his third pro season. "I always wanted to be an all-star," he noted. "I've worked on my game so hard. I want to be an outstanding player so bad that, you know, that is the goal I've set the whole time. I'm just glad people recognize it."*

Becoming the Face of the Franchise

Raptors management made a number of important changes prior to the start of the 2004-05 NBA season. They hired a new coach and general manager, for instance, and acquired center Loren Woods so that Bosh could move to the power forward position. When Toronto traded veteran star Vince Carter early in the season, Bosh emerged as the new face of the team. "Not many people get to go into an organization and become the cornerstone of the franchise, to have a chance to be built around," he stated. "I recognize that."

Bosh and Orlando Magic forward Dwight Howard struggle for the rebound, 2005.

Bosh started 81 games during his second NBA season and increased his averages to 16.8 points and 8.9 rebounds per game. In February 2005 he became the third-youngest player in NBA history to record his 1,000th career rebound. Despite his contributions, however, the Raptors continued to struggle. Toronto posted a 33-49 record for the second season in a row to finish fourth in the newly formed Atlantic Division and miss the playoffs. Some analysts began speculating about how long Bosh would be satisfied to be the best player on a bad team. But Bosh insisted that the Raptors would improve over time. "I'm trying to win in an organization where people didn't really think about winning that much," he acknowledged. "I took the challenge here. Yeah, we weren't that good when I got here, but we're going to be good while I'm here."

Prior to the start of the 2005-06 NBA season, the Raptors recognized Bosh's importance to the team by naming him captain. He responded by increasing his season averages to 22.5 points, 9.2 rebounds, and 2.6 assists per game. He surpassed 2,500 career points in November 2005 and 1,500 career rebounds the following month. NBA coaches acknowledged his contributions by naming him as a reserve player on the Eastern Conference All-Star Team. Bosh expressed delight at achieving his dream of playing in the NBA All-Star Game in only his third pro season. "I always wanted to be an all-star," he noted. "I've worked on my game so hard. I want to be an outstanding player so bad that, you know, that is the goal I've set the whole time. I'm just glad people recognize it."

Although the Raptors benefited from a strong rookie season by first-round draft pick Charlie Villanueva, the team continued to depend heavily on Bosh. When he went down with a severely sprained thumb in March 2006, Toronto lost 10 of the last 11 games of the season. The Raptors ended up with the fifth-worst record in the NBA at 27-55 and failed to make the playoffs once again. Although Bosh had contributed an impressive 77 double-doubles (games in which he posted double-digit statistics in both points and rebounds) during his first three NBA seasons, Toronto had lost a total of 153 games during that time. Despite the frustrating results, Bosh showed his loyalty to the team by signing a three-year contract extension worth an estimated $63 million at the end of the season. "It was real tough at first, but that's all about being a competitor," he explained. "No matter how bad things get, you've got to keep going."

Showing Personality and Gaining Fans

This faith in the Raptors proved well-founded during the 2006-07 season. With Bosh averaging a team-leading 22.6 points and 10.7 rebounds per game, Toronto finished on top of the Atlantic Division with a 47-35 record. His strong performance earned him a starting forward position on the Eastern Conference All-Star Team. The Raptors made the playoffs for the first time in five seasons, but they were eliminated in the first round by the New Jersey Nets. Still, Bosh expressed satisfaction with the team's improvement. "I knew that success wasn't going to happen right off the bat," he stated. "I had to continue to work, to go through the hard times and remember that feeling so I won't go back. I don't want to lose it. As much as it hurt, I knew it was all for a plan. Losing those close games every day, working as hard as you can and still come up short. But at the end of the day it's all about growing up. That helps you to grow up quickly and be a better person and a player."

In 2007-08 Bosh had another solid season, averaging 22.3 points and 8.7 rebounds per game. He hoped that his numbers would result in another All-Star Game start. As the voting process went on, however, he learned that he trailed far behind fellow Eastern Conference forwards LeBron James and Kevin Garnett. Partly as an attempt to close the gap, and partly as a way to raise his public profile, Bosh decided to make a direct appeal to NBA fans on the Internet. He filmed a clever video in which he wore a black cowboy hat and bolo tie and pretended to be a used-car salesman. Speaking rapidly in a Southern accent, Bosh encouraged fans to vote for him on the All-Star Game ballot. He posted the video on YouTube and on his personal web site. It became an instant online sensation, attracting hundreds of thousands of viewers. Before long it appeared on major television sports networks and news programs across the United States and Canada, including ESPN and CNN.

Many people were surprised by Bosh's decision to openly lobby for votes. No NBA player had ever publicly campaigned to be on the All-Star Team before, and some people complained that it shifted the emphasis of the selection process from performance to popularity. But most people found his video so funny and charming that they dismissed such concerns. "I didn't want to make a regular, boring video, because no one would watch. There wouldn't be any word of mouth," he explained. "It has become bigger than I could have imagined. The Internet is the most powerful tool in the world. It's everywhere." Although the video increased Bosh's total by 500,000 votes, he still finished one million votes behind James and Garnett and had to settle for being named to the All-Star Team as a reserve. Nevertheless, it proved to be a valuable experience for Bosh. He showed a goofy, playful side to his personality, gained thousands of new fans, and even received an offer to launch his own YouTube channel.

Aside from Bosh's growing popularity, 2007-08 turned out to be a disappointing season for the Raptors. The team struggled to overcome injuries to key players and limped into the playoffs with a 41-41 record. Although Bosh averaged 24 points per game during the first-round series, the Raptors fell to the Orlando Magic in five games.

Winning an Olympic Gold Medal

In the summer of 2008 Bosh was thrilled to have an opportunity to represent the United States at the Olympic Games in Beijing, China. Continuing to reach out to fans through the Internet, he published a daily blog de-

Bosh battles for a loose ball between Daniel Gibson (left) and Anderson Varejao (right) in a 2008 game against the Cleveland Cavaliers.

scribing his experiences at the Games, which included a tour of the Great Wall of China. During the men's basketball tournament, Bosh came off the bench to average 9.7 points and a team-leading 6.1 rebounds per game. Team USA posted a perfect 8-0 record in Olympic competition and defeated Spain in the finals to claim the gold medal.

As the 2008-09 NBA season got underway, the Raptors continued to struggle with frequent personnel changes and injuries to key players. In fact, the team got off to such a slow start that Toronto replaced its head coach after 17 games. Bosh performed well despite all the upheaval, posting a career-best average of 22.7 points per game to go along with 10 rebounds, 2.5 assists, and 1.0 blocks. He was selected to the All-Star Team for the fourth straight year but was forced to miss the game with a knee injury. The Raptors finished the season with a disappointing 33-49 record to rank fourth in the division and miss the playoffs.

During the 2009 off-season, Bosh made major changes to his diet and workout regimen in an effort to improve his game. He ended up adding 20 pounds of muscle to his frame, thus increasing his playing weight to a formidable 250 pounds. "I always hear people saying Toronto needs to get a big man to protect Chris Bosh inside. I heard that a lot, and maybe I believed it," he explained. "But finally, I thought, I can't wait on nobody else. I can't wait on this imaginary figure who might come and make everything OK. Why don't you protect yourself?"

Bosh decided to commemorate the physical changes to his body, along with what he viewed as his mental and spiritual growth, by getting his first tattoo. He documented the experience on film and released it on DVD as *First Ink* in 2009. In addition to showing the real-life story of the tattoo, *First Ink* also featured Bosh playing various characters in a series of silly skits. In one amusing episode, he drives around Toronto and pretends to confront anti-fans who made negative comments about Chris Bosh on the Internet. Bosh viewed the DVD as another way to connect with fans and generate publicity. "I don't have as much popularity as the other guys, so I guess some avenues that came to them or that they deserved didn't come to me like that," he noted. "So I was forced to be more creative. Either sit there and be dormant or do something fun, take something and elevate it and make it better, keep it moving. It's worked out so far."

"The stereotype of a leader is one who talks and peps people up and things like that, but in actuality you have to listen to your teammates," Bosh explained. "If you're just talking the whole time, you may say some things in ways that they may not like. And you may not get along. It's very important to listen first and then react based off what you heard."

Becoming a Free Agent

As the 2009-10 NBA season got underway, many people wondered whether it would be Bosh's last year in Toronto. Raptors management offered him a contract extension over the summer, but he refused to sign it. Although Bosh insisted that he had not yet made up his mind, the media speculated that he would choose to become a free agent and field offers from more prominent and successful NBA teams. "I honestly have not made a decision, but I know what people think—I know they think that if you want to be a star player you have to be in some other market," he acknowledged. "But with all the technology that is out there now, I have been able to reach a lot of people in this market and beyond. And besides, I am not very predictable. I wouldn't assume anything when it comes to me."

Both before and during the season, Raptors management made a number of roster moves in an effort to turn the team into a contender. Although the idea was to convince Bosh to stay, the personnel changes had a negative impact on team chemistry. As usual, Bosh rose above the fray and turned in another outstanding season, averaging a career-high 24.0 points and 10.8 rebounds per game. "It's funny because, when you look at it, my numbers right now are about two points and one rebound better than they were last year," he noted. "I spent a lot of hours for those two points and one rebound. But that separates you from being OK to being great. Think about it. A guy who averages 18 points and 9 rebounds is a good player. But 20 and 10? That's great."

Bosh earned a spot on the All-Star Team for the fifth straight year, and he surpassed Vince Carter as the Raptors' all-time leading scorer with 9,421 career points. In April 2010, however, he took an accidental elbow to the face from Cleveland Cavaliers forward Antawn Jamison. The blow resulted in broken facial bones that required surgery and brought his season to a premature end. Without their leader, the Raptors faltered down the stretch and were edged out for the final spot in the playoffs by the Chicago Bulls. By the end of the 2009-10 season—his seventh in a Raptors uniform—Bosh ranked as the franchise's all-time leader in several statistical categories, including points, rebounds, blocks, minutes played, and free throws. Over the course of 509 professional games with the Raptors, he averaged 20.2 points, 9.4 rebounds, 2.2 assists, and 1.18 blocks per game. He also shot an impressive 49.2 percent from the field, 79.6 percent from the foul line, and 29.8 percent from three-point range.

Joining the Miami Heat

Once the 2009-10 NBA season came to a close, Bosh's contract with the Raptors expired. He officially became a free agent, able to re-sign with Toronto or offer his services to any other NBA team. As Bosh considered his options, fans and sportswriters speculated about his future. On July 9, 2010, he announced that he had decided to leave the Raptors and play for the Miami Heat. He signed a six-year contract worth over $100 million. Bosh described it as "the most difficult decision of my life … mostly because Toronto has been so great to me. I've loved every minute here."

Bosh explained that one of the main factors influencing his decision was that moving to Miami gave him the chance to play with Dwyane Wade, a close friend from the Olympic team who was a star guard for the Heat. "We've wanted to play with each other and we have a golden opportunity to do that," he noted. Two days after Bosh announced his decision, free

Bosh with his new Miami Heat teammates, LeBron James (left) and Dwyane Wade (right), 2010.

agent forward LeBron James revealed that he planned to leave the Cleveland Cavaliers and sign with Miami as well. James's decision meant that three of the top five picks from the 2003 NBA draft were on the Heat roster. Analysts pointed out that as the star players on their former teams, Bosh, Wade, and James had each been routinely double-teamed by opposing defenses. Now that all three played for the same team, however, defending them would pose a serious challenge. "There's no question about it, they become the favorites along with [the Boston Celtics] to win the East," said Orlando Magic coach Stan Van Gundy. "You have three guys, all-stars, in the prime of their careers. That's a heckuva team to match up against." (For more information on Wade, see *Biography Today Sports,* Vol. 14; for more information on James, see *Biography Today,* Sep 2010.)

At the same time, though, the Heat faced some challenges incorporating the new stars. Miami Coach Erik Spoelstra had to design an offensive system that would create quality scoring chances for James and Bosh as well as Wade. "We don't want to reinvent their games," Spoelstra said. "These guys have played together, they have high basketball IQs, and they're versatile. I don't want to restrict them, but take advantage of their skills." Some analysts worried that Miami would have trouble finding good supporting players, since the three stars signed such big contracts that the team had very little money left under the league's salary cap. Others predicted that

Bosh, James, and Wade would have trouble getting along and working together as a team, since they were all used to being the premier player on their former teams.

As the 2010-11 NBA season got underway, it appeared that the doubters might be right. The three stars struggled to figure out how to play together, and Miami limped to a 9-8 record to start the season. "We're stuck on a treadmill right now," Bosh admitted. "We believe in each other and we believe that eventually we're going to get better. Sometimes, you just have to let the pain teach you something." Ultimately, the Heat's formidable talent prevailed. With Bosh contributing 18.7 points and 8.3 rebounds per game, Miami went on to post an impressive 58-24 record on the year. The Heat entered the playoffs as the second seed in the Eastern Conference behind the Chicago Bulls, and many NBA insiders regarded the team as favorites to win the championship.

Coming Up Short

As predicted, the Heat looked unstoppable through the first three rounds of the 2011 NBA playoffs. Bosh and his teammates disposed of the Philadelphia 76ers, the Boston Celtics, and the Chicago Bulls—winning each 7-game series by an impressive 4-1 margin—to reach the NBA Finals, where they faced the Dallas Mavericks. To the surprise of many fans, the first few games of the Finals turned into a defensive struggle between the two high-powered offensive teams. Miami took Game 1 by a score of 92-84, but Dallas came back to win Game 2 by a score of 95-93. In Game 3, Bosh made a clutch jump shot in the closing seconds to lift the Heat to an 88-86 victory and a 2-1 series lead. Miami appeared poised to take control of the series, needing only to win two games at home to capture the NBA title.

Unfortunately for Bosh, the Mavericks went on a hot streak and conquered the tough Heat defense with outstanding shooting. Dallas beat Miami three games in a row to win the series 4-2 and claim the first NBA championship in franchise history. Many basketball fans across the country were delighted to see the Mavericks win the title at the expense of the superstar-filled Heat. Bosh, on the other hand, was overcome with emotion after the final buzzer sounded on his much-anticipated first season with Miami. As he left the court and made his way to the locker room, he fell to his knees, sobbing, and had to be helped up by teammates.

Although Bosh performed well in the playoffs, virtually matching his season averages with 18.6 points and 8.5 rebounds per game, he expressed deep disappointment with the outcome of the season. "We've got a lot of

Bosh defending against the Dallas Mavericks' Dirk Nowitzki during the NBA Finals, 2011.

work to do," he stated. "We've got to go back to the drawing board. It hurts to come this far and come up short. It's disappointing, but hopefully we can use this for motivation going forward." Bosh also praised the great teamwork displayed by the Mavericks. "Hands down they were the better team in this series," he noted. "They played together well, and they deserve everything they got."

Since joining the Heat, Bosh has received praise for maintaining the humble, hardworking demeanor he has shown throughout his career while also playing a quietly effective leadership role. "The stereotype of a leader is one who talks and peps people up and things like that, but in actuality you have to listen to your teammates," he explained. "You have to know what they like, you have to know their tendencies, and the only way you do that is by observing what they do, and listening to them and seeing what kind of person they are. If you're just talking the whole time, you may say some things in ways that they may not like. And you may not get along. It's very important to listen first and then react based off what you heard." Miami fans hoped that Bosh's quiet leadership would help the Heat work together to earn an NBA championship.

HOME AND FAMILY

Bosh has a daughter, Trinity, who was born in late 2008. Trinity lives with her mother, Allison Mathis, in Maryland. Mathis was Bosh's girlfriend for several years, but their relationship ended before Trinity was born. In March 2009 Mathis filed a high-profile lawsuit against Bosh seeking full custody of Trinity and financial support. They eventually settled the matter out of court. Bosh sees his daughter as much as possible and says that he enjoys fatherhood. "It changes your outlook on life," he stated. "Makes you realize what things are important." In August 2010 Bosh announced his engagement to Adrienne Williams. They have homes in Miami and Dallas.

HOBBIES AND OTHER INTERESTS

In his spare time, Bosh enjoys reading. He is also learning to speak Spanish by working with a tutor several times per week. His biggest off-court interest, however, involves computers. Bosh set up a custom computer in his home to operate his sophisticated entertainment center, which includes music, television, and multiple video game systems. He also founded a company, Max Deal Technologies, to provide technology solutions for homes and businesses. "He's a computer geek trapped in an NBA player's body," said NBA deputy commissioner Adam Silver.

Bosh was one of the first NBA players to make extensive use of technology to connect with fans and market himself. In addition to his personal web site and YouTube channel, Bosh has long used social media such as Facebook and Twitter to inform and entertain people. "I have reached a whole lot of people I wouldn't have reached because of the technology that is out there now," he acknowledged. "I think that helped raise my profile beyond basketball."

The NBA recognized Bosh's leadership in the field by inviting him to sit on an expert panel at the annual NBA Technology Summit. "Bosh has become a template for the way other athletes approach their fans," wrote Sean Deveney in the *Sporting News.* "He has altered the way we perceive our world-famous athletes and altered the way those athletes present themselves to the world." Bosh even filed a lawsuit on behalf of fellow athletes and celebrities to reclaim 800 Internet domain names—including ChrisBosh.com—that had been nabbed by a notorious cybersquatter. "That dude was messing things up," he declared. "Everyone should have their own name." Bosh won the case and returned the domain names to their rightful owners.

Bosh is active in charity work through the Chris Bosh Foundation, a non-profit organization dedicated to promoting social enrichment, education, and physical fitness among youth. Upon signing a contract extension with the Raptors in 2006, Bosh made a $1 million commitment to various community programs in Toronto. He is also a member of the Hoop Heroes program, which provides after-school sports programs for middle-school children in cities across the United States.

HONORS AND AWARDS

McDonald's High School Basketball All-American: 2002
Mr. Basketball for the State of Texas: 2002
NCAA Atlantic Coast Conference Rookie of the Year: 2003
NCAA Freshman All-America Team (U.S. Basketball Writers Association): 2003
NBA All-Star Team: 2006-2011
NBA Sportsmanship Award: 2008
Olympic Games, Men's Basketball: 2008, gold medal (with Team USA)
Magic Johnson Award (Pro Basketball Writers Association): 2010

FURTHER READING

Periodicals

Current Biography Yearbook, 2010
Macleans, Feb. 8, 2010, p.14
New York Times, Nov. 19, 2010, p.B13
Sporting News, Dec. 30, 2002, p.13; June 30, 2003, p.53; Dec. 22, 2003, p.67; Mar. 1, 2010, p.20
Sports Illustrated, Dec. 22, 2003, p.58; Feb. 4, 2008, p.44; Dec. 7, 2009, p.42; July 19, 2010, p.38; Oct. 25, 2010, p.72; Dec. 6, 2010, p.98
Sports Illustrated Kids, Nov. 2010, p.20
Toronto Star, Feb. 10, 2006, p.C2; Apr. 6, 2007, p.D7; Jan. 3, 2010, p.S1
USA Today, Jan. 15, 2008, p.C7

Online Articles

http://sports.espn.go.com/nba/playoffs/2011/news
(ESPN, "The Less Glamorous Life of Chris Bosh," June 6, 2011)
http://www.miamiherald.com
(Miami Herald, "Miami Heat's Chris Bosh Ignores Bashing," Feb. 20, 2011)

http://www.nytimes.com
(New York Times, "For Bosh, Trip Home Reflects a Road Back," June 4, 2011)
http://sportsillustrated.cnn.com
(Sports Illustrated, "Ever-Improving Bosh Fuels Raptors' Unexpected Rise," Feb. 6, 2007; "The Plot Starts Here Showtime Starts Here," July 19, 2010; "Measure of a Champion," July 19, 2010; "After Finals Failure, Where Do Heat Go from Here?" June 13, 2011)

ADDRESS

Chris Bosh
Miami Heat
American Airlines Arena
610 Biscayne Boulevard
Miami, FL 33132

WORLD WIDE WEB SITES

http://www.chrisbosh.com
http://www.nba.com/heat/roster/heat_player_chris_bosh

Robert Bullard 1946-

American Sociologist and Environmental Justice Activist
Author of Numerous Books, including *Dumping in Dixie: Race, Class and Environmental Quality*
Director of the Environmental Justice Resource Center at Clark Atlanta University

BIRTH

Robert Doyle Bullard was born on December 21, 1946, in Elba, Alabama. His father, Nehemiah Bullard, was a laborer. His mother, Myrtle Bullard, was a homemaker. Bullard is the fourth of five children. He has three brothers, Joe, Jimmy, and Leon, and one sister, Bettye.

YOUTH

Bullard grew up in an environment of strict racial segregation that was enforced throughout much of the southern U.S. at that time. Bullard explained,"I grew up in the all-black Mulberry Heights neighborhood located in Elba, Alabama. Elba was a typical southern small town with rigid racial boundaries where blacks and whites seldom interacted—except in a work setting. In the 1950s and 1960s, nearly every aspect of life in this small town was separate or segregated, including the public schools, parks, playgrounds and swimming pools, and libraries. The local public library was for 'whites only.' Our 'black library' was located at the segregated high school—that closed at 3:00 PM."

"I grew up in the all-black Mulberry Heights neighborhood located in Elba, Alabama. Elba was a typical southern small town with rigid racial boundaries where blacks and whites seldom interacted," Bullard recalled. "Nearly every aspect of life in this small town was separate or segregated, including the public schools, parks, playgrounds and swimming pools, and libraries. The local public library was for 'whites only.'"

This system of racial discrimination and the laws that enforced it were known as "Jim Crow." Under Jim Crow, African Americans were treated as second-class citizens. Bullard's childhood experiences with Jim Crow made him aware of how a person's race affected their access to housing, education, jobs, and transportation. Later in his life, Bullard drew upon his early experiences to understand how American communities grew and developed over time. "My upbringing did not shelter me from the fact that all societies are not created equal, [including] access to paved roads, sewer, and water. Nobody had to get me a movie ticket to see this. I saw it with my own eyes. And some of this exists today, the residual of Jim Crow in southern rural communities.

"I think growing up in the Jim Crow South, during a period in our nation's history where African Americans were largely judged as not equally qualified, made me want to excel and do more than 'average.' My parents always instilled in me and my siblings that we should never strive to be 'equal,' but we should strive to be 'better' and have that 'extra edge' that will set us apart from the pack," Bullard said. "My parents made sure my siblings and I had lots of books and magazines to read. They were strong believers in education and reading. Not being able to enter the Elba Library or check out a book did not stop me from writing 15 books." In fact, reading and writing were among Bullard's favorite things to do when he was young.

As a child, Bullard also enjoyed hiking, camping, and being outdoors. "I did not have video games or computers growing up," he recalled. "Most of my recreation and fun activities were outside—even in the heat of South Alabama. My parents always had a vegetable garden and fruit orchard which I enjoyed working and watching the plants grow and mature."

EDUCATION

Throughout school, Bullard's favorite subjects were history, government, geography, and English composition. He particularly enjoyed assignments that involved writing.

Bullard attended Alabama Agricultural and Mechanical University (Alabama A&M), where he studied history, government, and sociology. (Sociology is the study of human society and social systems such as culture, class, and race relations.) He earned a master's degree in sociology from Atlanta University (now Clark Atlanta University) and a doctorate degree (PhD) in sociology from Iowa State University.

CAREER HIGHLIGHTS

Over the course of a career spanning more than 30 years, Bullard has become known as the father of the environmental justice movement. Environmental justice is the equal right of all people to enjoy a safe and healthy place to live, work, and play. Environmental justice is based on the idea that environmental activists should be interested in the living conditions of people in cities in addition to protecting and conserving nature. As Bullard explained, "Environmental justice incorporates the idea that we are just as much concerned about wetlands, birds, and wilderness areas, but we're also concerned with urban habitats, where people live in cities, about reservations, about things that are happening along the U.S.-Mexican border, about children that are being poisoned by lead in housing and kids playing outside in contaminated playgrounds."

The area near the Shell Refinery in Norco, Louisiana, known as Cancer Alley, was one example of environmental problems in poor neighborhoods. Some homes were only 12 feet from the refinery, and many residents developed respiratory problems. According to Bullard, "The playgrounds in Norco, La., in Cancer Alley, are across from a huge Shell refinery. You stay there 15 minutes and you can't breathe."

Bullard is a pioneer in the fields of environmental justice research, scholarship, and activism. He sees no difference between the fight against racism and the fight for environmental protection. He is the author of many books on topics like environmental racism, industrial pollution, unfair land use, and unequal access to safe housing, transportation, and jobs. His work brings attention to the fact that poor minorities suffer the most from the world's environmental problems.

Many of Bullard's studies and reports have shown that racial segregation has resulted in hazardous waste sites being located in minority communities. "Environmental justice really is based on the premise that no community should become the dumping ground for things other people don't want.... We all produce garbage, but we all don't live next to a garbage dump," Bullard said. "You don't have to be a rocket scientist to understand that rich people throw away more than poor people, yet the poor get the burden and health risks of living near the landfills."

Getting Started

Before getting involved in environmental justice, Bullard worked as an urban planner. Urban planning is the design of cities and towns, including public spaces, business and residential areas, parks and recreation spaces, and roads. In 1978, he became an assistant professor of sociology at Texas Southern University in Houston. He intended to teach part-time while also conducting research in sociology.

By that time, Bullard decided that he wanted to model his career after W.E.B. Du Bois, an African-American civil rights activist, sociologist, historian, and author. "From my earliest moments in academia, I wanted to make sure I kept my feet grounded in the community while publishing in mainstream journals and cutting-edge publications that ... looked at racism and African Americans. I wanted to make sure my research was used, like Du Bois's, and that it pushed the envelope, whether it was smart growth, transportation, or housing."

Bullard's career in environmental justice began somewhat unexpectedly. His wife at that time, Linda McKeever Bullard, was an attorney. She asked Bullard to work on research for an important legal case against the creation of a city garbage dump in the middle of an African-American neighborhood in Houston called Northwood Manor. He agreed.

Bullard was surprised by the results of his research. "My students and I found that 100 percent of city-owned landfills in Houston were located in predominantly black neighborhoods, even though African Americans accounted for only 25 percent of the population. I expanded that research to include the entire southern United States," he remembered. "I got hooked. I started connecting the dots in terms of housing, residential patterns, patterns of land use, where highways go, where transportation routes go, and how economic development decisions are made. It was very clear that people who were making decisions—county commissioners or industrial boards or city councils—were not the same people who were 'hosting' these facilities in their communities. Without a doubt, it was a form of apartheid where whites were making decisions and black people and brown people and people of color, including Native Americans on reservations, had no seat at the table."

Bullard credits his ex-wife as "the single most important person that set me on the three-decade path of environmental justice. Although we did not live in Northwood Manor, Linda and I both felt assaulted by what was being proposed and by the discriminatory waste facility siting pattern that occurred over the previous five decades—with African-American Houston neighborhoods [getting] the bulk of the city's garbage.

"Even when you control for how much money people make and the price of housing, race still comes out as the number one factor in determining

Bullard's 1990 book Dumping in Dixie *became a groundbreaking work in the new field of environmental justice.*

where toxic facilities are located," Bullard stressed. "Race permeates everything, in terms of housing, education, where people can live, land-use decisions, transportation, and mobility. And often, the fact that so many people of color live near facilities that other people don't want is based on historical factors that resulted in residential segregation and affected the decisions of housing commissions."

The 1979 lawsuit *Bean v. Southwestern Waste Management Corp.* was the first to use the 1964 Civil Rights Act to fight environmental discrimination in the location of a waste facility. "We made that connection," Bullard claimed. "You have a right to breathe clean air, you have a right to drink clean water, you have a right for your food not to be poisoned—just as you have a right to fair employment and equal opportunities in education."

Creating a National Movement

By the early 1980s, a national environmental justice movement was taking shape. In 1982, an organized protest against the creation of a hazardous waste dump in Warren County, North Carolina, brought renewed attention to the existence of environmental racism. The dump was to be located in a mostly African-American rural community. Members of the community were united in their opposition to the plan, and they staged a dramatic public protest to stop it. "The Warren County case brought home the 'in-your-face' politics of waste facility siting in the nation," Bullard declared. "The people said, 'No.' But more important, over 500 people went to jail trying to keep this dump out of the black community. Young school children, old people, and people from all walks of life put their bodies in front of dump trucks to protect their community."

In 1990, Bullard published *Dumping in Dixie: Race, Class, and Environmental Quality*. In this groundbreaking book, he documented disturbing trends in waste facility location throughout the U.S. and includes a call to action for environmental activists. It is widely regarded as the first publication to fully explain the concept of environmental justice. *Dumping in Dixie* was generally praised by critics, with a review in *Contemporary Sociology* calling it "provocative and helpful." In recognition of his pioneering work, the National Wildlife Foundation honored Bullard with a Conservation Achievement Award.

In 1991, Bullard helped to organize the first National People of Color Environmental Leadership Summit in Washington, DC. This event brought together representatives from more than 300 different organizations in the U.S., Puerto Rico, Canada, and Mexico. The goal was to unite people of color to work on issues related to environmental and economic justice, civil rights, and health. According to Bullard, "Out of this summit came 17 principles of environmental justice that laid the framework for how we would work together among ourselves, with grassroots groups, networks, and how we would relate to the national environmental groups."

Bullard's research and activism during these years resulted in significant changes to U.S. federal government operations. In 1991, the U.S. Environmental Protection Agency (EPA) Office of Environmental Equity was created. This office focused on environmental justice issues and produced the influential report "Environmental Equity: Reducing Risks for All Communities." Then President Bill Clinton expanded the EPA's Office of Environmental Justice and created the National Environmental Justice Advisory Council. In 1994, President Clinton signed an executive order to address environmental injustice in federal laws related to civil rights and environmental issues. Bullard was invited to the White House to witness the signing of this historic order.

"Environmental justice really is based on the premise that no community should become the dumping ground for things other people don't want.... We all produce garbage, but we all don't live next to a garbage dump," Bullard said. "You don't have to be a rocket scientist to understand that rich people throw away more than poor people, yet the poor get the burden and health risks of living near the landfills."

Environmental Justice Resource Center

By 1994, Bullard was teaching sociology at Clark Atlanta University in Georgia. There he founded the Environmental Justice Resource Center to organize and inform activists. The Environmental Justice Resource Center presents environmental protection as a civil rights and social justice issue that affects people of color and low-income communities more than others. "We have to work even harder to hold the ground," Bullard said, "and for the notion that equal justice is for all communities and that we're all created equal."

Through the Environmental Justice Resource Center, Bullard was able to raise awareness of the many ways that environmental problems affect every part of life. His extensive research and analysis of waste facility loca-

Bullard shown in his office at Clark Atlanta University with enlarged covers of two of his books. He has written and edited books on several topics related to environmental justice, including Atlanta's public transit system policies.

tion decisions, environmental laws, regulations, and public policies revealed that these environmental problems tended to accumulate over time. Once a waste facility was located in a particular community, it became easier to place another one there, and then another. The combined effect of multiple facilities in one area is devastating.

Bullard explained the hazards of these multiple problems like this: "It's not just the landfill, it's not just the incinerator, it's not just the garbage dump, it's not just the crisscrossing freeway and highway, and the bus barns that dump all that stuff in these neighborhoods—it's all that combined. Even if each particular facility is in compliance, there are no regulations that take into account this saturation. It may be legal, but it is immoral. Just like slavery was legal, but slavery has always been immoral.

"Whether it's by design, or whether it's by default, or whether it's by accident, the negative health impacts are the same. So we're not even arguing about the intentionality anymore. What we're saying is, if a kid is being impacted by lead, or by industrial pollution, or whatever—whether the community was there first or the plant was there first, the kid can be just as sick. So that should not be an argument. The good question is, 'What are we going to do about it?'"

The Environmental Justice Resource Center also highlights issues of race and class in environmental decision-making. "We strongly believe that people of color must speak for themselves and do for themselves," Bullard explained. "We are seeing an increase in the number of grassroots people of color environmental and economic justice groups emerge across the U.S., Puerto Rico, Canada, and Mexico. This is also the case in the Caribbean, Latin America, Asia, and Africa. Trans-boundary and international collaborations are forming among nongovernmental organizations to address global human rights, environmental, and economic justice issues." In this way, environmental justice has become a global issue.

"You have a right to breathe clean air, you have a right to drink clean water, you have a right for your food not to be poisoned—just as you have a right to fair employment and equal opportunities in education."

In the years since founding the Environmental Justice Resource Center, Bullard has made tremendous progress in raising awareness of the relationship between civil rights and environmentalism. Bringing civil rights and environmental activists together produces benefits across many different parts of modern society. "The environmental justice movement has basically redefined what environmentalism is all about," he explained. "It basically says that the environment is everything: where we live, work, play, go to school, as well as the physical and natural world. And so we can't separate the physical environment from the cultural environment. We have to talk about making sure that justice is integrated throughout all of the stuff that we do.

"A lot has changed in 20 years," Bullard observed. "We have strong regional and ethnic-based environmental justice networks and grassroots groups. We have an array of environmental justice courses being taught at colleges and universities all across the country. Several law schools have legal clinics that work on [environmental justice] issues. We even have four university-based environmental justice centers. We have made a lot of progress. But we still have a lot of work to do."

Future Plans

While some progress has been made, Bullard notes that race is still the biggest factor in the location of hazardous waste sites. In 2007, his research showed that more than half of the nine million people living within two miles of U.S. hazardous waste facilities were minorities. "Environmental racism is alive and well. Racism is making some of us sick—mentally and physically.... Where you live can impact your quality of life. In the real

Bullard has been active in many human rights causes, including this 2005 march in Atlanta, Georgia, to commemorate the 40th anniversary of the Voting Rights Act.

world, all communities are not created equal. Blacks, whether rural, urban, or suburban, are more likely than whites to live in polluted environments, and lack health insurance and access to health care. In general, black communities receive less environmental protection than white communities."

As a result, Bullard has no plans to stop working on issues related to environmental justice. His focus remains on empowering people to create change and to work for safe, healthy communities. "Our communities are under siege. These threats are real—not imagined. All you have to do is turn on the television or read the newspaper and the reality hits home loud and clear," Bullard declared. He has a clear idea of what will be required in the future. "As a group, black people need a laser-like focus on such issues as environmental and economic justice, public health, livable communities, pollution prevention, brownfields redevelopment, clean production, transportation, air quality, and urban sprawl just to name a few areas."

Bullard also sees a need for more young people to join the environmental justice movement. A new generation of leaders is needed. "Young people should understand that every successful social movement in this country has had a youth and student component. This was true for the civil rights movement, women's movement, anti-war movement, environmental movement, and others. Movements need young people to grow and thrive.

Young people must be educated, trained, and mentored to take over the leadership reins from the elders."

In particular, Bullard would like to see more young people of color working on environmental justice issues. "It's a great field. The opportunities are unlimited," he remarked. "It's an area where you can have not only a great career, but a great impact. The latter is where a legacy can be left. The field is growing and advancing. It's important that minority students have a significant stake in what happens in communities of color—not to say that every black student lives in a black neighborhood—but you can have an impact, whether on a reservation, a barrio, or an ethnic enclave.... We have to be researchers and advance the field, but if you can get elected to office or direct an environmental office—government or organization—you can contribute beyond the individual level and have a huge impact.

"The best advice I have for young people is to set your sights on a goal you would like to achieve and work hard to get there. Do not let anyone tell you or convince you that you can't excel. Set your sights high," Bullard said. "There is nothing you can't achieve if you set your mind to it. Most of the people who have made advancements in our society were not 'sprinters' [work for the short term] but were 'marathon runners' [work for the long term]. In the struggle for environmental justice, we need more young people who are willing to be marathon runners."

MAJOR INFLUENCES

Bullard has many personal heroes and people who have inspired him. At the top of the list are his parents. He also counts his grandmother among those who have had a big impact on his life. Bullard described his grandmother as "a strong advocate of education, of standing on your own two feet and not letting anybody ride your back. She instilled that in me, in my father, and my parents also instilled it in me."

In addition, Bullard said, "Educators, scholars, and activists have always been a big hit with me!" He named W.E.B. Du Bois as "the number one intellectual, scholar, teacher, researcher, and political activist who has influenced my academic career." Bullard has expressed admiration for many African-American leaders from the past: civil rights leader Martin Luther King Jr., religious leader and activist Malcolm X, voting rights activist and civil rights leader Fannie Lou Hamer, and writer, speaker, social reformer, and anti-slavery activist Frederick Douglass. "The people who came before me ... really combined telling the truth and not letting things come back and get you—repercussions—just because you're standing for social justice."

MARRIAGE AND FAMILY

Bullard was married to Linda McKeever Bullard, an attorney. The marriage ended in divorce.

HOBBIES AND OTHER INTERESTS

Bullard enjoys gardening in his spare time.

SELECTED WRITINGS

Books

Dumping in Dixie: Race, Class, and Environmental Quality, 1990
Sprawl City: Race, Politics, and Planning in Atlanta, 2000 (editor, with Glenn S. Johnson and Angel O. Torres)
Highway Robbery: Transportation Racism, New Routes to Equity, 2004 (editor, with Glenn S. Johnson and Angel O. Torres)
The Quest for Environmental Justice: Human Rights and the Politics of Pollution, 2005
Growing Smarter: Achieving Livable Communities, Environmental Justice, and Regional Equity, 2007
Race, Place, and Environmental Justice after Hurricane Katrina: Struggles to Reclaim, Rebuild, and Revitalize New Orleans and the Gulf Coast, 2009
Environmental Health and Racial Equity in the United States: Strategies for Building Environmentally Just, Sustainable, and Livable Communities, 2011

Periodicals

"Victims of Their Environment," *Atlanta Journal and Constitution*, Jan. 19, 1995, p.A11
"It's Not Just, Pollution," *Our Planet*, Sep. 2001
"Toxic Waste Dumpers Prefer to Poison Poor People," *Atlanta Journal and Constitution*, Nov. 28, 2002
"Environmental Justice for All," *New Crisis*, Jan./Feb. 2003, p.24
"The Color of Toxic Debris," *The American Prospect*, Mar. 2009, p.A9

HONORS AND AWARDS

Conservation Achievement Award (National Wildlife Foundation): 1990
CNN People You Should Know (CNN): 2007
Environmental Leaders of the Century (Newsweek): 2008
100 History Makers in the Making (TheGrio.com): 2010

FURTHER READING

Periodicals

Atlanta Magazine, Mar. 2007
E: the Environmental Magazine, July/Aug. 1998, p.10
Earth First! Journal, July 1999
National Catholic Reporter, June 16, 2006, p.A2
Sierra, Nov./Dec. 2005, p.28
Smithsonian, June 2008, p.33

Online Articles

http://www.ejrc.cau.edu
(Environmental Justice Resource Center, "Robert Bullard," undated; "Why Blacks Should Be Concerned About the Environment: An Interview with Dr. Robert Bullard," Nov. 1999)
http://www.greenamerica.org/pubs/caq/articles/Fall2007/robertbullard.cfm
(Green America, "Our Interview with Robert Bullard," Fall 2007)
http://www.grist.org
(Grist, "Meet Robert Bullard, the Father of Environmental Justice," Mar. 14, 2006)
http://www.sptimes.com/2007/09/09/Opinion/The_world_s_a_dirty_p.shtml
(St. Petersburg Times, "The World's a Dirty Place When You Are Poor," Sep. 9, 2007)
http://www.thegrio.com/black-history/thegrios-100/thegrios-100-robert-bullard.php
(TheGrio.com, "TheGrio's 100: Robert Bullard, Father of Environmental Justice Inspires Next Generation," Feb. 2, 2010)

ADDRESS

Robert Bullard
Environmental Justice Resource Center
Clark Atlanta University
223 James P. Brawley Drive
Atlanta, GA 30314

WORLD WIDE WEB SITE

http://ejrc.cau.edu

Steven Chu 1948-

American Scientist and U.S. Secretary of Energy
Nobel Prize-Winning Physicist Who Discovered Pioneering Techniques in the Study of Atoms, Molecules, and DNA

BIRTH

Steven Chu was born on February 28, 1948, in St. Louis, Missouri. His parents were Chinese students who came to the U.S. to attend the Massachusetts Institute of Technology. They decided to remain in the U.S. when China's civil war made it unsafe to return there. Chu's father, Ju Chin Chu, was a chemical engineer and professor at Washington University in St. Louis. His mother, Ching Chen Li, studied economics. Chu has an older brother named Gilbert and a younger brother named Morgan.

YOUTH

In 1950, when Chu was two years old, his father took a position teaching at Brooklyn Polytechnic Institute. The family moved to Garden City, a Long Island suburb of New York City. At that time, there were only two other Chinese families living in Garden City.

As a young boy, Chu liked to build things. He began building model airplanes and ships from kits in the summer between kindergarten and first grade. "I don't know what it was, but since I was very young I loved building things," he remembered. "I loved building things with my hands. I would be given for Christmas a model set of airplanes or boats and things, and I loved to put them together."

"Since I was very young I loved building things," Chu remembered. "I loved building things with my hands. I would be given for Christmas a model set of airplanes or boats and things, and I loved to put them together."

By the fourth grade, Chu had moved on to building his own creations using Erector Sets, a toy construction system. Erector Sets include small metal pieces that are connected together using screws, nuts, and bolts. Mechanical parts such as pulleys, gears, and electrical motors can be used to create working models. "Unlike Lego blocks, you actually have to screw something together, it wasn't all pre-designed to make a boat or something like that," he explained. "I loved doing those things." Chu recalled spending "many happy hours constructing devices of unknown purpose, where the main design criterion was to maximize the number of moving parts and overall size."

"Now, it turns out that working with your hands and building things gives you a spatial intuition that turned out to be invaluable once I became a scientist. I could see things in my head very clearly and rotate them around. This idea of picturing things geometrically has always been a part of my thinking.... I only discovered later that most physicists do that."

Chu's other interests included reading, writing, chemistry, and sports. He experimented with making his own rockets, using his lunch money to buy

An early photo of Chu in a laser lab.

parts and supplies. One summer, he and a friend made money using their chemistry sets to test their neighbors' soil for acidity and missing nutrients. When he wasn't involved with these activities, Chu joined informal neighborhood games of touch football, baseball, basketball, and ice hockey. He was always interested in learning new things, often exploring topics on his own. "I taught myself tennis by reading a book," he claimed, "and in the following year, I joined the school team as a 'second string' substitute, a position I held for the next three years." Later, Chu taught himself to pole vault using bamboo poles that he got from the local carpet store. "I was soon able to clear eight feet, but was not good enough to make the track team."

EDUCATION

Although he was always interested in learning new things, Chu found most of his schoolwork boring. It wasn't until high school that he began to find any classes interesting. "Geometry was the first exciting course I remember. Instead of memorizing facts, we were asked to think in clear, logical steps," he recalled. "I took immediately to the sport of proving theorems." Chu also enjoyed his high school English classes, where reading assignments often led to "binges" where he voluntarily went on to read more books by the authors he liked.

Chu's interest in physics and math began in his senior year of high school. He took advanced placement courses in these subjects, and his teachers became his early mentors. He particularly enjoyed his physics class, in which he was encouraged to conduct his own experiments. Chu spent half of his senior year working on an ambitious physics project that involved the construction of a working pendulum. He used the pendulum to make precise measurements of gravity. "The years of experience building things taught me skills that were directly applicable to the construction of the pendulum," he maintained. "Ironically, 25 years later, I was to develop a refined version of this measurement using laser-cooled atoms."

"Early in his career Chu worked at Bell Labs, a prestigious research facility where his group had complete freedom in their work. They had "no obligation to do anything except the research we loved best," he explained. "The joy and excitement of doing science permeated the halls. The cramped labs and office cubicles forced us to interact with each other and follow each others' progress. The animated discussions were common during and after seminars and at lunch and continued on the tennis courts and at parties. The atmosphere was … electric.""

Education was highly valued by Chu's family. "Virtually all of our aunts and uncles had PhDs in science or engineering, and it was taken for granted that the next generation of Chus were to follow the family tradition." Chu performed well in school, maintaining an A-minus average. By his family's standards, however, this performance was appalling. Chu describes himself as the "academic black sheep" of his family. "In comparison to my older brother, who set the record for highest cumulative average for our high school, my performance was decidedly mediocre," he admitted. "I studied, but not in a particularly efficient manner. Occasionally, I would focus on a particular school project and become obsessed with what seemed to my mother to be trivial details instead of apportioning the time I spent on school work in a more efficient way.… I've never been that good at apportioning time. When I got really excited about something, I would dig into it. It turns out that is a quality that the best researchers have."

SOME TERMINOLOGY

Atom — An atom is a basic form of matter that is made up of a nucleus surrounded by electrons.

Molecule — A molecule is a group of at least two atoms held together in a specific arrangement.

DNA — DNA is deoxyribonucleic acid, the genetic code that dictates the individual characteristics of all living things.

Chu's attitude about school changed once he started college. He attended the University of Rochester, a small research university in New York. There he was free to choose his own courses, and he enrolled in a series of introductory physics and math classes. Chu enjoyed those classes so much that he immediately committed himself to studying physics. Schoolwork became the focus of his obsessive energy. "All of a sudden, the things they wanted me to do were very natural," he explained. He earned a Bachelor of Arts degree (BA) in mathematics and a Bachelor of Science degree (BS) in physics from the University of Rochester in 1970. He then attended the University of California at Berkeley for graduate school. In 1976, Chu earned his doctoral degree (PhD) in physics from UC-Berkeley.

CAREER HIGHLIGHTS

As a Nobel Prize winner, Chu is known all over the world as an innovative scientist. Throughout his career, he has expanded the boundaries of scientific research and experimentation. His early discovery of pioneering techniques in the study of microscopic particles such as atoms, molecules, and DNA contributed to breakthroughs in many different scientific disciplines. Chu's more recent work in climate science and alternative energy laid the foundation for advances in those fields as well. In this way, his groundbreaking work with some of the smallest matter in existence has led to scientific and technological advancements on some of society's biggest issues.

The First Breakthrough

In 1978, Chu went to work at Bell Labs, a prestigious research facility operated by the AT&T company. In this position, he was part of an elite group of young scientists who had complete freedom in their work. Chu explained that his group had "no obligation to do anything except the research we loved best. The joy and excitement of doing science permeated the halls. The cramped labs and office cubicles forced us to interact with each other and follow each others' progress. The animated discussions were common during and after seminars and at lunch and continued on the tennis courts and at parties. The atmosphere was ... electric." Chu's supervisor instructed him to take at least six months to decide what type of work to pursue. During this time, he researched many potential topics and spent hours reading in the library.

Chu flourished in this open, collaborative environment. For his first project, he and a colleague planned an extremely difficult experiment. They wanted to measure the energy levels of an atom called positronium, which is one of the most basic types of atoms. Chu explained that "a precise measurement of its energy levels was a long standing goal ever since the atom was discovered in 1950." The problem was that positronium atoms exist for only a fraction of a second, making them exceptionally difficult to study. At the time, there were 12 published studies documenting failed attempts to observe positronium atoms. Chu's supervisor strongly discouraged him from pursuing the experiment, warning him that he could be ruining his career chasing an impossible result. But Chu was stubborn. After two years of effort, he finally succeeded in obtaining the precise measurements he hoped for. This early success was the first of many to come.

Building an Atom Trap

In 1983, Chu became the head of electronics research at Bell Labs and began the work that would lead to his Nobel Prize. A colleague was studying atoms and needed a way to slow them down in order to capture more detailed information about the properties of individual particles. Atomic particles are always moving at extremely high speeds—several thousand miles per second—and at that time it was impossible to catch and hold atoms for examination. Chu set his mind to the task, determined to find a way.

At that time, it was known that fast-moving atoms would stick to laser beams due to a force similar to static electricity. It was also known that atomic particles moved somewhat slower when they were cold. Previous attempts to trap atoms were based on the idea that atoms could be held by a laser beam and then slowed down by supercooling. Once they were slowed, the atoms could be studied. In theory, this approach should have worked. In practice, however, the atoms didn't stick to the laser beam long enough to be cooled. A new approach to the problem was needed.

An atom trap.

Chu worked on this problem for a long time without success. The breakthrough finally came late one evening in 1985 as he sat alone in his lab, thinking about trapping atoms as he watched snow falling outside the window. Chu recalled that something about the snowfall triggered a new thought. "The conventional wisdom at that time was first you hold the atom with light and then you make it cold so you can do what you want with it," he explained. "My idea was to reverse this by cooling the atom first, then grabbing it with light."

Though his colleagues were somewhat skeptical that this approach would work, Chu went ahead with his plan. He set up six laser beams in three pairs, pointed at each other at 90-degree angles. In this way, an atom placed in the middle of this system was trapped. With this setup, an atom becoming unstuck and moving away from any one of the laser beams would become stuck on another one of the laser beams. No matter which way the atoms moved, they were trapped by the surrounding laser beams.

Once the atoms were trapped, they could then be cooled. As the atoms were cooled to a temperature just above absolute zero, a glowing cloud about the size of a pea formed, containing about a million super-cooled atoms. The trapped and cooled atoms were then slow enough to be observed and manipulated. "Once you get an atom really cold, so it's moving as fast as an ant walks, a fraction of an inch per second, then very, very weak forces can push them around, and you can do what you want with them—for example, using electric or magnetic fields, or light," he explained. "You can hold them, you can push them around, you can do things that you simply cannot do when they're whizzing around like supersonic jet airplanes." Chu's technique came to be known as an "atom trap" because it confines atoms to a small space. The atom trap was also described as "optical molasses" because beams of laser light (optics) were used to make atoms sluggish, as if they were stuck in slow-moving molasses.

Although many researchers had wished for the ability to slow down atoms for detailed study, the full implications of this breakthrough were not yet realized. Chu recalled, "I told my boss, 'Guess what? I just trapped an atom.' He said, 'Great. What are you going to do with it?' I said, 'I don't know, but it's great.'"

Developing Uses for the Atom Trap

Chu and other researchers then set to work developing uses for the atom trap. One of the first outcomes of the atom trap was the proof of one of Albert Einstein's theories. If the atom trap experiment was continued over a period of time, it was found that a group of atomic particles could be collected. These particles formed a new state of matter that Einstein predicted in 1927. This matter was a very thin gas made up of slowly moving particles, with properties that made it different from the other four known states of matter (solid, liquid, gas, and plasma).

Further uses of the atom trap were soon found, and atom traps are now used in many different types of scientific experiments. Atom traps have also improved the precision time-keeping of the atomic clocks that determine the world's official time. "The ability to hold onto and control and manipulate these atoms means, for example, you can toss them up; they can turn around due to gravity in a vacuum where there are no other atoms around, and you can make better atom clocks," Chu argued. "So all of a sudden, you can measure changes in gravity so accurately that it's going to become competitive with the current ways of measuring changes in gravity, which is useful in all exploration. You can probably put it on an airplane or a helicopter. And with global positioning satellites to tell you the height and changes in distance ... it opens up the opportunity to map gravity drains and pockets of oil, diamonds, things of that nature, minerals, on a very fast-moving platform like a slow-moving plane or helicopter. So there are real practical implications."

"

"Once you get an atom really cold, so it's moving as fast as an ant walks, a fraction of an inch per second, then very, very weak forces can push them around, and you can do what you want with them," Chu explained. "You can hold them, you can push them around, you can do things that you simply cannot do when they're whizzing around like supersonic jet airplanes."

"

In 1987, Chu left Bell Labs to become the chairman of the physics department at Stanford University. In continuing his work on laser cooling and atom trapping, he began to explore atomic experiments in chemistry and biology. He developed another new method of using laser beams to work with atomic particles. Chu found that laser beams could be used to trap the ends of molecules and hold onto them long enough for their properties to be studied. This technique became known as "optical tweezers" because the beams of light allowed scientists to pick up and manipulate microscopic particles.

Chu (left) receives the 1997 Nobel Prize in Physics from King Carl XIV Gustaf of Sweden (right).

The first use that Chu imagined for optical tweezers was to aid in the study of DNA. At that time, DNA was difficult to examine closely because of its double helix structure. Even under a powerful microscope, the structure and properties of DNA were obscured by its spiraling twisted shape. Chu used optical tweezers to uncoil DNA and stretch it out into a single straight strand. In that form, it became easier to observe and study the structure and elements of DNA. The optical tweezer technique is now widely used in biology research.

Winning the Nobel Prize

In 1997, Chu was awarded the Nobel Prize in Physics for his work in developing methods to cool and trap atoms with laser light. The award recognized his contribution to new techniques that increased scientific understanding of atomic matter. He shared the award with two other scientists, Professor Claude Cohen-Tannoudji and Dr. William D. Phillips, who had expanded on his breakthrough.

Global Warming and Climate Change

Around this time Chu was becoming more concerned about global warming and the related climate change problems. He became convinced that new energy options were desperately needed to control and reduce greenhouse gas emissions. Chu believed that these new options would be discovered and developed through scientific research and experimentation. "The first industrial revolution allowed us to transition from muscle power, humans and animals, to using carbon-based fuels," he argued. "The unintended consequences were direct air pollution—sulfur dioxide, nitrogen oxides, particulate matter, smog. And we used science to clean that up. This is a much more serious problem: namely, how do we get our energy in a much more carbon-free manner?"

Chu developed an interest in finding solutions to the problems that would result from global climate change. Scientific evidence indicated that global warming could result in a substantial increase in the Earth's temperature if left unchecked. Chu felt that continuing with current energy usage and emissions could have catastrophic results. "In the business-as-usual scenarios … there's a 50 percent chance we may [have an increase of] five degrees centigrade," he observed. "We know what the Earth was like five or six degrees centigrade colder. That was called the Ice Age. Imagine a world five degrees warmer. The desert lines would be dramatically changed. The West is projected to be in drought conditions.... We can adapt to one or two degrees. More than that, there is no adaptation strategy."

In 2004, Chu was asked to consider becoming the director of the Lawrence Berkeley National Laboratory. This lab was owned by the U.S. Department of Energy and operated by the University of California. At first, he wasn't interested. "My first answer was no. I didn't have aspirations to be a big bureaucrat." But then, Chu explained, "It just sort of happened. I followed the path first from going and doing the science, to getting very concerned about some issues that affect us all as a society, to finally saying, I can't sit idly by and occasionally give a talk on this. I really have to get proactive and put my money where my mouth is and do a career shift because it is that important." He soon realized the potential benefit in taking the position. "If I really was interested in doing something about climate change, this would be a good platform. If I could get some of the best scientists to Lawrence Berkeley and get them to shift their interest, it might have some impact."

As the head of the Lawrence Berkeley National Laboratory, Chu was determined to make a difference on climate change issues. "Stronger storms, shrinking glaciers and winter snowpack, prolonged droughts and rising sea levels are raising the spectre of global food and water shortages. The ominous signs of climate change we see today are a warning of dire economic and social consequences for us all, but especially for the poor of the world. The path to finding solutions is to bring together the finest, most

Chu with students at the Lawrence Berkeley National Laboratory.

passionate minds to work on the problem in a coordinated effort, and to give these researchers the resources commensurate with the challenge."

At Lawrence Berkeley, Chu launched several major long-term research projects that are expected to lead to significant breakthroughs in alternative energy options. He believed that alternative energy exploration should be as important today as space exploration was in the 1960s and 1970s. "Sustainable energy is the equivalent of the U.S. moon shot," he declared. "If you look at the funding in the United States during Kennedy's era and followed by Lyndon Johnson, what the United States invested in the Apollo program, money of that magnitude, I am confident, would reveal a lot of breakthroughs in energy technologies, efficiency technologies and new forms of energy."

Science and Politics

Chu's commitment to working on energy issues and his reputation as one of the top scientists in the country combined to make him President Barack Obama's choice for U.S. Secretary of Energy. In announcing Chu's selection, President Obama said, "Steven has blazed new trails as a scientist, teacher, and administrator, and has recently led the Berkeley National Laboratory in pursuit of new alternative and renewable energies." Chu is the first person of Chinese descent to serve as Secretary of Energy, and the first Nobel Prize winner to hold such a high-ranking position. Chu was sworn into office on January 21, 2009.

The Secretary of Energy directs the U.S. Department of Energy, which is responsible for a range of energy, environmental, and national security issues. The Department is the largest source of funding for physical science research in the U.S. It operates 17 national research laboratories, manufactures and maintains America's nuclear weapons, and manages the environmental clean-up of nuclear waste. In addition to these responsibilities, Chu was given specific goals by President Obama: reduce America's dependence on fossil fuels, rebuild the nation's electrical grid, and address the challenges of climate change. Chu commented on his duties as Secretary of Energy by explaining, "I do not underestimate the difficulty of meeting these challenges. But I remain optimistic that we can meet them. I believe in the dynamism of our country and our economy. And as a scientist, I am ever-optimistic about our ability to expand the boundaries of what is possible."

"

"Science is really about describing the way the universe works in one aspect or another in all branches of science—how a life form works, how this works, how that works. You're really trying to understand what's around you. You have to have a natural curiosity for that.... It's remarkable what simple curiosity can lead to."

"

At the Department of Energy, as at Lawrence Berkeley, Chu began by recruiting top scientists to leave their chosen fields of research and focus on energy issues. "They say that necessity is the mother of invention and this is the mother of all necessities," he declared. "So we're going to get the mother of all inventions. And it's not going to be just one, it has to be many." Chu has said many times that sustainable energy solutions will require Nobel-level breakthroughs in certain critical areas. "Solar technology will have to get five times better than it is today, and scientists will need to find new types of plants that require little energy to grow and that can be converted to clean and cheap alternatives to fossil fuels." Chu also believes that electric batteries will have to improve substantially.

With the determination he has displayed throughout his career, Chu insists that these goals are attainable. "I think science and technology can generate much better choices. It has, consistently, over hundreds and hundreds

DEPARTMENT OF ENERGY
UNITED STATES OF AMERICA
Mic OFF

of years." Along with the development of new energy options, Chu believes that energy conservation and efficiency are critical components of a sustainable energy policy. "First and foremost…we should start using the energy we have more wisely. For example, in buildings. Forty percent of the energy that we use in the United States is in buildings, roughly 20 percent in commercial buildings and 20 percent in residential buildings. A tremendous amount of improvement can be made. We have the possibility of designing buildings that can reduce the energy consumption in commercial buildings by … 50, 60, 80 percent."

One of the biggest challenges Chu has faced as Secretary of Energy is working with members of Congress, particularly those who do not believe that global warming is a problem. Chu has made it part of his mission to educate Congress on the science of climate change and the consequences of ignoring it. Whenever he is faced with resistance from individual legislators, Chu invites them to meet with him to discuss their position. "I say, 'Come to my office and we'll talk about it.' At the very least you can put a little doubt in their minds. If they're so sure [global warming is caused by] natural causes, they may be less sure."

Chu has been widely recognized in the scientific world. He has written or co-written more than 200 scientific papers and has gathered a devoted following for his lectures on climate change. He is a member of the American Academy of Arts and Sciences, the National Academy of Sciences, the American Philosophical Society, the Chinese Academy of Sciences, Academica Sinica, the Korean Academy of Sciences and Technology, and the Copenhagen Climate Council. He holds honorary degrees from 10 universities. In 2009, Chu was named as one of *Time* magazine's 100 people who most affect the world.

In thinking about the future of scientific research and discovery, Chu sees great potential in the next generation of scientists. He had this to say when asked for his advice to young people interested in a career in science: "You've got to be very interested in what you're doing. You have to attack it with a passion. You can't give up. You have a plan, but if during the execution of whatever plan you had something comes along, keep an open mind." In Chu's opinion, curiosity is perhaps the most important characteristic of a great scientist. "Science is really about describing the way the universe works in one aspect or another in all branches of science—how a life form works, how this works, how that works. You're really trying to understand what's around you. You have to have a natural curiosity for that." Chu sums up his own achievements by simply saying, "It's remarkable what simple curiosity can lead to."

HOBBIES AND OTHER INTERESTS

Chu enjoys bicycling, swimming, cooking, and playing tennis and bridge.

MARRIAGE AND FAMILY

Chu met his first wife, Lisa Thielbar, when they were both graduate students at the University of California Berkeley in the early 1970s. They had two sons, Geoffrey and Michael, before their marriage ended in divorce. In 1997, Chu married Jean Fetter, a physicist.

HONORS AND AWARDS

Broida Prize for Laser Spectroscopy (American Physical Society): 1987
King Faisal International Prize for Science (King Faisal Foundation): 1993
Member, National Academy of Sciences: 1993
Arthur L. Schawlow Prize in Laser Science (American Physical Society): 1994
William F. Meggers Award for Spectroscopy (Optical Society of America): 1994
Science for Art Prize (LVMH Moet Hennesy Louis Vuitton): 1995
Guggenheim Award: 1996
Humboldt Senior Scientist Award (Alexander von Humboldt Foundation): 1996
Nobel Prize in Physics (Royal Swedish Academy of Sciences): 1997
Member, Chinese Academy of Sciences: 1998
Newsmaker of the Year (Nature): 2009
Public Policy Leadership Award (Asia Society): 2009
Arthur L. Schawlow Award (Laser Institute of America): 2010

FURTHER READING

Periodicals

Current Biography Yearbook, 2009
Economist, July 4, 2009, p.60
Nature, Dec. 24/31, 2009, p.978
New York Times, June 30, 1998; Oct. 23, 2007; Dec. 23, 2008; Feb. 12, 2009; Mar. 23, 2009; Apr. 19, 2009
Newsweek, Apr. 13, 2009; Apr. 20, 2009; Apr. 5, 2010, p.42
Popular Science, July 2009, p.54
Rolling Stone, June 25, 2009, p.58
Time, Dec. 2, 2008; Apr. 30, 2009; Aug. 24, 2009, p.30
U.S. News & World Report, Dec. 16, 2008; Apr. 2010, p.44
Wired, May 2010, p.104

Online Articles

http://www.lbl.gov/Publications/Director/index-Chu.html
(Berkeley Lab,"Obama Picks Berkeley Lab Director Steven Chu for Energy Secretary,"Jan. 29, 2009)
http://www.topics.nytimes.com
(New York Times,"Steven Chu,"multiple articles, various dates)
http://nobelprize.org/nobel_prizes/physics/laureates/1997/chu-autobio.html
(NobelPrize.org,"Steven Chu: Autobiography,"1997)
http://www.stanford.edu/group/chugroup/steve_personal.html
(Stanford University,"Steven Chu,"Oct. 18, 2005)
http://www.topics.time.com/time/topics
(Time,"Steven Chu,"multiple articles, various dates)
http://www.content.usatoday.com/topics
(USA Today,"Steven Chu,"multiple articles, various dates)

ADDRESS

Steven Chu
U.S. Department of Energy
1000 Independence Ave. SW
Washington, DC 20585

WORLD WIDE WEB SITE

http://www.energy.gov

Chris Colfer 1990-

American Actor
Plays Kurt Hummel on the Award-Winning
Television Show "Glee"

BIRTH

Christopher Colfer was born on May 27, 1990, in Fresno, California. His parents are Tim and Karyn Colfer. He has a younger sister named Hannah.

YOUTH

Colfer grew up in Clovis, California, a small town near Fresno in the San Joaquin Valley of Central California. He knew at a very young age that he wanted to become a professional actor. Beginning when he was about three years old, he often entertained his family by performing shows for them. His parents were very supportive and encouraged him to audition for roles in plays at the local community theater. "I was every little boy role in every production," Colfer recalled. He was Chip in the local theater's stage version of Disney's *Beauty and the Beast.* When he was eight years old, he received a standing ovation for his portrayal of Snoopy in the play *You're a Good Man, Charlie Brown.* He later played the role of Kurt von Trapp in a musical production of *The Sound of Music.*

"

Colfer was a frequent target of school bullies, who shouted insults and called him names as he passed by in the halls. "I had nothing but tough times in high school," he recalled. "But I was the kind of kid, very much like Kurt, who was so driven and set in what I wanted to do with my life and my future that I pretended that nothing they said bothered me."

"

EDUCATION

In school, Colfer's love of theater and the performing arts made him an outsider in the conservative community of Clovis. Rather than hanging out with friends or going out to socialize, he preferred to stay at home and write. He also spent a lot of time taking care of his younger sister, who suffered from severe epilepsy.

By the time Colfer entered Clovis East High School, his status as a social outcast was firmly in place. "The best way I can describe myself in high school was that I was kind of like a social llama," he remarked. "Like, where does the llama go? A llama's not a cow. It's not a horse. It might hang out with the duck once in a while, but it really has no place to belong. I was a social llama." He was a frequent target of school bullies, who shouted insults and called him names as he passed by in the halls. "I had nothing but tough times in high school," he recalled. "But I was the kind of kid, very much like Kurt, who was so driven and set in what I wanted to do with my life and my future that I pretended that nothing they said bothered me."

Colfer found ways to express his creativity by participating in a number of different school activities. He was the president of his high school writers' club, editor of the school's literary magazine, and a member of the competitive speech and debate teams. He held numerous championship titles in forensics (public debate) and creative interpretation (public performance of an original creative work).

Colfer was also involved in his high school's theater and drama programs. In 2003, he began working with an acting agent. He began going to auditions, but did not receive any roles. In his senior year of high school, Colfer wrote, directed, and acted in a spoof of the musical *Sweeney Todd.* His production, titled *Shirley Todd,* was set in the modern-day punk rock scene of London, England, and reversed the genders of the original roles.

At one point while he was in high school, Colfer decided that he wanted to learn how to use Japanese *sai* swords, the three-pronged martial arts daggers featured in the 2005 movie *Elektra.* "I bought the swords on eBay and I taught myself in my bedroom and in my living room," he admitted. "I broke lamps and my parents' coffee table, which I still haven't replaced. I'm a horrible son. It still has a huge sword imprint on it." Colfer graduated from Clovis East High School in 2008.

CAREER HIGHLIGHTS

After high school, Colfer enrolled in classes at Fresno City College. He continued to go to acting auditions in Los Angeles, hoping to be cast in a movie or television show despite his lack of acting experience. "I've never had any professional training anywhere, just high school and community theater shows," Colfer explained.

When Colfer first auditioned for a part on the TV show "Glee," the show's concept and full cast of characters were still under development. He tried out for the part of Artie, performing the song "Mr. Cellophane" from the musical *Chicago.* He was so nervous during the interview that he assumed he would not get the job. His agent called later that evening to say that the producers did not want to cast him as Artie, but that they were interested in him for a different role.

In his audition, Colfer had impressed the show's producers so much that they decided to create a new character especially for him. The role of gay teen Kurt Hummel was originally inspired by Colfer's own personality. As the character was developed, he worked with the writers to make Kurt a multi-dimensional role that avoided gay clichés and stereotypes. "I see these gay characters on other programs, and they're always loud and flamboyant," he declared. "In high school—especially in a conservative town—someone wouldn't be like that. That's why I made Kurt more internal and superior, rather than external and annoying." Many of Colfer's experiences as a social outsider in high school influenced the creation of Kurt's storylines, particularly with regard to anti-bullying themes.

Colfer as Kurt Hummel.

"Glee" made its TV debut in 2009. The show is set in the fictional William McKinley High School in a small Ohio town. The story focuses on the experiences of the members of the New Directions glee club, a show choir whose musical performances combine singing and dancing. The members of New Directions, who are seen as the school's misfits and geeks, are bullied and ridiculed by most of the other students and even some of the faculty. In each episode, glee club members perform at least six different songs as they prepare for various show choir competitions.

"Glee" Becomes a Hit

"Glee" quickly became a phenomenal success, attracting viewers of all ages. In its first season, "Glee" was the No. 1 TV series for teen viewers and consistently ranked in the top three TV shows among adults. Colfer seemed unsurprised by the show's remarkable success. "The show has struck a chord with an audience that never had anything to relate to before," he commented. "I know personally, because I am that audience, I'm one of those kids. It's the first time that the performing arts have been put in a good light and been encouraged."

The show's runaway success has been driven by its unique combination of fun, entertaining musical performances, and complicated, emotionally charged stories. Some of the more serious storylines have involved Colfer's character Kurt as he struggles to come to terms with himself as a young gay man. In one early episode, Kurt joins the school's football team in an attempt to win the approval of his traditional, sports-loving father. When Kurt kicks the winning field goal in an important game, he gains the courage to tell his father that he is gay. Kurt's father responds by telling his son that he'll love him no matter what.

The episode's sensitive handling of a significant moment in Kurt's relationship with his father was particularly powerful because it represented one of the few times that the struggles of gay teens were portrayed on broadcast network TV. "I really think that my character has gotten the best material. The fact that a father accepts his gay son for who he is needs to be seen, and probably should have been seen a lot sooner," Colfer observed. "I love the dramatic scenes that I get to do in the show because it's fun. It's like candy. You get to be gritty and gross, and any time Kurt's having an emotional breakdown, I'm loving it. Good fun for me."

Colfer's skill in navigating such difficult dramatic moments has made Kurt the unexpected breakout character in the large ensemble cast. *Rolling Stone* noted that Kurt "may be the most honest and inspirational portrait of a gay teenager ever attempted on TV" and praised Colfer for portraying Kurt "with a pitch-perfect mix of arrogance and vulnerability—high school personified." *Entertainment Weekly* called Kurt "one of the most socially relevant characters on TV," and "a new kind of gay hero … one who's loved as

Colfer with Mike O'Malley, who plays his father, Burt Hummel, on "Glee."

much for his boa wearing as he is for fending off bullies." The reviewer credited Colfer's "poignant, but often … gleeful depiction of a modern gay teen," concluding that "Colfer has turned into 'Glee's' musical and emotional show-stopper."

The popularity of Kurt's character and storylines ultimately resulted in the addition of the new character Blaine (played by Darren Criss), Kurt's friend and potential love interest. "When we made the announcement that Kurt was getting a boyfriend, people went [crazy], they were so excited." Viewers instantly loved the onscreen chemistry between Kurt and Blaine. In 2010, the most downloaded song from the bestselling *Glee Christmas* album was the duet "Baby It's Cold Outside" sung by Kurt and Blaine. "I think it's extremely important for gay youth out there to see that it's actually ok and that they are being represented in these shows," Colfer said. He believes it is "extremely important that there is this character in pop culture. Because Kurt is strong, he's brave, he's a hero. He's not a constant punchbag or punchline. He's someone that people can look up to."

Inspiring Others

Though he initially tried to keep his personal life private, Colfer publicly acknowledged that he was gay after "Glee" began to air. Since then, Colfer has helped to inspire other gay teens. "With all due respect to my castmates, they don't get the letters like I get—the letters that not only say 'I'm your biggest fan' but also 'Kurt saved my life' and 'Kurt doesn't make me feel alone' from seven-year-olds in Nebraska. When I was growing up, there wasn't a character like this. I think what makes Kurt so special is he's finding himself in front of our eyes," Colfer said. "I had a little boy, I don't know if he was gay. He was six and no one knows they're gay when they're six. He came up to me and gave me a hug and then broke down crying. Then I started crying. I got a message from a boy in Nebraska who said watching Kurt makes me feel like I'm not alone. I just think the vulnerability of the character is what touches people and makes them love him."

"I think the craziest thing for me personally—and this has happened like 150 times—is where someone will come out to me and they'll tell me I'm the only person they've come out to," Colfer said. "Had you told me when I was walking down the halls being picked on and harassed, in a matter of four years I'd be put in a position where the character I'd be playing on TV would be inspiring so many people in that same situation, it would have been mind-blowing. Everything happens for a reason, so maybe it was good I went through all of that because now it all comes from a personal place."

Achieving Success

Colfer's performance as Kurt has been recognized and honored by the entertainment industry. In 2009, he shared the Screen Actors Guild Award for Outstanding Performance by an Ensemble in a Comedy Series with the rest of the "Glee" cast. In 2010, Colfer was nominated for a 2010 Emmy Award for Outstanding Supporting Actor in a Comedy Series and a Screen Actors Guild Award for Outstanding Performance by a Male Actor in a Comedy Series. The show has been nominated for numerous awards, winning four Emmys in 2010 along with a Peabody Award, the Golden Globe Award for Best Television Series, and the People's Choice Award for Favorite TV Comedy.

In 2011, Colfer won the Golden Globe Award for Best Performance by an Actor in a Supporting Role in a Series, Miniseries, or Motion Picture Made for Television. In his acceptance speech, he dedicated the award to all the young people who struggle each day just to be themselves. "To all the amazing kids who watch our show and the kids that our show celebrates, who are constantly told 'no' by the people in their environment, by bullies at school, that they can't be who they are or have what they want because of who they are—well, screw that, kids!"

"Glee" is broadcast in countries all over the world, with more than 14 million viewers in the U.S. alone. The cast members have toured to sold-out

Colfer with castmates in a scene from "Glee" (from left): Heather Morris (Brittany Pierce), Amber Riley (Mercedes Jones), Kevin McHale (Artie Abrams), and Jenna Ushkowitz (Tina Cohen-Chang).

shows throughout the U.S. and around the world. In a relatively short period of time, music releases of "Glee" cast performances have amassed two platinum and two gold records, multiple Grammy Award nominations, and more than 16 million downloads of individual songs. "Glee" also holds the record for the most songs by a group to reach the *Billboard* Hot 100, beating out previous record-holder The Beatles. The 2010 release of the "Glee" *Christmas* album became the No. 1 soundtrack of that year.

Colfer has remained modest about all of the awards and critical acclaim. Though he dreamed of becoming an actor since childhood, he did not expect success to come so quickly. "I'd always wanted to eventually do something on Broadway or do something on TV, but I never thought it would be a mix of both. I'm very fortunate."

HOME AND FAMILY

Colfer currently has a home in Los Angeles.

SELECTED CREDITS

"Glee," 2009-

HONORS AND AWARDS

Screen Actors Guild Award: 2010, for Outstanding Performance by an Ensemble in a Comedy Series, for "Glee" (shared)
100 Most Influential People in the World (Time magazine): 2011
Golden Globe Award: 2011, for Best Performance by an Actor in a Supporting Role in a Series, Miniseries, or Motion Picture Made for Television

FURTHER READING

Periodicals

Advocate, Oct. 6, 2009
Entertainment Weekly, Nov. 12, 2010, p.46; Jan. 28, 2011, p.34
Los Angeles Times, Sep. 9, 2009, p.D1
People, Nov. 12, 2009; Oct. 2010, p.42
Rolling Stone, Apr. 15, 2010, p.42; Sep. 16, 2010, p.51
USA Today, Nov. 11, 2009, p.14b
Washington Post, Apr. 11, 2010, p.Y3

Online Articles

http://www.people.com
(People, "Glee's Chris Colfer Reveals Real-Life Story Behind Kurt's Diva Moment," Nov. 12, 2009)
http://www.tvguide.com
(TV Guide, "Chris Colfer: Biography," undated)

ADDRESS

Chris Colfer
Coast to Coast Talent Group
3350 Barham Boulevard
Los Angeles, CA 90068

WORLD WIDE WEB SITE

http://www.fox.com/glee

Suzanne Collins 1964-

American Writer for Young Adults
Author of the Award-Winning Novel Series *The Underland Chronicles* and *The Hunger Games*

BIRTH

Suzanne Collins was born in 1964 in New Jersey. Collins rarely grants interviews and is reluctant to give out much information about her personal life. She has revealed that her father served in the U.S. Air Force and has discussed how military life shaped her childhood, but she has not revealed any information about her mother. The youngest of four children, Collins has two older sisters and one older brother.

YOUTH

Collins's childhood was shaped by her father's career in the Air Force. She describes herself as a "typical military brat." She and her family moved around a lot when she was young, living in many different homes on or near military bases in the U.S. and overseas. The family spent the longest stretch of time living in Brussels, Belgium. (Belgium is a small country in Western Europe that borders Germany and France.)

———— " ————

Collins heard a lot about military history from her father. "He would take us frequently to places like battlefields and war monuments," she recalled. "It wasn't enough to visit a battlefield, we needed to know why the battle occurred, how it played out, and the consequences. Fortunately, he had a gift for presenting history as a fascinating story. He also seemed to have a good sense of exactly how much a child could handle, which is quite a bit."

———— " ————

Collins's father was a military historian who held a doctorate degree in political science. He sometimes held teaching positions at military academies, and during these times the family would live at the base where he taught. One of Collins's earliest childhood memories is of sitting on a hill at West Point Military Academy and watching the cadets go through drill exercises on the field below.

Collins's father shared his love of military history with his children. "He would take us frequently to places like battlefields and war monuments," she recalled. "It was very important to him that we understood about certain aspects of life. So, it wasn't enough to visit a battlefield, we needed to know why the battle occurred, how it played out, and the consequences. Fortunately, he had a gift for presenting history as a fascinating story. He also seemed to have a good sense of exactly how much a child could handle, which is quite a bit."

As a young girl, Collins enjoyed gymnastics and spending time outdoors, particularly in the woods. She loved reading and was a big fan of Greek and Roman mythology. Growing up, her favorite novels were *A Tree Grows in Brooklyn* by Betty Smith, *1984* by George Orwell, *A Wrinkle in Time* by Madeleine L'Engle, *Lord of the Flies* by William Golding, and *Dandelion Wine* by Ray Bradbury.

EDUCATION

Collins attended Indiana University, where she earned bachelor's degrees in theater and telecommunications—and where she also met her future husband, Cap Pryor. She then moved to New York City and attended New York University, where she earned a master's degree in dramatic writing.

Melissa Joan Hart in a scene from "Clarissa Explains It All," a popular Nick TV show that Collins wrote for at the beginning of her career.

CAREER HIGHLIGHTS

After earning her master's degree, Collins worked for a short time at an organization in New York City that provided services for adults with learning disabilities. A few years later, she began writing plays for adult audiences. In 1991, she began working as a writer for children's television shows. Collins was a member of the writing team for several popular shows on the Nickelodeon cable network, including "Clarissa Explains It All," "The Mystery Files of Shelby Woo," "Little Bear," "Oswald," and "Clifford's Puppy Days." She also worked as a writer for the show "Generation O!" on the Kids WB network. In 2001, she co-wrote an animated Christmas TV special called "Santa, Baby!"

The Underland Chronicles

Collins got the idea for her first novel around the time she was working on the "Generation O!" TV show. One day, she was thinking about the book *Alice in Wonderland* and how the story takes place in the countryside. She thought that children growing up in cities would be much more likely to fall down an open manhole than go down a rabbit hole like Alice did in that story. Collins began to imagine what would happen if a young person accidentally discovered a secret world hidden underneath a big city. As the story took shape in her mind, she started writing *Gregor the Overlander,* the first of what would eventually be five books in *The Underland Chronicles* series.

Gregor the Overlander, published in 2003, tells the story of Gregor, an 11-year-old boy who lives in New York City with his family. One day, he follows his two-year-old sister Boots through an air duct in their laundry room. When they come out at the other end of the duct, they find themselves in a strange underground world. The Underland is populated with extraordinary creatures like giant cockroaches, bats, spiders, and rats, all of which can talk. "I liked the fact that this world was teeming under New York City and nobody was aware of it," Collins explained. "That you could be going along preoccupied with your own problems and then whoosh! You take a wrong turn in your laundry room and suddenly a giant cockroach is right in your face. No magic, no space or time travel, there's just a ticket to another world behind your clothes dryer."

Humans also live in the Underland, and Gregor is surprised to learn that everyone there has been waiting for him to arrive. It seems that his father, who has been missing for more than two years, may be trapped in the Underland. Gregor and his sister set out to rescue their father with the help of several new friends: the rat Ripred, the cockroach Temp, and a human girl named Luxa. The inventive story of Gregor's adventures in the Underland captured the imagination of readers and was also praised by critics. As *Kirkus Reviews* tersely summarized, "Creature depictions are soulful and the plot is riveting; Underland's dark, cavernous atmosphere is palpable. Explanation and subtlety balance perfectly. Wonderful." *Booklist* called *Gregor the Overlander* "a well-written, fast-moving, action-packed fantasy.... Collins creates a fascinating, vivid, highly original world and a superb story to go along with it, and Gregor is endearing as a caring, responsible big brother who rises triumphantly to every challenge. This is sure to be a solid hit with young fantasy fans."

Gregor and the Prophecy of Bane, the second book in *The Underland Chronicles,* was published in 2004. In this story, Gregor finds himself drawn back to the Underland to rescue his little sister Boots, who has been kidnapped by giant cockroaches. Gregor discovers that both he and Boots have important roles to play in an ancient prophecy about a powerful white rat that threatens the existence of the Underland. The story unfolds with plenty of adventure, danger, conflict, and loss as Gregor embarks on the journey to rescue his sister from her captors. "Collins crafts another edge-of-the-seat quest," wrote *Kirkus Reviews.* "Gregor's resolution of the prophecy will surprise and delight readers—who will be equally delighted to see a new prophecy in Gregor's luggage when he returns home. Yessss!"

Gregor and the Curse of the Warmbloods, published in 2005, is the third book in the series. This time, a deadly plague threatens the residents of the Underland as well as the "real" world above. Gregor is called upon to help find a cure for the disease, which threatens several of his Underland friends as well as a member of his own family. With Gregor's loved ones in great danger, the tone of *Gregor and the Curse of the Warmbloods* is darker than

The first book in The Underland Chronicles *series.*

the previous books in the series. According to *Horn Book Magazine,* "This immensely readable installment won't disappoint fans of the first two books.... Character development, plotting, pacing, and description all shine; suspenseful chapter endings propel the story forward to its shocking and sobering conclusion."

Gregor and the Marks of Secret, the fourth book in the series, was published in 2006. This story finds Gregor setting out to solve a mystery involving the mice that live in the Underland. In the process, he learns a terrible secret. "As the series continues, Gregor is faced with increasingly difficult quests and choices as the Underland breaks into a massive global war," Collins remarked. "His struggle to survive—both physically and spiritually—forms the arc of *The Underland Chronicles."* Many reviewers, including *Horn Book Magazine,* praised the novel. "Collins keeps the tension and the stakes high; vivid description, expert pacing, and subtle character development all enhance this gripping fantasy adventure. At the conclusion, we leave Gregor heading into what promises to be an interspecies conflict of epic proportions. 'Who would he be...if he survived?' Readers will have to wait for the fifth (and final?) book to find out."

Gregor and the Code of Claw, the final book in *The Underland Chronicles,* was published in 2007. In this story, Gregor finally learns the truth about the Prophecy of Time and his role in fulfilling that prophecy. With his mother and sister trapped in the Underland, and a fearsome army of rats gathering for battle, Gregor must find a way to save everyone. But time is running out, and there is a code to be cracked, a mysterious new princess, and an impending war. As the story races to its conclusion, readers find out if Gregor has the courage and strength to save the Underland world. "Perhaps Collins's greatest achievement in these tales is the effortless introduction of weighty geopolitical ethics into rip-roaring adventure," said *Kirkus Reviews.* "It seems as elusive in the Underland as up above, but Gregor and his companions, including the unforgettable rat Ripred, may yet find a way. The resolution is bittersweet but faintly hopeful—a fitting end for an unflinchingly gutsy series whose deftly drawn characters have always lived dangerously."

The Hunger Games

By the time Collins completed the final book in *The Underland Chronicles* series, she already had the idea for a new book. She envisioned a trilogy (a series of three books) that would tell the story of a brutal futuristic world. In this world, children are randomly chosen to participate in a barbaric annual reality TV competition that ends with a fight to the death—the win-

The first book in The Hunger Games *series.*

ning competitor is the last one left alive. *The Hunger Games* became the title of the series as well as its first book. The series is a dark story of survival that breaks new ground in young adult fiction. The story unfolds through the viewpoint of a resourceful and courageous teenaged girl named Katniss Everdeen, who was called "the most important female character in recent pop culture history" by *The Atlantic.*

Collins first got the idea for *The Hunger Games* while watching TV. "I was channel surfing between reality TV programming and actual war coverage when Katniss's story came to me. One night I'm sitting there flipping around and on one channel there's a group of young people competing for, I don't know, money maybe? And on the next, there's a group of young people fighting an actual war. And I was tired, and the lines began to blur in this very unsettling way, and I thought of this story."

As Collins developed the idea for the story, she also began to incorporate several themes that became crucial to the plot: the horrors of war, particularly for young people; the insidious influence of reality TV and celebrity culture; and repression and rebellion in a dictatorial society. She married these themes with her childhood love of mythology. In ancient Greek mythology, the city of Athens lost a war against the kingdom of Crete. Every seven years after that, Crete forced Athens to sacrifice seven boys and seven girls to the Minotaur—a monster that was half man and half bull. "Even as a kid, I could appreciate how ruthless this was," Collins recalled. "Crete was sending a very clear message: 'Mess with us and we'll do something worse than kill you. We'll kill your children.' And the thing is, it was allowed; the parents sat by powerless to stop it." This went on until Theseus, the son of the king of Athens, volunteered to take the place of one of the boys chosen for this sacrifice. Theseus became famous when he fought and defeated the Minotaur. Collins imagined a futuristic version of Theseus and the Minotaur to create Katniss and her world. She was also inspired by stories of ancient Roman gladiators, the slaves who were forced to fight one another for the entertainment of Roman citizens.

The Hunger Games, published in 2008, is the first book in the series. This story is set in the distant future and focuses on Katniss, a 16-year-old girl who lives with her mother and younger sister. They live in the poorest of the 12 districts of Panem, a nation that evolved from the remains of North America after a terrible calamity. Most of its citizens are forced to work to support the wealthy residents of the Capitol, the tyrannical rulers of Panem. Many years before Katniss was born, the people in the districts went to war against the Capitol and suffered a terrible defeat. As part of their surrender, each district was forced to agree to send one boy and one girl to participate in "The Hunger Games," an annual televised competition. The 24 competitors, known as "tributes," are selected by lottery. They are taken to the Capitol and locked in an arena where they must fight one another until only one is left alive. The winner is awarded riches and freedom.

An expert hunter and archer, Katniss becomes a tribute for her district. *The Hunger Games* tells the story of her experiences before, during, and immediately after the gruesome competition. As the *New York Times Book Review* described her, "The 17-year-old girl at the center of the revolution is a great character without being exactly likable. Katniss is bossy, moody, bratty, demanding, prickly. She treats the world with an explosive aggression that is a little out of the ordinary, to say the least.... She is mesmerizing in her way of defying authority, antisocial, courageous, angry, self-involved and yet somehow sweepingly sympathetic."

"*The 17-year-old girl at the center of the revolution is a great character without being exactly likable,*" *wrote the* New York Times Book Review. "*Katniss is bossy, moody, bratty, demanding, prickly. She treats the world with an explosive aggression that is a little out of the ordinary, to say the least.... She is mesmerizing in her way of defying authority, antisocial, courageous, angry, self-involved and yet somehow sweepingly sympathetic.*"

The Hunger Games captivated readers and critics alike. The book was an immediate success, selling more than 2.9 million copies and spending more than 100 consecutive weeks on the *New York Times* bestseller list. Horror writer Stephen King called the book "a violent, jarring, speed-rap of a novel that generates nearly constant suspense.... I couldn't stop reading." *Twilight* author Stephenie Meyer said that "I was so obsessed with this book I had to take it with me out to dinner and hide it under the edge of the table so I wouldn't have to stop reading. The story kept me up for several nights in a row, because even after I was finished, I just lay in bed wide awake thinking about it.... *The Hunger Games* is amazing." Rick Riordan, author of the Percy Jackson series, wrote that "*The Hunger Games* is as close to perfect an adventure novel as I've ever read. I could not put it down. Collins has transformed the ancient Labyrinth myth into a terrifyingly believable tale of future America. Readers will be hungry for more." *Horn Book Magazine* also praised the book, saying "The plot is front and center here—the twists and turns are addictive, particularly when the romantic subplot ups the ante—yet the Capitol's oppression and exploitation of the districts always simmers just below the surface, waiting to be more fully explored in future volumes. Collins has written a compulsively readable blend of science fiction, survival story, unlikely romance, and social commentary."

Catching Fire

Catching Fire, published in 2009, is the second book in the series. The story begins with the aftermath of Katniss's shocking act at the conclusion of *The Hunger Games.* It seems that Katniss has set off a rebellion among residents of the districts, which has angered the leaders of the Capitol and threatened the safety of her family. As the district rebellion grows, she finds herself becoming its reluctant leader. She also finds herself in a romantic triangle, as she grows closer to both Peeta and Gale.

Catching Fire soon became as popular as its predecessor. This highly anticipated sequel simultaneously held the No. 1 position on the bestseller lists of *USA Today,* the *New York Times,* the *Wall Street Journal,* and *Publishers Weekly.* It won rave reviews, including these comments from *Booklist:* "Collins's crystalline, unadorned prose provides an open window to perfect pacing and electrifying world-building, but what's even more remarkable is that aside from being tremendously action-packed [science fiction] thrillers, these books are also brimming with potent themes of morality, obedience, sacrifice, redemption, love, law, and, above all, survival.... If you were dying to find out what happens after the last book, get ready for pure torture awaiting the next."

Mockingjay

The third and final book in the series, *Mockingjay,* had readers on the edge of their seats even before it was published. The cliffhanger ending of *Catching Fire* left fans begging for any clues about Katniss's fate. By the time *Mockingjay* was being readied for publication, the anticipation was so high that the publisher imposed strict secrecy measures. Going against the normal book release process, no advance copies of *Mockingjay* were made available for review before publication. Collins was not allowed to talk about any part of the story, and not even her husband was allowed to read the finished book until after it was published.

Mockingjay, the final chapter in *The Hunger Games* series, was published in 2010. By now, a revolution has begun, and the Capitol is striking back—and is specifically threatening Katniss and those closest to her. As the story races to its dramatic conclusion, Katniss faces even more challenges and

Mockingjay *provided a satisfying conclusion to Katniss's story.*

must gather all of her courage to make it through alive."In Katniss, Collins has crafted a heroine so fierce and tenacious that this reader will follow her anywhere," wrote the *Christian Science Monitor.* "Being the Mockingjay comes with a price as Katniss must come to terms with how much of her own humanity and sanity she can willingly sacrifice for the cause, her friends, and her family," wrote *School Library Journal.* "Collins is absolutely ruthless in her depictions of war in all its cruelty, violence, and loss, leaving readers, in turn, repulsed, shocked, grieving and, finally, hopeful for the characters they've grown to empathize with and love. *Mockingjay* is a fitting end to the series."

"In Katniss, Collins has crafted a heroine so fierce and tenacious that this reader will follow her anywhere," wrote the **Christian Science Monitor.**

Once again, praise for the novel was high, both on its own merits and also as the conclusion to the series, as in this review from *Publishers Weekly.* "This concluding volume in Collins's *Hunger Games* trilogy accomplishes a rare feat, the last installment being the best yet, a beautifully orchestrated and intelligent novel that succeeds on every level.... In short, there's something here for nearly every reader, all of it completely engrossing."This review from *Booklist* added more praise."Collins does several things brilliantly, not the least of which is to provide heart-stopping chapter endings that turn events on their heads and then twist them once more," wrote *Booklist.* "But more ambitious is the way she brings readers to questions and conclusions about war throughout the story. There's nothing didactic here, and sometimes the rush of events even obscures what message there is. Yet readers will instinctively understand what Katniss knows in her soul, that war mixes all the slogans and justifications, the deceptions and plans, the causes and ideals into an unsavory stew whose taste brings madness. That there is still a human spirit that yearns for good is the book's primrose of hope."

Success of the Series

Since the initial publication of *The Hunger Games,* the series has become extremely popular with both young adult and adult readers. *The Hunger Games* books have been published in 41 countries around the world. According to the *New York Times Book Review,* the series owes its phenomenal success to many factors."The specifics of the dystopian universe, and the fabulous pacing of the complicated plot, give the books their strange, dark charisma.... The trilogy balances seriousness with special effects, a fundamental furious darkness with fast-paced storytelling, so that the books manage to be simultaneously disturbing and fun. They contain a sharp satire of celebrity culture, mindless tabloidism, and decadence, as well as crusading teenagers trying to save the world; but they also resist our hunger for clear definitions of good and evil, our sentimental need for a worthwhile cause, our desire for happy or simple endings, or even for the characters we like not to be killed or tortured or battered or bruised in graphic ways. Like the evil Capitol that controls and shadows its world, the trilogy tends to use the things we are attached to against us."

Based on the runaway success of the books, *The Hunger Games* series is being developed into several movies. Collins is deeply involved in creating the first screenplay, which is not expected to follow exactly along with the story presented in the book. "When you're adapting a novel into a two-hour movie you can't take everything with you," Collins acknowledged. "The story has to be condensed to fit the new form. Then there's the question of how best to take a book told in the first person and present tense and transform it into a satisfying dramatic experience. In the novel, you never leave Katniss for a second and are privy to all of her thoughts, so you need a way to dramatize her inner world and make it possible for other characters to exist outside of her company.... A lot of things are acceptable on a page that wouldn't be on a screen." Many key parts have been cast: Jennifer Lawrence will play Katniss; Josh Hutcherson will play Peeta; Liam Hemsworth will play Gale; Woodie Harrelson will play Haymitch Abernathy; Elizabeth Banks will play Effie; and Lenny Kravitz will play Cinna. The first *Hunger Games* movie is scheduled to be released in 2012, with the sequel to be released in 2013.

Controversy over *The Hunger Games* Books

Although they have been extremely popular bestsellers, *The Hunger Games* books have also been the subject of much controversy and criticism. In 2010, the American Library Association listed *The Hunger Games* books among the top ten most frequently challenged books. (A "challenged book" is a book that someone has tried to have banned or removed from shelves in schools and libraries, usually because of objections to the book's content.) Some book reviewers feel that the dark tone and graphic violence of the story are too much for young readers. One *Wall Street Journal* book critic called *The Hunger Games* series "hyper-violent," and criticized the books for presenting images that may make destructive, harmful behavior seem normal.

Katniss (Jennifer Lawrence) and Gale (Liam Hemsworth) in a scene from the first Hunger Games *movie.*

In responding to this criticism, Collins argues that young readers are very capable of understanding the books' complicated subject matter. "I think right now there's a distinct uneasiness in the country that the kids feel," she observed. "Dystopian stories are places where you can play out the scenarios in your head—your anxieties—and see what might come of them. And, hopefully, as a young person, with the possibilities of the future waiting for you, you're thinking about how to head these things off."

Collins believes the violent parts of *The Hunger Games* are a necessary part of the story. "This is not a fairy tale; it's a war," she declared, "and in war, there are tragic losses that must be mourned." Collins also believes that adults need to have more conversations with young people about violence, war, and the challenges of determining how much of "reality" TV is actually real and not scripted. "There's this potential for desensitizing the audience so that when they see real tragedy playing out on the news, it doesn't have the impact it should," she contended. "It all just blurs into one program. And I think it's very important not just for young people, but for adults to make sure they're making the distinction. Because the young soldiers dying in the war in Iraq, it's not going to end at the commercial break. It's not something fabricated, it's not a game, it's your life."

"One of the reasons it's important for me to write about war is I really think that the concept of war, the specifics of war, the nature of war, the ethical ambiguities of war are introduced too late to children. I think they can hear them, understand them, know about them, at a much younger age without being scared to death by the stories," Collins argued. "If we introduce kids to these ideas earlier, we could get a dialogue about war going earlier and possibly it would lead to more solutions. I just feel it isn't discussed, not the way it should be. I think that's because it's uncomfortable for people. It's not pleasant to talk about. I know from my experience that we are quite capable of understanding things and processing them at an early age."

According to Collins, it was her father's passion for military history and his ability to share it with his children that formed these experiences. "My dad was career Air Force, a Vietnam vet, and a doctor of political science. He felt very strongly about educating his children about war. And in turn, I feel drawn to creating stories for kids that might help them understand it." For Collins, that's become the basis of the many stories beloved by her fans. "A lot of people tell writers to write about what they know. And that's good advice, because it gives you a lot of things to draw on. But I always like to add that they should write about things that they love. And by that I mean things that fascinate or excite them personally."

MARRIAGE AND FAMILY

Collins lives in Sandy Hook, Connecticut, with her husband, Cap Pryor; their two children; and two cats.

SELECTED WRITINGS

The Underland Chronicles

Gregor the Overlander, 2003
Gregor and the Prophecy of Bane, 2004
Gregor and the Curse of the Warmbloods, 2005
Gregor and the Marks of Secret, 2006
Gregor and the Code of Claw, 2007

The Hunger Games Series

The Hunger Games, 2008
Catching Fire, 2009
Mockingjay, 2010

HONORS AND AWARDS

100 Books for Reading and Sharing (New York Public Library): 2003, for *Gregor the Overlander*

Best Book of the Year (*Publishers Weekly*): 2008, for *The Hunger Games;* 2009, for *Catching Fire;* 2010, for *Mockingjay*
Best Book of the Year (*School Library Journal*): 2008, for *The Hunger Games*
Best Young Adult Book of the Year (*Kirkus Reviews*): 2008, for *The Hunger Games;* 2009, for *Catching Fire;* 2010, for *Mockingjay*
Editors' Choice (*Booklist*): 2008, for *The Hunger Games;* 2009, for *Catching Fire;* 2010, for *Mockingjay*
Editors' Choice (*New York Times Book Review*): 2008, for *The Hunger Games;* 2009, for *Catching Fire*
Notable Book (*New York Times*): 2008, for *The Hunger Games;* 2010, for *Mockingjay*
Cybils Award for Young Adult Fantasy & Science Fiction: 2008-2009, for *The Hunger Games*
Best Books for Young Adults (American Library Association): 2009, for *The Hunger Games;* 2010, for *Catching Fire*
Indie Bound Young Adult Book of the Year (American Booksellers Association): 2009, for *Catching Fire*
Top Ten Best Books (*People*): 2009, for *Catching Fire*
Top Ten Fiction Books (*Time*): 2009, for *Catching Fire*
Best of 2010 (*Christian Science Monitor*): 2010, for *Mockingjay*
Entertainers of the Year (*Entertainment Weekly*): 2010
Teen Choice Book of the Year (Children's Book Council, Children's Choice Book Awards): 2010, for *Catching Fire*
Teen Top Ten (American Library Association—Young Adult Library Services Association): 2010, for *Catching Fire*
The Time 100: The World's Most Influential People (*Time*): 2010
The Year's Most Transporting Books (National Public Radio): 2010, for *Mockingjay*

FURTHER READING

Periodicals

Entertainment Weekly, Dec. 12, 2010; Aug. 20, 2010; May 27, 2011
New York Times, Apr. 8, 2011
New York Times Book Review, Sep. 8, 2010
New Yorker, June 14, 2010
Publishers Weekly, June 9, 2011
School Library Journal, Sep. 2008; Aug. 2010
Time, Apr. 29, 2010
USA Today, Sep. 1, 2009
Wall Street Journal, June 4, 2011; June 9, 2011

Online Articles

http://www.ew.com
(Entertainment Weekly, "Hunger Games Central," multiple articles, various dates)
http://insidemovies.ew.com/2011/04/07/hunger-games-suzanne-collins-gary-ross-exclusive
(Entertainment Weekly, "Team 'Hunger Games' Talks: Author Suzanne Collins and Director Gary Ross on Their Allegiance to Each Other, and Their Actors," Apr. 7, 2011)
http://www.nytimes.com
(New York Times, "Survivor," Sep. 8, 2010; "Suzanne Collins's War Stories for Kids," Apr. 8, 2011)
http://www.newyorker.com
(New Yorker, "Fresh Hell: What's Behind the Boom in Dystopian Fiction for Young Readers?" June 14, 2010)
http://www.publishersweekly.com/pw/by-topic/childrens
(Publishers Weekly, "Are Teen Novels Dark and Depraved—or Saving Lives?" June 9, 2011)
http://www2.scholastic.com
(Scholastic, "Q&A with *Hunger Games* Author Suzanne Collins," undated; "Suzanne Collins Biography," undated)
http://www.teenreads.com/authors/au-collins-suzanne.asp
(Teen Reads, "Suzanne Collins," Aug. 2010)
http://online.wsj.com
(Wall Street Journal, "Darkness Too Visible," June 4, 2011; "Why the Best Kids Books Are Written in Blood," June 9, 2011)

ADDRESS

Suzanne Collins
Scholastic, Inc.
555 Broadway
New York NY 10012

WORLD WIDE WEB SITE

http://www.suzannecollinsbooks.com

Paula Creamer 1986-

American Golfer
Winner of the 2010 U.S. Women's Open

BIRTH

Paula Creamer was born on August 5, 1986, in Mountain View, California, and raised in Pleasanton, California. Both towns are near San Francisco. She is the only child of Paul Creamer, a commercial airline pilot and former Navy pilot, and Karen Creamer.

YOUTH

As a young child, Creamer enjoyed gymnastics, but she didn't have the ideal body type for the sport. "I was too tall for the

"

As a young child, Creamer enjoyed gymnastics, but she didn't have the ideal body type for the sport. "I was too tall for the bars and the beam," she remarked. "I really just did floor exercises. I later became an acrobatic dancer.... I was good. We traveled all over and won lots of big events."

"

bars and the beam," she remarked. "I really just did floor exercises. I later became an acrobatic dancer.... I was good. We traveled all over and won lots of big events." One day while attempting an acrobatic trick, Creamer took a bad fall. "I landed on my neck, and I heard something crack and pop, and I thought I was paralyzed," she remembered. Although she wasn't seriously injured, thoughts of that fall haunted her. "It was never really the same," she said. "I didn't like tumbling anymore. Then I found golf, and it was a blessing."

Creamer's father golfed, and the family lived next to the Castlewood Country Club, where there are two championship golf courses and an excellent youth golf program. Her father introduced her to the basics of the game when she was 10 years old. It was obvious she was naturally talented, and she liked it immediately. "I had great teachers who made it fun," she recalled. Her average score quickly dropped from 90 to the low 80s and then the low 70s. (The object of golf is to get the ball in the hole with as few strokes as possible, and the total number of strokes is the player's final score.) By the age of 11, Creamer had won 18 junior tournaments.

EDUCATION

Creamer's education was a bit unusual. She became intrigued with the Leadbetter Academy in Bradenton, Florida, which specializes in developing talented young golfers. She convinced her parents to take her there for a visit and some instruction. "I thought it was the most unbelievable place," she said. "Leaving, I was so depressed because I wanted to stay." In 2000, the whole family relocated so she could attend Leadbetter full-time. "It was like a fairy tale. It has everything you need to become the player you want to be. You aren't forced to do anything; it's up to you. It has physical fitness, media training, and mental training," she said. Creamer also attended the Pendleton School, a private school attended by many elite young athletes who train in the area. She graduated from Pendleton in 2005.

GOLF SCORING

In golf scoring, players keep track of how many "strokes" it takes them to hit the ball from the tee to the cup; the fewer strokes, the better. "Par" refers to the standard number of strokes it should take a player to complete each hole. For example, most golf courses include short holes, which are usually designated as "par 3," as well as longer holes, which are designated as "par 5." On a regulation, 18-hole golf course, par for all holes will add up to 72.

On the professional golf circuit, most tournaments take place over four days. Each day, all the players shoot one "round" of 18 holes. After the first two rounds, they often cut the field to the top 60 or 70 golfers (players either "make the cut" or "miss the cut"). After all four rounds, the scores are totaled and the player with the lowest score wins the tournament. This format is called "stroke play." There are many tournaments on the women's professional golf tour, but the most prestigious are the four major, or "Grand Slam," events: the Kraft Nabisco Championship, the LPGA Championship, the U.S. Women's Open, and the Women's British Open.

Many amateur tournaments and team tournaments (like the Solheim Cup) use a different scoring system, called "match play." In this system, golfers play one-on-one over 18 holes. Whoever takes the fewest strokes on a hole scores a single point; if the two golfers tie they split the point. They keep a running tally of holes; if Player A has won 5 holes and Player B has won 3 holes, Player A is considered "2 up." A match can end before 18 holes if one player mathematically eliminates the other. In this case, the final score is listed as two numbers: the first indicating how many up the winner was, the second showing how many holes were left over. The highest winning score in match play is thus "10-and-8," meaning the winner won the first 10 holes, so they did not need to play the last eight. If a round of 18 holes ends in a tie, the match goes to "sudden death" on extra holes—meaning that the first player to win a hole wins the match.

"The Pink Panther"

While Creamer was a student at Leadbetter, one of her friends gave her the nickname the Pink Panther, after the all-pink cartoon character of the same name. Pink outfits and accessories are her trademark, both on and off the golf course."I've always loved pink,"she explained."I love how feminine it is, and at the same time it's kind of a power color." She also gained a reputation as a fierce competitor, intensely focused on her game.

While attending Pendleton and Leadbetter, Creamer competed at the highest levels of amateur and junior golf. She won 19 national tournaments as an amateur, including 11 sanctioned by the American Junior Golf Association (AJGA). In 2002, she was part of the winning U.S. team in the Junior Solheim Cup, one of the most prestigious events in junior golf.

CAREER HIGHLIGHTS

Outstanding Amateur

Creamer's 2003 season was one of the most outstanding ever played by an amateur golfer, male or female. She won seven junior tournaments and made the semifinals for two major competitions, the U.S. Girls' Junior and the U.S. Women's Amateur. If they qualify, amateur golfers can play in a limited number of events on the professional golf tour run by the Ladies Professional Golf Association (LPGA). Creamer qualified for the U.S. Women's Open, but she did not make the cut to play in the final round. She did make the cut in two other LPGA competitions, however. She also played at the Junior Solheim again that year, and the U.S. took second in the event. At the end of the season, she was named Player of the Year by the American Junior Golf Association and Junior Player of the Year by *Golfweek* and *Golf Digest*. That year also saw an important improvement in her game. She was already impressive at hitting the ball off the tee, and she knew how to keep her cool even when playing a high-stakes game. Her weakness was her "short game," the shots taken close to or on the green. To reach the level of play that would take her to the top of competition, Creamer needed to sharpen her short game, and she did.

Creamer had another impressive year in 2004. In March, she played in the Kraft Nabisco Championship, one of the four "majors" in women's golf. Sponsors of tournaments can invite promising players to take part, paying their entry fees as well. This is known as a "sponsor's exemption." Creamer had a sponsor's exemption for the Kraft Nabisco, and she tied for the 45th spot in the final standings.

The Kraft Nabisco was an important turning point for Creamer. Being on the course with older players she admired, she found herself feeling starstruck, rather than focusing on playing her best game. That showed in her higher scores. "I had to get stronger," she recalled. "But mentally that was a big thing to overcome, to believe in myself and be able to compete at that level." She worked hard to change her attitude before her next event, the

Creamer made the semifinals at the U.S. Women's Amateur during her outstanding 2003 season, when she was just 17.

ShopRite LPGA Classic in Abescon, New Jersey. She finished second, losing to Cristie Kerr by just one shot on the final hole.

Creamer continued to play strongly in 2004 and was chosen for the U.S. team for the 33rd Curtis Cup. Held every other year, the two-day tournament is the greatest prize in the world of women's international amateur golf. In 2004, the U.S. team was the youngest in the history of the event, with five teens on the squad and no player over the age of 25. The U.S. won, defeating Ireland and Great Britain. Creamer's 2-0 victory over Emma Duggleby of England in the singles division was a strong contribution to the team's overall performance.

One of Creamer's teammates was Michelle Wie, a talented golfer from Hawaii who was only 14 at the time. The two already had a rivalry on the golf course, but they became friends while on the Curtis Cup team. "When we were off the golf course, we didn't talk about golf," Creamer said. "I love shopping and fashion, and she loves it, too. We have a lot in common. We were on the plane, drawing outfits and designing clothes."

Creamer competed in seven LPGA tour events in 2004, usually playing on sponsor's exemptions, and she made the cut in every one. In addition to her fine performances in the ShopRite and the Curtis Cup, she finished 13th in the U.S. Women's Open. She and Wie tied with the best amateur scores in the event. Creamer was 18th in the Canadian Women's Open, and she went to the World Amateur Team Championship as part of the U.S. squad, which took second place. Her 2004 season earned her the Nancy Lopez Award from the LPGA, given each year to the best amateur in women's golf.

Turning Pro

The difference between amateur and professional status is important in golf. Amateurs can only accept a limited amount of prize money each year. If they break this rule, they can have their amateur status taken away. Most professional golfers earn their living by teaching golf, but the top players can qualify to play in major tours sponsored by the LPGA, the Professional Golf Association (PGA), and other organizations. Talented junior golfers usually continue to play as amateurs during college before deciding whether or not to turn pro. A golfer as talented as Creamer, however, might qualify for the pro tour without playing first for a college team.

In 2004, Creamer took part in the LPGA Qualifying School, a series of tournaments that is also known as "Q-School." Those who prove them-

Creamer's dominating play at the 2004 Daytona Beach LPGA Qualifying School (Q-School) earned her a spot on the pro tour.

selves in Q-School win a spot on the pro tour, but if things do not go well, participants may hold on to their amateur status. Creamer decided that if she didn't do well in Q-School, she would remain an amateur, enter college, and play collegiate golf. Her real desire was to win a spot on the pro tour, however. "I want to be the No. 1 player in the world," she stated in 2004. "And if I turn pro, I want to win my first year out there. Those are lofty goals, but I mean what I say, and I'm going to do everything I can do to get there."

Creamer dominated the 2004 Q-School. In December, at the LPGA final qualifying tournament in Daytona Beach, Florida, she became the youngest winner and the first amateur winner in the history of the event. Her victory was decisive—she took the final round by five strokes. Soon afterward, she declared herself a professional. She wrapped up her studies at Pendleton and joined the LPGA pro tour in February 2005, at age 18. "Going to college and getting your degree is so important. I wanted to experience that. I really did," she said. "[But] I wanted to be the No. 1 player in the world instead of the No. 1 collegiate player."

LPGA Rookie of the Year

Being part of the LPGA tour and having the opportunity to watch and play against so many other world-class players was an incredible learning experience for Creamer. Always goal-oriented, she first set her sights on qualifying for the Kraft Nabisco Championship, held late in March, one of the four majors. In 2004, she had played in the Kraft Nabisco on a sponsor's exemption. In 2005, she earned her way into the tournament by placing in the top 15 money-winners from the first three LPGA events of the season. She finished in a five-way tie for 19th place.

A few months later, Creamer became the youngest winner in the history of a multi-round LPGA event, triumphing in the Sybase Classic on May 23, 2005, just a few days before her official graduation from high school. Much of the final round was played in cold rain, and at one point, it seemed Creamer's game was falling apart, but she defeated Gloria Park and Jeong Jang by just one stroke. Two months after Sybase, she took the Evian Masters in France with an eight-shot win. That made her the youngest winner ever on the Ladies European Tour, and the prize money pushed her career earnings over the million-dollar mark. She was the youngest LPGA player to earn that much, and she had done so more quickly than any other player.

Creamer's rookie season had other highlights. She won twice on the Japanese LPGA tour and took third place at the LPGA Championship. She also qualified for a spot on the U.S. team for the Solheim Cup. Each year, the Solheim pits the top 12 U.S. players against the top 12 European players. Creamer was the youngest player ever to compete in the event, which the U.S. won that year. When the season ended, her rookie earnings stood at $1.5 million and she was ranked the second-best player on the LPGA tour.

It was not surprising when she was named the LPGA Rookie of the Year. This award is based on a point system, and Creamer stood more than 500 points ahead of her closest rival. "Paula has played incredibly well during her rookie year and has displayed poise and maturity beyond her years," said Carolyn Bivens, who was commissioner-elect of the LPGA at that time. "She has consistently played at the highest level and has set a new performance standard for rookies."

Injuries and Experience

Being a top-ranked pro golfer presented new challenges. Creamer's schedule was hectic. Professional events are held more frequently than amateur events, leaving less time for practice. She faced the distractions of celebrity parties and endorsement deals with many companies, including Kraft, TaylorMade, Adidas, and Bridgestone. She also sprained ligaments in her hand in 2006. She went without a win that year, and her ranking fell to 11th.

In 2007, Creamer had two LPGA wins and was part of the U.S. Team for the Solheim Cup. She made the winning stroke for the Americans in the final round at the Solheim. Her LPGA ranking rebounded to third that year. The 2008 season saw further improvement. She won four times on the tour, earned $1.8 million in prize money, and set a course record score of 60 while winning the Jamie Farr Owens Corning Classic in Sylvania, Ohio. At the end of the season, she was once again ranked the second-best player in the LPGA.

Asked if she regretted not attending college, Creamer said, "No. I can honestly say that. These have been the best five years of my life. There is so much I want to do in women's golf and I'm living my dream.... I will go back and get my degree, there's not a doubt in my mind. But when you have opportunities like I did, you have to take advantage of them.

”

As 2008 drew to a close, however, Creamer developed serious health problems that troubled her into the next year. During a trip to Mexico she suffered severe abdominal pain, but doctors didn't know what was wrong. Over the next months she endured pain, vomiting, weight loss, and weakness. She was tested for many different illnesses and tried different medications, but doctors were unable to determine the cause of the problems. Her weight went up and down, and her strength deteriorated. Minor illnesses became major because her body's immune system was weakened. Her health problems persisted the next year and at times forced her to withdraw from competition or play in pain. She had no wins in 2009, and her ranking fell to ninth. Her health eventually came back, although doctors still didn't know why. "They still have no idea what was wrong with me, which is a scary thought knowing that it could come back," Creamer acknowledged. Dealing with these health issues was difficult for her. "It was hard," she said of this period. "But I feel like it made me a lot stronger, mentally, and it put things in perspective. It was a year of learning."

Triumph in the 2010 U.S. Open

Creamer had high hopes for the 2010 season, but it had barely started when she was forced to withdraw from the LPGA Thailand event because

After several years battling illness, Creamer came back strongly in 2010, winning the U.S. Women's Open.

of a thumb injury. At the end of March, she underwent surgery on a damaged ligament. She thought she might have to take the whole season off, but her doctor let her return to play four months after surgery. It was the longest she had ever gone without playing golf since she had taken up the game. Even during her layoff, she was preparing mentally for the 65th U.S. Women's Open, to be held in July in Oakmont, Pennsylvania. She got back on the course just four weeks before the Open.

Creamer's performance over the four days of play in the Women's Open was commanding. She started the final round with a three-stroke lead and never fell below two shots. She won by four shots, with a final-round score of just 69. Her total score was 281, three under par. She played three subpar rounds in a row, something accomplished only once before in Oakmont's history. Creamer had finally claimed her first victory in an LPGA majors. Due to her injury, she limited her play for the rest of the season, but she still finished with a ninth-place ranking and $875,140 in winnings.

Creamer was not such a commanding presence during 2011. By mid-September, she had not won a tournament. She tied for second in the RR Donnelley LPGA Founders Cup in March; she tied for third in the LPGA State Farm Classic and the Wegmans LPGA Championship, both in June; and she took fourth in the Safeway Classic in August; her other finishes were even lower. In the U.S. Women's Open, where she was the defending champ, she tied for 15th.

But a mediocre season didn't diminish Creamer's love for the sport. She describes herself as "energetic, cheerful, competitive, and determined." She loves golf and encourages children to get involved with it. "You learn so many lessons: control, adversity, time management, integrity, honesty. And you can have so much fun doing something you love. You can't beat that."

Asked if she regretted not attending college, Creamer said, "No. I can honestly say that. These have been the best five years of my life. There is so much I want to do in women's golf and I'm living my dream.... I will go back and get my degree, there's not a doubt in my mind. But when you have opportunities like I did, you have to take advantage of them."

HOME AND FAMILY

Creamer lives in Isleworth, an exclusive community just outside Windermere, Florida, in the greater Orlando area. Isleworth includes a championship golf course, and many top golfers have homes there. In 2009, Creamer bought her own house, seven doors away from the one where her parents live. She says her focused and competitive nature are much like her father's.

HOBBIES AND OTHER INTERESTS

Creamer loves to get her hair done, get manicures, and go shopping. She enjoys getting dressed up and looking at the latest fashion trends. She has said that if she weren't devoted to golf, she would like to have a career in fashion design. She is also interested in nutrition and fitness.

Creamer also enjoys watching TV and movies. She likes the TV programs "America's Next Top Model," "Newlyweds," and "CSI." Her favorite golf movie is *Happy Gilmore.* Other favorite movies include *Shrek, Pretty Woman, Curly Sue,* and *Dirty Dancing.*

HONORS AND AWARDS

AJGA Player of the Year: 2003
Golf Digest Junior Player of the Year: 2003
Golfweek Junior Player of the Year: 2003
Golf Digest Amateur of the Year: 2004
Golfweek Amateur of the Year: 2004
LPGA Nancy Lopez Award: 2005
LPGA Rookie of the Year: 2005
U.S. Women's Open (LPGA): 2010

FURTHER READING

Periodicals

Golf Digest, Jan. 2006, p.110; Dec. 2011, p.123
Golf Fitness, Nov.-Dec., 2008, p.14
USA Today, Dec. 14, 2004, p.C3; June 28, 2006, p. C12

Online Articles

http://www.golfdigest.com
(Golf Digest,"Interview with Paula Creamer,"Mar. 1, 2010)

ADDRESS

Paula Creamer
IMG
1360 East 9th Street, Ste. 100
Cleveland, OH 44114

WORLD WIDE WEB SITES

http://www.lpga.com

Lucas Cruikshank 1993-

American Actor, Writer, and Comedian
Creator of the Fictional Character Fred Figglehorn
Producer and Star of the Hit Web Video Series "Fred" and the Film *Fred: The Movie*

BIRTH

Lucas Cruikshank was born on August 29, 1993, in Columbus, Nebraska, a small rural town near Omaha. The fourth of eight children, he has two brothers and five sisters. His father, David, works as an engineer. His mother, Molly, is a nurse.

YOUTH

Cruikshank grew up in a farming community, in a house that was surrounded by cornfields on three sides. For as long as he can remember, he wanted to be an actor. He enjoyed putting on shows and performing with his brothers, sisters, and cousins during family vacations and other gatherings. Cruikshank's first videos were recordings of these performances. "I've been doing videos for as long as I can remember," he said. "I've always been messing around with cameras wherever I could find them. Whether it was my mom's camera or a friend's camera."

By the time he was nine years old, Cruikshank was downloading movie scripts from the Internet and acting out the stories. "I always had dreams of being an actor," he explained. "I had a really strong drive. I was looking online for auditions in Nebraska. I wanted to do it so bad."

By the time he was nine years old, Cruikshank was downloading movie scripts from the Internet and acting out the stories. "I always had dreams of being an actor," he explained. "I had a really strong drive. I was looking online for auditions in Nebraska. I wanted to do it so bad." He found opportunities to act on stage with local theater groups. He appeared in productions of *High School Musical, Aladdin,* and *Grease.*

EDUCATION

Cruikshank attends Lakeview High School in Columbus, Nebraska. In addition to English, math, and science, he also studies Spanish, journalism, and drama. He has had the same classmates since the third grade. "I go to a really small, country school," he commented. "So I've been in school with them since third grade. They all know me as the same Lucas before the YouTube videos took off."

Cruikshank's parents support his dream of a career in acting, though they have insisted that school must come first. Even with the growing popularity of his videos and other projects, he is realistic about the importance of his education. "My parents obviously always have school come first," he stated. "I have to do my homework before I can do any of the other stuff with Fred. It's not that big of a deal." After graduating, Cruikshank plans to go to college to study drama and writing.

Cruikshank as Fred Figglehorn.

CAREER HIGHLIGHTS

By the time he was a teenager, Cruikshank had developed a reputation as a successful entertainer of children and teens. He is the writer, producer, director, and star of the popular Web video series "Fred," which has attracted one of the biggest groups of viewers on YouTube. The "Fred" video series documents the life, adventures, and mishaps of Fred Figglehorn, a fictional character created and performed by Cruikshank. "Fred" began as a hobby that Cruikshank thought would be just for fun. But within just four years, "Fred" grew into an entertainment phenomenon that includes the original video series, a full-length movie, two albums of music, and a line of merchandise including clothing, stickers, posters, and mugs. The "Fred" YouTube channel was the first ever to reach one million subscribers.

Creating Fred Figglehorn

Cruikshank first got the idea for the character of Fred Figglehorn when he was 13 years old. "I got a digital video camera for my 13th birthday so I started making up these random characters," he recalled. "I just loved writing and acting. So I recorded a few videos with this camera and Fred was one of them."

Fred Figglehorn is a hyper, overexcited, loud-mouthed, fast-talking six-year-old with an annoying high-pitched voice. He loses his temper easily and yells about everything. Cruikshank uses digital video editing software to distort his own voice into Fred's trademark screech. He also speeds up the videos to make Fred appear even more frantic and agitated. Cruikshank explained that the inspiration for Fred came from watching his younger brothers. "They were crazy little kids, and I exaggerated what they did and made Fred like them."

In June 2006, Cruikshank uploaded the first Fred videos to YouTube. "YouTube was just being created when I was 13 and back then it was mostly just vloggers [video bloggers]," he said. "I thought it was so weird how people did that so Fred was kind of poking fun at that." Cruikshank thought it would be funny to create a fictional video blogger who was a little boy. The concept was that each video would feature Fred ranting to his webcam about the different things that were going on in his life.

Cruikshank originally created the videos for his friends and family members to enjoy. He was surprised when complete strangers began leaving comments on the Fred videos posted on YouTube. "I didn't really understand YouTube at the time," he admitted. "I didn't know that millions of people could watch your video. I just thought that the friends I sent it to could watch it. So I was really surprised when I posted 'Fred' and it totally blew up."

At that time, Cruikshank shared a YouTube channel called JKL Productions with two of his cousins. Each person contributed videos on different topics, most having nothing to do with Fred Figglehorn. Their collective channel soon began attracting a large number of viewers interested in seeing Fred's latest antics. YouTube soon offered the three cousins a partnership to place ads on the pages with the most viewers. At the height of its popularity, JKL Productions' ad revenue from YouTube averaged $2,000 each month.

The "Fred" Channel

In May 2007, Cruikshank created the "Fred" channel on YouTube and set a goal of posting a new Fred video every two to three weeks. By this time, he had created Fred's whole world. Although there was no real plot or much of an ongoing storyline to the video series, there was a cast of characters and a background story. Fred's mother struggles with alcoholism and the challenges of parenting while his father is in prison. Fred's only friend is geeky Bertha, and he nurtures a crush on his neighbor Judy, who is pretty and popular. None of these characters ever appears in the videos. Instead, viewers learn about Fred's world through the stories he tells to the camera.

"Fred" videos are based on simple ideas drawn from everyday life experiences. Some of the most popular videos include "Fred Goes Swimming," "Fred Goes to the Dentist," and "Fred Sees a Therapist." Cruikshank begins the process of making each video by first coming up with the title. He then develops a story outline for each title, but does not write anything before filming. "I know the general idea of what the video will be—beginning, middle, and end—and then from there, I pretty much [improvise] it. I've never really scripted anything with Fred." With only his ideas for what Fred will say and do, Cruikshank usually records each video in one try. He then edits the video and posts it online.

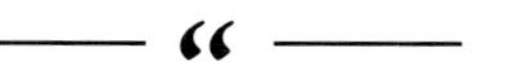

Cruikshank was surprised when complete strangers began leaving comments on the Fred videos posted on YouTube. "I didn't really understand YouTube at the time," he admitted. "I didn't know that millions of people could watch your video. I just thought that the friends I sent it to could watch it. So I was really surprised when I posted 'Fred' and it totally blew up."

”

In creating each video, Cruikshank caters to his target audience of children and teens. He has attracted a loyal and devoted group of fans, although not everyone appreciates Fred's screechy voice and high-speed commentary. "It's an acquired taste," Cruikshank acknowledged. "I think the kids like it because it's funny, and they also like it because they could relate to the things that Fred goes through. Like, Fred doesn't have any friends, or maybe how he doesn't have a dad in his house, or something like that. So there's a lot of things you could relate to Fred. I think that adults, for the most part, hear the voice and automatically push it away, because it's so in your face. They don't really give it a chance."

Response to "Fred"

Response to "Fred" has included both positive and negative reactions. The video series has gotten many hateful comments from YouTube viewers, but Cruikshank ignores the negativity. "I think online, like on YouTube and stuff, people could pretty much say whatever they want. They have no filter in their brain, because no one knows who they are. They're totally anonymous, so they could say whatever they want. But when they're in person with me, they wouldn't say those things, because I can actually see who they are. They're not another name on a comments list."

Cruikshank appearing as Fred on an episode of "Hannah Montana," shown here with Emily Osment and Miley Cyrus.

Entertainment critics have praised Cruikshank's work even if they don't always understand Fred's appeal. A reviewer for *BusinessWeek* recognized Cruikshank's talent with the comment that "adults don't get it, kids can't get enough of it." A *Los Angeles Times* reviewer said that he "has more range than a parent might guess from the shrill voice emanating from the family computer," and concluded that "in the land of positive-message-laden kids TV, Fred is a force for giddy anarchy."

In response to the conflicting feedback from his admirers and detractors, Cruikshank said, "I really try not to focus on any of that—the comments, or the views, or the subscribers, or any of that. It kind of changes how you think. I'd rather just be thinking about the creative part of it."

The "Fred" Channel has become wildly and unexpectedly successful, gathering a huge number of subscribers and millions of viewers for each video. This success has created new opportunities for Cruikshank. He has appeared as a guest star on the popular television shows "iCarly" and "Hannah Montana." In 2009, he won the Teen Choice Award for Choice Web Star. Around the same time, he also created a line of Fred merchandise, and sold more than 800,000 T-shirts within one year. In addition, he released the CD *It's Hackin' Christmas with Fred* in 2009, containing four tracks: two original songs along with Fred's version of "Jingle Bells" and "The 12 Days of Christmas."

Fred: The Movie

With the explosive popularity of the "Fred" series, Cruikshank began getting offers for movies and television shows based on the character. At first he was reluctant to make any deals. "Lots of people came to me with ideas: they wanted to do a TV show, a movie, products. They wanted to make Fred mainstream. At first I was really leery because I was scared someone was going to get a hold of it and totally make it something it wasn't. I feared they'd take all of the creative control." But once he had a chance to think about the opportunities, Cruikshank started to change his mind. "It hit me one day that a Fred movie could be really cool because the fans would get to see so many of the characters, like Judy, Kevin, Bertha and the mom—the whole Fred world."

In 2010, *Fred: The Movie* debuted on the Nickelodeon cable television network. It drew 7.6 million viewers, making it the year's No 1 cable television movie for kids. *Fred: The Movie* stars Cruikshank as Fred, "iCarly" star Jennette McCurdy as Bertha, wrestler John Cena as Fred's dad, and Siobhan Fallon as Fred's mom. The story opens with Fred feeling devastated because his beloved Judy, played by British pop star Pixie Lott, has moved away. Fred decides to set off on an adventurous journey to Judy's new house. Along the way, he meets many challenges, overcomes some large obstacles, and hatches a plan to get revenge on his arch-rival Kevin, who is also Judy's boyfriend. The movie release was accompanied by the full-length music album *Who's Ready to Party?*, which included some tracks featured in the film. In December 2010 *Fred: The Movie* was released in theaters across the United Kingdom.

Making a movie about Fred allowed Cruikshank to do things he had not been able to do in the video series. "In the movie, you get to see it from a different point of view," he explained. "On YouTube, it's just Fred's point of view, just him and his webcam when he's video blogging. In the movie, you get to see more layers than you get to see in the videos." Another difference is that in the movie, Fred is portrayed as a teenager. "I feel that Fred has always been a 15-year-old—or 14-year-old, or whatever. The thing is, he's still, like, trapped in the mentality of a six-year-old. Obviously, when you watch the videos, I don't look like a six-year-old. I think that he's just trapped in the mentality of a six-year-old." Despite his initial reluctance to take Fred to the big screen, Cruikshank said the movie "turned out better than I ever could have expected."

Cruikshank has earned recognition from the entertainment industry. In 2010, he was named by *Hollywood Reporter* as one of the 50 Most Powerful Players in Digital Media. He was also named by *Variety* as one of the Top

Cruikshank as Fred with Pixie Lott as Judy in a scene from Fred: The Movie.

Ten Comics to Watch. However, not everyone at *Variety* agreed with that assessment. A *Variety* review of *Fred: The Movie* warned that audiences would have reason to be "absolutely horrified" by Cruikshank's "deliberately irritating character," calling his success "inexplicable" and "unfathomable." "I made the movie for the fans," Cruikshank responded. "I didn't make it for the critics. All of my fans really liked it. We tested the movie before we put it out. We had a bunch of test audiences with kids, the core demographic, and it tested amazingly. I think we did the job pretty well."

Future Plans

As a result of his success with Fred Figglehorn, Cruikshank has several new projects planned, including a sequel to *Fred: The Movie*. Nickelodeon has also signed him to star in a new television sitcom called "Marvin, Marvin," about a high school student who has trouble fitting in because he is from another planet. Cruikshank will also star in the upcoming film *Emo Boy,* based on the graphic novel series about a boy who believes he has special EMO "extra-sensitive emotional" powers. And he is also planning to produce more Fred videos, though he admits "I think Fred's almost done. I mean, I've been doing it for four years, and it seems so much longer to me than four years. I think it's time."

"Everything that is happening is really exciting to me," Cruikshank said. "When I first started making videos on YouTube I got a bunch of haters who tried to discourage me by saying to stop making videos. If I would have stopped then none of this would have ever happened. You have to focus on the positive and have fun with it." He is still surprised by all of the opportunities available to him. "I never expected any of this—I lived in Nebraska. It shows that, seriously, anything can happen. Fred Figglehorn? Who knew?"

HOME AND FAMILY

Cruikshank lives in Nebraska with his family, four dogs, two cats, and two cockatiels. He travels frequently to Los Angeles for meetings, filming, and other work. "I think it's awesome living in Nebraska. I like going out to California, but I love coming home and living a totally normal life with my family and friends."

WORKS

"Fred," 2006- (YouTube video series)
It's Hackin' Christmas with Fred, 2009 (CD)
Fred: The Movie, 2010 (movie)
Who's Ready to Party? 2010 (CD)

HONORS AND AWARDS

Choice Web Star (Teen Choice Awards): 2009
50 Most Powerful Players in Digital Media (*Hollywood Reporter*): 2010
Ten Comics to Watch (*Variety*): 2010

FURTHER READING

Periodicals

Girls' Life, Oct./Nov. 2010, p.58
Los Angeles Times, Sep. 16, 2010
New York Times, Dec. 8, 2009
Omaha World Herald, Sep. 18, 2010, p.E1
USA Today, Sep. 17, 2010, p.D9
Washington Post, Sep. 15, 2010, p.A19

Online Articles

http://www.avclub.com
(The A.V. Club, "Lucas Cruikshank, a.k.a. 'Fred'," Oct. 26, 2010)
http://gigaom.com
(NewTeeVee, "Fred Speaks to NTV (Squeaky Voice Not Included)," June 25, 2008)

http://www.people.com
(People,"Five Things to Know About Lucas Cruikshank," Sep. 18, 2010)
http://www.seventeen.com
(Seventeen,"Everything You Ever Wanted to Know about Lucas Cruikshank (YouTube's Fred!)," Dec. 2, 2009;"Meet Fred Star Lucas Cruikshank," no date)

ADDRESS

Lucas Cruikshank
The Collective
8383 Wilshire Blvd., #1050
Beverly Hills, CA 90211

WORLD WIDE WEB SITE

http://lucascruikshank.org

Jason Derülo 1989-

American Singer and Songwriter
Creator of the No. 1 Hits "Whatcha Say" and "In My Head"

BIRTH

Jason Derülo was born Jason Joel Desrouleaux (pronounced day-ROO-low) on September 21, 1989, in Miramar, Florida. His parents, Joel and Jocelyne Desrouleaux, had immigrated to the United States from the Caribbean nation of Haiti. To support Jason and his older brother and sister, their father worked for the federal government and their mother worked as a bank manager and an immigration officer. Jason Desrouleaux changed the spelling of his last name to "Derülo" when he became a professional performer to make it easier for his fans to pronounce.

YOUTH

Derülo grew up in Broward County, Florida, near Fort Lauderdale and just north of Miami. He was interested in music from a young age, especially after he discovered singer Michael Jackson. "I was a huge Michael Jackson fan growing up," he recalled. "I studied his videos and copied all his moves. I'd also practice singing Usher and Justin Timberlake songs while doing their moves." Even at a young age, Derülo felt a drive to perform. And with a large extended family living in south Florida, there were plenty of opportunities to perform for his family. "Really, my only musical influence—as I was growing up—was school and television," he explained. "Because I didn't have anybody in my household that sang, or did any kind of performing, AT ALL! So for me, it all really came from the inside. I just always had this desire to sing and perform. And with me having tons of cousins—my grandmother had 15 kids—there was always a birthday! And so I'd be singing and dancing at every family function! You know, it was a huge love of mine that I just continued doing for years and years."

"I just always had this desire to sing and perform," Derülo recalled. "And with me having tons of cousins—my grandmother had 15 kids—there was always a birthday! And so I'd be singing and dancing at every family function!"

Derülo soon wanted a wider audience than just his family, and at age seven he entered his first talent show. At first, he was struck by stage fright. "I remember being backstage and saying, 'I'm not going out there. There are people out there!'" he recalled. "This guy had to pick me up and literally place me on the stage. Then the music came on, and I started singing 'Ben' by Michael Jackson, and I was fine." His family supported his interest in music by enrolling him in a performing arts school, starting in third grade. That was the age he also started writing songs. His first song was a ballad called "Crush on You," which he never shared with the girl that inspired it.

In performing arts school, Derülo studied all kinds of music, from classical and opera to jazz and musical theater. He took a variety of dance classes, including ballet and tap, training he would later use while performing with a professional hip-hop dance company. He spent his free time writing songs; he recorded demos in his mother's car by soundproofing the vehicle and singing into his laptop computer. When he was 12 years old he met Frank Harris, a law student and former basketball player. Derülo had been cut from his junior high school basketball team, so he was practicing on a neighborhood court, and Harris offered to help him improve his game. After having trouble competing with Harris, Derülo told him, "Basketball isn't my thing anyway, I'm a singer." Harris realized the young man wasn't bragging about his musical talents and offered to contact some friends in the New York music industry on his behalf. The contacts helped Derülo sell some of his songs to professionals, and Harris became his manager. For Derülo, it was his first step on the road to becoming an internationally famous performer.

EDUCATION

Derülo attended Dillard School of the Arts, a public high school in Fort Lauderdale, Florida, that was also a performing arts magnet school. (The school is now called Dillard Center for the Arts.) There, he had lead roles in musical productions and also played on the basketball team. After graduating from Dillard in 2005, he moved to New York City to attend the prestigious American Musical and Dramatic Academy (AMDA), a post-secondary school that offers two- and four-year programs. He enrolled in its intensive two-year musical theater program, where he studied dance (including tap), singing, and acting. He graduated from AMDA in 2006 with a certification in musical theater.

CAREER HIGHLIGHTS

Winning the Apollo Theater Competition

After graduating from AMDA, Derülo was offered a part in the Broadway musical *Rent,* the long-running rock musical about struggling artists in New York. It was a prestigious job—*Rent* won both the Pulitzer Prize for drama and the Tony Award for best musical after its 1996 opening—but it would have required a year-long commitment to the role. Derülo decided to chase his dream of becoming a recording artist instead.

The same year Derülo graduated from AMDA, he competed in a talent competition at the famous Apollo Theater in New York's Harlem neighborhood. Amateur Night at the Apollo first debuted in 1934 and was the forerunner to talent competitions like "Star Search" and "American Idol." Contestants could perform any kind of act, but they risked being booed off the stage—audiences at the Apollo have long been known for expressing their

A 2009 portrait of Derülo.

opinions quite forcibly. "Once you play there, you can play anywhere," Derülo recalled of the competition. He participated in the 2006 season, which was televised as "Showtime at the Apollo," and won the overall top prize. He thought he was on his way to success, but "actually, the Apollo didn't really help me out at all, and I was surprised," he remembered. "I was really excited. I thought everything would start happening for me. But it was when I started writing songs for people that the doors opened."

Derülo's manager helped him secure a deal with Rondor Music Publishing, and Derülo started writing songs for other performers. He was still a teenager when Birdman, a rapper from New Orleans, recorded his song "Bossy" in 2007. Derülo also contributed vocals to the track. These efforts led to work writing for rhythm & blues (R&B) singer Cassie and rapper Big Daddy Kane. Derülo also contributed vocals to the 2007 song "My Life," which he co-wrote for Miami rapper Pitbull. Later he wrote songs for Grammy-winning rapper Lil Wayne, chart-topping girl group Danity Kane, and teen rapping sensation Sean Kingston. Although his songwriting was getting him work, he hated giving up his songs to other performers. "It was killing me," he noted. "I had a huge attachment to the songs I was writing, but I had to give them up to make a quick buck. Being in music, I was just hoping something would happen, that someone would notice me."

> *"I'm not just an urban artist," Derülo stressed. "I want to make music for the world. I want to break musical barriers and not be pigeonholed by the color of my skin to do a certain kind of music."*

One person who noticed Derülo was producer J.R. Rotem, who had signed Kingston as the first artist to his new Beluga Heights label. Rotem's brother had discovered Derülo through his MySpace page and brought him to Rotem's attention. The producer invited Derülo to come out to Los Angeles to explore his abilities as a songwriter. After hearing him sing in the studio, however, Rotem saw his potential as a performer. Derülo, in turn, felt something click when working with Rotem. "We recorded six songs that night and even though other labels were putting their offers on the table, the music was so compelling that I didn't leave without signing a deal with J.R.," he recalled. When Rotem brought Beluga Heights into a partnership with giant entertainment company Warner Brothers, Derülo was the first artist he planned to promote. The deal introduced Derülo to

Kara DioGuardi, the songwriter and former judge on "American Idol" who was also a Warner Brothers senior vice president in charge of developing talent. With support from her and Rotem, Derülo began creating a great song to introduce himself to the world.

Inspiration for His First Hit Single

Because Derülo was young, he often looked beyond his own experiences for song material. One day his older brother called, upset because his girlfriend had left him. He had cheated on her, but he still loved her and wanted her back. "Because the way he told it to me was so compelling," Derülo said, "I was like, 'If you explain it to HER the way you've just done to ME, maybe she'll give you another chance.'" At the time, Derülo and Rotem were playing around with a sample by British artist Imogen Heap, known for her experimental electronic style. Derülo explained how he came across Heap's music: "I'm the kinda guy that goes into the record store and just picks up any random CD just 'cause I've never heard of it before. And Imogen Heap is one of those people that I just picked up." Her 2005 song "Hide and Seek" contained a lyric addressed to a cheating lover: "Whatcha say? That you only meant well? Of course you did." Derülo took the sample, combined it with his brother's situation, and came up with the song "Whatcha Say."

"Whatcha Say" was released as a single in summer 2009 and became a huge success, selling 3.6 million copies. It hit No. 1 on both the *Billboard* Hot 100, which measures radio airplay and sales, and the *Billboard* Pop 100, which measures airplay on mainstream Top 40 stations. The single also reached the Top 10 in England, Canada, Australia, Sweden, Switzerland, Germany, and Japan. When the single finally dropped from the Pop 100 No. 1 after four weeks, it was replaced by Iyaz's "Replay," a song Derülo had co-written for his Beluga Heights label mate. Gradually, he became more comfortable having other performers sing his songs. "It was a little frustrating for me, because these artists got to be the voice while I was behind the scenes, where I always wanted to be the person delivering my lyrics and stuff," he admitted. "It feels really good that I can do that at this stage. I feel really comfortable writing for other people now." He even enjoyed the challenge of matching a song to a performer's personality.

Derülo's success with his first single led to more opportunities. He got an offer to tour with Lady Gaga, who was the biggest new artist of 2009 and the top-selling artist of 2010. He spent the first weeks of 2010 opening for the glamorous and inventive singer. "She's a really great performer and it forced me to step my game up," he noted. "It's just amazing that I'm on the same show with her." Not long after finishing his tour with Gaga, Derülo

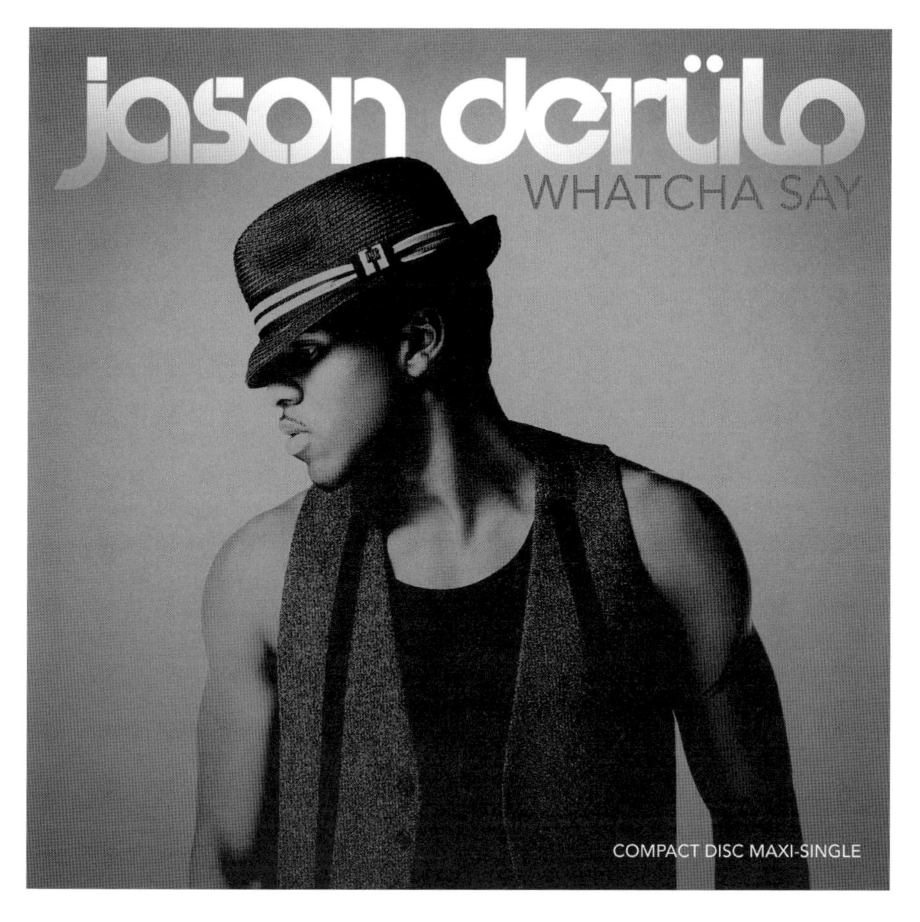

Derülo's first single hit No. 1 on the Billboard charts.

released a second single. "In My Head" sold 2.8 million copies, hit No. 5 on the Hot 100, and followed "Whatcha Say" to the No. 1 spot on the Pop 100 chart. The top placement made Derülo the first male solo artist in the 17-year history of the radio airplay chart to have his first two singles hit No. 1.

In early 2010 Derülo also got a chance to show off his acting skills, appearing in MTV's television movie *Turn the Beat Around.* The movie followed the struggles of a young dancer trying to hit the big time by bringing disco music to a new nightclub. Derülo played a pop star searching for new dancers to perform in his video. "I was really proud of that film because I got the role before I had the musical success," he related. After his single "Whatcha Say" became popular, they changed the role so he was playing himself instead of a character. "It started out I was playing a pop star with a made-up name and now I'm the real pop star!" Throughout the first half of 2010, Derülo got more national exposure with television appearances on "American Idol" and several daytime and late-night talk shows, like "Ellen" and "The Tonight Show."

First Album and First Solo Tour

Derülo released his first album in March 2010, the self-titled *Jason Derülo.* He had waited to release the album, as he explains here. "I wanted people to get to know me as an artist first," he said. "Dropped another single first, and they can see the versatility, because I reinvent myself on each song. You can't really get to know somebody after one song, so I didn't want to drop my album before they were ready for it." Derülo had devoted a lot of effort to the album, working 20-hour days and recording 300 songs in the studio with Rotem before choosing the best nine. "I worked really, really hard on this album to make sure that every single song could stand on its own, and every single song could potentially be a single, and every single song a reinvention, just totally different," he said. Although he could have brought in guest artists for some of the tracks, he decided to establish his own voice and let his music stand on its own.

The album included a wide variety of musical styles. "At one point I was doing straight rock, at another point I was doing Euro dance stuff," Derülo recalled. "I realized I didn't have to choose." The singer noted that although he is African American, "I'm not just an urban artist.... I want to make music for the world. I want to break musical barriers and not be pigeonholed by the color of my skin to do a certain kind of music." The album peaked at No. 11 on the *Billboard* 200 Album chart and stayed on the chart for seven months. According to *Guardian* critic Caroline Sullivan, "He's followed an increasingly well-trodden path to R&B success by first serving an apprenticeship as a songwriter (for Lil Wayne, Diddy, et al.), so he's got the craft of making modern, hyper-slick tunes nailed."

Derülo continued his success on the charts with his third single from the album, "Ridin' Solo," which hit No. 9 on the Hot 100 and stayed on the chart for seven months. A fourth single, the tender ballad "What If," also hit the Top 40 of the pop charts. After opening for the Black Eyed Peas on some of their summer concerts, he set off on his own tour as a headliner. He played dates in Asia, Australia, Europe, and the United States throughout the last half of 2010. "Jason Derülo has got the whole contemporary soul pop package," *Boston Globe* contributor Sarah Rodman said about one tour stop. "He can sing (well enough), he moves beautifully, and he writes songs of such breezy joy it's as if they're made of air, smiles, sugar, and

Derülo at the 2010 MTV Video Music Awards.

electronic handclaps." Derülo finished off 2010 by winning a Teen Choice Award for Choice R&B Album and earning MTV Music Video award nominations for best new artist and best male video, both for the dance-heavy video for "In My Head."

Current Plans

Derülo promised something different for his second album, *Future History*, scheduled for release in late 2011. "I've literally been around the world and back," he said. "I've experienced a lot of ups and downs. I've grown as an artist. There's a totally huge side of my artistry that people have yet to see, so I'm looking forward to the near future." He planned to expand his style by working with other producers as well as Rotem. His method of writing remained the same, though. "I never write songs down—I feel like the pen dilutes the music," he explained. "I get a concept, go into the [recording] booth and just start singing. I start off with a melody and then figure out the words to match." He co-wrote the first single, "Don't Wanna Go Home," with producers the Fliptones. According to Jeff Fenster, Warner Bros. executive vice president of A&R, this dance track connected so quickly because "it's a reactive uptempo song with great melodies and a familiar sample from one of the best house records ever [Robin S's 'Show Me Love']. And Jason's delivered a cool, convincing vocal performance that cuts through the clutter."

"I don't feel like I'm competing with other artists," Derülo noted. "I'm just going to try and be the best I can be. And when I get to that level, well, I'll figure out a way to get better."

Although Derülo has had a fantastic start as a singer, he wanted to remind his fans that he is a triple-threat performer: a singer who is trained also in acting and dance. "While music is very much at the forefront for me now," he said, "in the long-term I can see the acting becoming equally important in my career." He hoped to guest-star on the musical show "Glee," perhaps portraying a character who was a class clown, like he was in high school. Whatever his future brings, he plans to work hard and learn from his peers. "I don't feel like I'm competing with other artists," Derülo noted. "I'm just going to try and be the best I can be. And when I get to that level, well, I'll figure out a way to get better."

HOME AND FAMILY

Although Derülo now makes his home in Los Angeles, he often spends time with his family in the Miami area. "I was one of those kids who couldn't be far from home," he said of his years at school in New York. "I'm still like that." While touring, he travels with his brother and cousin, and tries to fly his mom out for a visit every month.

HOBBIES AND OTHER INTERESTS

Derülo doesn't have much time for hobbies, but he does enjoy using social media like Twitter and Facebook to interact with his fans. He also enjoys movies, especially comedies. He is quick to donate his time and money to charity, a habit he said he learned from his generous mother. As a youth, he grew out his hair for five years and then donated 14 inches of hair to Locks of Love, a charity that makes wigs for cancer patients. He has worked with other cancer charities as well, and has visited children's hospitals while on tour. The singer has also donated money and worked with charities that benefit his family's homeland of Haiti; after the January 2010 Haiti earthquake, he performed at several concerts where the proceeds benefited the victims.

SELECTED CREDITS

Recordings

Jason Derülo, 2010

Television Appearances

"Showtime at the Apollo," 2006
Turn the Beat Around, 2010 (TV movie)

HONORS AND AWARDS

Season Finale Grand Championship ("Showtime at the Apollo"): 2006
Teen Choice Awards: 2010, for Choice Music Album-R&B, for *Jason Derülo*
BMI Pop Awards: Pop Songwriters of the Year (shared with J.R. Rotem and Lady Gaga), for "In My Head," "Replay," "Ridin' Solo," and "Whatcha Say"

FURTHER READING

Periodicals

AMDA Alumni Spotlight, fall 2010, p. 2
Baltimore Sun, Sep. 30, 2010

Billboard, Oct. 10, 2009, p. 86
Boston Globe, Sep. 30, 2010
Guardian (London), Feb. 26, 2010, p.9
Jet, Jan. 11, 2010, p.22
Miami Herald, Dec. 27, 2009
New York Times, Mar. 6, 2010, p.C1
USA Today, Mar. 15, 2010, p. 3D

Online Articles

http://www.beatweek.com
(Beatweek Magazine,"Jason Derülo Interview,"Mar. 9, 2010)
http://www.billboard.com
(Billboard,"Jason Derülo Takes Off with 'Whatcha Say' Single," Oct. 6, 2009; "Jason Derülo Makes History on Pop Songs Chart," Apr. 12, 2010; "Jason Derülo Recording 'Dark Material' for Sophomore Album," Sep. 24, 2010)
http://www.bluesandsoul.com
(Blues and Soul Magazine,"Jason Derülo: Whatcha Think?" Nov. 30, 2009)
http://www.cnn.com
(CNN,"Jason Derülo: The Man behind the Hit," Dec. 23, 2009)
http://www.goerie.com
(Erie Times-News,"Pop/R&B Star Jason Derülo Performs at Gannon," Apr. 22, 2010)
http://www.mtv.com
(MTV,"Jason Derülo," Oct. 1, 2010)
http://www.popeater.com
(Popeater,"About to Pop: Jason Derülo," Nov. 12, 2009)
http://www.singersroom.com
(Singers Room,"Jason Derülo: Perfect Timing," Dec. 22, 2009)

ADDRESS

Jason Derülo
Beluga Heights/Warner Bros. Records Inc.
PO Box 6868
Burbank, CA 91510

WORLD WIDE WEB SITE

http://www.jasonderulo.com

Nina Dobrev 1989-

Bulgarian-Canadian Actress
Star of "Degrassi: The Next Generation" and "The Vampire Diaries"

BIRTH

Nina Dobrev was born Nina Constantinova Dobreva on January 9, 1989, in Sofia, Bulgaria. She uses a shortened form of her last name for her acting credits. Her father is a computer specialist, and her mother is an artist. She has an older brother, Aleksander.

YOUTH

The Dobreva family moved from Bulgaria to Canada when Nina was two years old, and she grew up in Toronto, Ontario. She has always loved performing. "My parents didn't know what to do with me because I was so high energy," she remembered. As a young girl, she became involved in rhythmic gymnastics. In this sport, teams perform routines that blend dance and gymnastics using such objects as hoops, ribbons, and balls. Dobrev earned a place on Canada's national team and represented her country in international competition.

"

Dobrev's parents encouraged their children to be self-reliant. "My parents gave us chores and wanted us to work for everything," she remembered. "We never got anything handed to us. I bought my first car. I learned that if I want something in life, I have to take the necessary steps and measures to achieve what I want."

"

Dobrev's parents lived on a modest income, and they encouraged their children to be self-reliant. "My parents gave us chores and wanted us to work for everything," she remembered. "We never got anything handed to us. I bought my first car. I learned that if I want something in life, I have to take the necessary steps and measures to achieve what I want." During high school, she had two jobs and juggled the demands of work, school, and her various lessons and activities. She described herself as very self-motivated: "When I wanted to do gymnastics, it was all me, and my parents just signed me up. And when I wanted to do the acting thing, I would take an hour bus ride downtown for auditions and classes.... I've always been driven."

EDUCATION

Dobrev attended public schools in Toronto. When she was old enough, she auditioned for and was accepted to the Wexford Collegiate School for the Arts, a performing-arts high school. Wexford is a part of Toronto's public school system, but students must earn the right to attend. Dobrev found Wexford competitive and challenging, and her acting career began to take shape there. She also studied at the Dean Armstrong Acting School in Toronto. After high school, she started at Toronto's Ryerson University, majoring in sociology, but she left in 2008 to focus on acting.

CAREER HIGHLIGHTS

After signing with a talent agent, Dobrev quickly moved from modeling to television commercials and then to movie auditions. She had small parts in the films *Repo! The Genetic Opera, Away from Her,* and *Playing House,* all released in 2006. Her big break came that same year when she was cast in the Canadian television series "Degrassi: The Next Generation."

"Degrassi: The Next Generation"

"Degrassi: The Next Generation" was the fourth in a series of TV shows that began in 1979 with "The Kids of Degrassi Street." Although fiction, "The Kids of Degrassi Street" was a realistic portrayal of the lives of a group of kids in Toronto. School-aged children are often played by older actors, but in "Degrassi," the actors were about the same age as their characters. They wore ordinary clothes and were shown without a lot of makeup—blemishes and all. On the air until 1986, the program became a huge favorite in Canada. In 1987, an updated version premiered, titled "Degrassi Junior High." Many of the actors returned, but with slightly different characters and storylines. In 1989, the cast and characters appeared in a new version of the show, "Degrassi High," which aired until 1991. All of the "Degrassi" shows were praised for their depiction of young people and the tough problems they face, including drug abuse, racism, and pregnancy.

"Degrassi: The Next Generation," a new series, premiered in 2001, ten years after the last episode of "Degrassi High." "Degrassi: The Next Generation" had the same concept and setting as the previous shows, but the cast and characters were almost entirely new—with a few former cast members returning in adult roles. The earlier "Degrassi" programs had picked up an international following over the years, thanks to reruns shown in the United States, Europe, and around the globe. When "Degrassi: The Next Generation" was released, there was a huge audience of fans already waiting for it. It was an immediate success. The subject matter continued to be dramatic, featuring episodes about school shootings, cyberstalking, eating disorders, and other serious issues. As commentor Ben Neihart wrote in an article for the *New York Times Magazine,* "'Degrassi: The Next Generation' confronts controversy in a way that American network television wouldn't dream of."

Dobrev joined the cast of "Degrassi: The Next Generation" in 2006. She appeared in just a few episodes that year, but she became a regular cast member in 2007 and stayed with the show until 2009. She played Mia Jones, a student who transfers to Degrassi from Lakehurst, a rival school. Mia wants to join the cheerleading squad, but when Darcy, the squad cap-

Dobrev appeared as Mia Jones on "Degrassi: The Next Generation" for several seasons.

tain, learns that Mia has a two-year-old child, she refuses to let her on the team. Subsequent episodes revealed that at her old school Mia was a "party girl" who became much more responsible after the birth of her daughter, Isabella. Abandoned by Isabella's father, an older student at Lakehurst, Mia raises the baby with help from her mother. At Degrassi, Mia eventually begins a relationship with a boy named J.T. She is devastated when he is stabbed and killed by another student.

The next season showed Mia dealing with Isabella's father and his attempts to get back into their life, as well as Mia's attempt to develop a new relationship. The following year showed Mia leading a somewhat more carefree life when her mother takes more responsibility for Isabella's care. Mia finally wins a spot on the cheerleading squad, but bigger things quickly develop after she is discovered by a modeling agency and begins a part-time career as a model. For much of the rest of the season, Mia struggles to balance the demands of her career as a model with the responsibilities of being a student and a mother. She drops out of school, but eventually goes back when she realizes that she will need an education when her modeling career ends. That plot twist reversed at the beginning of the ninth season of "Degrassi." Offered an opportunity for a major modeling contract, Mia leaves for Paris, entrusting Isabella to her mother. Dobrev left the cast at that point, although she was mentioned in later episodes and appeared in the 2009 television movie *Degrassi Goes Hollywood.*

Dobrev's experience on "Degrassi" was very important to her, teaching her to work like a professional. "It was my constant, no matter what movie I would do on hiatus or whatever," she said. "They really sort of taught me all the groundwork and got me started."

Working in Films

During time off from production of "Degrassi," Dobrev kept busy with other projects. She had a part in the film *Fugitive Pieces,* which opened the Toronto International Film Festival in 2007. In this story, set during World War II, Dobrev plays Bella, the older sister of the main character, Jakob. When the Nazis attack their village in Poland, Jakob sees his father shot and Bella dragged away by soldiers. Jakob survives, but the results of the brutality he experienced stay with him. Bella continues to appear to him as a vision, years after he last saw her in real life.

Dobrev played a larger role in *The Poet,* also released in 2007 (also released as *Hearts of War*). Like *Fugitive Pieces, The Poet* takes place during World War II. The story is set in Poland in 1939, just as Germany is about to invade the country. Dobrev plays a young Jewish woman, Rachel, who becomes involved in an unlikely love triangle. She is already engaged to a Jewish man, but when she is rescued during a blizzard by a Nazi soldier, the two find themselves falling in love. "Unpredictable, tear-jerking sequences will have viewers surprised about how a tragic story can be so beautiful," said Erika Carmona, reviewing the movie for *Home Media Magazine.*

The year 2007 also saw Dobrev in the television movies *My Daughter's Secret* and *Too Young to Marry.* The following year she appeared in two more made-for-TV movies, *Never Cry Werewolf* and *The American Mall.* In *The American Mall,* produced for MTV, Dobrev played Ally, a girl who works for her mother in a music store at the local mall. Her musical dreams and her romance with Joey, one of the mall's janitors, are threatened by the spoiled daughter of the mall's owner. Some reviewers compared the lighthearted movie to *High School Musical.*

"The Vampire Diaries"

By 2009, Dobrev felt she needed to leave Toronto for Los Angeles, California, to be part of the entertainment industry. One of her first goals was to audition for a lead role in a new television series being developed, "The Vampire Diaries," based on the popular book series by L.J. Smith. The basic premise involves a girl named Elena who is caught up in a love triangle with two brothers, both of whom are vampires. The actress chosen for this role would also play the part of a vampire, Katherine, who bears an uncanny resemblance to Elena. "I really had to fight for the role because there were so many girls who wanted to play Elena," Dobrev remembered. She was ill at the time of her first audition, and the producers were not impressed by her performance.

After her audition, Dobrev returned to Toronto, where she was filming a supporting role in the movie *Chloe.* She couldn't stop thinking about "The Vampire Diaries," however, and her poor audition for the show. She put together another audition and sent it to the producers on a DVD. She didn't know that, in the meantime, CW network executives had decided to hire someone else for the part of Elena. Once they saw Dobrev's DVD, however, they knew she would be perfect in the role. She was hired. "I was very lucky, and I still feel like I have the coolest character—or characters—on TV," she said. Although she had just moved to Los Angeles, Dobrev now found herself packing up again and getting ready to move her home base to Atlanta, Georgia, where "The Vampire Diaries" is filmed.

"The Vampire Diaries" is set in the fictional town of Mystic Falls, Virginia. Elena Gilbert is a high-school student whose parents were killed in a car ac-

Dobrev in her two roles on "The Vampire Diaries" as Elena (left) and as Katherine (right).

cident. She lives with her aunt, who is only a little older than Elena, and her younger brother Jeremy. Elena is deeply saddened by the loss of her parents, and she worries about Jeremy, who gets involved with drugs. Visiting her parents' graves at the cemetery one day, Elena meets a young man named Stefan Salvatore (played by Paul Wesley). They feel an attraction for each other, but Elena has no idea that Stefan is a vampire. He and his brother Damon (played by Ian Somerhalder) lived in Mystic Falls in the 1860s, and they have returned because of a beautiful, ruthless vampire named Katherine Pierce, who also lived there and who is also played by Dobrev. Stefan fights his vampire nature and does not feed on human blood, but Damon embraces his urges, preying on the people of Mystic Falls.

"The Vampire Diaries" was created by Kevin Williamson, who also created the teen drama "Dawson's Creek" (for more information on Williamson, see *Biography Today Authors,* Vol. 6). Initially, "The Vampire Diaries" focused on the romantic tension between the characters. The plot quickly became more action-oriented, and viewers learned that vampires are not the only supernatural creatures in Mystic Falls. It was revealed that Damon hoped to release Katherine from a tomb where she had been imprisoned by the spell of a witch many years ago.

There are similarities between "The Vampire Diaries" and the popular "Twilight" series of books and movies created by author Stephenie Meyer. According to Dobrev, who is a big fan of the "Twilight" series, "I'll be honest: When I first read the pilot synopsis, I remember thinking, 'Oh, this is just Twilight on TV.'" Her opinion changed when she saw that Williamson had unique ideas about the vampire genre, including a willingness to make fun of it. "We began shooting and it kind of grew a life of its own. It's such a huge departure from how it originally came across," Dobrev said. Reviewing the show for the *Atlanta Journal and Constitution,* Rodney Ho said that "[Williamson] makes the show work, his witty dialogue courses through the action-packed series." "The Vampire Diaries" immediately became the most popular program on the CW network, averaging 3.7 million viewers a week and winning renewal for another season.

Dobrev enjoys playing her two characters—one sweet, the other ruthless. "As Katherine, I can get away with a lot more and say a lot more and be a little bit more edgy and bad. She has a very playful personality. As soon as I put on the heels and they start curling my hair, I'm in the zone," she explained. "As Elena, it's the same thing: I put on the Converse and jeans and a T-shirt, and I feel like this strong, young woman, figuring herself out. That's who she is: she's figuring herself out and she's growing." Cast members don't know about new plot twists until they get their scripts, so they are in almost as much suspense as their fans. "We live and play day by day, and we're just as shocked and surprised as the viewers are by what happens next," Dobrev said.

The series—and Dobrev's performance—have won accolades from fans and critics. In a review for *Entertainment Weekly,* Ken Tucker wrote, "The second-season premiere of 'The Vampire Diaries' proves once again why this series is one of prime time's more cleverly constructed, well-acted nighttime soap operas." Tucker called Elena/Katherine "the series' yin and yang of good and evil, purity and villainy. Dobrev has really risen to the challenge of portraying these two, managing to confuse viewers as to who's who when Katherine wants to impersonate Elena for some mischief."

Other Projects

Dobrev has continued to work in movies, even while committed to "The Vampire Diaries." She has had roles in *The Roommate,* a movie about an obsessed college student; *The Killing Game,* about gladiators forced to fight for an online audience; and *The Perks of Being a Wallflower,* a romantic drama. "I've always wanted to constantly challenge myself and play different characters in different genres, whether it's action, drama, romantic

Dobrev with Paul Wesley as Stefan Salvatore (left) and Ian Somerhalder as Damon Salvatore (right), her co-stars on "The Vampire Diaries."

comedy or a period piece," Dobrev declared. "I'll never take a part just for a paycheck or to fill time. I want to do projects that I really enjoy."

HOME AND FAMILY

Living in Atlanta while "The Vampire Diaries" is filmed, Dobrev sticks close to fellow cast members Paul Wesley and Ian Somerhalder. "They're wonderful guys and it's a real pleasure to work with them," she says. "I look at them like my brothers. They always have my back and are looking out for me. Prior to living here, I'd never really lived on my own." As for dating, she said: "I don't need a boyfriend to be happy. If I meet someone and I want to be with him, then I will be. I'm very confident in being single until I find someone who I'm extremely crazy about and who I want to devote my time and love to. Until then, I will just be on my own and I am totally fine with that." She has a tabby cat named Jammers.

"I've always wanted to constantly challenge myself and play different characters in different genres, whether it's action, drama, romantic comedy or a period piece," Dobrev declared. "I'll never take a part just for a paycheck or to fill time. I want to do projects that I really enjoy."

MEMORABLE EXPERIENCES

In 2007, Dobrev and five other cast members from "Degrassi: The Next Generation" traveled to Africa with Free the Children, an organization that helps young people in North America to work on projects that improve the lives of children in other parts of the world. Their mission was to help construct an addition to a school in Kenya. A documentary about their experience was made and shown on MTV in Canada. Dobrev remains an enthusiastic supporter of Free the Children. "Every single person can change a child's life," she said. "I really believe in the cause and I try to promote it and spread the word as much as possible."

FAVORITE BOOKS AND MOVIES

Dobrev is a fan of "The Lord of the Rings," "Harry Potter," and "Twilight" movies and books. "I've read all the 'Harry Potter' books and I've watched all the movies," she said. "When I went to London, I got to visit the set.... It was the Hogwart's set and I sat in Dumbledore's chair."

HOBBIES AND OTHER INTERESTS

When Dobrev has free time, she takes part in active sports, including volleyball, yoga, soccer, horseback riding, windsurfing, swimming, scuba diving, rock climbing, and snowboarding. She also enjoys yoga. She loves to travel. She is fluent in French and Bulgarian as well as in English. She is interested in fashion design, and she enjoys making jewelry out of antique silverware.

ACTING CREDITS

Away from Her, 2006
"Degrassi: The Next Generation," 2006-2009 (TV series)
Fugitive Pieces, 2007
MTV Presents: Degrassi in Kenya, 2007 (documentary)
The Poet, 2007 (also released as *Hearts of War*)
Too Young to Marry, 2007 (TV movie)
The American Mall, 2008 (TV movie)
Never Cry Werewolf, 2008 (TV movie)
Chloe, 2009
Degrassi Goes Hollywood, 2009 (TV movie)
"The Vampire Diaries," 2009- (TV series)
The Killing Game, 2011
The Roommate, 2011
The Perks of Being a Wallflower, 2012

HONORS AND AWARDS

Teen Choice Awards: 2010 (two awards), Choice Movie Breakout Star-Female and Choice TV Actress: Science Fiction/Fantasy; 2011, Choice TV Actress: Science Fiction/Fantasy

FURTHER READING

Periodicals

Atlanta Journal and Constitution, May 10, 2010, p.D1
Entertainment Weekly, Sep. 10, 2010, p.78
Girls' Life, Oct.-Nov. 2010, p.54
Home Media Magazine, Apr. 20, 2009, p.13
New York Times, Aug. 11, 2008, p. E2; Sep. 10, 2009, p.C1
New York Times Magazine, Mar. 20, 2005, p.40
Seventeen, Apr. 2010, p.136

Online Articles

http://www.portraitmagazine.net
(Portrait, "From 'Degrassi' to 'The Vampire Diaries' Leading Lady," Apr. 12, 2011)

ADDRESS

Nina Dobrev
Innovative Artists Talent and Literary Agency
1505 10th Street
Santa Monica, CA 90401

WORLD WIDE WEB SITES

http://www.cwtv.com/shows/the-vampire-diaries
http://www.teennick.com/shows/degrassi

© Andy Goldsworthy/Courtesy Galerie Lelong, New York. Photo: Melanie Einzig/Museum of Jewish Heritage, New York.

Andy Goldsworthy 1956-

British Sculptor, Photographer, and Environmentalist
Environmental Artist Who Creates Sculptures for Natural Settings

BIRTH

Andy Goldsworthy was born on July 25, 1956, in Cheshire, England, to Scottish parents. His father, F. Allin Goldsworthy, was a math professor at the University of Leeds. As a result, Goldsworthy spent his formative years near Leeds, in Yorkshire.

YOUTH

Throughout his childhood, Goldsworthy loved to play and work outdoors. His parents were strict Methodists and instilled in him a strong work ethic. While laboring on a farm outside Leeds during his teen years, he found himself drawn to the beauty of the landscape. "I was always going to be an artist, since I was a kid, but the impact that farming had was tremendous," he said. "It's a very sculptural activity. Not just dry stone walls but stacking bales [are like] big minimalist sculptures, beautiful and enormous. Plowing a field is like drawing lines on the land, painting the fields—it's incredibly visual."

"While laboring on a farm outside Leeds during his teen years, Goldsworthy found himself drawn to the beauty of the landscape. "[The] impact that farming had was tremendous," he said. "It's a very sculptural activity. Not just dry stone walls but stacking bales [are like] big minimalist sculptures, beautiful and enormous. Plowing a field is like drawing lines on the land, painting the fields—it's incredibly visual.""

His time as a farmhand provided Goldsworthy with an unconventional but indispensable education. "[What] I did on the farm is where the origins of my art came from and was as important to me as art college as a formative experience," he remembered. "Among other things the work I have done … represents a reconciliation between my art and my experiences on the farm."

EDUCATION

In order to pursue his passion for art, Goldsworthy enrolled at Bradford College of Art in 1974, and continued his studies at Preston Polytechnic (which was later renamed the University of Central Lancashire). But art school stressed indoor painting, and he missed the inspiration of the outdoors. "I felt an increasing concern for environmental issues, and a disillusionment with the kind of art I was then producing," he explained. "I had to discover my own nature, and then a work process that would use my nature like a tool."

Goldsworthy found a kindred spirit when artist Richard Long visited the school to give a presentation. Renowned for his unique style of Land Art (which is sometimes referred to as Earth Art), Long is a pioneer in the use of natural elements like ice, stone, earth, wood, and water to create art-

An undated shot of Goldsworthy in his studio.

works that exist as part of the landscape. Other notable proponents of Earth Art include Americans James Turrell and Michael Heizer. Freed from studio work, Goldsworthy began to use this style of art along the shore at Morecambe Bay. "I began working outside within three months of starting there," Goldsworthy said about art school. "You know how in art school everybody is working in their cubicles. Every day I went from that to Morecambe, where I had a flat.... Morecambe Bay is this fantastic flat space that greeted me every day when I got off the train from Lancaster. I was drawn to that space and began working there." Using stones along the shore, he created his first works of natural art at Morecambe Bay, temporary structures that would crumble in the tides.

Goldsworthy continued exploring this type of work throughout his time at art school. He graduated from Preston Polytechnic in 1978 with a Bachelor of Arts degree (BA) in Fine Arts.

CAREER HIGHLIGHTS

Developing His Approach to His Art

After finishing college, Goldsworthy worked as a groundskeeper for an estate on the border of Scotland. During these early years, during and right after college, he recognized his calling as an artist. For Goldsworthy, this meant becoming aware of the depth of his relationship with the natural world. "I want an intimate physical involvement with the earth," he stated. "I must touch. I take nothing out with me in the way of tools, glue, or rope, preferring to explore the natural bonds and tensions that exist within the earth. The season and weather conditions determine to a large extent what I make. I enjoy relying on the seasons to provide new materials." He also learned the value of trial and error, a lesson that has stayed with him throughout his career. "I make one or two sculptures each day I go out," he remarked. "From a month's work, two or three pieces are successful. The 'mistakes' are very important. Each new sculpture is a result of knowledge accumulated through past experience."

"I want an intimate physical involvement with the earth," Goldsworthy stated. "I must touch. I take nothing out with me in the way of tools, glue, or rope, preferring to explore the natural bonds and tensions that exist within the earth. The season and weather conditions determine to a large extent what I make. I enjoy relying on the seasons to provide new materials."

Goldsworthy soon began creating artistic works using a wide array of natural materials, including stone, wood, water, snow, ice, mud, and even flower petals. But he didn't receive much attention for this art at first. Because his landscape sculptures are often designed to be altered or destroyed by the deteriorating effects of weather, and because they are situated in remote outdoor locations, they are not always suitable for traditional artistic showcases like galleries or museums.

Often, the only way to preserve the appearance of his pieces is to photograph them. Goldsworthy has acknowledged that photographs can sometimes be the best way to show his art. "It's a very appropriate way to describe some of the works," he stated. "In the neutral space of a gallery, the light doesn't change, [the works] are just held in suspension when really they need to go from darkness into the light. The sun needs to penetrate and catch the bronze in just such a way at just such a moment. Photographs can show us that." To illustrate this point, he began selling books of photographs documenting his work in the 1980s.

Goldsworthy has embraced the fact that some of his works last only a short period of time. According to the artist, time plays a central role in his work. "Time gives," he explained. "Time gives growth, it gives continuity, and it gives change. And in the case of some sculptures, time gives a patina to them." He has placed equal emphasis on the natural materials that he uses. "There is life in a stone," he stated. "Any stone that sits in a field or lies on a beach takes on the memory of that place. You can feel that stones have witnessed so many things."

Goldsworthy has emphasized that he treasures the act of creation above all else. "My sculpture can last for days or a few seconds—what is important for me is the experience of making. I leave all my work outside and often return to watch it decay," he explained. "We're always wanting to hold onto things as they are. But that's not the nature of life or things, is it?"

Getting Recognition for His Art

During the first half of the 1980s, Goldsworthy continued to refine his craft, living and working in Yorkshire, Lancashire, and Cumbria (all in England). He began to attract attention in the British arts community, receiving a Northern Arts Award and a Yorkshire Arts Award from Arts Council England and Trinity Guildhall. In 1985 he moved to Scotland to pursue new artistic opportunities.

Goldsworthy's first brush with widespread recognition came in 1989 when he created *Touching North,* a group of four large snow arches constructed at the North Pole. "The North Pole project that I did was at the ultimate destination of north," he explained. "It was a way of following winter to its origin. I really like that because I am an artist who likes to work with materials at their source to understand them." In 1994 he created a similar series of arches near his home in Dumfriesshire, Scotland. Entitled *Herd of Arches,* the piece consists of seven arches made from pinkish-brown sandstone blocks that came from a local quarry. Since that time, he has gone on to construct arches in a variety of locations and with a variety of materials. That has become a common practice for Goldsworthy: to take a certain shape or a type of structure—like arches, walls, and cairns—and to reimagine that structure in different areas in new ways.

In 1996 Goldsworthy received a government grant to create a large-scale project called *Sheepfolds.* Set in the countryside of northern England, the project entailed the creation of a series of stone enclosures modeled after ancient sheep shelters. It was a very painstaking process that required the cooperation of the landowners, but he finally finished *Sheepfolds* in 2003. In total, the project consists of 46 separate structures and covers the entire county of Cumbria.

Sheepfolds met with some controversy when newspapers reported that Goldsworthy was given a large portion of public funds to complete the work. In addition, some of the landowners in the area did not want their property to become part of the project. But Goldsworthy looked upon the opposition as a growth experience. "It's very humbling to work … where some people don't want me," he confided. "But it's good for an artist to do that, instead of just working on private commissions where people really want you and do everything for you."

Working in the United States

Goldsworthy first established his reputation in the United States with *Storm King Wall,* a piece that he constructed in 1997 at the sculpture park at the Storm King Arts Center. Inspired by the stone walls built by European colonists centuries earlier, *Storm King Wall* extends 2,278 feet across New York's Hudson Valley. In tribute to the craftsmanship of the colonists, he built the wall without mortar, carefully balancing stone upon stone. But the hard work paid off. William Zimmer of the *New York Times* raved, "It's undeniably a grand creation: the wall, though low, makes its mark as being as relentless as the Great Wall of China." To Goldsworthy, working in the Hudson Valley was not very different from working at home. "My art came out of the British landscape which is heavily worked by people, so that's important to my work," he said. "The East Coast of America is also quite interesting for similar but different reasons. Once there were stone walls that ran through fields there, and now there are secondary woods; you can feel the presence of the farmer in the past."

As his reputation in the United States increased, Goldsworthy began to receive commissions from prestigious American institutions. One such commission came from Stanford University, where he created *Stone River* in 2001 as part of the outdoor art collection at the Cantor Center for Visual Arts. This 320-foot sculpture is made of sandstone blocks from university buildings that had been destroyed in earthquakes in 1906 and 1989. The wall-like piece is set in a trough and snakes through a natural area. "I describe the form as a river…. It is the flow, not the water, that is important—a river of wind, animals, birds, insects, people, seasons, climate, stone, earth, color." "It raises questions about the purpose and place of art and about humankind's relationship to the past and to the land," said Thomas K. Seligman, the director of the Cantor Arts Center. "The graceful undulations and richly hand-worked stones evoke and interact with the environment in an elegant and engaging way."

In 2001-02, Goldsworthy created *Three Cairns,* a piece that incorporates elements of permanence and impermanence. Cairns are typically piles of

Stone River *is one of several pieces that explore the stone wall. Iris & B. Gerald Cantor Center for Visual Arts at Stanford University. Courtesy of Andy Goldsworthy and Haines Gallery.*

stones left on the side of the road. Goldsworthy's cairns are eight-foot tall oval structures that are made of limestone pieces put together without mortar; the weight of the stone holds it together. Goldsworthy created three permanent cairns for the Neuberger Museum of Art (Purchase, New York), the Museum of Contemporary Art (San Diego, California), and the Des Moines Art Center (Des Moines, Iowa). These three pieces are intended to connect the East Coast, the West Coast, and the Midwest. In addition, he also created three temporary cairns, also for the East Coast (New Rochelle, New York), West Coast (Pigeon Point, California), and Midwest (Grinnell College, Iowa). All three were destined to be destroyed by natural forces: the temporary pieces for the East and West were created at low tide in tidal zones and then were destroyed by incoming water; the piece for the Midwest was placed in the prairie and allowed to erode a bit over several months, then destroyed by a controlled prairie fire. "His are not mere stacks of stones marking a trail," commentator Donna Seaman said about the cairns, "but rather elaborately constructed and gracefully balanced egg-shaped forms that bring into focus the beauty of their surroundings."

In 2003 Goldsworthy was commissioned by the Museum of Jewish Heritage in New York City to create *Garden of Stones,* a memorial set on the museum's roof. The piece consists of hollowed-out boulders into which Holocaust survivors placed dwarf chestnut-oak saplings. *New York Times* critic Jason Edward Kaufman was greatly moved by the piece, pointing out its universal relevance. "The metaphor of life surviving in adverse conditions is immediately accessible," Kaufman claimed, "and might just as easily serve the symbolic needs of, say, a Christian or Buddhist shrine." Goldsworthy wanted *Garden of Stones* to contain a quiet optimism symbolized by the relationship between the trees and the planters. "Amidst the mass of stone the trees will appear as fragile, vulnerable flickers of life—an expression of hope for the future," he explained. "The stones are not mere containers. The partnership between tree and stone will be stronger for having grown from the stone."

The following year, Goldsworthy was commissioned to make another rooftop creation in New York City, this time for the Metropolitan Museum of Art. The resulting piece, *Stone Houses,* is made up of two columns of balanced granite stones, each surrounded by wooden domes with spaced slats. Adding a personal touch to the project, he had the stones shipped all the way from a beach near his Scotland home.

In 2005, Goldsworthy completed *Roof,* a series of similar domes, at the National Gallery of Art in Washington, DC. According to the National

Two views of Garden of Stones, *a rooftop piece at the Museum of Jewish Heritage in New York City: one view in 2003, shortly after its installation (top), and another view in 2010, after some time has elapsed (bottom). © Andy Goldsworthy/Courtesy Galerie Lelong, New York. Photo: Melanie Einzig/Museum of Jewish Heritage, New York.*

Gallery's website, the piece "follows a trajectory that includes Neolithic burial chambers and dwelling cairns, ancient Roman and Byzantine structures, Enlightenment architecture and modern public buildings." *Roof* consists of nine hollow domes of stacked slate that stand over five feet high and 27 feet in diameter. The museum wanted something that spoke to the history of the area. Goldsworthy accomplished this by choosing the same kind of stone used to construct much of the city and by taking inspiration from the many domed buildings in the capital. "The dome structure and its rich associations gain new meaning in Andy Goldsworthy's work," declared Earl A. Powell III, the director of the National Gallery of Art. "This site-specific installation will call attention to the materials and forms that define our nation's capital, underscoring the natural origins of our urban and cultural environment."

"My sculpture can last for days or a few seconds—what is important for me is the experience of making. I leave all my work outside and often return to watch it decay," Goldsworthy explained. "We're always wanting to hold onto things as they are. But that's not the nature of life or things, is it?"

Also in 2005, Goldsworthy was hired to install a series of paving stones at the entrance of the de Young Museum in San Francisco. Once again, he had the stones brought over from Britain, this time from the Leeds area where he was raised. The artist drew the inspiration for this project, entitled *Drawn Stone,* from the 1989 earthquake that damaged the original buildings that housed the de Young Museum. To remind audiences of the power and fragility of the earth, he carefully crafted a long, snaking crack through the stones and boulders of the courtyard, creating a seating area for museum patrons.

While working in America, Goldsworthy established a relationship with the Galerie Lelong in New York City. His sixth exhibition at Lelong, *White Walls,* was notable for containing a multimedia element. He created the 2007 sculpture by covering the gallery walls with white porcelain clay shipped from Cornwall, England, covering an expanse 13 feet high and more than 140 feet long. Over the course of the exhibition, the wall slowly began to crumble, leaving debris along its base. Once again, Goldsworthy wanted to display the effect of time on his art, and visitors were encouraged to witness the work's slow decay. In a different room, the artist showed a 37-minute film called *Stone Shadow Fold,* which provided another perspective on time. The film depicts Goldsworthy lying on a slab of stone as snow slowly falls on and around him. After the snow accumulates, he stands up and walks away, leaving a bare spot on the stone in the shape of his body. The camera lingers on that image as the snow begins to fill in the space where his body was, removing all trace of Goldsworthy from the stone. Writing for the *New York Times,* critic Bridget L. Goodbody characterized *Stone Shadow Fold* as "a poignant meditation on the brevity of human life and the brutal eternity of nature's processes."

In 2006 Goldsworthy visited the Presidio Forest, a park near San Francisco that is part of the National Park Service. He was so impressed by the forest's centuries-old eucalyptus and cypress trees that he returned in 2008 to construct *Spire,* a towering structure made from mature, felled trees. Formally, the piece echoes one of his earliest creations, *Memories,* a group of spires consisting of mature trees located in England's Grizedale Forest. Creating *Spire* was a different experience for Goldsworthy in that he designed the piece, but did not actually work on it. "I sat at the bottom, in a director's chair, with a pair of binoculars and a walkie-talkie, telling the crew where to put the logs, which is something I've never done before," he explained. "It was a really strange experience, and exhausting, in some ways more exhausting to do it by direction than doing it myself."

Projects at Home and in France

In 2002 Goldsworthy began working on a series of stone arches throughout the countryside near his Scotland home. Called *Striding Arches,* the piece is considered an expansion of the idea behind *Herd of Arches.* Standing atop a series of rolling hills, the arches give the illusion of peacefully strolling. Indeed, Goldsworthy designed the arches to "walk the hills alongside people." "What really matters is energy, the energy of the stone on the move in the landscape," he stated.

In 2007, the Yorkshire Sculpture Park in West Yorkshire, England, held a retrospective of Goldsworthy's work in recognition of his remarkable career. The event consisted of permanent outdoor sculptures along with temporary installations, paintings, and archival material. Along with a number of his earlier pieces, the exhibition featured new structures like *Hanging Trees,* a stone wall enclosure supporting fallen oaks; *Shadow Stone Fold,* a sheep enclosure made from locally quarried rock; *The Leaf Stalk Room,* a screen or curtain made out of 10,000 horse-chestnut leaf stalks; and a series of rooms made out of stone, wood, and clay. Goldsworthy viewed the retrospective as an excellent way to connect with his audience and let people experience his

This cairn from the Neuberger Museum of Art in New York is part of the piece Three Cairns. *Andy Goldsworthy,* East Coast Cairn, *2001. Collection Friends of the Neuberger Museum of Art, Purchase College, State University of New York. Museum purchase with funds from the Roy R. Neuberger Endowment Fund, the Klein Family Foundation, Sherry and Joel Mallin, Douglas F. Maxwell and other private donations. Photo credit: Jim Frank. © Andy Goldsworthy/Courtesy Galerie Lelong, New York.*

work in person. "Here in the Yorkshire Sculpture Park is an opportunity, with a gallery and the outdoors, to make work that people can see, lay on, touch and engage in without photography as a medium," he enthused.

In 2011 Goldsworthy created *Aldernay Stones,* a multi-piece site-specific work. It's located on the island of Aldernay, part of the Channel Islands, an archipelago in the English Channel that is quite near northwestern France. His work is part of the "Art and Islands" project, an attempt to promote the Channel Islands as an art destination and to bring together these disparate islands by bringing an artist to each island to interpret its individual character. The installation features 12 boulders, each about five to six feet in diameter and weighing three tons, which Goldsworthy created in a mold with rammed earth. They are linked by a 16-mile walking path. As he described his plan, "Each stone will be made with earth containing materials and objects. These will be incorporated into each stone as it is being constructed and might be rocks, branches, bones, tools, seeds, clothes, beach debris or anything else. These materials will be revealed as the stones wear away.... It will be a project that reveals itself over time through the process of erosion, which I hope will be relevant to a small island." The stones were placed in a variety of locations—in an underground bunker used during World War II and on beaches and headlands—and will weather differently over time, reflecting the natural environment. "I think anybody who lives here has to have some understanding of the climate, the changes, the light," Goldsworthy commented. "It's an extraordinary place to live in and I hope these stones reflect some of those qualities."

In the Provence region of southeastern France, near the town of Digne-les-Bains, Goldsworthy has been working on a long-term art installation project that continues to the present day. "As long as I can walk," he claimed, "and the people in Digne are still involved, the project will continue." He first visited the area in 1994 as a guest artist at the Musée Gassendi. After that time, he returned to the area for many long visits and began and created a wide variety of works there. In 1999 he created his renowned sculpture *River of Earth,* a wall made of locally sourced clay that he created at the Musée Gassendi. In 2002 he began work on a vast project in the nearby countryside, which is dotted with mountainous terrain, abandoned farms, and villages.

Called "Refuges D'Art," this project encompasses a series of permanent artworks linked by a 100-mile walking trail along ancient footpaths. Along these walking paths Goldsworthy has renovated a number of historically significant ruined buildings in the French countryside, repurposing them to house his sculptures. For example, in the farmhouse called Le Ferme de Belon, he constructed a group of white stone arches inspired by the site's

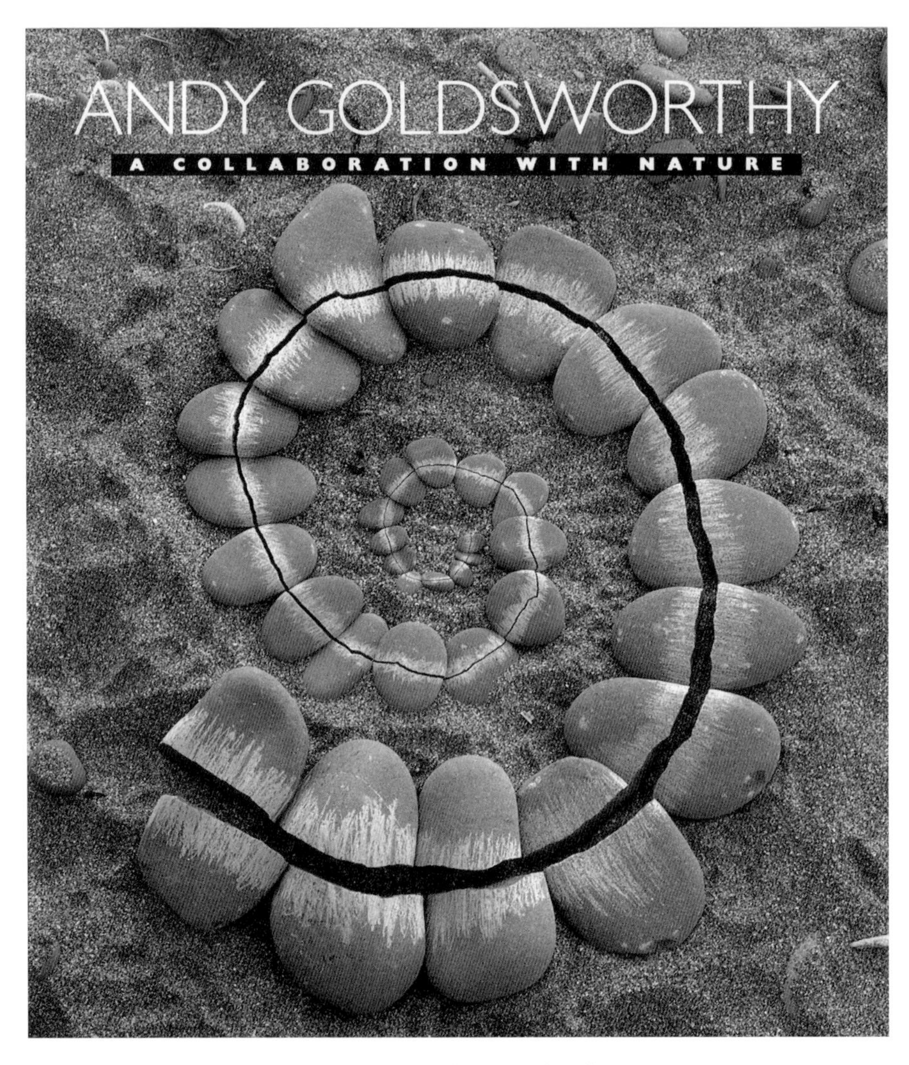

In his books, Goldsworthy uses photographs, diary excerpts, essays, and other explanatory text to document his work.

history as a hiding place for resistance fighters during World War II. The footpath leads up the mountainside to a restored barn at Col de l'Escuichiere, the site of an old coalmine surrounded by oak trees and rare stone. Visitors can follow a ten-day walking itinerary to explore the sites, some of which were specifically renovated to house hikers. Goldworthy plans to continue working in the area. "What has evolved is a project that goes beyond art as an object to be looked at," he explained, "to something that is part of a landscape to be lived in."

Sharing His Work through Film and Books

As Goldsworthy's reputation grew, he caught the attention of German filmmaker Thomas Riedelsheimer. Goldsworthy agreed to become the subject of a documentary for the director, and the resulting film was released in 2001 as *Rivers and Tides: Andy Goldsworthy Working with Time.* Riedelsheimer went about filming the artist at work in Scotland, Canada, America, and France. The film shows the sculptor tending to *Storm King Wall* and creating pieces like *Ice Snake,* a curving piece of ice on a river in Nova Scotia that slowly melted under the sun's heat.

Capturing the process of creation and disintegration was part of the filmmaker's plan. "We both liked the idea of dealing with time," Riedelsheimer commented. "[Goldsworthy] does the photography, which deals very much with the frozen moment, but I can do the photographs in motion—what happens before them, what happens after them." This emphasis on the fading quality of some of Goldsworthy's works impressed critics. "As the film's images accumulate, the movie becomes a sustained and ultimately refreshing meditation on surrender to the idea of temporality," Stephen Holden wrote in the *New York Times.* "If Mr. Goldsworthy's humility in the face of change reminds us that all is vanity, his playfulness also reminds us that a fervent engagement in the moment is in its own way infinite." Writing in *Entertainment Weekly,* reviewer Nicholas Fonseca praised its depiction of "the soft-spoken artist as he painstakingly molds nature's tools (stones, leaves, icicles) into eye-popping installations that may or may not survive by the time he finishes.... Goldsworthy is a marvel, with his unflinching dedication to creating art that's at once ephemeral and eternal." Other critics were equally taken by *Rivers and Tides,* and the film went on to win the Golden Gate Award at the San Francisco International Film Festival.

Goldsworthy's works are typically difficult to see, so early in his career he started taking photographs of his sculptures to make them accessible to people who would otherwise never get to see them. He has published these photos in a series of collections that include explanatory text written by art critics or Goldsworthy himself, as well as interviews with the artist, diary excerpts, and critical commentary. The books serve to document and "preserve" his work. The books have received favorable responses from reviewers and readers alike. Critics have characterized the process of reading Goldsworthy's books as an emotionally affecting experience and have praised the books for providing deep insight into his artistic methods. "He writes of failures and frustrations as well as successes," W.B. Holmes wrote in *Choice,* "and we see how one project leads to another over the days and years."

Reviewing his book *Time,* Donna Seaman provided a summary that could apply to all of his work: "The earth is Goldsworthy's medium, and he works quiet, fleeting miracles as he creates exquisitely delicate and temporal sculptures out of leaves, twigs, ice, petals, feathers, sand, water, and stone," Seaman wrote in *Booklist.* "Left open to the forces of time and change, each piece succumbs to the inevitable process of dissolution, an integral aspect of Goldsworthy's lyrically sacrificial art, and he captures these transformations in elegant photographs.... [In diary entries] he writes eloquently about the why and how of his magical work, articulates his fascination with change and decay, and describes the challenges of working in such volatile settings as beaches and woods in winter. By reversing Western art's tradition of creating works that will last long after the artist has gone, Goldsworthy celebrates beauty's transitory nature."

MARRIAGE AND FAMILY

In 1982 Goldsworthy married Judith Gregson. The couple had four children and shared a home in Penpont, a small town in Dumfriesshire, Scotland. They later divorced. He lives in Penport with his current partner, Tina Fiske, an art historian whom he met when she took on a project to catalogue and digitize photographs of his early work.

HOBBIES AND OTHER INTERESTS

When he is not busy creating works of art, Goldsworthy enjoys fishing. Even when he is working, he often takes a break to watch videos about his favorite pastime. Also, he takes one week every year to vacation with his family on the Scottish coast. Yet even during his time off, Goldsworthy finds an outlet for his creativity. "During my holiday, I work on the beach," he stated. "A lot of the most recent work on the beach has been made in anticipation of its inevitable collapse when the sea comes in."

Goldsworthy's close bond to the land has fostered a passion for its preservation. Aside from being works of art, he sees his pieces as examples of a healthy relationship with nature. Goldsworthy hopes that his art draws attention to the perils of environmental exploitation and destruction. "In many ways my approach to the earth has been a reaction against the abuse of the land by the industrial farmer," he explained.

SELECTED WORKS

Sculptures

Memories, 1984
Touching North, 1989

Herd of Arches, 1994
Sheepfolds, 1996-2003
Storm King Wall, 1997-98
Ice Snake, 2001
Stone River, 2001
Three Cairns, 2001-02
Striding Arches, 2002-08
Garden of Stones, 2003
Stone Houses, 2004
Drawn Stone, 2005
Roof, 2005
White Walls, 2007
Spire, 2008
Aldernay Stones, 2011

Photography Books

Andy Goldsworthy: A Collaboration with Nature, 1990
Hand to Earth: Andy Goldsworthy Sculpture, 1976-1990, 1990
Stone, 1994
Wood, 1996
Arch, 1999
Time, 2000
Wall, 2000
Passage, 2004
Enclosure, 2007

HONORS AND AWARDS

North West Arts Award (Arts Council England and Trinity Guildhall): 1979
Yorkshire Arts Award (Arts Council England and Trinity Guildhall): 1980
Northern Arts Award (Arts Council England and Trinity Guildhall): 1981; 1982
Scottish Arts Council Award: 1987
Northern Electricity Arts Award: 1989
Honorary Degree from the University of Bradford: 1993
Officer of the Order of the British Empire: 2000
South Bank Show Award: 2008, Visual Arts, for exhibition at Yorkshire Sculpture Park

FURTHER READING

Books

Malpas, William. *Andy Goldsworthy: Touching Nature*, 1995

Periodicals

Current Biography Yearbook, 2000
Los Angeles Times, May 5, 2003, p.E1; Dec. 21, 2004, p.F6
Nature, Jan. 15, 1998, p.235
New York Times, Sep. 14, 2003, p.2.35; Nov. 2, 2008, p.AR19
New Yorker, Sep. 22, 2003, p.126
Odyssey, Jan. 2010, p.22
Scholastic Art, Apr./May 2005, p.6
Smithsonian, Feb. 1997, p.94; Nov. 2005, p.46

Online Articles

http://www.kqed.org
(KQED Public Media, Spark,"Andy Goldsworthy," undated)
http://www.nga.gov
(National Gallery of Art,"Andy Goldsworthy: Roof," undated)
http://www.topics.nytimes.com
(New York Times,"Andy Goldsworthy, multiple articles, various dates)
http://www.pbs.org
(Public Broadcasting Service, Art Beat,"Andy Goldsworthy's 'Spire,'" Jan. 7, 2009)
http://www.time.com
(Time,"Q&A with Andy Goldsworthy," Apr. 13, 2007)

ADDRESS

Andy Goldsworthy
Harry N. Abrams, Inc.
115 West 18th Street
New York, NY 10011

WORLD WIDE WEB SITES

http://www.goldsworthy.cc.gla.ac.uk
http://www.sculpture.org.uk/artists/AndyGoldsworthy

Jay-Z 1969-

American Rapper, Entrepreneur, and Record Executive
Creator of"Empire State of Mind"
Founder of Roc-A-Fella and Former Head of Def Jam Records

BIRTH

The rapper known by the stage name Jay-Z was born Shawn Corey Carter on December 4, 1969, in Brooklyn, New York. He was the youngest of four children born to Gloria Carter, who worked as a clerk for an investment company, and Adnes Reeves. He had one older brother, Eric, and two older sisters, Michelle and Andrea.

YOUTH

Carter grew up in Brooklyn, a borough of New York City. As the youngest of four kids, he enjoyed being the center of attention, gaining fame in his neighborhood when he taught himself to ride a two-wheeled bike at age four. His family moved to Brooklyn's Marcy housing project when he was about six years old. Although the projects were known for poverty, crime, and drugs, young Shawn had the support of both parents and stayed out of trouble. He did well at school and his teachers considered him a good kid. Not only did he enjoy reading, he loved to make up his own rhymes. To learn new words to put in his raps, he even read the dictionary. "I had this green notebook that I used to write in incessantly," he recalled. "I would walk through the Marcy projects, where everyone's playing basketball, with my notebook, and that was not a cool thing. You went to school because you had to, but you did not carry books." As a youth he began performing his raps on street corners. His outgoing personality and cool, confident style led to the nickname "Jazzy." For his rap career, Carter later shortened this nickname to Jay-Z.

Things changed for Carter when he was 12 years old. His parents split up, and his father left the family. Feeling abandoned, Carter started drifting into trouble. As he explained in his song "December 4th" from *The Black Album,* "Was a kid torn apart once his pop disappeared/ I went to school got good grades could behave when I wanted/ But I had demons deep inside that would raise when confronted." These were the same years when crack cocaine, a cheap and very addictive drug, was invading the inner city, and it seemed as if everyone in his neighborhood was either using crack or dealing it. If people found other ways to escape the projects, Carter recalled, "they never came back to share the wisdom of how they made it." By the time he was 16, he had started dealing drugs on the street. He hadn't aspired to become a drug dealer. "You aspire to the lifestyle you see around you," he explained. "You see the green BMW, the prettiest car you've ever seen. You see the trappings of drug dealing, and it draws you in." Eventually, however, "I started seeing people go to jail and get killed, and the light slowly came on. I was like, 'This life has no good ending.'" Looking for another way out of the projects, he turned to music.

EDUCATION

Carter attended Eli Whitney High School in Brooklyn until it closed; then he attended George Westinghouse High School in Brooklyn, where his classmates included future rappers Notorious B.I.G. and Busta Rhymes. He later moved to Trenton, New Jersey, where he attended Trenton Central High School, but he never graduated. Although he became successful with-

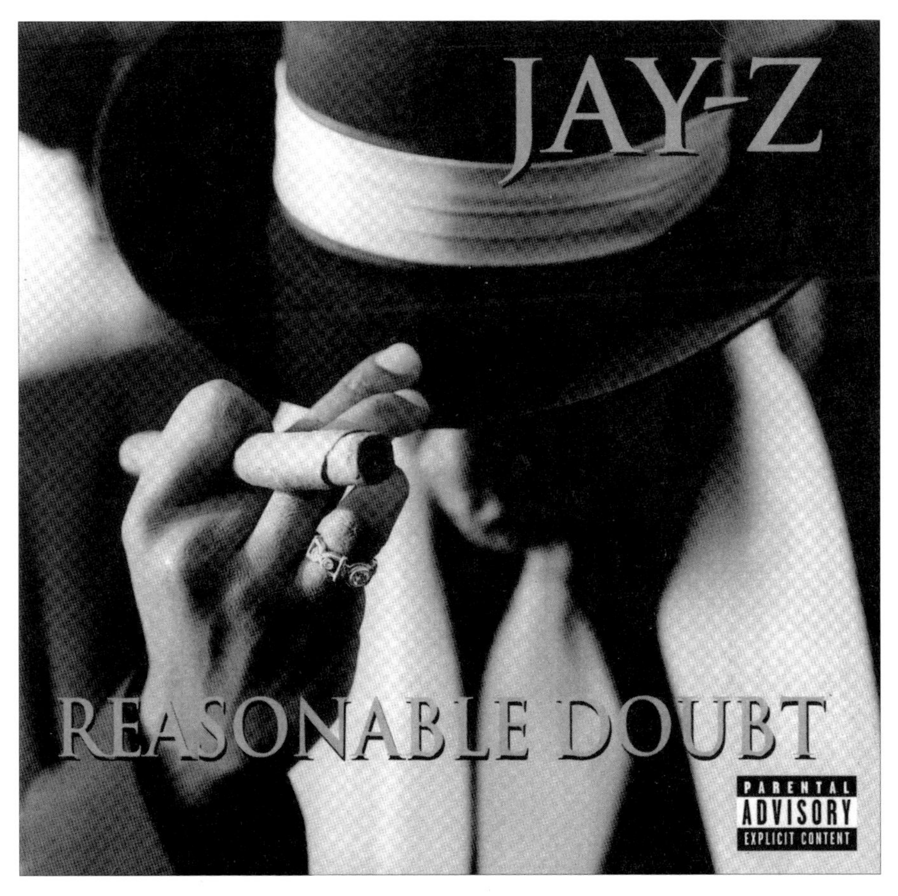

Jay-Z released his first album, Reasonable Doubt, *in 1996.*

out higher education, he notes that it took a lot of hard work and good fortune. He frequently visits urban schools to urge kids to stay in class, telling them: "There are only about 10 to 20 rappers that are in the game making money with album after album. Do the math and get your education."

CAREER HIGHLIGHTS

Getting Started as a Rapper

Carter knew that there was little future on the streets—most drug dealers ended up dead or in jail. "You can't run on the streets forever," he said of those times. "What are you going to be doing when you're 30 years old, or 35 or 40? I had a fear of being nothing—that pretty much drove me." He had never stopped rapping, although he no longer carried around a notebook, holding all his rhymes in his memory instead. He thought about giving a music career a shot, but he didn't trust record company executives. That distrust derived, in part, from watching his friend, Jaz-O, make a record and a couple of videos in the late 1980s. Carter, recording as Jay-Z, had contributed to his friend Jaz-O's album, even spending two months with him recording in London, England. Jay-Z saw how the record label broke promises to his friend, who saw little of the profits from his work. When Jay-Z recorded a 12-inch single titled "In My Lifetime" in 1995, he sold it himself out of his car. The next year he and friends Damon Dash and Biggs Burke decided to form their own record company, which they called Roc-A-Fella Records. They produced another Jay-Z single, which did well enough to get a distribution deal with Priority Records.

> *Jay-Z knew that there was little future on the streets—most drug dealers ended up dead or in jail. "You can't run on the streets forever," he said of those times. "What are you going to be doing when you're 30 years old, or 35 or 40? I had a fear of being nothing—that pretty much drove me."*

Roc-A-Fella brought out Jay-Z's first album, *Reasonable Doubt,* in 1996. The album featured a guest rap from popular rapper Notorious B.I.G., as well as a vocal from R&B superstar Mary J. Blige on the single "Can't Knock the Hustle." The album became very popular in New York City, generating enough sales to land in the Top 25 of the *Billboard* album chart. In recent years, *Rolling Stone* magazine called it "one of hip-hop's foundational records." Jay-Z's songs were typical of the "gangsta" rap genre, telling stories of his life on the streets and rapping about living the high life. His songs were filled with curse words and racial epithets. But Jay-Z's skill with language was undeniable, and he was open and honest about the darker side of the gangsta lifestyle as well. After his first album, he later said, "There were cats coming up to me like, 'You must have been looking in my window or following my life.'... It was emotional. Like big, rough hoodlums, hardrock, three-time jail bidders with scars and gold teeth just breaking down. It was something to look at, like, I must be going somewhere people been wanting someone to go for a while."

For his second album, *In My Lifetime, Vol. 1* (1997), Jay-Z worked with Sean "Puff Daddy" Combs and other producers to create a more mainstream sound with crossover appeal. The album reached No. 3 on the *Billboard*

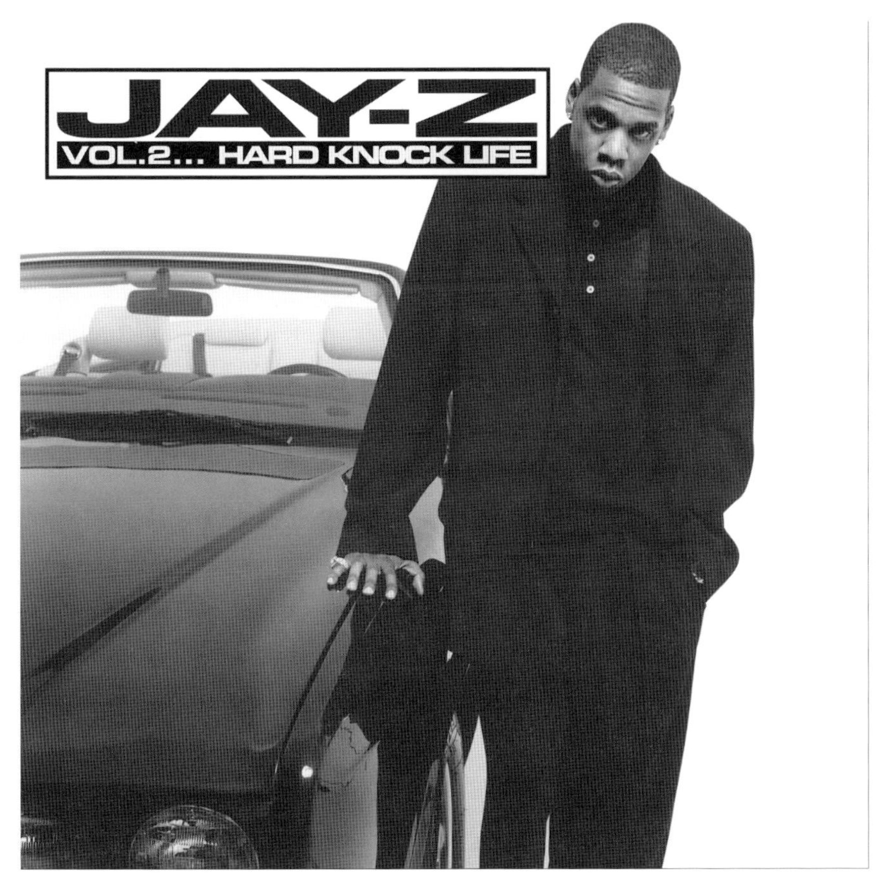

Hard Knock Life *became Jay-Z's first No. 1 album.*

album chart despite having only one Top 100 single, "The City Is Mine," a tribute to Notorious B.I.G., who had been murdered recently. Although many tracks boasted of Jay-Z's skill with words and the ladies, it also contained songs like "You Must Love Me," in which he apologized for hurting his family and others. "The first album dealt with things on the outside—the cars, the jewelry, the clothes … things you could see," he noted. "Now that everyone got to know that, I'm gonna take 'em a little deeper. Now we can explore and get to the heart of Jay-Z."

Jay-Z's breakthrough into crossover success came with *Vol. 2: Hard Knock Life* (1998), his first No. 1 album. The album had his first Top 20 single, the track "Can I Get A…", which also appeared on the soundtrack for the popular action film *Rush Hour* and earned the rapper his first MTV Video Award. The title track reached No. 15 and sampled a song from the Broadway musical *Annie:* "It's a hard knock life/ for us/ instead of treats/ we get tricked/ instead of kisses/ we get kicked." *Vol. 2: Hard Knock Life* earned Jay-Z his first Grammy Award, for best rap album, but he didn't attend the ceremony. At that time rap music was not widely respected, and Jay-Z believed that the Recording Academy gave rap music only token respect. To prove the growing appeal of rap, Jay-Z used his new success to create a hip-hop-only lineup for his Hard Knock Life Tour in 1999, performing with DMX, Ja Rule, Method Man, and other rappers. Despite conventional wisdom that hip-hop stars needed to tour with R&B acts to be accessible, Jay-Z's tour sold out all 52 performances. The successful tour was recorded for the documentary *Backstage,* which appeared in theaters in 2000.

In fewer than five years Jay-Z had become one of the world's best-selling rappers, without any hint of the violence that surrounded other hip-hop artists. That changed in late 1999, after an incident following a release party for Jay-Z's third album, *Vol. 3: The Life and Times of S. Carter.* Jay-Z crossed paths with a rival producer, Lance "Un" Rivera, who Jay-Z thought was bootlegging his new CD. Their encounter ended with Rivera in the hospital with stab wounds and Jay-Z charged with assault. Jay-Z denied any involvement, but later pled guilty in exchange for no jail time. "Where I grew up, I saw a lot of people get wronged," he explained. "No matter how much you believe in the truth, that's always in the back of your mind." The charges had little effect on his musical success, however. *Vol. 3: The Life and Times of S. Carter* was another No. 1 album for Jay-Z, selling more than three million copies. The single "Big Pimpin'" reached the Top 20, while superstar vocalist Mariah Carey performed on "Things That U Do." Jay-Z returned the favor that year by appearing on Carey's No. 1 hit, "Heartbreaker."

Focusing on Business and the Roc-A-Fella Brand

After his brush with the law, Jay-Z decided to avoid people and situations that might get him into trouble and focus on business instead. From the time he had partnered with Dash, they envisioned Roc-A-Fella as a diverse business that would include not just music but movies, fashion, and other lifestyle products. The company sold a 50 percent stake in the music division to the major label Def Jam in 1997 and established the Rocawear clothing line in 1999. Jay-Z's fifth album, *The Dynasty: Roc La Familia* (2000), featured other artists signed to the Roc-A-Fella label, giving them exposure on another No. 1 Jay-Z album. Roc-A-Fella Films released its first film in 1998, *Streets Is Watching,* based on the rapper's rise to fame, and then released a pair of street-set feature films that featured Jay-Z in small cameo roles. As rap songs often name-check brand-name alcohol and jew-

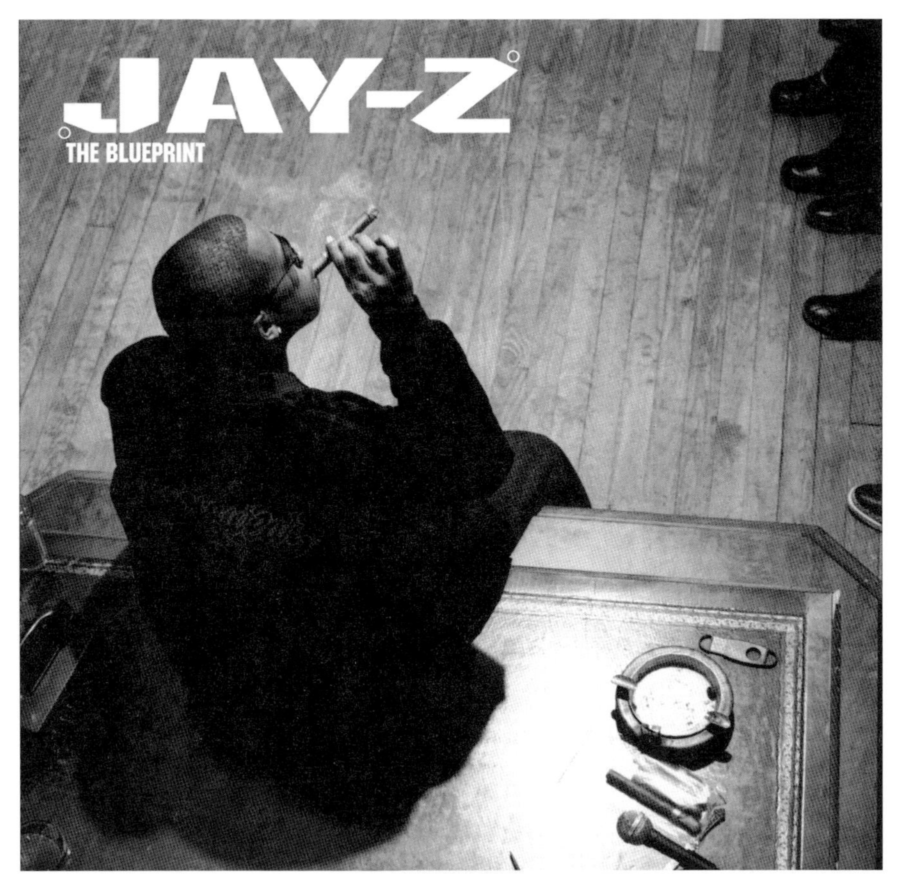

The Blueprint *debuted at No. 1 and became an instant classic.*

elry, Roc-A-Fella became the exclusive distributor for the Scottish vodka brand Armadale in 2002. That year Jay-Z also signed a deal with Reebok, becoming their first non-athlete to have a signature shoe; the line, S. Carter, became Reebok's fastest-selling shoe ever. In 2003, Jay-Z extended his business interests further by co-founding a high-end sports bar in Manhattan, the 40/40 Club.

In the meantime, the rapper continued his domination of the record charts. His 2001 album, *The Blueprint,* debuted at No. 1, selling over 400,000 copies the first week despite being released on September 11, 2001, when terrorists attacked the World Trade Center in New York and the Pentagon in Washington, DC. (Jay-Z responded by immediately donating $45,000 to the Red Cross, then giving $1 from each ticket sold on that fall's tour to the charity Hip Hop Has Heart and the New York Fire

Department.) Many critics considered *The Blueprint* an instant classic, fueled by old-school soul samples and production by up-and-comer Kanye West. It produced two Top 20 singles, "Girls, Girls, Girls" and "Izzo (H.O.V.A.)," which at No. 8 became his highest-charting single yet. The album was also notable for starting a verbal feud with fellow rapper Nas. The two performers traded insults for the next few years—but through their music only, as neither wanted any violence like the shootings that took the lives of rival rappers Notorious B.I.G. and Tupac Shakur. Later that year Jay-Z became the first rapper to be featured on MTV's acoustic music program "Unplugged," with the Roots as his backup band. Reviewing the show in the *Village Voice,* Selwyn Hinds noted that "hip-hop with live instrumentation has seldom sounded this good."

"Jay-Z attributed his success running Def Jam to his love for music. "I'm not just a guy behind a desk trying to make numbers," he said. "I'm an artist in my own right trying to get them to be more creative. After that, success is a by-product of doing the job right.""

Jay-Z didn't slow down in 2002, releasing two more albums that year. The first was a collaboration with soul singer R. Kelly, *The Best of Both Worlds.* The second release was actually a double album: *The Blueprint 2: The Gift and the Curse,* which debuted at No. 1 and quickly sold three million copies. The album had two Top 10 singles, the No. 8 "Excuse Me Miss" and the No. 4 "'03 Bonnie and Clyde," a duet with singer Beyoncé. While *The Blueprint 2* sold well, some critics observed that the quality of songs didn't extend over two discs, and Jay-Z released a condensed version of the album on a single disc, *The Blueprint 2.1.* Still, the rapper continued to dominate the airwaves. In February 2003, the cable network Showtime produced a live broadcast of his concert from Memphis, Tennessee, making it the first time a hip-hop artist had performed a full-length concert on live television. He was all over the radio in the summer of 2003, between appearances on Pharrell's No. 5 hit "Frontin'" and Beyoncé's No. 1 summer anthem "Crazy in Love." The latter song earned the rapper two Grammys (he attended the awards show this time) and two MTV Video Music Awards.

Despite this success, rumors began to spread that Jay-Z was considering retirement. He had achieved everything he could in rap music and wondered whether he had more to say. "I may have told, in my whole career, maybe 10 stories," he admitted. "I deal with the same topics [over and over] in different ways." He finally announced that his late 2003 release, *The Black Album,* would be his last. It was another No. 1 debut for the rapper, generating Top 10 singles "Change Clothes" and "Dirt Off Your Shoulder," as well as the Grammy winner for Best Rap Solo Performance, "99 Problems." If this was Jay-Z's last album, Chuck Arnold noted in *People,* "he goes out on top with this awesome display of his dope, deft skills.... After the relative disappointment of last year's spotty *The Blueprint 2: The Gift & the Curse,* Jay-Z delivers highlight after highlight here with whatever style he attempts." A documentary that followed the recording of the album, as well as Jay-Z's "final show" at Madison Square Garden, was released in theaters in 2004 as *Fade to Black.*

Moving into the Board Room

In 2005, Jay-Z began a new phase of his career, becoming the head of the major label Def Jam Records. "I've done just about everything rapping, so now I have to push the envelope on the executive side," he said. The deal included Def Jam buying out his share of Roc-A-Fella Records, while giving Jay-Z ownership of his recording masters. It was the first time a hugely successful performer had taken over a prominent record label, but Jay-Z felt qualified for the job. "The business of business has always been something I focused on, and rightly so.... Whatever job you have, be it hustling on the street or working at the mall, you gotta have a plan for when it's over." Most observers felt he had more hits than misses as an executive. He signed his ex-rival Nas and Kanye West, his former producer who had become a No. 1-selling rapper in his own right. He broke new acts that included rapper Young Jeezy (No. 2 debut album); R&B singer Ne-Yo (Grammy-winning debut album); and Barbadian singer Rihanna, who became an international pop star. Jay-Z attributed his success running Def Jam to his love for music. "I'm not just a guy behind a desk trying to make numbers," he said. "I'm an artist in my own right trying to get them to be more creative. After that, success is a by-product of doing the job right."

Jay-Z continued overseeing other business interests, as well. He had bought out his partner Dash's share in Rocawear, to which he still contributed ideas. "We know how we like our stuff," he remarked. "If I see something that I like, I'll maybe take it and alter it to my specifications. Fashion pirates—that's what they call us!" By 2005, the company was earning $400 million in annual sales. The rapper fulfilled a lifetime dream in 2004 when he bought a share in the National Basketball Association's New Jersey Nets; he hoped to move the pro basketball team to his hometown of

Two views of Jay-Z: as a rapper; and as a business leader and philanthropist.

Brooklyn. Jay-Z also had several lucrative endorsement deals, including partnerships with beer brewer Anheuser-Busch, Swiss watchmaker Audemars Piquet, and laptop computer company Hewlett-Packard. By 2006, Jay-Z's personal worth was estimated to be $320 million.

Even though he had retired from solo recording after 2003, Jay-Z remained an active collaborator with other artists. His second album with R. Kelly, *Unfinished Business,* debuted in 2004 and hit No. 1. The two artists planned a tour in 2004, but when Kelly proved unreliable Jay-Z booted him off the tour and finished the dates alone, attracting such guest artists as Mary J. Blige, Snoop Dogg, and P. Diddy. In 2004 he also released *Collision Course,* an extended play CD, in collaboration with alternative metal band Linkin Park. *Collision Course* was another No. 1 album for Jay-Z, and the track "Numb/Encore" earned him a Grammy for Best Rap/Sung Collaboration. In 2005, he promoted and performed in the "I Declare War" concert with his rival, Nas. Instead of exchanging insults, the two rappers shook hands at the end of the concert and performed a medley of their songs. Showing that rap rivals could resolve things peacefully was important, Jay-Z noted, in contrast with the unsolved murders of the rappers Notorious B.I.G. and Tupac Shakur. "Everybody talks about Big and Pac and how that ended," Jay-Z explained. "We talked about showing a different side and what it would mean to the culture of hip-hop. It was bigger than just us and our trivial little beefs. Hopefully, it shows another way."

Jay-Z also thought it was important to use his wealth and celebrity to help the less fortunate. After Hurricane Katrina devastated New Orleans in 2005, he and Sean "Diddy" Combs donated a million dollars to the American Red Cross's relief efforts and publicly called on others to contribute as well. The following year, the rapper teamed with the United Nations to promote awareness of the global water crisis. Jay-Z toured developing countries and met with young people who didn't have safe access to fresh water. "As I started looking around and looking at ways that I could become helpful, it started at the first thing, water, something as simple as water," he said. He promoted the issue during a world tour, and MTV filmed his visits to African villages, where his donations helped build pumps. The experience was moving, he related. "I've given money and written checks, but when you're on the ground and you turn on the faucet and the village gets water for the first time, it's like nothing else." He hoped the film of his experience, "Water for Life," would inspire his listeners to consider how they could get involved and help others.

Making a Musical Comeback

Because Jay-Z remained an active performer during his time as Def Jam president—including a 2006 single with Beyoncé, "Déjà Vu," that hit No. 4—rumors began to fly that he would return to recording his own material. The rapper made his comeback official with the late 2006 release of *Kingdom Come.* His decision to record again "wasn't like a defining moment," he remarked. "Something, when you love it, is always tugging at you and itching at you, and I was putting it off and putting it off. I started fumbling around to see if it felt good." The CD included several thoughtful songs, including tracks inspired by a painting, Hurricane Katrina, and the loss of his nephew in a car crash. "As you mature you realize that being vulnerable isn't weak. You realize that a man is himself," he explained. The CD received mixed reviews from fans and critics. But according to Jay-Z, "It's what I wanted to do. I was trying to show that hip-hop can talk about different things." The album still became his ninth No. 1, spawning one Top 10 single, "Show Me What You Got."

After joining Rihanna for the hottest single of summer 2007, "Umbrella," Jay-Z released another album, *American Gangster.* The CD was inspired by the Denzel Washington film of the same title that traced the rise and fall of a heroin dealer in the 1970s. Jay-Z considered his *American Gangster* a "concept CD" that told a story, his vision of how his life might have turned out if he hadn't left dealing drugs for rapping. "It's really about why [you deal drugs], and the paranoia, and all the emotions you go through," he explained. "I wasn't dealing with that on my latter albums because that was-

Jay-Z and Alicia Keys performing their hit "Empire State of Mind" at the 2009 MTV Video Music Awards.

n't the life I was living. I didn't think I would ever be able to be in that place again. The movie gave me a chance to revisit those emotions." Much of the album was produced by Combs, and many critics considered it a return to form for the rapper.

Feeling he had proved himself as an executive, Jay-Z left his position with Def Jam at the end of 2007 to focus on his music. He signed a 10-year deal with music promoter Live Nation for concerts, recordings, and merchandise that was reportedly worth $150 million. The deal included the formation of his Roc Nation label. In 2009 Jay-Z released *The Blueprint 3,* which became his 11th album to hit No. 1 on the *Billboard* charts. With that feat he passed Elvis Presley to become the solo artist with the most No. 1 albums in history, and the second most overall only to the Beatles. The rapper felt he still had something to prove, that he could get older and still be musically relevant. "For me to still be able to compete at that level at my age, that's rarefied air," he said. "It's never been done." Jay-Z earned three Grammys for songs off the album, including Best Rap Solo Performance for "D.O.A. (Death of Auto-Tune)" and Best Rap Song and Best Rap/Sung Collaboration for "Run This Town," which featured Rihanna and Kanye

West. The highlight of the CD was his first No. 1 single, "Empire State of Mind," a duet with R&B singer Alicia Keyes. New Yorkers adopted the song as an anthem for the city, and Jay-Z performed it at a commemorative concert on the eighth anniversary of the terrorist attacks on 9/11, which raised money for the families of police and firefighters lost during the attacks.

Jay-Z followed up his award-winning album by going out on tour in 2010, headlining the Coachella Valley Festival in California and the Bonnaroo Festival in Tennessee. He put on a series of special joint performances with rapper Eminem at stadiums in Detroit and New York, and made a special appearance with Irish rock band U2 in Australia. *Forbes* magazine named him hip-hop's biggest moneymaker in 2009-2010, with total earnings of $63 million, more than twice as much as his nearest rival. By late 2010 his business interests included owning five more 40/40 Clubs worldwide; serving as chief executive officer of Rocawear; breaking ground on a Brooklyn sports complex for the Nets; joining actors Will and Jada Pinkett Smith as producers of the hit Broadway musical *Fela!,* which received 11 Tony Award nominations in 2010; and releasing the 2010 book *Decoded,* a memoir that also included interviews with people close to him and discussions of selected lyrics. Jay-Z shared this secret to his success: "There's the gift, there's the spirit, and there's the work—all three have to come together. If one of those things is off, it can stop you from becoming who you were meant to be."

> *His goal with all his work, Jay-Z has said, is "to represent hip-hop culture positively.... Rap is what took me out of my situation, and now I must care for it. I have to leave it as I found it—or better—for the next generation of kids. Then maybe they can change their situation like I did."*

In 2011, excitement built when critics and fans learned that Jay-Z and Kanye West would be collaborating on an album, *Watch the Throne,* which soon became the most anticipated release of the year. With two of the biggest names in hip-hop as collaborators, some commentators said, the album couldn't possibly live up to the hype. Indeed, responses to the album varied widely. Some complained that the album was cluttered and disjointed, and many commented on the emphasis on wealth at a time of great economic hardship for many, what writer Jennifer Lena described as "Two fatuous, wealthy rappers celebrating their good fortune in the face of

Jay-Z and Beyoncé enjoy a New Jersey Nets basketball game.

massive global inequality." Others praised the rappers' use of social commentary and revealing lyrics about their own lives. "Though the title suggests pomposity and majesty, *Throne* is lyrically well-balanced and accessible," Brad Wete commented in *Entertainment Weekly*. "There are opulent raps dripping with swag for sure, but also plenty that smack of militancy, worry, and grief." That view was also expressed by Claire Suddath in *Time* magazine. "Dig deep into *Throne,* past the bacchanal celebration of the finer things in life, and you'll find the album's heart: two men grappling with what it means to be successful and black in a nation that still thinks of them as second class," Suddath wrote. "A listen of *Throne* is enough to drown out the haters. What could have been a forgettable mishmash or, considering the egos involved, a bombastic vanity project, is instead a beautifully decadent album by two of hip-hop's finest artists—men with a lot of things to say and a lot of money to spend. And as Kanye explains in the opening track, 'We probably spend it all 'cause pain ain't cheap.'"

Jay-Z continues to inspire both admiration and controversy. While some have argued that his self-made success and business smarts made him a role model, others have complained that his music, like much of hip-hop, does nothing but glorify money and violence. Jay-Z countered that when he hears those critics, he knows they haven't listened beyond the hit tracks on his CDs. He explained that a song like "I Just Wanna Love U (Give It to

Me)," a Top 20 hit with lyrics about girls and drugs, "plays on the radio for eight months, a year, but nobody picks up 'Soon You'll Understand,'" which contains lyrics like "I wanted things like bling bling, ice/ I was wrong in hindsight." Besides, he noted, "I don't think people should imitate what they see. It's entertainment, and I trust the listener is smart enough to know that. I'm just a human being. I do wrong things too and I hope you don't follow me; hope you see what I do and go, 'That was wrong, Jay, I'm going over here, I'm gonna do this." His goal with all his work, Jay-Z has said, is "to represent hip-hop culture positively.... Rap is what took me out of my situation, and now I must care for it. I have to leave it as I found it—or better—for the next generation of kids. Then maybe they can change their situation like I did."

MARRIAGE AND FAMILY

Rumors about Jay-Z's romantic involvement with superstar singer and actress Beyoncé began in the late 1990s, well before the two first collaborated on Jay-Z's 2002 single "'03 Bonnie and Clyde." Their next collaboration, on Beyoncé's 2003 single "Crazy in Love," was that summer's biggest hit. Despite being spotted together at various awards shows, basketball games, and other high-profile events over the years, neither of them publicly commented on their relationship, preferring to keep it private. In 2008, however, Jay-Z and Beyoncé revealed that they had married on April 4, in a private ceremony in the groom's luxury apartment in New York City. Instead of exchanging rings, the couple got matching "IV" tattoos on their ring fingers; the number four symbolized their birthdays (9/4 for Beyoncé and 12/4 for Jay-Z) and their wedding date (4/4). In 2011, the couple made news at the MTV Video Music Awards when Beyoncé confirmed she was pregnant with their first child. (For more information on Beyoncé, see *Biography Today,* January 2010.)

HOBBIES AND OTHER INTERESTS

As someone who makes a career out of using words, Jay-Z is an avid reader. He is also a huge basketball fan who regularly attends games around the NBA—not just those of his home team, the Nets—and has made personal friends of several basketball stars.

Jay-Z is also heavily involved in sponsoring and supporting several charities. His Shawn Carter Scholarship Fund has provided college tuition to inner city kids, including those who have been incarcerated; the Jay-Z Santa Claus Toy Drive has given holiday gifts to kids in Marcy Housing Projects; and Team Roc, a charity arm of Roc-A-Fella, has raised money to benefit underprivileged children in New York City. Jay-Z is quick to perform at benefit concerts or to design a signature watch or shoe to be auctioned for charity.

Recipients of these efforts have included charities that benefit AIDS patients, underprivileged children, and disaster relief; after the 2010 earthquake in Haiti, Jay-Z performed and recorded for the charity Hope for Haiti. "I just think [charity work] is the right thing to do," he commented. "If you have more than enough, then you should spread the wealth a little bit."

SELECTED WORKS

Recordings

Reasonable Doubt, 1996
In My Lifetime, Vol. 1, 1997
Vol. 2: Hard Knock Life, 1998
Vol. 3: Life and Times of S. Carter, 1999
The Dynasty: Roc La Familia, 2000
The Blueprint, 2001
Jay-Z: MTV Unplugged, 2001
The Best of Both Worlds, 2002 (with R. Kelly)
The Blueprint 2: The Gift and the Curse, 2002, selections released as *The Blueprint 2.1,* 2003
The Black Album, 2003
Unfinished Business, 2004 (with R. Kelly)
Collision Course (EP), 2006 (with Linkin Park)
Kingdom Come, 2006
American Gangster, 2007
The Blueprint 3, 2009
Watch the Throne, 2011 (with Kanye West)

Featured Appearances on Top-Ten Singles

Foxy Brown, "I'll Be," 1996
Mariah Carey, "Heartbreaker," 1999
R. Kelly, "Fiesta (Remix)," 2001
Beyoncé, "Crazy in Love," 2003
Pharrell, "Frontin'," 2003
Beyoncé, "Déja Vu," 2006
Rihanna, "Umbrella," 2007
T.I., "Swagga Like Us," 2008

Films

Streets Is Watching, 1998
Backstage: Hard Knock Life Tour, 2000 (concert film)
Paper Soldiers, 2002
State Property, 2002

Fade to Black, 2004 (concert film)

Books

Decoded, 2010 (memoir)

HONORS AND AWARDS

Billboard Music Awards (*Billboard* magazine): 1999, for Rap Artist of the Year

Grammy Awards (The Recording Academy): 1999, Best Rap Album, for *Vol. 2: Hard Knock Life*; 2004 (two awards; with Beyoncé), Best R&B Song and Best Rap/Sung Collaboration, both for "Crazy in Love"; 2004, Best Rap Solo Performance, for "99 Problems"; 2006, Best Rap/Sung Collaboration (with Linkin Park), for "Numb/Encore"; 2008, Best Rap/Sung Collaboration (with Rihanna), for "Umbrella"; 2009, Best Rap Performance by a Duo or Group (with T.I., Kanye West, and Little Wayne), for "Swagga Like Us"; 2010 (three awards), Best Rap Solo Performance, for "D.O.A. (Death of Auto-Tune)," and Best Rap Song and Best Rap/Sung Collaboration (with Rihanna and Kanye West), for "Run This Town"; 2011 (three awards), Best Rap Peformance by a Duo or Group (with Swizz Beatz), for "On to the Next One," Best Rap/Sung Collaboration and Best Rap Song (with Alicia Keys), for "Empire State of Mind"

MTV Video Music Awards (MTV): 1999, Best Rap Video (with Ja Rule and Amil), for "Can I Get A…"; 2003 (two awards), Best Female Video and Best R&B Video (with Beyoncé), both for "Crazy in Love"; 2004 (four awards), Best Rap Video, Best Direction, Best Editing, and Best Cinematography, all for "99 Problems"; 2007 (two awards), Video of the Year and Monster Single of the Year (with Rihanna), both for "Umbrella"

Soul Train Music Award: 2000, Sammy Davis Jr. Entertainer of the Year

BET Awards (Black Entertainment Television): 2001, Best Male Hip-Hop Artist; 2004 (two awards), Best Male Hip-Hop Artist and Best Duet/Collaboration (with Beyoncé), for "Crazy in Love"; 2009 (four awards), Best Live Performer, Lyricist of the Year, MVP of the Year, and Hustler of the Year; 2010 (four awards), Best Live Performer and Best Collaboration, Best Hip Hop Video, and Perfect Combo Award (all with Alicia Keyes), for "Empire State of Mind"

American Music Awards: 2004, Favorite Rap/Hip-Hop Artist; 2009 (two awards), Favorite Rap Artist and Favorite Rap/Hip-Hop Album, for *The Blueprint 3*

People's Choice Award: 2010, Favorite Music Collaboration (with Rihanna and Kanye West), for "Run This Town"

FURTHER READING

Periodicals

Billboard, Aug. 30, 1997, p.20
Current Biography Yearbook, 2002
Entertainment Weekly, May 30, 2003, p.26; Nov. 5, 2004, p.11; Sep. 22, 2006, p.34; Nov. 2, 2007, p.36
Fortune, Nov. 17, 2005, p.110
Jet, May 31, 2004, p.54; Aug. 28, 2006, p.38
New York, May 21, 2005
New York Times, Sep. 6, 2000, p.B5; Sep. 17, 2009, p.C1
New Yorker, Dec. 6, 2010
Newsweek, July 12, 2004, p.75; Dec. 4, 2006, p.63
O: The Oprah Magazine, Oct. 2009
People, Apr. 5, 1999, p.161; Dec. 8, 2003, p.47
Rolling Stone, Jan. 20, 2000, p.15; June 24, 2010, p.42
Teen People, June 16, 2002, p.54
Time, Aug. 9, 2011
USA Today, Jan. 25, 2006, p.D2; Nov, 21, 2006, p.D5; Sep. 2, 2009, p.D5
Vibe, Dec. 2000
Village Voice, Jan. 15, 2002
Wall Street Journal, Oct. 22, 2010, p.D1
Washington Post, Jan. 2, 2000, p.G1

Online Articles

http://www.allmusic.com
(All Music Guide,"Jay-Z,"June 14, 2010)
http://www.billboard.com
(Billboard,"Jay-Z,"Aug. 31, 2010)
http://www.hiphoparchive.org
(HipHop Archive,"Jay-Z Timeline,"Aug. 31, 2010)
http://www.rollingstone.com/music/artists/jay-z
(Rolling Stone,"Jay-Z,"no date)

ADDRESS

Jay-Z
Live Nation
9348 Civic Center Drive
Beverly Hills, CA 90210

WORLD WIDE WEB SITE

http://www.jay-z.com

Angelina Jolie 1975-

American Actor and Humanitarian
Star of the Movies *Girl, Interrupted*; *Lara Croft: Tomb Raider*; *Mr. & Mrs. Smith*; and *Kung Fu Panda*
Goodwill Ambassador for the United Nations High Commissioner for Refugees

BIRTH

Angelina Jolie Voight was born on June 4, 1975, in Los Angeles, California. Her father, Jon Voight, is an Academy Award-winning actor. Her mother, Marcheline Bertrand, was an actor and homemaker. Jolie has one older brother named James Haven Voight. When Jolie was 16 years old, she stopped using her famous father's last name in order to pursue an acting career independent of his reputation."I dropped my name because it was important that I become known as my own person."

YOUTH AND EDUCATION

Jolie's parents separated before her first birthday and divorced in 1978 when Angelina was about three years old. After the divorce, Jolie's mother took her and her brother to live in Palisades, New York. As a child, Jolie had very little contact with her father.

As a young girl, Jolie liked to play dress up. She loved wearing clothing and costumes that were very feminine, frilly, and sparkly. She created elaborate skits, plays, and theater games with her brother and friends. Her mother made costumes, and her brother would sometimes film her performances with his video camera. Though Jolie enjoyed acting on make-believe stages as a child, she was not interested in movies at all. "Growing up, I couldn't have cared less about movies. [My brother James] had to drag me to them."Despite her lack of interest, when Jolie was about seven years old her father gave her a small role in the 1982 movie *Lookin' to Get Out*, which he co-wrote. She appeared in one brief scene.

"

Though Jolie enjoyed acting on make-believe stages as a child, she was not interested in movies at all. "Growing up, I couldn't have cared less about movies. [My brother James] had to drag me to them."

In 1986, when Jolie was 11 years old, her mother moved the family to Beverly Hills, California. Her father did not provide much financial support to his children and ex-wife, and the family had to depend only on her mother's income. They lived in small apartments and wore secondhand clothes. Jolie did not fit in very well with her Beverly Hills classmates. She was teased a lot at school because she wore eyeglasses and had braces on her teeth for a while. Classmates also made fun of her for being too skinny and for having big lips. For Jolie, that was a turning point."At some point, I got closed off, darker."

By the time she was a teenager, Jolie was involved in the Los Angeles punk and grunge music scene. She dyed her hair purple, dressed in scruffy black clothes, and began collecting knives. She was obsessed with death and wanted to become a funeral director. She began experimenting with drugs when she was about 14. "I had a lot of sadness and distrust. I came very close to the end of my life a few times," Jolie later explained. "I think now that if somebody would have taken me at 14 and dropped me in the middle of Asia or Africa, I'd have realized how self-centered I was, and that there was real pain and real death—real things to fight for, so that I wouldn't have been fighting myself so much. I wish, when I was thinking about suicide, I'd have seen how many people are dying each day that have no choice in the matter. I would have appreciated the fact that I had a choice."

Jolie dropped out of public school in 1989 and enrolled in acting classes at the Lee Strasberg Theatre Institute in Beverly Hills. There she studied method acting, an approach that requires actors to draw upon their own personal memories and life experiences to feel the emotions of their characters. Jolie appeared in several productions but left the Strasberg Institute after about a year. She felt that she was too young to have had enough life experience to properly use the method acting approach.

In 1990, Jolie returned to Beverly Hills High School. She completed her coursework early and graduated in 1991, when she was 16 years old. By then, she knew she wanted a career as a movie actor. She moved into her own apartment and began private acting lessons with her father. At that time, Jolie also started modeling with Finesse Model Management. Working as a fashion model gave her more confidence in her appearance and valuable experience being photographed and filmed.

CAREER HIGHLIGHTS

In the early 1990s, Jolie acted in several music videos and five films produced by her brother for his film school classes. She auditioned for and won small roles in several movies and stage plays. Her first major role was in the 1995 crime thriller *Hackers,* starring an ensemble cast of unknown young actors. Jolie played the role of Kate Libby, a young hacker who works with a group of friends to stop an evil genius from releasing a dangerous computer virus. At the same time, the group must hide from Secret Service agents who believe they are responsible for creating the virus. *Hackers* received mixed reviews from movie critics. Most reviewers complained that the plot moved too slowly and the characters were not believable. However, film critic Roger Ebert said that *Hackers* was "well directed, written, and acted" and that Jolie in particular was "convincing and engaging."

Early Success

Jolie's performance in *Hackers* gave her the exposure she needed to win more movie roles. In the late 1990s, she appeared in several theatrical re-

Jolie in stills from three early films: George Wallace *(top),* Hackers *(middle), and* Girl, Interrupted *(bottom).*

leases and made-for-television movies. In 1997 she appeared in *George Wallace,* a television drama about the life of former Alabama governor George Wallace. Jolie played Wallace's wife Cornelia in this story set during the battle to end racial segregation in the southern U.S. She won her first Golden Globe award for that performance. In 1998, she appeared in the lead role of the HBO movie *Gia.* This movie told the story of the tragic life and death of 1970s supermodel Gia Carangi. *Variety* praised Jolie's portrayal of Carangi as "a multi-faceted revelation," and her performance garnered a Screen Actors Guild Award and another Golden Globe award.

In 1999, Jolie appeared in *Girl, Interrupted,* a drama about a group of women confined to a mental hospital in the late 1960s. The movie was based on a 1993 memoir by author Susanna Kayson about her own stay in a mental institution and the women she met there. The movie focused on the experiences of Susanna, played by Winona Ryder, the movie's star. Jolie played a rebellious, loud patient named Lisa who befriends Susanna. To the surprise of many critics, she outshone Ryder. The *New York Times* said that Jolie's "ferocious, white-hot performance captures the scary allure of this daredevil and brutal truth-teller," and the *Boston Globe* called her performance "high-voltage." Jolie won her second Screen Actors Guild Award, her third Golden Globe, and an Oscar. She was just 24 years old.

That same year, Jolie appeared in *Pushing Tin,* the story of a group of air traffic controllers that was not successful with critics or at the box office. She followed that with a small role alongside Nicolas Cage in *Gone in 60 Seconds,* a 2000 action drama about a group of car thieves who must steal 50 cars in one night in order to stop a major crime lord from killing one of their own. Many movie critics panned it, with a reviewer for *Variety* calling it "perfectly dreadful in every respect." But the action sequences, special effects, and car chases made the movie a hit with theater audiences.

Lara Croft: Tomb Raider

Jolie's first major starring role was as the title character in the highly anticipated 2001 action film *Lara Croft: Tomb Raider.* The movie was based on *Tomb Raider,* the most successful video game series of the 1990s, which included five games that ultimately sold more than 20 million copies worldwide. At the time Jolie was cast in the movie, the daredevil adventurer Lara Croft was one of the most recognizable video game characters in the world.

To prepare for this physically demanding role, Jolie had to transform herself into an action hero. "I felt like this little geek, this scrawny young actress from L.A.," she said about arriving on the movie set. "I was extremely

Jolie's performance as Lara Croft made her an international superstar.

out of shape. I had not gone to the gym in years. And then through all the training, my body had changed and my mind had changed because I had a totally different focus." She followed a special weight training routine and diet program. She studied kickboxing, learned to race motorbikes and dog sleds, and trained with various weapons. Jolie did most of her own stunts in the movie, including complicated gymnastic moves while hanging from a bungee cord.

Lara Croft: Tomb Raider is the action-packed story of the global search for a legendary artifact called the Triangle of Light. Lara races a group of mercenaries to locate this ancient artifact, which was broken into two pieces and hidden long ago in order to prevent anyone from accessing its great power. If the two pieces are joined together at the precise moment that all the planets in the solar system are in perfect alignment, the holder of the triangle will be able to travel through time. Lara must locate the pieces of the artifact and prevent the mercenaries from using its power to implement their own evil plans. *Lara Croft: Tomb Raider* did not fare well with movie critics. *Variety* called the film "flat and unexciting," while *Entertainment Weekly* said it was a "temple of numb." In spite of such poor reviews, the movie was a huge hit with fans. It became one of Paramount movie studio's highest grossing films, earning $275 million worldwide. And some critics praised Jolie's performance. "Jolie makes a splendid Lara Croft, although to say she does a good job of playing the heroine of a video game is perhaps not the highest compliment," said Roger Ebert of the *Chicago Sun-Times.* "Ever the living fireworks display, Angelina Jolie kicks butt in *Tomb Raider,*" Karen S. Schneider wrote in *People.*

For Jolie, the film proved to be a turning point, both professionally and personally. Playing Lara Croft was her first real breakout role and launched her on the road to becoming an international superstar. It was also the first time that a woman had played a major action hero, and the movie's box-office success proved that a female lead could carry an action movie. In addition, it marked a change in her personal life, as she became more aware of and involved in human rights issues.

Working with the United Nations

Filming *Lara Croft: Tomb Raider* required Jolie to travel to many locations around the world, including some remote parts of Cambodia, a country near Vietnam in Southeast Asia. There she first learned about the terrible living conditions of most Cambodian villagers. Thousands of unexploded land mines are still buried in the ground throughout the country, left there during several decades of war in the late 20th century. Unexploded land mines last long after a war is over. Many Cambodian people have been killed or severely injured by stepping on a mine, which is a particular threat for these who live in rural areas. According to the BBC, "Cambodia's chronic mine contamination problem means the threat of death or serious injury is a daily reality for most people here." Jolie was appalled by this and became determined to help the Cambodian people and others in similar situations.

Jolie began to educate herself by reading reports from the United Nations (UN) on global poverty and the harsh living conditions of refugees around the world. "I remember sitting up for two days straight and reading everything obsessively," she stated. Soon after, she approached the UN to find out what she could do to help.

The UN sent Jolie on her first mission, a goodwill trip to the African nation of Sierra Leone. Sierra Leone has been ravaged by civil war for many years, resulting in a large number of refugees who have either fled or been driven from their homes. Jolie was shocked by what she observed on that trip. "I had no idea what a difficult life was. It was as if someone slapped me across the face and said, 'Oh, my God, you silly young woman from California, do you have any idea how difficult the world really is for so many people?' I got out of myself pretty quickly, being in the middle of a civil war."

In 2004 Jolie traveled as a UN goodwill ambassador to Darfur, a region in Sudan that has been the site of an ongoing violent civil war. Here, she is shown talking to children at a displaced persons camp.

Within a few months, Jolie returned to Cambodia on another goodwill trip for the UN. She slept in barracks with the other aid workers, distributed food, washed dishes, and did other jobs as needed. She was most interested in learning all she could by listening and observing. In 2001, Jolie was officially appointed as a goodwill ambassador for the UN High Commissioner for Refugees. In this position, Jolie was able to continue visiting troubled parts of the world as both a fact-finder and an aid worker. That year, she visited Pakistan in South Asia and Tanzania in Africa, and made return trips to Sierra Leone and Cambodia. In 2002, she visited Namibia and Kenya in Africa, Thailand in Southeast Asia, Ecuador in South America, and Serbia in Eastern Europe.

These trips made a huge impact on Jolie. As she met and spoke with refugees in all of these countries, she realized that they "have seen so much, they've felt so much pain—lost more than anyone could bear, and yet they contain joy of life and appreciation for small things we often forget."This realization inspired Jolie to continue doing as much as she could to help people in desperate situations. She also gained a new understanding of her place in the world."I would never complain again about the stupid things I used to complain about, or be self-destructive, or not realize on a daily basis how lucky I am to have a roof over my head and enough food to eat."

Humanitarian missions and trips around the world were taking up more and more of Jolie's time. Acting began to take a secondary role in her life. She appeared in a few movies, but none did very well with critics or moviegoers. In 2002, she filmed *Lara Croft Tomb Raider: The Cradle of Life,* a sequel to *Lara Croft: Tomb Raider* that was released in 2003. In this movie, Lara is on the hunt for the mythical Pandora's Box, which contains forces of unimaginable evil. Pandora's Box is also sought by a mad scientist with plans to create biological weapons, and Lara must find the box before he does. The movie was scorned by critics but became a hit with fans.

"

As Jolie spoke with refugees dealing with unthinkable hardships, she gained a new understanding of her place in the world."I would never complain again about the stupid things I used to complain about, or be self-destructive, or not realize on a daily basis how lucky I am to have a roof over my head and enough food to eat."

"

Jolie continued her humanitarian work in 2003, visiting the island nation of Sri Lanka in South Asia, Russia in Northern Europe, Jordan and Egypt in the Middle East, and Tanzania in Africa. During all of her travels, she kept journals of her experiences, thoughts, and impressions. In 2003, Jolie published *Notes from My Travels,* a book based on these journals. In a review of the book, British anthropologist Jane Goodall praised her efforts. "Angelina is living proof of the power we all have—every one of us—to make a difference," Goodall said. "I was deeply moved by her descriptions of individual refugees struggling to live with dignity and hope, and found her personal commitment to be an inspiration." Also in 2003, Jolie received the United Nations Correspondents Association Citizen of the World Award in recognition of her work to bring attention to the challenges faced by the world's refugees.

Jolie continued her travels in 2004, when she made her first humanitarian visits within the U.S. She visited three camps in Arizona for immigrants seeking asylum in the U.S. (Asylum is the term used to describe the shelter or protection provided to people who would face risk of death or great harm if they returned to their home country.) Jolie also visited Sudan in Africa, Lebanon in the Middle East, and made a return trip to Thailand.

By this time, Jolie had begun using a large portion of the money she earned from acting to fund her trips. She also began donating millions of dollars to hospitals, schools, children's charities, and refugee organizations. "The reality is I make a ridiculous amount of money to be an actor. And I love being an actor, but I don't need that money," she acknowledged. "Just to have a bunch of money—what do you do with it? What is your life about? But if you know exactly what you're doing with it, and you can see it changing other people's lives, there's a reason for it." For Jolie, the money now had a worthwhile purpose. "I'm able to take the money and see a hospital built or build a well somewhere.... It makes me all that more eager to go to work and be successful because I can do good things."

Appearing in Animated Films

Jolie's next movie project was the 2004 animated feature *Shark Tale*. In this story, a gangster family of sharks suffers a loss when Frankie, next in line to head the crime family, is accidentally killed. Oscar, a lowly nobody fish voiced by Will Smith, takes credit for the murder—even though he didn't kill Frankie—and promptly becomes famous as a "shark slayer." As Oscar takes advantage of his new-found fame, he is pursued by the glamorous gold-digger Lola, voiced by Jolie. Lola is only interested in Oscar because of his celebrity status, and Oscar soon finds that he must make some difficult choices about the direction his life will take. Jolie enjoyed giving Lola a voice, explaining, "One, it's just fun to go to work in your pajamas with no makeup on.... But it's funny to see yourself as a fish. They showed me the pictures of all the different fish, and I saw my fish, and it was so apparent to me very quickly that that was my fish."

Jolie returned to voice acting in 2008 with the role of Tigress in the animated feature film *Kung Fu Panda*. This is the story of a big, bumbling, pot-bellied, black and white panda bear named Po, voiced by Jack Black. Po works in his father's noodle shop but really wants to be a martial arts star. The problem is Po doesn't know anything about martial arts. Through a series of accidents and unexpected events, Po is thought to be the long-awaited Dragon Warrior, the one who will save the town from a menacing, unbeatable enemy. By naming Po as the Dragon Warrior, the ancient sage Oogway passes over other candidates who are much more qualified, including Tigress. Po learns that once he deciphers the Secret of the Dragon Scroll, he will have to battle Tai Lung, the most powerful kung fu master ever known. Though movie reviewers gave *Kung Fu Panda* a mixed reception,

Jolie voiced the character of Tigress in Kung Fu Panda.

the film was a hit with fans and with reviewer A.O. Scott from the *New York Times*: [*Kung Fu Panda*] was a rambunctious, whimsical blend of action, jokiness and sentiment, lifted above the kiddie-cartoon mean by its shiny, playful look and Mr. Black's endlessly adaptable charm."

Jolie reprised her role as Tigress in *Kung Fu Panda 2*, released in 2011. In this sequel, Po joins forces with a group of kung fu masters, including Tigress (Jolie), to battle an old enemy who now has a deadly new weapon. Once again, critics offered both positive and negative responses, including this comment from Roger Ebert: "*Kung Fu Panda 2* is exactly as you'd expect, and more. The animation is elegant, the story is much more involving than in the original, and there's boundless energy.... What's best about this sequel is that it's not a dutiful retread of the original, but an ambitious extension."

Mr. & Mrs. Smith

Jolie's next big role was in the 2005 action-adventure-comedy film *Mr. & Mrs. Smith*. This movie tells the story of Jane Smith, played by Jolie, and her husband John Smith, played by Brad Pitt. On the surface, the Smiths appear to be an average married couple. But each hides a very big secret—they are both professional killers for hire. They have managed to keep their true occupations secret from each other for years, until each receives information about their next job: Mr. and Mrs. Smith have been hired to kill each other. Fast-paced action unfolds as each attempts to carry out these orders, while trying to figure out what the other one is up to. *Mr. & Mrs. Smith* was widely praised by critics and enjoyed by moviegoers. Jolie won three Teen Choice Awards and an MTV Movie Award for her performance.

The chemistry shared onscreen by Jolie and Pitt spilled over into real life, as the couple dealt with tabloid rumors that they had become romantically involved while making the movie. Though both denied having an affair, Pitt soon divorced Jennifer Aniston, his wife of seven years, and moved in with Jolie and her children. Pitt also joined Jolie in her humanitarian work, traveling with her on many official trips and also donating large sums to charitable causes.

Over the following years, Jolie continued to alternate making movies with doing humanitarian work. In 2005, she was honored once again by the UN, which gave her the Global Humanitarian Action Award. In accepting the award, Jolie reaffirmed her commitment to serving those in need."Second to my children, spending time with refugees and other persons of need around the world has been the greatest gift." In 2006, she took a break from movies in order to focus on her family and her work with the UN. In 2007, Jolie had a part in the epic *Beowulf*, about an ancient warrior who fights against monsters. She also starred in *A Mighty Heart*, based on the memoir of Mariane Pearl, the widow of journalist Daniel Pearl, who was kidnapped and publicly executed by terrorists. As she divided her time between making movies and humanitarian work, Jolie made refugee aid trips to Chad in Africa, Syria in the Middle East, Iraq and Afghanistan in Asia, and made a return trip to Thailand.

Recent Films

In 2008, Jolie appeared in the conspiracy thriller *The Changeling*. This movie is based on the true story of Christine Collins, played by Jolie. Collins is a Los Angeles woman whose nine-year-old son Walter goes missing in 1928. Five months later, the Los Angeles Police Department is under intense pressure to find the boy and close the case. Miraculously, Walter is suddenly found. A staged reunion is planned, with reporters and photographers on hand to capture the moment. During this reunion, Collins realizes that the boy being returned to her is not her son. She confronts the police, trying to point out the mistake. The police respond by committing her to the psychiatric ward of the county hospital, to keep her quiet and avoid exposing what really happened. Jolie's performance in *The Changeling* earned her an Academy Award nomination for Best Actress. Though she did not win the Academy Award that year, by the end of 2008 Jolie was the movie industry's highest-paid female actor. At that time, she was earning an average of $15 million per movie. She continued to use her income to fund her charitable work.

In 2010, Jolie starred in two major films: *Salt* and *The Tourist.* In the spy thriller *Salt* she played the title character, a role originally written for Tom

Jolie with Johnny Depp in a scene from The Tourist.

Cruise and rewritten for Jolie after Cruise declined the role. The story unfolds during a routine interrogation of Russian defector Orlov, who reveals that for many years the Russian government has maintained a network of secret agents within the U.S. These agents were chosen as children and raised their whole lives to become sleeper agents, waiting to trigger a massive attack against the U.S. Orlov then unexpectedly names the CIA agent Evelyn Salt as one of these secret agents. Salt denies this accusation, but then goes on the run to evade her CIA colleagues. Her motives become even more suspect as the plot develops, and audiences must try to figure out the truth. *Salt* received mixed reviews, with some calling it predictable and others calling it enjoyable fun. "*Salt* knows how to stay one step ahead of you in devious, if jaw-droppingly contrived, ways. The movie is fun," Owen Gleiberman wrote in *Entertainment Weekly*. "The movie builds nuts-and-bolts suspense into the question of who Salt is [and] which side she's on.... *Salt* has enough high-octane reversals to keep you guessing right to the end."

In *The Tourist,* Jolie played Elise, a glamorous mystery woman. The movie focuses on the strange events that happen after she deliberately entices a man named Frank, played by Johnny Depp, an American math teacher on vacation in Italy to mend his broken heart. It seems that Elise has chosen Frank to stand in for her former lover, who has been hiding from the police and an angry mobster for the past two years. Elise hopes to use Frank as a decoy to trick the police long enough to retrieve a secret stash of money and escape with it. Elise receives puzzling instructions from her lover in hiding, and as she tries to follow his instructions, a series of plot twists unfolds to keep audiences guessing about how this case of mistaken identity will be resolved. *The Tourist* did not fare well with movie critics, many of whom decried the stilted dialogue, tedious plot, and poor direction, as well as the stars' lack of chemistry and wooden acting. "Stardom can take a terrific story and turn it into a festival of preening earnestness and precious mugging," reviewer Mick LaSalle wrote in the *San Francisco Chronicle.* "Give them a couple of mirrors and have them play the love scenes to their own reflections, and their ardor would be more convincing." Still, Jolie received a Golden Globe nomination for her performance in the film.

— " —

"No matter where you live or how old you are, you can decide to change your life. That's amazing," Jolie said. "I believe everyone has a choice: to be a person who does nothing, or a person who does something to make the world better. Maybe you can't fix it. But at least you didn't do nothing."

— " —

Future Plans

Over the course of her career to date, Jolie has appeared in more than 35 movies. In the past nine years, she has made more than 30 goodwill trips on behalf of the UN. Her future plans are to continue dividing her time between acting and humanitarian work, although she is not sure how many more movies she wants to make. "I like acting. It's not the most important thing in my life. Acting helped me as I was growing up. It helped me learn about myself, helped me travel, helped me understand life, express myself, all those wonderful things. So I'm very, very grateful, it's a fun job. It's a luxury.... But I don't think I'll do it much longer."

Jolie has expanded her influence by funding various humanitarian projects through the Jolie-Pitt Foundation, which channels financial donations to charitable organizations around the world. She plans to continue working to raise awareness of causes that are close to her heart, particularly those that benefit the world's refugees. She also works to make progress on international laws governing war crimes. "I am a strong believer that without justice there is no peace. No lasting peace, anyway," she said. "I'm somebody who's very curious about the International Criminal Court.... I think people that do horrible

Jolie with a family on a recent trip to Bosnia, part of her work as a Goodwill Ambassador for the United Nations High Commissioner for Refugees.

things should be held accountable." She has become a familiar voice in Washington, DC, as she pushes U.S. politicians to take action. "In my early 20s I was fighting with myself. Now I take that punk in me to Washington, and I fight for something important," Jolie explained. "As much as I would love to never have to visit Washington, that's the way to move the ball."

"No matter where you live or how old you are, you can decide to change your life. That's amazing," Jolie said. "I believe everyone has a choice: to be a person who does nothing, or a person who does something to make the world better. Maybe you can't fix it. But at least you didn't do nothing."

MARRIAGE AND FAMILY

In 1996, Jolie married Jonny Lee Miller, her costar in the movie *Hackers*. The couple divorced in 2000. Less than one month after the divorce was final, Jolie married Billy Bob Thornton, her costar in the movie *Pushing Tin*. The couple divorced in 2003. In 2005 Jolie got involved with Brad Pitt. They remain unmarried.

In 2002, Jolie adopted a son, Maddox Chivan, from a Cambodian orphanage. Maddox was born on August 5, 2001. In 2005, Jolie adopted a daughter,

Zahara Marley, from an Ethiopian orphanage. Zahara was born on January 8, 2005. Also in 2005, Pitt officially adopted Jolie's children as his own, with the children taking the last name Jolie-Pitt. On May 27, 2006, Jolie gave birth to a daughter named Shiloh Nouvel Jolie-Pitt. In 2007, Jolie adopted a son, Pax Thien Jolie-Pitt, from a Vietnamese orphanage. Pax was born on November 29, 2003. On July 12, 2008, Jolie gave birth to twins, a son named Knox Leon Jolie-Pitt and a daughter named Vivienne Marcheline Jolie-Pitt.

Jolie travels with her family extensively throughout the world. Jolie and Pitt maintain several homes in different countries.

SELECTED MOVIES

Hackers, 1995
George Wallace, 1997
Gia, 1998
Girl, Interrupted, 1999
Pushing Tin, 1999
Gone in 60 Seconds, 2000
Lara Croft: Tomb Raider, 2001
Lara Croft Tomb Raider: The Cradle of Life, 2002
Shark Tale, 2004
Mr. & Mrs. Smith, 2005
Beowulf, 2007
A Mighty Heart, 2007
The Changeling, 2008
Kung Fu Panda, 2008
Salt, 2010
The Tourist, 2010
Kung Fu Panda 2, 2011

HONORS AND AWARDS

Golden Globe Awards: 1998, Best Performance by an Actress in a Supporting Role in a Series, Mini-Series or Motion Picture Made for TV, for *George Wallace*; 1999, Best Performance by an Actress in a Mini-Series or Motion Picture Made for TV, for *Gia*; 2000, Best Performance by an Actress in a Supporting Role in a Motion Picture, for *Girl, Interrupted*

Screen Actors Guild Awards: 1999, Outstanding Performance by a Female Actor in a TV Movie or Mini-Series, for *Gia*; 2000, Outstanding Performance by a Female Actor in a Supporting Role, for *Girl, Interrupted*

Academy Award (Academy of Motion Picture Arts and Sciences): 2000, Best Actress in a Supporting Role, for *Girl, Interrupted*

Citizen of the World Award (United Nations Correspondents' Association): 2003
25 Most Influential Philanthropists in the World (*Worth* magazine): 2003
Global Humanitarian Action Award (United Nations): 2005
People's Choice Awards: 2005, Favorite Female Action Movie Star; 2009, Favorite Female Action Star
Teen Choice Awards: 2005 (3 awards), Choice Movie Actress: Action Adventure/Thriller, Choice Movie Liar, Choice Movie Rumble (with Brad Pitt), for *Mr. & Mrs. Smith;* 2011, Choice Movie Actress-Action, for *The Tourist*
MTV Movie Award: 2006, Best Fight, for *Mr. & Mrs. Smith* (with Brad Pitt)

FURTHER READING

Books

Schuman, Michael A. *Angelina Jolie: Celebrity with Heart,* 2011

Periodicals

Biography, Oct. 2003, p.42
Christian Science Monitor, Sep. 8, 2010
Current Biography Yearbook, 2000
Entertainment Weekly, June 20, 2008
Marie Claire, July 2007, p.124
New York Times, Oct. 19, 2008; Nov. 21, 2008
Newsweek, Mar. 19, 2007
People, May 8, 2002, p.67; Sep. 5, 2005; Aug. 2, 2010, p.58
Time, Apr. 30, 2006; Apr. 30, 2009
Vanity Fair, Aug. 2010

Online Articles

http://www.allmovie.com/artist/angelina-jolie-36009/bio
(AllMovie, "Angelina Jolie Biography," no date)
http://www.nationalgeographic.com
(National Geographic, "Angelina Jolie on Her UN Refugee Role," June 18, 2003)
http://www.topics.nytimes.com
(New York Times, "Angelina Jolie," multiple articles, various dates)
http://www.newsweek.com/topics.html
(Newsweek, "The Secret World of Angelina Jolie: The One Part of Her Life We Don't Obsess Over," July 13, 2010)
http://www.people.com/people/angelina_jolie/biography
(People, "Angelina Jolie," no date)

ADDRESS

Angelina Jolie
Special Artists Agency
9465 Wilshire Blvd., Ste. 470
Beverly Hills, CA 90212

WORLD WIDE WEB SITES

http://www.un.org/works/goingon/refugees/angelina_story.html
http://www.unhcr.org/pages/49c3646c56.html

Victoria Justice 1993-

American Actress and Singer
Star of the Nickelodeon Series "Victorious"

BIRTH

Victoria Dawn Justice was born on February 19, 1993, in Hollywood, Florida. Her mother, Serene Justice, is of Puerto Rican descent, while her father, Zack Justice, is mostly Irish and Western European. Victoria's parents split up when she was still a toddler. Her mother later married Mark Reed, and they had a daughter, Madison, who is Victoria's half-sister.

YOUTH

Justice grew up in Hollywood, Florida, a city on the Atlantic coast between Fort Lauderdale and Miami that is known for its beautiful beaches. She was a natural performer from a young age. "I have always been the kid who at family gatherings would put on my tutu and my mom's lipstick, perform and make everybody watch me," she remarked. Although some child stars are pushed by their parents, it was Justice herself who insisted on exploring acting. She was eight years old when she saw an advertisement on television, turned to her mother, and said, "I can do that." Seeing her daughter's determination, Justice's mother found her an agent based in Miami. She quickly booked her first TV commercial, a national spot advertising the drink mix Ovaltine.

"I have always been the kid who at family gatherings would put on my tutu and my mom's lipstick, perform and make everybody watch me," Justice remarked.

——— ” ———

With her dark-eyed good looks, Justice soon was in demand as a model, as well. Sunny Miami is a major center for fashion photo shoots, and she was featured in ads for national clothing lines like the Gap, Guess, and Ralph Lauren. Her bubbly personality made her a natural. During one photo shoot, Justice recalled, the photographer wanted a girl to kiss one of the boy models. "And all the girls were like, 'I don't want to do it. Cooties!' And I was like, 'I'll do it! I'll do it!' I've always been pretty outgoing."

While she enjoyed modeling and working in commercials, Justice believed she could handle more complex acting jobs. Those jobs were to be found in California. In 2003, Justice's family decided to devote the summer to seeing if Victoria could make it there as an actress. She quickly landed the same agent who represented Miley Cyrus, and within three weeks Justice had secured her first job on television, a guest spot on the popular WB series "The Gilmore Girls." At age 10, she had taken her first steps on the path to becoming a television star.

EDUCATION

After moving to California, Justice attended the Millikan Middle School, a magnet school for the performing arts in Sherman Oaks. She spent one year at Cleveland High School in Reseda, but became too busy with her career to attend school regularly. She left after her freshman year and had private tutoring on the sets of her shows. Dedicated studying allowed her to pass her graduation exams early, and she earned a high school diploma when she was 16. "I love reading, and I've always loved school," she said. She has taken junior college classes and hopes to study at a university one day.

CAREER HIGHLIGHTS

Moving to California

During Justice's first stay in California at the age of 10, the experience of being on the set confirmed her love of acting. She and her family returned to Florida for the school year, with a plan to return the next summer and continue building her career. When Justice came back to California in the summer of 2004, she earned a part in an independent film, *When Do We Eat?,* in which she played the younger version of the main character's daughter in a flashback. The film was a comedy for mature audiences and wasn't widely released, but it provided Justice with more exposure. She booked a few more commercials and two roles in short independent films before landing a guest appearance on a new Disney Channel series, "The Suite Life of Zack & Cody." She taped her role as the crush of one of the two twin brothers shortly before heading back to Florida for school. When the series debuted in spring 2005, it became a big hit, and Justice's appearance in the second episode brought her lots of publicity.

Her family returned to California that summer, but soon decided that the constant moving back and forth wasn't allowing the young actress enough chances to develop her skills. When Justice was accepted into Millikan Middle School's musical theater program, they decided to move the whole family there year-round. Justice honed her talent in acting and singing classes at school while continuing to find jobs in commercials and other small parts, in the horror film *The Garden,* the holiday television movie *Silver Bells,* and the thriller *Unknown.*

Justice was 12 years old when she got her first big role, on the Nickelodeon show "Zoey 101." Jamie Lynn Spears (sister of singer Britney Spears) played Zoey, one of the first girls admitted to a formerly all-boys boarding school. In the second season, the show was looking for a new actress to join the cast. The Emmy-nominated show was very popular, and the part was a big one—Zoey's new roommate—so Justice was eager to land it. She auditioned, then got a callback to have a screen test. "You could tell from the first five seconds of the tape … she was just meant to be in front of a camera," series producer Dan Schneider said of her audition. She landed the part and began filming episodes of the series in 2005.

A shot of the ZOEY 101 Cast, Season 4. Back Row (L-R): Chase (Sean Flynn), Logan (Matthew Underwood), Michael (Christopher Massey). Middle Row (L-R): Quinn (Erin Sanders), Lola (Victoria Justice), Zoey (Jamie Lynn Spears). Floor: Dustin (Paul Butcher) in ZOEY 101 on Nickelodeon. Photo: Andrew Eccles/Nickelodeon. ©2007 Viacom International, Inc. All Rights Reserved.

Breaking Out on "Zoey 101"

Justice was introduced to "Zoey 101" audiences in the first episode of the second season, which was broadcast in fall 2005. Her character, Lola Martinez, first appeared in Zoey's room as a goth-type girl who seems very dark and sinister. As the show continues, however, the characters discover that Lola is "really an actress who is just having fun in an acting experiment," as Justice described her. Filming the episode "was a blast! I loved my wardrobe and I loved the way they introduced my character," she remembered. "The best part of that episode was when I had to improvise this voodoo chant. It was so funny because I was making all these weird sounds and none of us could keep a straight face!"

Lola quickly became a popular character, with her flamboyant personality and her funky sense of fashion bringing fun to every episode. The show continued to be one of Nickelodeon's most popular, with second-season episodes drawing over a million viewers between the ages of 9 and 11. Justice and her co-stars also earned critical acclaim, winning the Young Artists Award for best young ensemble performance in a TV series in both 2006 and 2007. Justice herself earned a Young Artists nomination for best supporting young actress in 2007. She played Lola in 52 episodes over three seasons, until the show ended in 2008.

While Justice was sad to leave behind the friends she had made during three years of filming "Zoey 101," she was excited to pursue new career opportunities. In the summer of 2008 she signed a talent deal with Nickelodeon that would have her star in her own series as well as make a record. She also starred in the Nickelodeon TV film *Spectacular!,* about a group of kids trying to rebuild their school's show choir. (The movie debuted in February 2009, before the Fox series "Glee" made show choirs a mainstream phenomenon.) Justice played the leader of the rival show choir, who was a bit of a snob. She was glad that her fans were "really going to get to hear me sing for the first time," she commented. While the movie didn't draw spectacular ratings, it showed Justice could act, sing, and dance.

Later that year Justice had her first starring role in a feature film, *The Kings of Appletown.* This family film involved two cousins (played by twins Dylan and Cole Sprouse from "The Suite Life of Zack and Cody") investigating a mystery; Justice played a suspect's daughter who is drawn into the search for the truth. Reviewer Elliot V. Kotek noted for *Moving Pictures Magazine* that "for pure acting chops that suggest a long future, set your sights on Victoria Justice as Betsy. In a supporting role, the young actress steals her scenes by providing heart to the film and shouldering an honesty with which an audience can empathize."

Justice in a scene from Spectacular!

Getting Her Own Television Show: "Victorious"

By this point Justice was developing success in TV shows and movies for the young adult audience. And she had come to the attention of Dan Schneider at Nickelodeon, the creator or producer of many of Nick's hit shows, including "The Amanda Show," "Drake and Josh" "Zoey 101," and "iCarly." While working with Justice on "Zoey 101," Schneider noticed that "her look and the way she carried herself, she had a great energy." She had only filmed a few episodes when he called the network and said, "I've got your next star." He set to work creating a show especially for Justice that would feature all her talents: acting, singing, and dancing.

"Victorious" debuted in February 2010, in a prime spot right after the Kids Choice Awards. It introduced Justice as Tori Vega, a science nerd who is overshadowed by her older sister Trina. Trina attends a high school for the performing arts and Tori is content to stay in her sister's shadow—until the day she fills in for Trina at the all-school talent show. After she stops the show with her singing and dancing abilities, Tori decides to transfer to Hollywood Arts, where the student body is filled with quirky and talented students.

For Justice, "Victorious" offered not just a starring role, but a chance to have lots of fun. "We always get to do really kooky things and get dressed up in weird outfits," she said. "There's always some funny, hilarious thing going on in the episodes, so I'm having an awesome time." At the same time, she thought fans would enjoy the show because of the characters. "They are normal kids dealing with normal problems, and they are really funny." Producer Schneider believed Justice's comic talents and willingness to do physical comedy would help her go far. "I see a mega-superstar waiting to explode—she's a rare combination of funny and pretty," he noted. "So many pretty girls don't want to be funny anymore." Reviewing the show for the *Fort Lauderdale Sun-Sentinel,* critic Tom Jicha also saw potential in the actress. "The series is geared toward teens and tweens," Jicha wrote, "but Victoria, who displays a maturity beyond her years, far outshines her material, singing and acting in the kind of role that launched Miley Cyrus."

Other Projects

Not long after her show debuted, Justice released the theme song as her first single, "Let It Shine." She has begun planning her first album and writing her own songs, with lyrics about "fun things that make me happy." The album is expected to be released in 2012. She also recently starred in the Nickelodeon TV movie *The Boy Who Cried Werewolf.* Justice played Jordan, a girl who moves with her brother and father to Wolfsberg, Romania, where they hope to sell the castle they inherited from a great-uncle. While a sinister caretaker tries to convince them to stay, Jordan gets accidentally transformed into a werewolf. She is working on two movies to be released in 2012: *The First Time,* about a teen couple and the problems they face when he falls for another girl, played by Justice; and *Fun Size,* about a smart and sarcastic teen girl who has to take her little brother trick or treating on Halloween but ends up losing him.

As Justice has become more popular with teen viewers, some media watchers have described her as competing with other young stars like Miley Cyrus, Miranda Cosgrove, and Selena Gomez. Justice said she doesn't think that way. "I'm not here to replace anybody," she explained. "I'm just doing what I love, and I am just hoping to be half as successful as the other girls out there. I am just doing my thing. I work hard, I put a lot of time and effort into [what I do]. And I think I've done pretty well so far." Acknowledging that some fans might consider her a role model, Justice said she takes the responsibility seriously. "When I'm doing something," she related, "I'm always going to think, 'Would my fans be proud of this? Is this something they would approve of?' It's always going to be in the back of my head, and I'm going to try to do the best I can."

Justice is looking forward to a long career in entertainment. Although she enjoys comedy—"I'm not afraid to get a pie in the face," she said—she also hoped to take on more dramatic roles in the future. "I love comedy, and I love the challenge of a really intense dramatic role." For the near future, her

Justice with the cast of "Victorious." (L-R, top row) Leon Thomas (Andre), Matthew Bennett (Robbie) and Rex, Ariana Grande (Cat), (bottom row, L-R) Danielle Monet (Trina), Victoria Justice (Tori), Elizabeth Gillies (Jade), Avan Jogia (Beck) in VICTORIOUS on Nickelodeon. Photo: Aaron Warkov/Nickelodeon ©2009 Viacom International, Inc. All Rights Reserved.

goal is "to make a TV show that people love and that can help kids learn from experiences and that kids can laugh at and … escape to if they're having problems. They can just turn on my show and enjoy themselves." To aspiring young performers hoping to follow in her footsteps, Justice recommended dedication and practice: "Find ways to keep training in your local area. There are always theater groups, local acting classes, vocal and dance classes, which will all help with your confidence in performing in front of an audience and sharpen your skills at the same time." For her, "the most important thing in an audition is to feel that you gave it your best." Most of all, she said, "You should always keep working hard and to never give up."

HOME AND FAMILY

Justice lives in California with her mother, stepfather, and sister; she also spends time with her father at his home in South Carolina. Because she has allergies, she never had pets until 2008, when she and her sister received two puppies for Christmas. The dogs are "chonzers," or Bichon Frise and Schnauzer mixes, named Sophie and Sammy.

HOBBIES AND OTHER INTERESTS

Like many teens, Justice enjoys spending time with friends; a typical outing might include dancing, shopping, or singing karaoke. She also likes reading and movies, and swims to keep fit. She has also participated in benefits for arts education, children's hospitals, and kids' health programs. Through Nickelodeon's "The Big Help" initiative, she encourages kids to get involved in environmental causes and their communities.

SELECTED CREDITS

Television

Silver Bells, 2005 (TV movie)
"Zoey 101," 2005-08
Spectacular! 2009 (TV movie)
"Victorious," 2010-
The Boy Who Cried Werewolf, 2010 (TV movie)

Movies

When Do We Eat?, 2005
The Garden, 2006
Unknown, 2006
The Kings of Appletown, 2009

Recordings

Spectacular! 2009 (contributor to soundtrack)
"Make It Shine," 2010 (single; theme from "Victorious")

HONORS AND AWARDS

Young Artist Award (Young Artist Foundation): 2006 and 2007, Best Young Ensemble Performance in a TV Series, for "Zoey 101"

FURTHER READING

Books

Bloom, Ronny. *Victoria Justice,* 2009

Periodicals

Fort Lauderdale Sun-Sentinel, Mar. 26, 2010
Girls' Life, Dec. 2009/Jan. 2010, p.46; Oct./Nov. 2011
New York Times, Mar. 26, 2010, p.C1
Teen Vogue, Sep. 2010
The Record (Ontario, Canada), Apr. 7, 2010, p. C5
Time for Kids, May 7, 2010
Washington Post, Aug. 26, 2009, p.C1

Online Articles

http://www.iesb.net
(IESB Movie News,"Exclusive Interview: Victoria Justice is VICTORIOUS on Nickelodeon," Mar. 31, 2010)
http://www.kidzworld.com
(Kidzworld,"Victoria Justice Interview," June 3, 2010)
http://www.peoplepets.com
(People Pets,"Victoria Justice's First Pets Arrived Under the Christmas Tree," May 5, 2010)
http://www.ryanseacrest.com
(Ryan Seacrest,"Victoria Justice: I'm Single and Looking," radio interview, Aug. 25, 2010)
http://www.seventeen.com
(Seventeen,"Victoria Justice to Star in *Spectacular!,*" Oct. 9, 2008)

ADDRESS

Victoria Justice
Nickelodeon
1515 Broadway
New York, NY 10036

WORLD WIDE WEB SITES

http://www.victoriajustice.net
http://www.nick.com

Elena Kagan 1960-

American Supreme Court Justice
Former Dean of Harvard Law School

BIRTH

Elena Kagan was born in New York City on April 28, 1960. Her parents were Robert Kagan, a lawyer, and Gloria Gittelman Kagan, a teacher. She has an older brother, Marc, and a younger brother, Irving.

YOUTH

Kagan's mother and father were both first-generation Americans, the children of Russian Jews who had immigrated to the

United States and settled in New York City. They were each the first in their families to attend college, and they believed passionately in the importance of education and critical thought. Gloria Kagan worked at Hunter College Elementary School, a school for gifted and talented children. She was known as a very demanding teacher. "She was a little more playful with her kids," remembered a neighbor. "Her kids were very driven, so she didn't have to nag them." Robert Kagan impressed on his children the importance of working for social justice. In his law practice, he helped to protect the rights of people who were being pushed out of their neighborhoods because of real-estate development. He also gave time and energy to environmental issues. Once he even tied himself to a tree in a city park to prevent some workers from wrongly cutting it down. Thoroughly analyzing and debating current events and issues was part of everyday life in the Kagan household.

Kagan described herself as "one of these students who go to law school for all the wrong reasons, because they can't figure out exactly what else they want to do."

EDUCATION

Kagan attended Hunter College Elementary School, where her mother taught. The school is not part of New York City's public school system; instead, it's run by Hunter College, a part of the City University of New York. There is no tuition fee, but students must demonstrate academic excellence to be accepted. Kagan continued on at Hunter College High School. Hunter is one of the most prestigious high schools in the United States, with a very high percentage of its graduates going on to top-ranked colleges and universities. Even though the school was full of high achievers, Kagan stood out. She was known as a confident, thoughtful, ambitious person, and she was elected president of the student body. She graduated in 1977. For her yearbook photo, she posed in a judge's robe, holding a gavel. Underneath her photo was a quote from Felix Frankfurter, a former Supreme Court justice: "Government is an art, one of the subtlest of arts."

Kagan next attended Princeton University in New Jersey, where she earned a Bachelor of Arts (BA) degree in history in 1981, graduating with highest honors. She was named the David M. Sachs Graduating Fellow, an award that funded two years of study in philosophy at Worcester College, part of Oxford University in England. There she earned her Master of Philosophy (MPhil) degree in 1983. Kagan next enrolled at Harvard Law School, which is frequently ranked the top law school in the United States.

Kagan described herself as "one of these students who go to law school for all the wrong reasons, because they can't figure out exactly what else they want to do." Nevertheless, she loved it immediately and excelled at her studies, as usual. "I really felt as if I had found something I was good at," she commented. She was eventually made the supervising editor for the *Harvard Law Review,* a position of great prestige, and she earned her Juris Doctor or Doctor of Law (JD) degree with high honors in 1986.

Kagan in a photo from her senior year in the Hunter College High School Yearbook, 1977. Kagan is wearing judge's robes.

CAREER HIGHLIGHTS

The Role of the Judiciary in the U.S. Government

As set out in the Constitution, the U.S. government comprises three branches: the executive branch, the legislative branch, and the judicial branch. Each branch has specific responsibilities. The executive branch includes the president and the vice president. It also includes the Cabinet, a group of presidential advisers who are the heads of federal departments and agencies, including the departments of state, treasury, defense, justice, education, and others. The legislative branch is the Congress, including both the House of Representatives and the Senate. The Congress creates laws, collects taxes, declares war, ratifies treaties, and approves the president's nominations for certain positions, including federal judges. The judicial branch includes the nation's courts.

The federal judicial system has three different levels. The lower courts, the level at which most cases are originally tried, are the 91 District Courts. After a case is tried, if one side disagrees with the decision of the District Court and wants to appeal it, the case would go to the next level, the Court of Appeals. There are 12 Courts of Appeals (also called Circuit Courts) covering the 50 states and the District of Columbia. The appeals (or appellate) court judge reviews the lower court's decision and either sustains it (agrees) or overturns it (disagrees). After that step, the case could be taken to the Supreme Court, the highest court in the land. The decision of the Supreme Court is final. At all three levels in the U.S. judicial system, federal judges are nominated by the president, confirmed by the Senate, and serve for life.

Becoming a Law Clerk

Kagan's first job after graduating from Harvard Law School was as law clerk for Abner Mikva, who sat on the U.S. Court of Appeals in the District of Columbia Circuit Court. This court is generally considered the second most powerful in the nation—only the Supreme Court itself is more important. As a law clerk, Kagan assisted the judge by doing research, analyzing issues, and writing opinions on legal questions related to current cases.

In 1987, Kagan became a law clerk at the Supreme Court. She worked for Thurgood Marshall, who had been serving as a Supreme Court justice for 20 years at that time. Marshall was a key figure in the civil rights struggles of the 1950s and the 1960s. As a lawyer for the NAACP, he worked on a wide range of legal cases that advanced the civil rights cause. In 1954 he argued before the Supreme Court in probably his most important case, *Brown v. Board of Education,* in which the Supreme Court banned school segregation. He was the first African American to serve as solicitor general, the government's top lawyer, and also the first African American to serve as a justice on the U.S. Supreme Court. Marshall affectionately nicknamed Kagan "Shorty."

In 1988, Kagan began working for the presidential campaign of Michael Dukakis, a Democrat who was then the governor of Massachusetts. When George H.W. Bush, a Republican, defeated Dukakis and became president of the United States, she temporarily set aside her plans to work in government. Going into the private sector instead, she became an associate at Williams & Connolly, a law firm in Washington, DC.

Professor and Presidential Advisor

Kagan didn't stay in legal practice for long. She switched to the academic world in 1991, when she took a position as assistant professor at the University of Chicago School of Law. There she met Barack Obama, who was then a state senator for Illinois. Like her, he had graduated from Harvard Law School, and he too was doing some teaching at the University of Chicago School of Law. Although they were both Harvard graduates, they had not attended at the same time, and their first meeting was at the University of Chicago.

In 1993, Bill Clinton replaced George H.W. Bush as U.S. president. Clinton nominated Ruth Bader Ginsburg to a seat on the Supreme Court, and he

Kagan playing in a 1992 trivia contest with a colleague at the University of Chicago Law School, where she was a law professor.

asked Kagan to come to Washington to serve as special counsel to the U.S. Senate Judiciary Committee during Bader's confirmation hearings. When a U.S. president nominates someone for a seat on the Supreme Court, that person must also be approved by the Senate, and hearings are held by the Senate Judiciary Committee to interview the nominee and review his or her qualifications. Ginsburg was ultimately appointed, making her the second woman to serve on the Supreme Court (the first was Sandra Day O'Connor).

After the hearings concluded, Kagan returned to the University of Chicago, where she became a tenured professor in 1995. New opportunities continued to take her away from her teaching post, however, when President Clinton asked her to serve as the associate counsel to the president. The person who fills this post helps to advise the president on all legal matters having to do with the White House and the presidency. Kagan took a leave of absence from University of Chicago, which continued on when in 1997 she became deputy assistant to the president for domestic policy and deputy director of the Domestic Policy Council. These positions gave her influence over law and policy concerned with public health, education, and other important areas of government.

While in Washington, Kagan earned a reputation as a hard worker with an amazing ability to read and absorb information and to use that information effectively when presenting arguments. She was known as a progressive thinker and a tough negotiator who could be a little impatient at times. She also showed her ability to build partnerships among people with different viewpoints and ideas.

Kagan worked with Republican senator John McCain to draft a bill that would allow the Food and Drug Administration (FDA) to regulate tobacco. She had been a cigarette smoker as a teenager, and she knew from personal experience that tobacco is very addictive. "I love smoking, and I still miss it," she stated. "It's completely clear to me how addictive this product is." Therefore, she felt it made sense for the FDA to regulate tobacco. This position was unpopular among many Republicans, yet Kagan managed to get the support of several key Republicans besides McCain. Despite this, the regulation did not pass at that time.

In 1999, President Clinton nominated Kagan for a seat on the U.S. Court of Appeals in the District of Columbia—the powerful court where she had first served her as a law clerk. The Senate Judiciary Committee, which oversaw the hearing process, was under Republican control at the time, and most of those opposed to Kagan's nomination were Republicans. The start of the hearing process was delayed for 18 months, at which point it officially expired.

Dean of Harvard Law School

In addition to being nominated to the U.S. Court of Appeals in 1999, Kagan had also begun to teach at Harvard Law School as a visiting professor. In 2001 she was made a full professor and appointed the Charles Hamilton Houston Professor of Law. The classes she taught focused mostly on civil procedure, constitutional law, and administrative law. She was known as a well-prepared and intelligent teacher who was very well liked by her students. In 2001, she published an article in the *Harvard Law Review* titled "Presidential Administration." It was named the top scholarly article of the year by the American Bar Association's Section on Administrative Law and Regulatory Practice.

Harvard Law had not always been a welcoming place for women, either as students or professors. Established in 1817, the school had not admitted female students at all throughout most of its history. The first class to include women graduated in 1953. Even after some women won admission to the school, they had to endure a great deal of hostility. Some of the professors refused to call on women at all in class, except on a day traditionally known as "Ladies Day." On this day, the few female students were put in a group in front of the class and made to answer rounds of relentless ques-

Kagan at the announcement of her position as dean of Harvard Law school, 2003, with former dean Robert C. Clark (left) and university president Lawrence Summers (center).

tioning from the professors and male students. Although this kind of discrimination did eventually die out, it wasn't until 1972 that Harvard Law had a tenured female professor on its staff.

Despite being consistently ranked at or near the top of all the law schools in the nation, Harvard had its share of problems. Having years of tradition was one of its strong points, yet it could also be a stumbling block. Outdated customs sometimes seemed to be too important in the decisions made concerning the school and its direction, and there was a lot of disagreement among various groups of faculty members. Class sizes were very large, and they were taught in a rigid style that had been established many years before.

Harvard University president Lawrence H. Summers felt that Elena Kagan was the person to lead the law school into a new era. On April 3, 2003, some 50 years after the first female-inclusive class had graduated, Summers appointed Kagan dean of Harvard Law School, the first woman to hold that position. He felt that she would bring a fresh perspective to the office, and that she would have a long-term vision for the school as well as meaningful short-term goals. Summers also felt confident that Kagan would be able to make progress with long-standing problems and find ways to work out compromises for groups that seemed unable to agree.

Kagan spent the next few months having personal meetings with each of the 81 members of the school's faculty. She wanted to hear what they had to say about the school and what aspects of the school they felt were most in need of reform. On July 1, 2003, she took over the office of dean. "I think it is a milestone, a great thing that shows how far Harvard has come and how far the legal profession has come, in terms of women's position," she stated.

Transforming Harvard Law School

Kagan felt that her appointment was a statement to the world indicating that Harvard was becoming a much more inclusive, progressive place. She was determined to make sure that trend continued. One of her goals was to expand the faculty. In doing so, she naturally looked for individuals who had demonstrated excellence in teaching, but she also looked for people who could bring fresh ideas and perspectives to the school. Harvard's teaching staff had a reputation of being made up mainly of political liberals. Kagan set out to hire men and women of varying ethnic backgrounds and political viewpoints. Her new hires included some well-known conservatives, including Jack Goldsmith, who had worked as a White House counsel for George W. Bush, and John Manning, an expert in administrative law.

Just as Harvard president Summers had expected, Kagan also made some quick, superficial changes at the law school that demonstrated her concern for the personal needs of individuals. For example, she began providing free coffee for students in all law school buildings, and free lunch was made available for faculty members. Courtyard and dining areas were remodeled to make them more inviting, with tables set up in ways that encouraged socialization. An area in front of the student center was turned into a beach volleyball court, which could be converted to a skating rink during the winter months. These small changes all did a lot to boost morale and create a feeling of unity, Kagan found. "As it turned out, you can buy more student happiness per dollar by giving people free coffee than anything else I've discovered."

Kagan showed a willingness to experiment that was new at Harvard Law. Instead of taking a long time to weigh each possible change against years of school tradition, Kagan simply asked herself if a change would improve things, or not. One major transformation she initiated was a complete review of the school's curriculum, which remained much the same as it had been when it was introduced in the 1870s. "It really is time to say, 'Is that really what students should be taking? Are they learning the set of competencies that they need to master in order to go out and be a great lawyer in today's world? How has the world changed in the last 100 and some years?'"

To get answers to those questions, Kagan formed a committee of eight people and gave them the task of studying Harvard's programs for three years. At the end of that time, the committee made many suggestions for overhauling Harvard's curriculum, including greater emphasis on international law, on complex problem-solving, and subjects such as cyber law. Faculty members voted on and approved the recommendations, leading to the modernization of Harvard Law School's program.

> *As dean of Harvard Law, Kagan initiated a complete review of the school's curriculum, which hadn't been overhauled since the 1870s. "It really is time to say, 'Is that really what students should be taking? Are they learning the set of competencies that they need to master in order to go out and be a great lawyer in today's world? How has the world changed in the last 100 and some years?'"*

Some of Kagan's other accomplishments as dean include planning for the construction of new facilities, encouraging students to pursue careers in public service, establishing more legal clinics that provide students with valuable courtroom experience, and increasing programs that help students to repay their educational loans. Although her work as dean was highly praised, she did endure a few controversies. In 2004 and 2005, two professors at Harvard Law were accused of plagiarism. Investigation into the charges resulted in the conclusion that the plagiarism had not been deliberate, and Kagan imposed no penalty on the accused teachers. Her detractors insisted that she was far too lenient with the professors and that any undergraduate in a similar situation would have been suspended or expelled.

Another controversy involved an issue concerning military recruiters on campus. A federal law passed in 1994, the Solomon Amendment, gives the secretary of defense the right to take away federal funding from universities that don't allow military recruiters to visit their campus. A number of prominent law schools opposed this law, however, because of the military's "Don't Ask, Don't Tell" (DADT) policy. Don't Ask, Don't Tell required that gays and lesbians serving in the military must keep their sexual orientation a secret. Many people viewed this as discrimination and therefore not in keeping with the non-discriminatory policies of Harvard and other law schools. In 2004, the U.S. Third District Court of Appeals said that the universities had the right to keep recruiters off campus, and that November, it was announced that Harvard Law would do so. In October, 2005, however, the Department of Defense said that it would withhold Harvard's federal funding, regardless of the Court of Appeals ruling. With the school set to lose about 15 percent of its annual budget—possibly as much as $5 million—Kagan backed down. Voicing her regrets publicly, she nevertheless reversed the decision to bar military recruiters.

In 2006, Summers announced he was planning to step down as Harvard's president. Kagan made no secret about being interested in taking over the position, and she was considered a very strong candidate for the job. That would have made her the first female president of Harvard, as well as the first female dean of the Harvard Law School. In the end, the job went to another woman—Drew Gilpin Faust, who had been dean of Radcliffe Institute of Advanced Study, another school within Harvard University.

Returning to Government Service

In 2008, Barack Obama, a Democrat, was elected president, marking a swing back to more liberal political trends. This boded well for Kagan's ambitions to work in Washington, which she had set aside when George W. Bush took office. She did not have long to wait. Shortly after his inauguration in January 2009, Obama nominated Kagan to be solicitor general. The solicitor general oversees any litigation in the Supreme Court and in the appellate courts in which the government is involved. That is highly significant, because the U.S. government is involved in approximately two-thirds of all cases decided by the Supreme Court each year. The solicitor general and staff prepare the cases and represent the government in court. There are nine justices on the Supreme Court, but the position of solicitor general is often referred to as the "tenth justice" because the job is so important. The job requires confirmation by the U.S. Senate, and Kagan was approved by a 61-31 margin. On March 19, 2009, she became the 45th solicitor general of the United States. She was the first woman appointed to the position.

Kagan had been solicitor general for only a little more than a year when, on May 10, 2010, President Obama nominated her for a seat on the Supreme Court. Justice John Paul Stevens was planning to retire the following month, and Obama thought Kagan was the person to take his place. Once nominated, Kagan stepped down from the position of solicitor general to wait for the Senate confirmation hearings to proceed.

An artist's drawing of Elena Kagan as U.S. solicitor general arguing a campaign finance reform case before the U.S. Supreme Court, 2009. Seated, from left, are justices Samuel Alito, Ruth Bader Ginsberg, Anthony Kennedy, John Paul Stevens, John Roberts (chief justice), Antonin Scalia, Clarence Thomas, Stephen Breyer, and Sonia Sotomayor. The Supreme Court does not allow cameras in the courtroom.

The Supreme Court

The Supreme Court is the most important court in the nation. The cases heard there start out in lower courts. They are appealed and taken to higher courts because of difficulties in reaching satisfactory decisions. Usually, it is because the laws involved are either difficult to interpret or controversial. If enough appeals are made, a case may eventually be taken all the way to the Supreme Court. About 100 cases are typically heard there each year, and the justices must consider them in light of the Constitution—the document that is the foundation for the laws of the United States. Cases are selected for their importance and for the impact they will have on the United States.

Reaction to Kagan's nomination was somewhat mixed. Some people objected to the idea that she might take a seat on the Supreme Court when she had never acted as judge in any other court. Although this situation was unusual, it had happened in the past, as recently as 1972. Because she had no experience as a courtroom judge, there was no record of her rulings for people to consider when trying to predict how she would interpret cases on the Supreme Court. Even her academic writings left few clues as to her personal opinions about controversial issues.

On the plus side, Kagan was known as a brilliant mind when it came to constitutional and administrative law. Letters in support of her appointment to the Supreme Court were written by the deans of more than one-third of the country's law schools. Her prior work in government, her accomplishments at Harvard, and her proven ability to work diplomatically with opposing groups were all seen as a good background for a Supreme Court justice. "Elena is open-minded, pragmatic, and progressive," said Walter Dellinger, who had been acting solicitor general during the Clinton administration. "Each of those qualities will appeal to some, and not to others. Her open-mindedness may disappoint some who want a sure liberal vote on almost every issue. Her pragmatism may disappoint those who believe that mechanical logic can decide all cases. And her progressive personal values will not endear her to the hard right. But that is exactly the combination the president was seeking."

Speaking on her own behalf, Kagan said at the time, "One of the things I would hope to bring to the job is not just book learning, not just the study that I've made of constitutional and public law, but a kind of wisdom and judgment, a kind of understanding of how to separate the truly important from the spurious." Regarding the appropriateness of allowing personal opinion to influence court rulings, she stated, "I think a judge should try to the greatest extent possible to separate constitutional interpretation from his or her own values and beliefs. In order to accomplish this result, the judge should look to constitutional text, history, structure, and precedent."

Confirmation hearings sometimes stir up a lot of controversy, but in Kagan's case, the process went very smoothly. On August 5, 2010, her nomination was confirmed by a vote of 63 to 37. She was just 50 years old, and appointments to the Supreme Court are for life, or until the justice chooses to retire. Therefore, Kagan could influence law in the United States for decades to come.

The swearing-in took place on August 7, 2010, in a two-part ceremony. It began in the justices' conference room, where just a few of Kagan's relatives witnessed it. Chief Justice John G. Roberts Jr. administered the constitutional oath for federal employees, in which Kagan swore to "support and defend the Constitution." After moving into a larger room, the chief justice administered the judicial oath, which includes the promise to "administer justice without respect to persons, and do equal right to the poor and to

Two views of Kagan joining the U.S. Supreme Court: taking the Constitutional Oath of Office, administered by Chief Justice John Roberts (top); and posing with current and former female Supreme Court justices—Sandra Day O'Connor (retired), Sonia Sotomayor, Ruth Bader Ginsberg, and Kagan.

the rich." A formal investiture ceremony took place at a session of the Supreme Court on October 1, 2010.

Because of her prior work as counsel for the White House, Kagan did not offer an opinion on many of the cases that were heard in the months immediately following her appointment. Her earlier involvement with a case could be seen as influencing her decision, so she "recused" herself, or disqualified herself, from any case she had worked on before joining the Supreme Court. As time passes, she is likely to be called on to make decisions in cases involving federal health care legislation, same-sex marriage, immigration issues, and questions regarding the balance of power between state and federal authorities.

For Kagan, a seat on the Supreme Court must surely be gratifying because of her deep love of the law. "I so love the law not just because it's challenging and endlessly interesting—although it certainly is that—but because law matters; because it keeps us safe; because it protects our most fundamental rights and freedoms; and because it is the foundation of our democracy."

HOBBIES AND OTHER INTERESTS

Kagan lives in Washington, DC. She enjoys opera and is a fan of the New York Mets.

HONORS AND AWARDS

Award for best scholarly article on administrative law (American Bar Association): 2001, for "Presidential Administration"

John R. Kramer Outstanding Law Dean Award (Equal Justice Works): 2008, for her efforts to encourage public service

FURTHER READING

Periodicals

Current Biography Yearbook, 2007

Education Week, May 19, 2010, p.23

Los Angeles Times, May 12, 2010, p.A1

Time, May 24, 2010, p. 28; July 5, 2010, p. 30

USA Today, May 11, 2010, p.A6; July 26, 2010, p. A9

Online Articles

http://spectator.org/topics
(American Spectator, "Elena Kagan," multiple articles, various dates)

http://www.csm.com
(Christian Science Monitor,"Elena Kagan Shows off Sense of Humor in Confirmation Hearings,"June 30, 2011)
http://www.nytimes.com
(New York Times,"At Harvard, Kagan Aimed Sights Higher,"May 26, 2010;"Elena Kagan,"October 4, 2010)
http://topics.nytimes.com
(New York Times,"Elena Kagan,"multiple articles, various dates)
http://www.time.com
(Time,"Judging Elena,"July 5, 2010)
http://content.usatoday.com/topics
(USA Today,"Elena Kagan,"multiple articles, various dates)
http://topics.wsj.com/index.html
(Wall Street Journal,"Elena Kagan,"multiple articles, various dates)

ADDRESS

Elena Kagen
The Supreme Court
One First Street NE
Washington, DC 20543

WORLD WIDE WEB SITES

http://www.supremecourt.gov
http://www.oyez.org/justices/elena_kagan

Jeff Kinney 1971-

American Author and Cartoonist
Creator of the *Diary of a Wimpy Kid* Series

BIRTH

Jeff Kinney was born on February 19, 1971, at Andrews Air Force Base in Maryland, near Washington, DC. His dad was a military analyst after having served in the U.S. Navy, while his mom earned her PhD in Early Childhood Education. Like his cartoon character Greg Heffley, Kinney is a middle child. He has an older brother, Scott, and a younger brother, Patrick. He also has an older sister, Annmarie.

YOUTH

Kinney grew up in Fort Washington, Maryland, in the area near Washington, DC. From a young age he wanted to become a newspaper cartoonist. Although he did not take art lessons, he spent a lot of time drawing and created his first cartoon in first grade. Growing up, he particularly admired the work of *Calvin and Hobbes* creator Bill Watterson, whom he has identified as an influence. Kinney enjoyed reading as a child and has cited Judy Blume's novel *Tales of a Fourth Grade Nothing* as his favorite, referring to it as "the gold standard in terms of creating kid characters who are believable and funny." As he got older, he liked fantasy books by Piers Anthony.

Kinney has described his youth as a "pretty typical childhood experience." He had strong observational skills as a boy, which he has linked to his ability to vividly recall the stories of his childhood and re-create the nuances of life as a middle school student in his books. "I have a good memory for what it was like to be a kid," he explained. "I'm often surprised when I hear that people can't remember their childhood. I feel like I remember every bit of mine." Readers might wonder if some of those childhood memories have found their way into his books. While *Diary of a Wimpy Kid* is not autobiographical, Kinney has said, "a lot of my family's DNA is in those books."

"

"I have a good memory for what it was like to be a kid," Kinney explained. "I'm often surprised when I hear that people can't remember their childhood. I feel like I remember every bit of mine."

"

One memorable episode from his youth was when his older brother, Scott, played a practical joke on him. On the first day of summer vacation, Scott woke him up at 2:00 a.m. and told him that he had slept through the entire summer—including the family trip to Disney World. Thinking it was the first day of school, Kinney got dressed and ate breakfast before realizing he was the victim of a prank. He documented the incident in the first *Diary of a Wimpy Kid* book.

Although Kinney does not consider himself to have been a "wimpy kid," he has said he was "an average kid with some moments of extreme wimpiness." "I was the orange cone for other kids to dribble around," he joked. For example, when he was on the swim team as a child, he used to skip practice to go catch tadpoles in the creek instead, until his mom caught him red-handed. He also used to hide from his swimming coach in the bathroom stalls, another childhood experience that he incorporated into his second book. "I would literally wrap myself in toilet paper so as not to get hypothermia," he said. "And I keep thinking that that's where Greg Heffley was born." Like his character, Kinney admits to having been mean and self-centered at times. "But I was also a good kid.... [Greg's] an exaggeration of my worse parts."

EDUCATION

Kinney has credited his fifth grade teacher, Mrs. Eleanor Norton, with bringing him out of his shell and nurturing his sense of humor. "She welcomed humor in the classroom. But she didn't settle for cheap laughs," he commented. "When we made a joke, she'd challenge us to come up with something funnier." Her encouragement had a lasting impact on the budding humorist. "I'll always remember the lessons she taught me," he affirmed.

After elementary school, Kinney attended seventh and eighth grade at Eugene Burroughs Middle School in Accokeek, Maryland, and later Bishop McNamara High School, an all-boys Catholic school in Forestville, Maryland. Upon graduation, he received an ROTC Air Force scholarship to Villanova University in Pennsylvania, where he studied for one year before transferring to the University of Maryland to study computer science. He developed an interest in federal law enforcement and switched his major to criminal justice, earning his bachelor's degree in 1993. Although he found the University of Maryland "huge and intimidating" at first, he eventually landed one of three comic-strip slots in the college newspaper, *The Diamondback*. That experience taught him the discipline of cartooning and what it was like to write for a large audience.

Kinney's comic strip, "Igdoof," was about an immature college freshman with poor study habits, a lack of finesse with women, and a fondness for booger jokes. Due to its popularity among some 30,000 university students, the comic was published in other campus papers across the East Coast. Kinney also sold "Igdoof" merchandise with the motto "Just Doof It." In addition to his work as a cartoonist, he also served as the paper's graphic editor and production manager. "I think *The Diamondback* is probably the best thing that ever happened to me," he said. "I made great friends and got exposure and experience."

BECOMING A WRITER

Based on the positive response to "Igdoof," Kinney was confident that he could become a professional cartoonist after college. He was able to attract the attention of the *Baltimore Sun* and the *Washington Post*, which both fea-

Kinney with two fans.

tured stories on him and the success of "Igdoof" on campus, but he was not able to persuade the national syndicates to publish his comic strip. "When I went out into the real world I was met with nothing but rejection letters," Kinney recalled. "The truth was that my drawings weren't professional grade." In 1995 he moved to Boston, where he worked as a layout artist at the *Newburyport Daily News* and later at a medical software firm. In 2000 he took a job as a computer-game designer at Pearson's Family Education Network, which publishes online parenting and teaching resources as well as educational games for kids.

Although his attempts to publish his comic strip after college were unsuccessful, Kinney kept writing, trying to stay motivated by keeping a daily journal. "The reason I started a journal was because I was wasting too much time watching television and playing video games, and I wasn't doing anything to pursue my cartooning aspirations. I thought that perhaps if I documented what I did every day, it would 'shame' me into spending more time working on my cartoons," he explained. "Ironically, keeping a journal was what inspired me to create [*Diary of a Wimpy Kid*]."

In 1998 Kinney drove by a billboard that featured a quote by Benjamin Franklin: "Well done is better than well said," it read. The message inspired him to turn off the television and start filling a sketchbook with his ideas.

He decided to write about his childhood in a way that he hoped would make people laugh, combining comics with the text of a middle school student's journal. "I wanted to write a story about all of the funny parts of growing up, and none of the serious parts. I had a pretty ordinary childhood, but lots of humorous stuff happened along the way," he said. After working on idea-development for four years, he completed the 77-page book in 2002, writing smaller and smaller so as not to run out of room. The final page of the book was so densely packed with text and drawings that it was nearly illegible. "It took me about four months to do one idea page at the end," he admitted. "It's funny but I wrote way, way too much. One idea page translates into about 150 pages in print."

In 2004 Kinney's boss at Family Education Network was looking for a solution to increase traffic to their website, Funbrain.com, during summer vacation. Kinney suggested that they post daily installments of the book he was working on, which ultimately became *Diary of a Wimpy Kid.* Although he intended it for adults, he thought his "novel in cartoons" was harmless enough for the Funbrain site, which is geared to elementary and middle school students and attracts 70,000 kids per day. It was an immediate hit, and after posting 1,300 pages online Kinney had attracted approximately 20 million readers. He found it gratifying to publish his work in an online format because of the instantaneous feedback he would get from readers around the world. When he would release an entry at 3:00 a.m., he would receive responses from young readers in China, Pakistan, Russia, and Greece within minutes.

Because of the popularity of *Diary of a Wimpy Kid* online, Kinney's employer sent him to the 2006 ComicCon convention in New York to scope out additional web content. Kinney brought a *Wimpy Kid* proposal along, just in case. As he was preparing to leave the convention, he ran into Charles Kochman from the publisher Harry N. Abrams, Inc. "It was like one of these moments from a movie," Kinney remembered. "In 30 seconds, [Kochman] said: 'This is exactly why we are here and what we are looking for.' It was really great and validating, and I think it only happens once in a lifetime."

"I took one look at the cover and the title, and I just absolutely fell in love with it," Kochman told the *Washington Post*. "He articulated visually and verbally something that everybody feels, whether they're 8 or 48," he said in *Entertainment Weekly.* Within weeks, Kochman offered Kinney a publication deal, with one caveat: in contrast to Kinney's concept of a single book as a nostalgic walk down memory lane for adults, Kochman and his publisher wanted to release *Diary of a Wimpy Kid* as a children's series. Together they agreed to publish three books.

Kinney's online comics eventually developed into the book Diary of a Wimpy Kid. *DIARY OF A WIMPY KID®, WIMPY KID™, and the Greg Heffley design™ are trademarks of Wimpy Kid, Inc. All Rights Reserved.*

CAREER HIGHLIGHTS

Diary of a Wimpy Kid

Written in a diary format with a font resembling handwriting on lined paper, *Diary of a Wimpy Kid* chronicles the daily struggles of Greg Heffley as he encounters the challenges that accompany the transition to junior high. In a series of short, episodic chapters, the book documents the humiliating and intimidating moments in Greg's life at school and home. It follows his misadventures with his best friend and sidekick, Rowley Jefferson, as they endure bullies, popularity contests, and a wrestling unit in gym class, among other trials. The simple drawings of Greg—who is illustrated as a stick-figure cartoon with an oversized head, three strands of hair, and a big nose—further the plot and are integral to the reader's understanding of the text.

To publish *Diary of a Wimpy Kid,* Kinney had to prepare approximately 700 jokes and complete 300 drawings. He has estimated that it takes him four hours to come up with one joke and one hour to complete each drawing. "It's hard to write and it's hard to draw. I'm very slow at both," he admitted. "But I always feel really satisfied when I see the finished product and know that kids are reading it." Instead of pen and ink, he now uses a plastic pen and a tablet computer to draw his artwork, which has sped up his writing process dramatically.

"

Kinney has estimated that it takes him four hours to come up with one joke and one hour to complete each drawing. "It's hard to write and it's hard to draw. I'm very slow at both," he admitted. "But I always feel really satisfied when I see the finished product and know that kids are reading it."

"

Response to the Book

The first *Diary of a Wimpy Kid* book debuted in print in April 2007. Within weeks it made the *New York Times* children's bestseller list, remaining there for more than three years. It reached the top of the chart in August 2007 and held onto the number-one slot until its sequel surpassed it. *Diary of a Wimpy Kid* has sold over 42 million print copies and has been translated into 33 languages.

As *Diary of a Wimpy Kid* and its main character, Greg Heffley, became popular among grade-school students, some parents and educators became wor-

In Diary of a Wimpy Kid, *Greg says he's writing a journal so he won't have to answer stupid questions when he becomes rich and famous (top); but in the meantime, he's stuck in middle school with a bunch of morons (bottom).*

ried. They have argued that Greg is not a positive role model—he is selfish, lazy, and judgmental, and his antics are both mean-spirited and disrespectful. "Greg is a deeply flawed protagonist," Kinney affirmed. "I think adults who voice complaints about Greg's shortcomings are missing the joke. Kids get that Greg isn't perfect, and I think that's why they like him." The author added: "He's a little bit narcissistic and he can be a crummy friend at times. But he's not a bad kid at all. He's just a not-fully formed person." Kinney has stated that his main goal was to make the character of Greg relatable and authentic so that kids did not sense that the book was written from an adult perspective. "If there is a lesson in the book," he cautioned, "it's to do the opposite of what Greg does."

"I think adults who voice complaints about Greg's shortcomings are missing the joke. Kids get that Greg isn't perfect, and I think that's why they like him," Kinney declared. "He's a little bit narcissistic and he can be a crummy friend at times. But he's not a bad kid at all. He's just a not-fully formed person."

Aside from concerns about the morality of his characters, some detractors have criticized Kinney for diluting the book with cartoons on every page. Many, including librarian Lisa Von Drasek, disagree. "It's not dumbing down the text," she told the *New York Times*. "The illustrations give more information. The kids who don't need illustration aren't losing anything by reading this, but kids who are visual learners have an added depth to the story they wouldn't have otherwise."

Diary of a Wimpy Kid has earned a positive reputation for its impact on reluctant readers, or those children—especially boys—who do not read for pleasure. Its visually appealing format has attracted millions of children who were either intimidated by or uninterested in books, including kids with learning difficulties. "I keep hearing from parents … who say these books were the breakthrough. It's very moving when parents come to me with tears in their eyes," Kinney stated. In 2009 he was named one of *Time* magazine's 100 Most Influential People in the World for encouraging millions of young people around the world to read.

Diary of a Wimpy Kid: The Sequels

The second book in Kinney's series, *Diary of a Wimpy Kid: Rodrick Rules,* was published in February 2008. Even before it was officially for sale, the highly anticipated and resoundingly successful book became a *New York Times* number-one bestseller. This volume depicts Greg Heffley's troubles with his older brother, Rodrick, who threatens to reveal Greg's most embarrassing secret. In October 2008 Kinney released the *Diary of a Wimpy Kid Do-It-Yourself Book,* an interactive companion text that asks the reader such questions as "What's the best dream you ever had?" and provides ruled and blank pages for kids to fill in their own stories and cartoons. It also includes 16 pages of full-color comics.

Kinney's third installment, *Diary of a Wimpy Kid: The Last Straw,* came out in January 2009. It, too, topped the children's bestseller list and received a favorable critical response, with a *Publisher's Weekly* critic hailing the return of "Kinney's spot-on humor and winning formula of deadpan text set against cartoons." The plot centers on family dynamics in the Heffley household, including the challenges of getting along with his brothers and enduring his overly enthusiastic mom and out-of-touch dad. It focuses on the conflict between Greg and his father, who is intent on making him manlier or else sending him off to military school.

In October 2009 Kinney published the fourth book in the series, *Diary of a Wimpy Kid: Dog Days.* It became the number-one bestseller on Amazon.com when it was released. This installment details Greg Heffley's summer vacation, including an embarrassing episode in the public pool locker room, a failed lawn-care business, a fight with his best friend, and miserable attempts at "family togetherness." *Publisher's Weekly* praised the author's "gift for telling, pitch-perfect details in both his writing and art," concluding that kids would likely "devour this book as voraciously as its predecessors."

Diary of a Wimpy Kid: The Movie

The phenomenon surrounding the *Diary of a Wimpy Kid* books soon caught the attention of Hollywood producers. In 2008, Fox 2000 purchased the film rights to Kinney's series and began work on bringing his first book to the silver screen. As executive producer, Kinney collaborated with the producer, director, and screenwriters to adapt his plots and characters for the film. "Jeff was an invaluable asset in the writing of this film," co-screenwriter Jeff Filgo stated. "He was always available for the inevitable question … 'Would Greg do this?' 'Would Rowley do that?' But he also read every outline and draft, and gave priceless feedback." In addition to helping add jokes and dialogue to the script, Kinney worked with the animators and brainstormed promotional ideas with the marketing department. Although it received mixed reviews, the 2010 film was a hit with young viewers, grossing $75 million in ticket sales worldwide. The movie starred

Greg learns the hazards of his plan to sit in the middle of a bunch of hot girls.

Zachary Gordon as Greg and Robert Capron as Rowley, both of whom were fans of the books. A second movie, *Diary of a Wimpy Kid: Rodrick Rules,* was released in 2011. It proved almost as popular as the first, grossing $71 million. Fans of the series are eagerly awaiting the third movie, *Diary of a Wimpy Kid: Dog Days,* to be released in August 2012.

In conjunction with the premiere of the film, Kinney released *The Wimpy Kid Movie Diary,* a nonfiction book that follows the author through the experience of creating his cartoon characters and the process of adapting his work into a live-action motion picture. The book offers a behind-the-scenes look at casting, props, special effects, stunts, and more. It also includes a range of photographs, script pages, storyboards, costume designs, and original artwork by the author. It too hit the top of the bestseller lists.

Current and Upcoming Projects

The fifth book in Kinney's wildly popular series, *Diary of a Wimpy Kid: The Ugly Truth,* was released in November 2010. In this volume, Greg is confronted with the pressures of adolescence, such as awkward physical changes, boy-girl parties, and the increasing responsibilities that come with leaving his childhood behind. "I feel like everything in the series has been leading up to the fifth book, which is about change and the different ways Greg and his best friend, Rowley, deal with it," Kinney explained.

In addition to the print books and his collaboration on the *Diary of a Wimpy Kid* film franchise, Kinney has talked about possibly creating an interactive "Wimpy World" online in which kids could interact with the characters, with a new storyline created specifically for the web.

When asked if he would ever write books on a different topic, Kinney said this: "I'll always like to write humor, and I'll always like to write for kids, and I'll always like to use comics. But I probably will take a stab at something else one day."

”

Kinney is also the creative force behind Poptropica.com, one of the internet's fastest-growing virtual worlds dedicated solely to publishing for kids. The site features eight interactive islands and attracts over 10 million young viewers each month.

What's next for Kinney? He has said that the lifespan of the *Diary of a Wimpy Kid* series is five to seven books, and the series is now reaching that mark. "I'll find out when I get to the end of five how good I feel. I'm certainly not going to carry it on just to carry it on. A good artist knows when to quit," he stated. In recent interviews, however, he has said: "I think that as long as the jokes are good, I should keep writing." When asked if he would ever write books on a different topic, he responded: "I'll always like to write humor, and I'll always like to write for kids, and I'll always like to use comics. But I probably will take a stab at something else one day."

MARRIAGE AND FAMILY

Kinney lives in Plainville, Massachusetts—a small town near the border of Rhode Island—with his wife and two young sons. His older son, Will, is a very creative boy with an interest in writing and drawing. His younger son, Grant, is an avid sports fan. Despite Kinney's busy schedule as an author and his full-time job as an online game designer, he makes it a priority to spend uninterrupted time with his family each day. He also helps coach his boys' soccer and baseball teams. He is close with his siblings, and still calls them to reminisce about funny childhood moments and ask whether they think a particular joke will work. "I had a blast talking on the phone with my siblings, remembering all of the things that happened to

A scene from the Diary of a Wimpy Kid *movie, where Fregley (left), Greg (middle), and Rowley (right) have been relegated to the lunchroom floor. Photo: Rob McEwan © 2010 Twentieth Century Fox Film Corporation. All Rights Reserved. DIARY OF A WIMPY KID®, WIMPY KID™, and the Greg Heffley design™ are trademarks of Wimpy Kid, Inc. All Rights Reserved.*

our family when we were growing up," he remarked. "I think if everyone would write down the funny stories from their own childhoods, the world would be a better place."

FAVORITE BOOKS

In addition to Judy Blume's *Tales of a Fourth Grade Nothing,* Kinney has identified a number of other favorite books, including Shaun Tan's graphic novel *The Arrival,* which he heralded as an "absolute masterpiece," and Marjane Satrapi's graphic novel *Persepolis,* which he admires for its expressive illustrations and educational value. He has also referred to Gary Jennings's historical novel *Aztec* as one of his favorite books of all time for its ability to capture his imagination, and has praised James Michener's novel *The Source* as a "compendium of the world's religions." For those interested in cartooning, he has recommended Scott McCloud's *Understanding Comics.*

HOBBIES AND OTHER INTERESTS

Although he has very little time to spend on hobbies, Kinney has said that he cherishes the time he spends with his kids. He enjoys traveling to New

Hampshire and swimming with his sons. He also likes to play volleyball and the Mario Kart video games. His favorite song is "Brownville Girl" by Bob Dylan, and his favorite movies include *Braveheart*; *Glory*; *Planes, Trains, and Automobiles*; and *A Christmas Story*. He has cited the series "Arrested Development" as "the best television show in history," and is also fond of reality shows. A kid at heart, Kinney still enjoys peanut butter and jelly sandwiches above any other.

WRITINGS

Diary of a Wimpy Kid, 2007
Diary of a Wimpy Kid: Rodrick Rules, 2008
Diary of a Wimpy Kid Do-It-Yourself Book, 2008
Diary of a Wimpy Kid: The Last Straw, 2009
Diary of a Wimpy Kid: Dog Days, 2009
The Wimpy Kid Movie Diary, 2010
Diary of a Wimpy Kid: The Ugly Truth, 2010

HONORS AND AWARDS

100 Most Influential People in the World (*Time* magazine): 2010
Kids' Choice Awards (Nickelodeon): 2010, Favorite Book, for the *Diary of a Wimpy Kid* series

FURTHER READING

Periodicals

Boys Life, Apr. 2010, p.22
Daily Variety, Mar. 24, 2011, p.4
New York Times, Oct. 13, 2009, p.D5
People, May 17, 2010, p.99
Scholastic Parent and Child, Sep. 2008, p.80
Time, July 18, 2011
Time for Kids, Oct. 2, 2009, p.7
USA Today, Jan. 28, 2008, p.D1; Jan. 13, 2009, p.D1
Weekly Reader News Edition 4-6, Mar. 25, 2011, p.11
WR News, Senior Edition, Oct. 9, 2009, p.7

Online Articles

http://www.npr.org
(National Public Radio, All Things Considered, "Cheese, Wimpy Kids, and the Perils of Middle School," Oct. 22, 2009; Fresh Air, "*Wimpy Kid*: A Hilarious Take on Middle School," Oct. 13, 2009)

http://nypl.org
(New York Public Library, "Author Chat with Jeff Kinney," Aug. 19, 2008)
http://www.powells.com
(Powell's Books, "Kids' Q&A: Jeff Kinney," undated)
http://www.projo.com
(Providence Journal, "The Man Who Made Being Wimpy Cool," Mar. 30, 2008)
http://www.time.com
(Time, "Kid Lit Unbound," July 18, 2011)
http://www.washingtonpost.com
(Washington Post, "Get Out of Here!" Mar. 3, 2009)

ADDRESS

Jeff Kinney
Amulet Books
Harry N. Abrams, Inc.
115 West 18th Street
New York, NY 10011

WORLD WIDE WEB SITES

http://www.wimpykid.com
http://www.abramsbooks.com

Lady Antebellum
Dave Haywood, Charles Kelley, Hillary Scott

American Country Music Trio

Winner of the Academy of Country Music Award for Top Vocal Group

EARLY YEARS

Lady Antebellum is a country music trio whose members are Dave Haywood, born in Augusta, Georgia, on July 5, 1982; Charles Kelley, born in Augusta, Georgia, on September 11, 1981; and Hillary Scott, born in Nashville, Tennessee, on April 1, 1986.

Dave Haywood and Charles Kelley

Dave Haywood is the son of Van and Angie Haywood and grew up in Augusta, Georgia. Haywood's father is a dentist who invented a tooth-whitening treatment. "In the dental world, he is a rock star," Haywood said of his dad. "He's the Bruce Springsteen of the dental world." When Haywood was growing up, the whole family was musical. His father taught him to play guitar when he was in the fifth grade, and his parents insisted he take piano lessons, even though he didn't want to do it.

Charles Kelley is the son of Gayle, a homemaker, and John, a doctor who also raised cattle. Like Haywood, Kelley grew up in Augusta, Georgia, in a family that encouraged music. When Charles was about 12 years old, his parents bought instruments for him and his brother Josh. The two brothers formed a band called The Sporks and played together in another group called Inside Blue. That early musical training paid off for Josh Kelley as well; he is now a successful singer-songwriter and pop musician.

> *"There's a convergence of talent and energy with the three of them," said producer Paul Worley. "Dave is the brains, Hillary's the heart, and Charles is the drive. They are all three creative people, but they don't overlap. The combination is powerful."*

Haywood and Kelley became friends in middle school, based on their shared interest in music. In fact, they played gigs at the Red Lion Pub in Augusta when they were only about 14 years old. They attended high school and college together, first Lakeside High School in Augusta, Georgia, and then the University of Georgia. They began writing songs at that time, but they weren't studying music—each of them earned a degree in finance.

Hillary Scott

Hillary Scott is the daughter of Linda Davis, a country singer, and Lang Scott, a musician. She grew up in the music business. Her mother and father were part of country star Reba McEntire's band during the 1990s. Scott's mother had some hits of her own, too, and shared a Grammy with McEntire for a dramatic duet they recorded, "Does He Love You." As a little girl, Scott thought about becoming a nurse, a veterinarian, a chef, and other professions, but spending a lot of time on the road with her parents helped prepare her for a future in music.

Because her parents were touring musicians, Scott was homeschooled when she was young, learning by watching videotapes while riding in the show's bus. She then attended the Donelson Christian Academy in Nashville, graduating in 2004. She later attended Middle Tennessee State University, where she studied the music business, but she dropped out of college to begin a music career in Nashville.

FORMING THE BAND

The band Lady Antebellum came together when all three band members were just starting out. Haywood and Kelley had graduated from the University of Georgia and had each landed jobs in the financial industry. Haywood moved to Atlanta, Georgia, and Kelley went to Winston-Salem, North Carolina. Neither of them really enjoyed the work they were doing. Meanwhile, Kelley's brother, Josh, had moved to Nashville and was establishing himself as a singer/songwriter. Charles Kelley eventually decided to join his brother and try to make his own mark in the music business. About three months after Kelley moved to Nashville, he called Haywood and said, "Man, you've got to come up here. This is the place to be. Quit what you're doing and come give it a shot while we're young." Haywood took his friend's advice, and soon they were both living at Josh Kelley's place and trying to make it as a singing/songwriting duo.

Scott had a different experience when she tried to break into the music business. Coming from a family of professional Nashville musicians, she had a lot of advantages when she was starting out. At the time Haywood and Kelley first got to Nashville, she was already working to establish a solo career. One night in 2006, in a Nashville music club, Scott noticed Kelley. She recognized him from his MySpace page, where she had been checking out his music. She introduced herself, and before the night was over, they had agreed to try writing some songs together. They began meeting, and soon Haywood joined them in their writing efforts.

Powerful Chemistry

Kelley and Haywood have said that at the time, they expected Scott to soon record a solo album, and they were just hoping to get one song on the album. After working together for a short while, however, the three of them all agreed they had great chemistry as writing partners. "We could write a song at lunch time and have it done as a demo that night," Scott said. The music they wrote reflected the great variety of music they loved, mixing country with elements of pop, rock, and soul.

As more time passed, they also realized that their voices worked well together. Kelley's rough tenor provided good counterpoint to Scott's sweet,

Haywood, Kelley, and Scott performing at a new artists' event in 2008.

smooth alto, and Haywood's backing harmonies and instrumental work supported the whole trio. They began to think they might have a future not only as songwriters, but also as a performing group. They came up with the name "Lady Antebellum" one day after a photo shoot at an old Southern plantation—the word "antebellum" refers to the American South before the Civil War. There is no real meaning behind the name, they simply liked the sound of it. (Fans of the group often shorten the name to "Lady A.")

They began posting their music demos on MySpace, and response to their work was very positive. They did some gigs opening for Josh Kelley at clubs in the Nashville area, and again, the audience response was enthusiastic. "Me and Charles couldn't get anything going under his name for a year," Haywood recalled. "Then, the first show we play [with Scott], we already have people who are flipping out about it. There was an energy that was created having the three of us there. I know for a fact it wasn't happening like that for us individually."

Scott agreed that performing with Kelley and Haywood was a completely different experience than being on her own. "We had so much fun," she said. "I never felt 100 percent confident being on stage alone with a band behind me. When the three of us got on stage together, we could interact together and there just wasn't as much pressure." Soon their career was really rolling. "It took on a life of its own," recalled Haywood. "There was no plan, we just kept churning out as many songs as we could."

CAREER HIGHLIGHTS

Lady Antebellum

In April 2007, the members of Lady Antebellum signed a recording contract with Capitol Nashville and began work on their first album, aided by award-winning songwriter Victoria Shaw and top producer Paul Worley. "There's a convergence of talent and energy with the three of them," Worley said. "Dave is the brains, Hillary's the heart, and Charles is the drive. They are all three creative people, but they don't overlap. The combination is powerful." The recording had the direct emotional appeal, great harmonies, and comfortable musical interplay that would come to define the group. Kelley and Scott shared lead vocals, while Haywood played guitar and sang harmony. Their reputation around Nashville was enough to earn them a nomination from the Academy of Country Music for the award for Top New Duo or Vocal Group, even though they hadn't yet released an album. They won the award later in the year.

The album, titled *Lady Antebellum,* was released on April 15, 2008. The trio had already built an audience for their music through their club dates, MySpace page, and their own web page. As a result of the advance publicity about the album and the existing enthusiasm about the group, *Lady Antebellum* shot to the top of the country album charts as soon as it was released, and the first single, "Love Don't Live Here," went to the top of the singles charts. The album was eventually certified platinum, meaning it sold more than one million copies.

Although their name recalls an earlier era in history, their sound is definitely modern country, showing the many musical influences Kelley, Haywood, and Scott have absorbed in their lifetimes. The music and emotion in the album ranged from "Love Don't Live Here," a song about a breakup, to the upbeat, romantic feelings called up by "Love's Lookin' Good on You"; the party song "Lookin' for a Good Time"; and the hard-driving "I Run to You."

The group hit the road for their first big tour in 2008 as the opening act for Martina McBride, one of country music's biggest stars. Although they were a tight writing and singing unit, they faced a new challenge in learning how to stage a show that would hold the audiences' attention in the big arenas where McBride played. They learned a lot while on the road with her, and kept building their fan base and improving their performances by

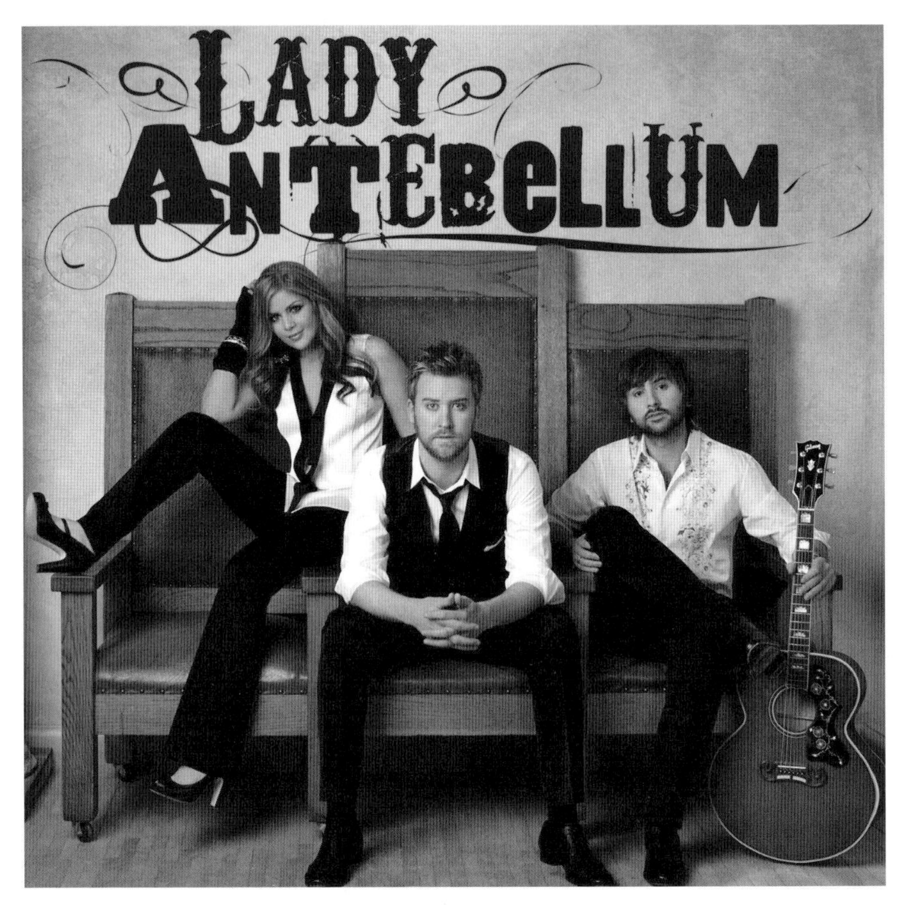

The group's first album, Lady Antebellum.

continuing to tour as an opening act for other big names, including Kenny Chesney, Taylor Swift, Josh Turner, Carrie Underwood, and Keith Urban. Their music reached even more people after they wrote "I Was Here," a song used in the NBC television network's coverage of the 2008 summer Olympic Games.

Need You Now

The members of Lady Antebellum had learned a lot about the music business in a very short time, and they looked forward to bringing their new knowledge and experience to their second album. Although they were incredibly busy on the road, they had already written so much that they had a huge selection of songs to choose from. They were getting close to finishing the second album in 2009 when Keith Urban asked them to tour with him.

Much as they wanted to complete their project, the opportunity to tour with Urban wasn't something they wanted to turn down. Albums frequently are released around Christmas in order to increase sales, but the public had to wait until early 2010 to hear Lady Antebellum's second release. The band members came to feel the delay was a good thing, as it gave them time to come up with some new songs they really liked. In addition to writing most of the material on the album, they co-produced it. The songs range from the title track, about separated lovers unwisely considering a reunion, to "American Honey," a nostalgic look at the simple pleasures in life, to "Hello World," an unusual song about a man who suddenly sees the world in a fresh light.

"The ultimate compliment is when someone comes up to us and says, 'That song really expresses what I really feel,'" said Scott. "And that's the beautiful thing about music. And we don't take it for granted at all."

”

January 2010 was a big month for Lady Antebellum. They were nominated for two Grammy Awards, one of the most prestigious prizes in the music world, and they were also asked to perform at the Grammy Awards ceremonies on January 31. Their second album, *Need You Now,* was released on January 26. The album itself debuted at the top of the Billboard Top 200 Albums chart, which includes all types of music—not just country. The first single from the album, also called "Need You Now," debuted at the top of the iTunes singles chart. The group performed "Need You Now" at the 2010 Grammys, where they won the award for Best Country Performance by a Duo or Group with Vocals, for the song "I Run to You," from the *Lady Antebellum* album.

"The Grammy performance completely flipped our world upside down," Haywood said. "That was an opportunity for us to be in front of an audience we have never been in front of, because that's an all-genre awards show. Our dressing room was next to the Black Eyed Peas and we're out there sitting next to Colbie Caillat and Lady Gaga.... The three of us feel incredibly overwhelmed and seriously very humbled."

But that was just the beginning. *Need You Now* was not only a solid success in the country music market, it also got airplay on pop radio stations, bringing many new fans to Lady Antebellum. More than three million copies of *Need You Now* have been sold. Reviewing the album for the *Los Angeles Times,* Ann Powers said that it describes "the moment in young adulthood when wild promise starts to give way to more realistic expecta-

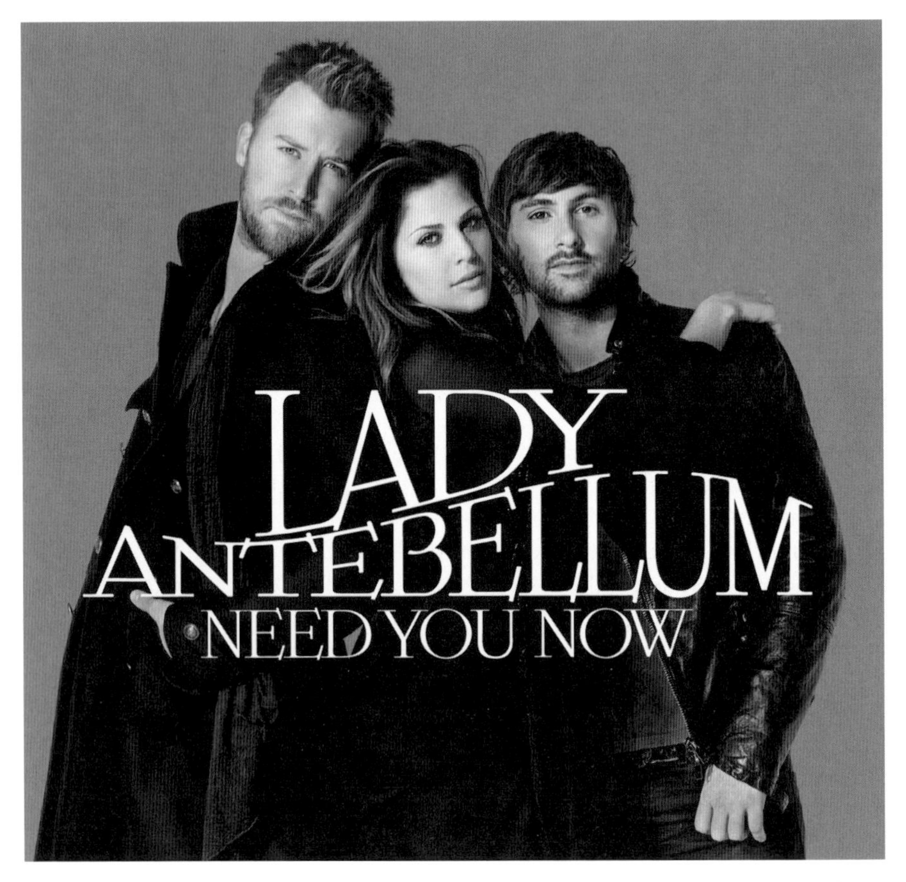

The group's second album, Need You Now, *won over both country and pop fans.*

tions." She added: "Scott has a gift for strongly expressing tentative feelings, like cautious hope on 'Perfect Day' and recovered self-respect in 'Ready to Love Again.'" According to Thom Jurek on allmusic.com, "The band's seamless, polished, and savvy brand of contemporary country is even more consistent than it was on their debut: it's virtually flawless in its songwriting, production, and performance."

The album and some individual songs went on to win a slew of major awards during 2010 and 2011, including six Academy of Country Music Awards, five Grammy Awards, and two Country Music Association Awards.

Crossover Success

Kelley, Haywood, and Scott are happy to have any new listeners appreciate their music, but they never set out to win pop music audiences. "We had no intentions of this ever crossing over," Kelley said. "Some pop stations just started playing 'Need You Now' after it had a little success at country radio. After seeing that, our record label started pursuing [pop airplay] a little more heavily, and EMI came in on it and showed a lot of support. It definitely surprised us all."

In addition to writing songs, spending time on the road, and performing, the members of Lady Antebellum are committed to staying in touch with their fans via the internet. They have songs and videos posted on their MySpace pages and Facebook, and they keep their own web site up to date, supplying a new "webisode" each week of funny, behind-the-scenes footage of what's going on with the band.

"We made a pact to try and process everything that's happening as much as we can, to not take it for granted. It seems like there's something new that happens every single day," said Scott, reflecting on the band's quick rise to stardom. "There's never going to be another time like this in our career, and we're soaking it up as much as possible. We're meeting as many people and shaking as many hands as we can. It's about getting the music in people's hands. We sign autographs after every show. The ultimate compliment is when someone comes up to us and says, 'That song really expresses what I really feel.' And that's the beautiful thing about music. And we don't take it for granted at all."

Own the Night

Lady Antebellum released their third album, *Own the Night,* in 2011. The release of *Own the Night* so soon after the wild success of *Need You Now* was considered a gutsy move by some critics, including Jessica Phillips in *Country Weekly*. "Recording the follow-up to an album that produced three chart-topping singles and sold three million copies is wrought with temptations—to veer off the rails in an attempt to create something different, or to basically replicate the previous album in hopes of a similar payoff. For the most part, Lady Antebellum strikes a nice balance between the two, keeping the penchant for bighearted ballads and the vocal chemistry between Charles Kelley and Hillary Scott intact."

Like their previous albums, many of the songs on *Own the Night* focused on all the experiences of love: how to find a soul mate, how to keep love alive, and how to suffer through the anguish when it's gone. "Musically speaking, the group's secret is the symbiotic blend of the voices of Hillary Scott and Charles Kelley that brings out the longing in songs they've written with a variety of collaborators," Randy Lewis wrote in the *Los Angeles*

Dave Haywood, Hillary Scott, and Charles Kelley.

Times. "Not surprisingly, everything sounds bigger, brighter and shinier than on Lady A's first two albums. That'll probably go over well with fans of grandiose country pop, but the all-stops-out production gradually loses impact. There's also a sameness of tempo and tone to a lot of the material." Several commentators considered the album a watered-down version of their previous music and noted that many of the songs veered closer to pop than country, a view echoed by critic Stephen Thomas Erlewine on allmusic.com. "*[Own the Night]* bears the sound of a band quite content with its position in the middle of the road," Erlewine argued. "Any lingering elements of country, whether twang or two-steps, have been banished and supplanted with a smooth soft rock designed to seep into the background wherever it's played. These songs of love won and lost tend to be so dreamy they verge on the sleepy, lacking any of the hushed urgency of *Need You Now* while retaining every ounce of its manicured prettiness."

HOME AND FAMILY

Kelley is married to Cassie McConnell, a Nashville publicist. Scott is engaged to drummer Chris Tyrrell, whom she met in 2010 while both were touring with Tim McGraw. Haywood is single.

Because the group is on tour a great deal, "home" is usually their large tour bus. Besides the band members, crew members travel on the bus as well. Most of them are male, too, so Scott has a small room of her own in case she wants some privacy. Because Kelley, Haywood, and Scott are together so much of the time, they have learned to be easygoing and not get upset about little things. If real problems or differences arise, "you can't be afraid to talk about things and hit them head-on. Don't let them grow into a big, huge thing that explodes," said Scott. "We always just kind of talk it out or give each other space and talk it out later. It's just like a friendship, only magnified because we're together all the time."

FAVORITE MUSIC

All three members of Lady Antebellum enjoy a wide range of musical styles. Kelley particularly admires country artists Keith Urban and Tim McGraw. Haywood likes the music of Keith Urban, Brad Paisley, Safetysuit, Paramore, The Eagles, Nirvana, Dave Matthews, and James Taylor. Some of the musicians Scott admires most are Beyoncé, Keith Urban, John Legend, Dave Barnes, Carole King, Trisha Yearwood, Maroon Five, Justin Timberlake, Ne-Yo, and Soulja Boy.

HOBBIES AND OTHER INTERESTS

Haywood, Kelley, and Scott all try to help with social causes. For example, they promote reducing waste by using water filters on their tour bus instead of drinking bottled water. After floods devastated parts of Tennessee, they took part in a fundraising concert that brought in more than $1.5 million for flood relief. The band also supports the Mocha Club, a project that aims to provide better living conditions for people in Africa.

RECORDINGS

Lady Antebellum, 2008
Need You Now, 2010
Own the Night, 2011

HONORS AND AWARDS

Academy of Country Music Awards: 2008, New Vocal Duet/Group; 2010 (three awards), Vocal Group of the Year, Single of the Year, for "Need You Now," and Song of the Year, for "Need You Now"; 2011 (three awards), Vocal Group of the Year, Album of the Year (as producers), for *Need You Now,* Album of the Year (as artists), for *Need You Now*

Country Music Association Awards: 2008, New Artist of the Year (Horizon Award); 2009 (two awards), Vocal Group of the Year and Single of the

Year, for "I Run to You"; 2010 (two awards), Vocal Group of the Year, Single of the Year, for "Need You Now"
Grammy Awards (National Academy of Recording Arts and Sciences): 2010, Best Country Performance by a Duo or Group with Vocals, for "I Run to You"; 2011 (five awards), Best Country Album, for *Need You Now*, Record of the Year, Best Country Performance by a Duo or Group with Vocals, Song of the Year, and Best Country Song, all for "Need You Now"
Country Music Television Awards: 2010, Group Video of the Year, for "Need You Now"; 2011, Group Video of the Year, for "Hello World"
Teen Choice Awards: 2010, for Choice Country Group; 2011, for Choice Country Group

FURTHER READING

Periodicals

Billboard, Jan. 9, 2010, p.28; Feb. 20, 2010, p.16
Entertainment Weekly, Feb. 26, 2010, p.48
Los Angeles Times, Jan. 26, 2010, p.D2
Toronto Star, Mar. 28, 2010, p.E4
USA Today, Mar. 10, 2010, p.D1

Online Articles

http://music.aol.com/artist
(AOL Music, "Lady Antebellum Biography," no date)
http://www.cmt.com/artists/az/lady_antebellum/artist.jhtml
(CMT, "Lady Antebellum," no date)
http://www.countryweekly.com
(Country Weekly, "Destined to Be Together," Apr. 21, 2008)
http://www.mixonline.com
(*Mix*, "Lady Antebellum on the Fast Track to Success," May, 2008)
http://www.msn.com
(MSN, "Lady Antebellum: Pop Goes the Country," no date)

ADDRESS

Lady Antebellum
Capitol Records, Nashville
3322 West End Avenue
Nashville, TN 37207

WORLD WIDE WEB SITES

http://ladyantebellum.com
http://www.myspace.com/ladyantebellum

Miranda Lambert 1983-

American Country Singer
Academy of Country Music 2011 Top Female Vocalist

BIRTH

Miranda Leigh Lambert was born on November 10, 1983, in Longview, Texas. Her parents are Richard Lee and Beverly June Hughes Lambert. Richard, who goes by the name of Rick, once worked as a narcotics officer for the Dallas police force. Later, he and his wife started a private detective agency. They have a son, Luke, who is about four years younger than Miranda.

YOUTH

The Lamberts moved from the eastern part of Texas to Dallas when Miranda was a baby. Their detective work brought them in contact with many women who had violent, abusive husbands or boyfriends. Sometimes, if these women didn't have a safe place to stay, the Lamberts would bring them to their own home. This meant there was a possibility of dangerous men coming to the house, and the Lamberts wanted to be sure their children knew how to protect themselves. They taught them how to react in a crisis situation and how to handle guns properly. Miranda received her first BB gun when she was only five years old.

When Lambert was six years old, her family fell on hard times. Her parents' detective agency went out of business. Unable to pay all their bills, they lost their home. They moved back to the eastern part of Texas, where they lived with relatives in Lindale for about a year. All the changes and uncertainty were very upsetting, and she would "cry every day," according to her mother. "I remember every detail about it, every tear," Lambert said of that time in her life. Eventually the family was able to rent a house—one that needed so many repairs that its owner had been thinking of tearing it down. They raised much of their own food, including rabbits and hogs, and Rick hunted to supply game meat for their meals.

The family had a lot of happy times despite these hardships. Rick worked part-time as a country singer, and the Lambert home was often the scene of casual parties with lots of music. Lambert grew up hearing and loving the sounds of classic country artists like Merle Haggard, Guy Clark, and Loretta Lynn. According to her parents, Lambert showed an instinctive grasp of music and could harmonize when she was only three years old. "My dad would play guitar, and I would sit on his lap and sing with him," she recalled. "I just grew up with it. It's in my blood."

MUSIC DREAMS

When she was 10 years old, Lambert had an experience that changed her life. "My parents took me to Dallas to see Garth Brooks," she remembered. "It was awesome. There I was in my braces screaming, 'Gaaaarrrth!' I was freakin' out." That concert ignited her dreams of being a country singer. Knowing that she was talented, and seeing that her passion for music was strong, her parents supported her in every way they could. They helped her to enter talent contests, and when she was 13 years old, they began taking her to Nashville each year for Fan Fair, an event where fans can hear and meet lots of top performers.

Lambert's dad gave her a guitar when she was 14, but she wasn't interested in it at first. When she was about 16, her parents sent her to a music-business seminar in Nashville. She had a chance to cut a "demo," or sample recording. When she went to the studio to make the demo, she was given four songs to sing. All of them had a pop-country sound that she did not like. When the session was over, she felt terribly disappointed with the result.

It was this experience that spurred Lambert both to learn to play guitar and to begin writing her own songs. She asked her dad to teach her some chords, and as soon as she knew three, she wrote her first song. "I just got so interested in it," she said. "I practiced four hours a day until my fingers would bleed. It came so naturally it was like sunbeams shining down on me. I always had to work at everything else. I never excelled in sports. In cheerleading, I was the last to learn the dance. I was terrible at school—if I made B's and C's my family was thrilled and jumping up and down. But with music it was, 'THIS is what I am supposed to be doing.'"

> *According to her parents, Lambert showed an instinctive grasp of music and could harmonize when she was only three years old. "My dad would play guitar, and I would sit on his lap and sing with him," she recalled. "I just grew up with it. It's in my blood."*

Even though she was just a teenager, Lambert had a lot of material to draw on when trying to write songs. Thanks to her parents' work as private investigators, she had seen and heard a lot about the dark side of life. Her compositions were often dark, gritty stories of betrayal and revenge—classic material for country music lyrics. Her music definitely showed the influence of the old-school country music she had grown up listening to, but it also had a modern, rock edge.

EDUCATION

Lambert attended Longview High School. By the time she was 17, she had formed her own band, Texas Pride. While still attending high school, she was hired to sing regularly at the Reo Palm Isle Ballroom, a famous country dance hall in Longview, Texas. With her music career picking up, Lambert chose to graduate early. "I'm not really a school person; I made it through high school barely passing, which is just fine by me. And I knew I would waste time in college, because I already knew what I wanted to do—I

Lambert performing at the Country Music Association Awards.

wanted to be in music, and I wanted to be in a band. And I figured the best way to do that was not waste money and time in a classroom." Seeing how focused and successful she already was, her parents supported her decisions. They decided to use money they had saved for her college education and put it toward her singing career instead. The last thing Lambert did in high school was to star in a musical, *Annie Get Your Gun.*

FIRST JOBS

Texas Star

In 2001, Lambert's parents helped her produce a CD titled *Miranda Lambert.* They bought a motor home and a trailer for equipment, and the whole family hit the road, traveling all over Texas so Lambert could sing in music clubs. Even her younger brother pitched in to help his sister's career, creating a web site to promote her appearances and sell her CD. Lambert learned a lot over the next couple of years, including how to deal with the rowdy, hard-drinking crowds that made up much of her growing fan base.

In January 2003, Lambert won the Texas round of competition for a new television show called "Nashville Star." It was based on the "American Idol" program, but featured country music. Some 8,000 people from all over the country were selected as initial contestants for "Nashville Star." After being chosen as the finalist from Texas, Lambert spent several months in Nashville to participate in the final rounds of televised competition. She made it all the way to the season finale, coming in third place.

Lambert was actually glad she placed third. "The winner had to go in right after the contest and make a record in a couple of weeks," she said. "I wasn't ready." She did sing backup vocals on the album made by the winner, Buddy Jewell. Soon after her performance on "Nashville Star," she was invited to meet with people from Sony, a major recording and entertainment company.

Contract with Sony

Lambert had already written a huge catalog of songs, and she knew she wanted to record her own work. She walked into the meeting with a confident attitude, as if she were already a star.

"All the Sony people were there," she remembered. "I sat down at the head of the table, crossed my hands and said, 'OK, this is who I am.... I'm from Texas. I write my own stuff. I have something to say. I'll never dance around on stage in a halter top. I will always play my guitar. Now, if you can't make a record that reflects me honestly, I'd rather just go home and play in Texas like I was.'" Sony executives liked her brash style. They offered her a contract, and she signed with Sony in September 2003. Sony executives gave her permission to go into the studio and make the record she wanted to make, without interference.

For the next few months, Lambert worked hard on her project. When she took her rough cuts back to the Sony executives, they were very happy with what they heard. Her debut single, released in 2004, was "Me and Charlie Talking," a wistful song about memories of young love. Although it wasn't a major hit, it was played on radio and got a good response. Lambert included it on her first Sony album, *Kerosene,* which was released in 2005. In the meantime, she went back on the road, playing music festivals and fairs.

CAREER HIGHLIGHTS

Songs of Revenge

Lambert wrote all but one of the songs on *Kerosene.* While "Me and Charlie Talking" had a gentle feeling, most of her music did not. The title song referred to taking fiery revenge on a cheating boyfriend. Because of the edgy nature of the lyrics, the singles from *Kerosene* didn't get a lot of radio airplay. Despite that, when the album was released, it started at the top of *Billboard* magazine's country music album sales chart. This would normally only happen to an album that had been heavily promoted by radio stations before its release, but Lambert already had a following, even without radio exposure. *Kerosene* was very well reviewed, and not just by country music lovers. It was named one of the 10 best albums of the year by *Rolling Stone,* a magazine that focuses on rock music. *Kerosene* eventually sold more than one million copies. In the summer of 2005, Lambert toured as the opening act for her hero, Merle Haggard. She also opened for several other country giants, including George Strait, Keith Urban, and Toby Keith. Onstage, she was as feisty and fiery as her lyrics.

Lambert's next album, *Crazy Ex-Girlfriend* (2007), expanded her persona as a dangerous woman. It was again full of hard-hitting, hard-edged lyrics. Once again, some radio stations were hesitant about playing it. The title track is about woman in a bar fight with an ex-boyfriend's new girlfriend. Another single, "Gunpowder and Lead," described a woman grimly waiting for the man who has been beating her, with a loaded shotgun in her hands. Even though it depicts a violent revenge, "Gunpowder and Lead" is seen by many people as sending a strong message about a woman's refusal to take any more abuse. "Gunpowder and Lead" was Lambert's first single to reach the Top 10 charts, and the album *Crazy Ex-Girlfriend* eventually reached the No. 6 spot on the *Billboard* Top 200 chart

for albums of all genres. While some may have had reservations about her lyrics, Lambert was named Top New Female Vocalist by the Academy of Country Music (ACM) in 2007, beating out Taylor Swift, and the CD was named Album of the Year at the 2008 ACM Awards. Reviewing the album for the *Washington Post,* J. Freedom du Lac called it "a stunning recording that's brimming with energy and personality."

In 2008 and 2009, Lambert went on tour with Blake Shelton, one of country music's most popular male singers, with whom she had been romantically involved since 2006. Later in 2009, she served as opening act for Kenny Chesney, another major country star, on his Sun City Carnival tour.

Revolution

In addition to touring in 2009, Lambert released her third album, called *Revolution*. It showed that there was more to her than just anger and revenge. "I was getting dangerously close to being shoved in that box of 'She's that crazy girl who kills people in her songs,'" she noted. "That's fine, but there's so much more to me than that." *Revolution* still gave listeners some of what they had come to expect from Lambert. "Sin for a Sin," which she co-wrote with Shelton, talks about a cheating man and a possible murder. The video for "White Liar" shows a wronged woman humiliating her cheating fiancé by leaving him at the altar and running off with the best man. Yet the album also included "Virginia Bluebell," a ballad; "Heart Like Mine," which describes some unconventional ideas about what it will be like to meet Jesus; and "The House That Built Me," a nostalgic look back at a beloved home.

"Lambert first heard "The House That Built Me" when Shelton played the demo for her in a car one night. "It was dark, and she wasn't saying anything," he remembered. "I looked over, and I could see from the dash lights that she was seriously bawling. I said, 'If that song means that much to you, you should record it.' The crying tripled after that."

Although "The House That Built Me" was not written by Lambert, it described her childhood home perfectly. She first heard it when riding in a car with Shelton. He was considering recording it and played the demo for her. "It was dark, and she wasn't saying anything," he remembered. "I looked over, and I could see from the dash lights that she was seriously bawling. I said, 'If that song means that much to you, you should record it.' The crying tripled after that."

The album—and specifically "The House That Built Me"—proved to be a huge success for Lambert, popular with fans and respected by critics. At the Country Music Association (CMA) Awards in 2010—which happened to be on her 27th birthday—she was named Female Vocalist of the Year, "The House That Built Me" won Music Video of the Year and Song of the Year, and *Revolution* won Album of the Year. To make the night even more special for Lambert, Shelton also took home two awards. Like *Kerosene* and *Crazy Ex-Girlfriend, Revolution* eventually sold more than a million copies. The accolades continued in 2011. At the Grammy Awards, Lambert won the Female Country Vocal award for "The House That Built Me," and at the Academy of Country Music (ACM) Awards, she won Top Female Vocalist and three awards for

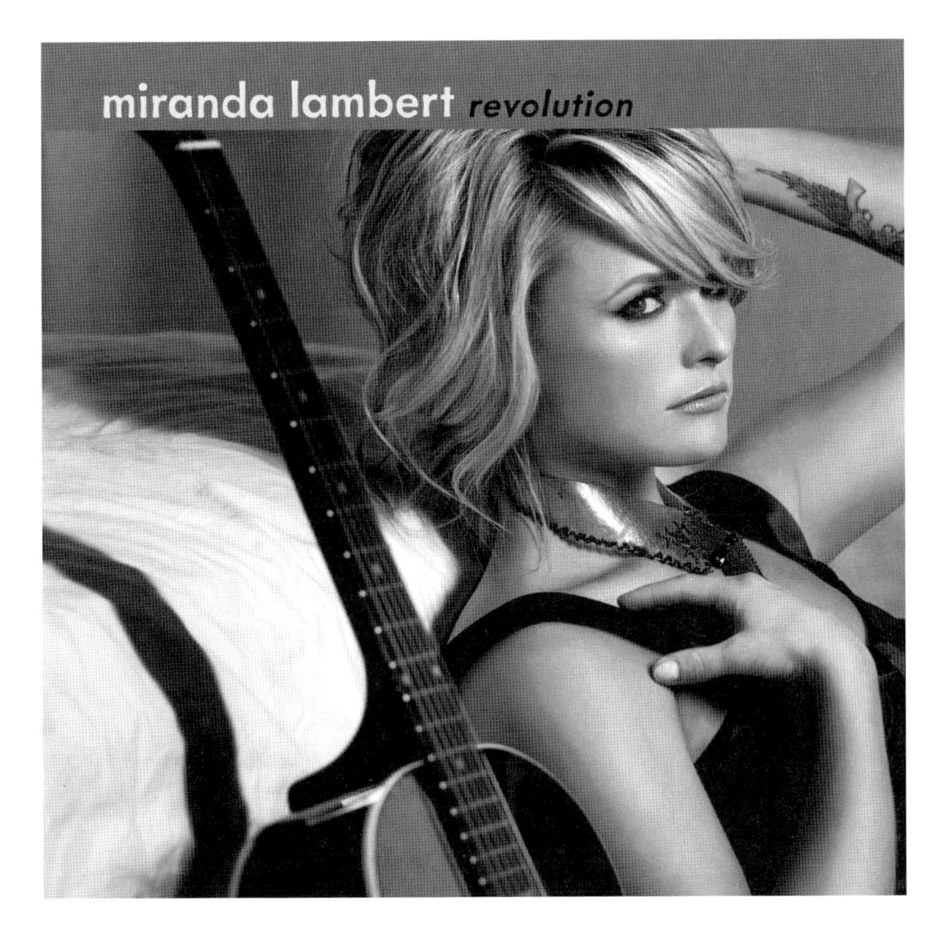

"The House That Built Me" (Single of the Year, Song of the Year, and Video of the Year).

In addition to her solo work, Lambert has put together a vocal trio called Pistol Annies. The group is made up of Lambert, Angaleena Presley, and Ashley Monroe, or as they call themselves, "Lone Star Annie," "Holler Annie," and "Hippie Annie." The group debuted on April 4, 2011, on the ACM television program *Girls' Night Out,* singing a song called "Hell on Heels." "Our music is honest and outspoken, just like us," Lambert said.

Lambert loves her career and hopes it will last a long time. "I want to shoot for a career like Reba McEntire's," she declared. "My ultimate goal is to be Loretta Lynn—I want to be that much of an influence, and I want to make an amazing record at 70 years old." Even if her high-profile career fades, though, she feels she'll always want to perform, even if she has to do it in small clubs and bars."Music is what I do; I can't do anything else."

Throughout her success, Lambert has remained close to her family and to her roots. Her mother and father still work with her, selling her merchandise. Her Christian faith is important to her."I grew up in church, and I've been a Christian my whole life. My mom always says I cut my teeth on a church pew," she declared."I know every day when I wake up, I have the Lord watching over me."

MARRIAGE AND FAMILY

Lambert and Blake Shelton were married on May 14, 2011, at the Don Strange Ranch in Boerne, Texas. They live in Tishomingo, Oklahoma, where they own hundreds of acres of farmland and woods. She said she expects that her greatest struggle will be to balance her life as an entertainer with a normal life,"not only as a wife, but as a person." She and Shelton hope that their love of ordinary farm routines and simple outdoor activities will help them keep their feet on the ground despite being a celebrity couple.

HOBBIES AND OTHER INTERESTS

Raised with guns, Lambert still appreciates and enjoys firearms. Her logo is two crossed pistols with angel wings, a design she also has tattooed on her arm. Explaining what the symbolism meant to her, she said: "I'm really a small-town Texas girl. I've got a good heart. I was raised right. But I also have a feisty side. I have this don't-take-any-crap attitude. The guns and wings represent both parts of my personality."

Lambert and her husband enjoy hunting together for deer, turkey, and hogs. At their wedding reception, they even served wild game that they had shot themselves. Besides hunting, they like most outdoor activities, including horseback riding, fishing, boating, and four-wheeling. Lambert works out with a personal trainer. She commented, "I LOVE to eat so I have to work out, which I don't love!"

Lambert is an avid hunter, but she is also an avid animal lover. In addition to horses and farm animals, she has several dogs and cats, all of them rescued from shelters. She founded the MuttNation Foundation, a charity that supports animal shelters in Texas. MuttNation's annual Cause for Paws benefit has raised hundreds of thousands of dollars for animal welfare.

RECORDINGS

Miranda Lambert, 2001
Kerosene, 2005

Crazy Ex-Girlfriend, 2007
Revolution, 2009

HONORS AND AWARDS

Academy of Country Music Awards: 2007, Top New Female Vocalist; 2008, Album of the Year, for *Crazy Ex-Girlfriend;* 2010 (three awards), Top Female Vocalist, Album of the Year, for *Revolution,* and Video of the Year, for "White Liar"; 2011 (four awards), Top Female Vocalist, Single of the Year, for "The House That Built Me," Song of the Year, for "The House That Built Me," and Video of the Year, for "The House That Built Me"
Country Music Association Awards: 2010 (four awards), Female Vocalist of the Year, Album of the Year, for *Revolution,* Song of the Year and Video of the Year, both for "The House That Built Me"
Country Music Television (CMT) Awards: 2010, Female Video of the Year, for "White Liar"; 2011, Female Video of the Year, for "The House That Built Me"
Grammy Award (National Academy of Recording Arts and Sciences): 2011, for Female Country Vocal, for "The House That Built Me"

FURTHER READING

Periodicals

Billboard, Sep. 12, 2009, p.16; Dec. 4, 2010, p.12
Boston Globe, Sep. 22, 2007, p. D3
Ladies' Home Journal, Mar. 2011, p.92
New York Times, Apr. 29, 2007, p.AR27
People, Nov. 11, 2009, p.46; Nov. 15, 2010, p.78
Redbook, Apr. 2011, p.158
Washington Post, May 15, 2007, p.C1

Online Articles

http://www.biography.com
(Biography, "Miranda Lambert Biography," no date)
http://www.theboot.com
(The Boot, "Miranda Lambert: Bio," no date)
http://www.cmt.com/artists
(CMT, "Miranda Lambert," no date)
http://www.lhj.com
(Ladies' Home Journal, "Miranda Lambert: Nashville's Shooting Star," Mar. 2011)

http://www.people.com/people/miranda_lambert/biography
(People,"Miranda Lambert: Bio," no date)

ADDRESS

Miranda Lambert
Sony/BMG
550 Madison Avenue
New York, NY 10022

WORLD WIDE WEB SITES

http://www.mirandalambert.com
http://www.pistolannies.com

Liu Xiaobo 1955-

Chinese Writer and Human Rights Activist
Winner of the 2010 Nobel Peace Prize

BIRTH

Liu Xiaobo was born on December 28, 1955, in Changchun, China, a large, industrial city in the northeastern part of the country and the capital of Jilin province. His parents were intellectuals, and his father was employed as a university professor. He has an older brother, Liu Xiaoguang, and a younger brother, Liu Xiaoxuan.

In Chinese names, the family name (what we would call the last name) is placed first, and the given name (what we would

CHINA UNDER COMMUNISM

Liu has lived his entire life under a communist government, which China adopted in 1949 after years of imperial rule. Communism is the name of a political system in which the government controls the economy. The communist philosophy dictates that all citizens should share equally in the country's resources. Therefore, under communism, the government eliminates private property and redistributes resources as it sees fit. It also controls the educations, careers, and cultural experiences of its people.

When Mao Zedong became president of the People's Republic of China (PRC) in 1949, he began reforming the agricultural system. He wanted to give land to the peasants and change the balance of power between landlords and workers. This plan, however, resulted in terrible bloodshed. In another attempt to improve agriculture and industry in China, Mao launched the Great Leap Forward economic program in 1958. The government created communes composed of many households that farmed together and pooled their profits. Despite the efforts of millions, the program was disastrous. Farmland became depleted and crops failed, poverty and starvation were widespread, and tens of millions died. Consequently, Mao stepped down as president of the PRC in 1959 but remained chairman of the Chinese Communist Party.

Fearing that he had lost the respect of the people, Mao made a final attempt to enact revolutionary change in China. He was determined to destroy the old ideas, customs, culture, and habits that he believed were corrupting the masses. In the mid-1960s he started the Great Proletarian Cultural Revolution, mobilizing students to criticize the views of political officials and intellectuals. Teachers, writers, and other professionals were considered threats to the revolution and were attacked if their work was interpreted as unpatriotic. Those accused of criticizing communism were labeled subversive. Many people were persecuted and sent to the countryside to be "reeducated," which meant they lived

call the first name) is placed last. So his family name is Liu, and his given name is Xiaobo. His name is alphabetized under Liu.

YOUTH

Little information is available about Liu's early life. After middle school, he moved with his parents to a rural area in Inner Mongolia, an autonomous region in northern China. The family lived there from 1969 to 1973 during in prison camps and were forced to do manual labor so they would support communist principles. Others were sent to prison or killed.

Following the communist takeover, the Chinese people lost many freedoms. They were told where to live, what work to do, even how many children to have. Today, China is still a one-party dictatorship, and many social and political restrictions remain in place. The Chinese government places severe limits on individual rights, including freedom of speech. There are no independent newspapers or TV stations—all are controlled and censored by the government—so the Chinese people have little access to independent news and few forums to present independent ideas. The Chinese government also restricts the Internet, limiting what web sites can be seen. It also controls the judicial system, which does not provide many rights and protections to the accused. In addition, police monitor the activities of those suspected of opposing government policy. The result of all these restrictions is that Chinese citizens face severe limits on many rights that Americans take for granted, including freedom of expression, freedom of association, freedom of religion, and due process under the law.

In China, those deemed counter-revolutionary are subject to harsh punishment. For example, dissidents opposed to government policy are censored and placed under police surveillance. Their phone lines and computers are monitored or disconnected. When government agents suspect someone of counter-revolutionary activity, he or she is arrested, interrogated, and often charged with subversion—undermining government authority. Many authors, human rights activists, and other intellectuals who have championed democracy have been detained and prosecuted with no hope for a fair trial. Imprisonment, torture, or even death is possible for those who oppose the government. Thus, although China's constitution states that the country belongs to the people, in practice Chinese citizens must follow the orders of the Communist Party or face extreme consequences.

the Great Proletarian Cultural Revolution—a social and political movement initiated by Communist Party Chairman Mao Zedong. It was a period of chaos, political upheaval, and violence. Many intellectuals were persecuted during this era, and many schools were closed.

Due to the Cultural Revolution, Liu was initially barred from pursuing an advanced education. As was typical of the educated youth of his generation, he was sent to the countryside at age 19 and spent two years working in a people's commune in his home province of Jilin. His close friend Yang Jianli, now in exile, talked about this time in Liu's life with the *Guardian.* "Some took it as suffering and thought they should reward themselves when they had power and money later. Liu Xiaobo took it as experience that helped him understand the real suffering of the Chinese people at the hands of the Chinese government." In 1976 Liu got a job as a construction worker in his hometown of Changchun, the automotive hub of China.

EDUCATION

In 1977, in the aftermath of the Cultural Revolution, the Communist Party reinstated the national university entrance exam. Students and intellectuals were allowed to return to universities, and Liu entered Jilin University to study Chinese literature. While in college, he and six of his schoolmates formed the poetry group The Innocent Hearts, and he became interested in Western philosophy. After graduating from Jilin University in 1982, he attended Beijing Normal University, earning a master's degree in Chinese literature in 1984. He lectured at Beijing Normal while completing his postgraduate studies and received his PhD (doctorate) in Chinese literature in 1988. Liu was the first student to obtain a doctorate degree in literature under the communist system.

CAREER HIGHLIGHTS

In 1987 Liu published his first book, the nonfiction bestseller *Criticism of the Choice,* in which he challenged the ideology of Professor Li Zehou, an influential voice in the intellectual community at the time. He also criticized the Chinese tradition of Confucianism, a system of ethical and philosophical principles based on the teachings of the ancient Chinese thinker Confucius. In 1988 Liu became a professor at Beijing Normal and worked as a visiting scholar at the University of Oslo, the University of Hawaii, and Columbia University in New York. In 1989 he published *The Fog of Metaphysics,* a comprehensive survey of Western philosophies. His academic career ended abruptly that same year when he returned home to participate in the developing pro-democracy movement.

Tiananmen Square Protests

On April 27, 1989, Liu cut short his lecture series at Columbia University and returned to Beijing to take part in the student-led pro-democracy demonstrations in Tiananmen Square. The pro-democracy movement was a response to the Chinese political system, where the Communist Party holds a monopoly on political and judicial power. The pro-democracy demonstrations in Tiananmen Square began with a student march through the capital city in memory of Hu Yaobang, a recently deceased political leader who favored social and economic reform. The students called for freedom, democracy, and human rights for Chinese citizens. After returning from the United States, Liu became an advisor to the student movement. One of a few professors to offer direct assistance to the protesters, he provided strategic guidance and gave speeches in support of their cause.

> *"I still want to tell the regime that deprives me of my freedom, I stand by the belief I expressed 20 years ago in my 'June Second Hunger Strike Declaration'—I have no enemies, and no hatred. None of the police who monitored, arrested and interrogated me, the prosecutors who prosecuted me, or the judges who sentenced me, are my enemies."*

On June 2, 1989, Liu staged a hunger strike with three other demonstrators to protest the use of military force to evacuate Tiananmen Square. He called for both the students and the government to abandon the ideology of class struggle in favor of a political culture based on dialogue and compromise. In a written statement issued at the start of the hunger strike and translated into English in London's *Independent* newspaper, the protesters urged the following: "We must do this because hatred can only produce violence and dictatorship. We must adopt the spirit of tolerance. We must begin to build up Chinese democracy with a democratic spirit of tolerance and concept of co-operation. Democratic politics is a politics without enemies, without hatred. Instead it means a politics based on mutual respect, mutual tolerance, and mutual compromise, through consultation, discussion, and the electoral process."

Liu was powerless to prevent bloodshed in Tiananmen Square, but he did play a critical role in preventing slaughter on an even larger scale. On June 3, the night before what turned out to be the most violent day in the demonstrations, Liu spoke to a group of workers. They were preparing to fight the troops, and he convinced them to disarm. Seizing and smashing a rifle during a rally, he emphasized the importance of peaceful, rather than violent, resistance. "Whatever extreme the government takes will help it dig its own grave," he argued. He negotiated the nonviolent retreat of sev-

Two views of the protests at Tiananmen Square: (top) demonstrators gathered in the square, with Liu at the right in sunglasses; (bottom) a Chinese man, crying and pleading for an end to the killing, trying to stop the tanks as they advanced into the square.

eral thousand protesters, brokering a deal with the army to allow the last demonstrators to evacuate the square in the final hours of the conflict. The following day, June 4, 1989, the army initiated a military crackdown, using tanks and guns to force the protesters out of Tiananmen Square. Following seven weeks of peaceful student protests, the Chinese army killed hundreds—possibly thousands—of demonstrators in an event that became known as the June 4th Massacre.

Witnessing the government's violent response to the Tiananmen Square protests was, as Liu put it, "the major turning point in my 50 years on life's road." On June 6, 1989, he was arrested for his role in the pro-democracy movement. He was expelled from Beijing Normal University three months later, and his writings were banned. The government issued publications and news reports denouncing him as the "black hand" and "madman" behind the movement. Reflecting back on the government's actions against him, Liu lamented the loss of the right to free speech. "Merely for publishing different political views and taking part in a peaceful democracy movement, a teacher lost his lectern, a writer lost his right to publish, and a public intellectual lost the opportunity to give talks publicly." Liu spent 19 months in detention before being convicted of "counter-revolutionary propaganda and incitement" in January 1991. He avoided a prison sentence on account of his "major meritorious action" in preventing further bloodshed in Tiananmen Square.

Human Rights Activism

Upon his release, Liu immediately resumed writing, focusing on the topics of human rights and politics. "Freedom of expression is the foundation of human rights, the source of humanity, and the mother of truth," he explained. "To strangle freedom of speech is to trample on human rights, stifle humanity, and suppress truth." Although his works were still banned in China, he published the memoir *The Monologues of a Doomsday's Survivor* in Taiwan in 1992. Despite the dangers of being an outspoken critic of the Chinese government, he remained dedicated to the pro-democracy movement. "Living in an authoritarian society, doing the pro-democracy work that I do, the possibility of being sent to prison at any time doesn't actually scare me too much. If it did, I wouldn't have kept on doing this kind of work for 19 years. What I'm afraid of is the way this can affect your family, the major problems it can cause them psychologically and in many other ways," he said. "The way I see it, people like me live in two prisons in China. You come out of the small, fenced-in prison, only to enter the bigger, fence-less prison of society. My phone, my computer, my whereabouts and so on are all monitored by the Chinese Public Security Bureau. For

Demonstrators protesting in Hong Kong after Liu was sent to a labor camp in October 1996 for his involvement in the Tiananmen Square protests and speaking out against the government.

myself, I firmly believe in the value of what I'm doing and I'm prepared to face the risks. But there are many times when it doesn't just affect you, there's also your wife, your parents, and other family members."

In May 1995 Liu was taken into custody for petitioning the government to initiate political reforms and reassess its response to the Tiananmen Square protests. Authorities held him under residential surveillance (house arrest) before arresting him in October 1996 for questioning the merits of China's single-party political system, criticizing China's policy toward Taiwan, and calling for a dialogue between the Chinese government and the Dalai Lama of Tibet. Liu was sentenced to three years in a reeducation-through-labor camp for "disturbing public order" through his statements. A labor camp of this type usually combines prison, back-breaking hard work, and political education, or an effort to force the person to change his beliefs, often used for political or religious prisoners.

In 1999, Liu was released from the labor camp. At the turn of the millennium, he continued to write articles on political reform in his country, and he published compilations of political criticism and poetry in Taiwan and Hong Kong. He also petitioned for freedom of expression and the release of prisoners. In addition, he sought compensation for the families of victims of the June 4th Massacre through his work with the Tiananmen Mothers, a support group formed by parents of students killed in the 1989 protests. In 2001 Liu established an Internet connection in his home, using this tool to distribute his writings. "The Internet is God's present to China," he said. "It is the best tool for the Chinese people ... to cast off slavery and strive for freedom." In 2004, however, authorities cut his phone line and Internet connection when he released an essay criticizing the government's use of "subversion" charges to silence authors and activists. He was detained overnight and thereafter subjected to regular police surveillance. Many saw this as a government crackdown on outspoken intellectuals.

From 2003 to 2007 Liu served as president of the Independent Chinese PEN Center, an association of independent writers. The organization's mission is to defend freedom of expression, which in other countries is a basic civil right. The group provides assistance to writers who are threatened, harassed, and convicted of crimes on account of their words. PEN is a worldwide association affiliated with the United Nations that works on behalf of authors who are persecuted for their opinions.

"Charter 08"

In 2008, Liu co-authored a manifesto entitled "Charter 08." This text was modeled after the Czech document "Charter 77," which called for political change in communist Czechoslovakia. At that time Czechoslovakia was one of many eastern European nations that were part of the Soviet bloc, under the control of the communist Soviet Union (USSR). "Charter 77" contributed to the downfall of the government in Czechoslovakia and the breakup of the Soviet bloc.

In preparing "Charter 08," the goal of the authors was to reach out to the Chinese people about a new direction for the country. "Charter 08" is a campaign for constitutional democracy that champions such basic individual rights as free speech, freedom of assembly, and freedom of religion. It also calls for an end to one-party rule and a new political system founded on the principles of democracy and human rights. The 4,000-word petition was originally signed by 303 intellectuals and has since been signed by more than 10,000 Chinese citizens from all walks of life, including political scientists, farmers, economists, artists, and even some government officials, revealing that the authors' views are shared by a broad cross-section of the Chinese public. "The Chinese people, who have endured human rights disasters and uncountable struggles across these same years," the manifesto states, "now include many who see clearly that freedom, equality, and human rights are universal values of humankind and that democracy and constitutional government are the fundamental framework for protecting these values."" Charter 08" was released on December 10, 2008, the 60th anniversary of the United Nations' adoption of the Universal Declaration of Human Rights, a document credited with inspiring the modern-day human rights movement. The Chinese government has since pulled "Charter 08" from the Internet. It was published in English in the *New York Review* on January 15, 2009.

On December 8, 2008, two days before "Charter 08" was formally released, police officers arrived at Liu's home with a warrant for his arrest. They stayed through the night to search the home and confiscated computers, books, and other personal belongings. "There were more than a dozen police," his wife, Liu Xia, told the *Los Angeles Times* by phone two days after his disappearance. "I am very frightened. Nobody can get in touch with him." Liu was sent to an undisclosed location in Beijing and held there for six months while authorities gathered evidence for his case. During his imprisonment, he didn't have access to a lawyer or writing materials. Nearly all of the original signatories of "Charter 08" were interrogated about his role in its preparation. In March 2009, when the police allowed Liu to meet with his wife, he revealed that he was being held in solitary confinement in a small windowless cell. Meanwhile, several prominent authors, scholars, lawyers, and human rights activists issued a letter to Hu Jintao, the president of China, calling for Liu's immediate release. Liu received the prestigious PEN/Barbara Goldsmith Freedom to Write Award in April 2009, while in prison.

Liu was officially arrested for "suspicion of inciting subversion of state power" on June 24, 2009, and was moved to the No. 1 Detention Center of Beijing City. The police turned over his case to the state prosecutor's office in December 2009; he faced charges for six articles he wrote on political reform over several years and his work on "Charter 08." His trial began on December 23, 2009. Several diplomats were in attendance, including ambassadors from the United States, Canada, Australia, and multiple European nations. Lu Xia, his wife, was forced to testify as a prosecution witness and could not attend the proceedings.

The short trial did not allow Liu to make his case. He pleaded not guilty, but he was not permitted a full defense during the two-hour trial. His counsel submitted a written statement arguing that he was denied the right of free speech enshrined in both international law and the Chinese constitution, which had been revised in 2004 to guarantee fundamental human rights. When Liu attempted to provide evidence in his own defense, the presiding judge interrupted him after 15 minutes for exceeding

Liu Xia, the wife of Liu Xiaobo, speaking to reporters in Beijing in December 2009 after he was sentenced to 11 years in prison for subversion for his work on the "Charter 08" manifesto calling for political reform.

the time limit. In his final statement, Liu spoke from the heart about his nonviolent beliefs. "I still want to tell the regime that deprives me of my freedom, I stand by the belief I expressed 20 years ago in my 'June Second Hunger Strike Declaration'—I have no enemies, and no hatred," he said. "None of the police who monitored, arrested, and interrogated me, the prosecutors who prosecuted me, or the judges who sentenced me, are my enemies.... For hatred is corrosive of a person's wisdom and conscience; the mentality of enmity can poison a nation's spirit, instigate brutal life and death struggles, destroy a society's tolerance and humanity, and block a nation's progress to freedom and democracy. I hope therefore to be able to transcend my personal vicissitudes in understanding the development of the state and changes in society, to counter the hostility of the regime with the best of intentions, and defuse hate with love."

For his role in organizing "Charter 08," Liu was found guilty of inciting subversion of state power on December 25, 2009. He was sentenced to 11 years in prison and two additional years without political rights, the longest sentence ever given for that charge. He released a statement after his sentencing. "For an intellectual thirsty for freedom in a dictatorial country, prison is the very first threshold," he observed. "Now I have stepped over the threshold, and freedom is near." A month later, his lawyers filed an appeal that concluded: "Liu Xiaobo is innocent, and any verdict that finds Liu Xiaobo guilty cannot withstand the trial of history." On February 11, 2010, the Beijing Municipal High People's Court rejected his appeal. On May 26, 2010, he was moved to Jinzhou Prison in Liaoning Province, about 300 miles northeast of his home in Beijing. His prison sentence expires on June 21, 2020.

Winning the Nobel Peace Prize

Upon learning of Liu's unexpectedly harsh sentence, human rights leaders around the globe came to his defense, urging his consideration for the Nobel Peace Prize. This honor, they argued, would not only recognize his valiant human rights efforts, but also inspire future rights activists in China and other nations. Furthermore, it would signal to China that the world is watching and intends to draw attention to the fundamental freedoms that the Chinese government denies its citizens.

On October 8, 2010, the Nobel Committee announced its selection of Liu as the 2010 Nobel Peace Prize winner for "his long and non-violent struggle for fundamental human rights in China.... Through the severe punishment meted out to him, Liu has become the foremost symbol of this wide-ranging struggle for human rights in China."

Liu was the first Chinese citizen to be awarded the prize and one of three to have received it while in prison. The announcement prompted strong reactions, both in China and abroad. The intellectual community was thrilled, viewing the prize as a turning point in the lengthy struggle for democracy in China. "The biggest benefit, in my opinion, would be that a prize for Liu Xiaobo would help millions of Chinese, both inside China and around the world, to see and feel more clearly that 'China' can be much more than the Chinese Communist Party," Professor Perry Link commented in *Time*. The Chinese government, on the other hand, was outraged. Foreign ministry spokesman Ma Zhaoxu responded: "To give the Peace Prize to such a person is completely contrary to the purpose of the award and a blasphemy of the Peace Prize."

Following the Nobel announcement, China launched an aggressive effort to characterize the award as an "obscenity." It claimed the prize should not be granted to a man considered both criminal and subversive. China viewed the award as a Western plot to undermine the Chinese Communist Party and pressured the international community to boycott the ceremony, convincing 19 ambassadors to decline the invitation. It also criticized the

Thorbjørn Jagland, chair of the Nobel Committee, at the Nobel Peace Prize ceremony in Oslo, Norway, December 2011. The empty chair, which holds the Nobel diploma and medal, symbolizes Liu's absence due to China's repressive policies.

Nobel committee for interfering with internal Chinese affairs and humiliating the country on the international stage. Nobel chairman Thorbjørn Jagland responded to these charges in a *New York Times* editorial."Liu's imprisonment is clear proof that China's criminal law is not in line with its Constitution," Jagland argued. "Governments are obliged to ensure the right to free expression—even if the speaker advocates a different social system. These are rights that the Nobel committee has long upheld by honoring those who struggle to protect them with the Peace Prize, including ... Rev. Dr. Martin Luther King Jr. for his fight for civil rights in the United States."

Inside China, authorities prevented Liu's supporters from leaving the country before the ceremony. Police placed some people—including his wife—under house arrest or surveillance. Chinese police wanted to prevent news of Liu's win from spreading to the citizens of China, so cyber police blocked access to news coverage of the Nobel Prize and barred Internet searches on his name. Additionally, Chinese journalists were instructed to report only on the basis of the official government press release. The government-owned *China Daily,* for example, labeled the award "a provocation" and "a Western plot to contain a rising China." To counter the Nobel Peace Prize, China created its own honor, the Confucius Peace Prize, which it awarded to former Taiwan vice-president Lien Chan the day before the official Nobel ceremony. Although Chinese law permits one family visit per month to prisoners, the government reportedly has blocked visits to Liu since shortly after the Nobel announcement. Upon visiting him in October, however, his wife reported that when he learned he was the recipient of the Nobel Peace Prize, he wept and dedicated it to the "Tiananmen martyrs."

On December 10, 2010, Liu was recognized at the Nobel Peace Prize ceremony in Oslo, Norway. An empty chair marked his absence, symbolizing China's policies to isolate and repress dissidents. The last time a detained recipient of the prize was unrepresented at the awards gala was in 1935 when Nazi Germany prevented pacifist Carl von Ossietzky from attending. "We regret that the laureate is not present here today," Jagland stated in his presentation speech. "He is in isolation in a prison in northeast China. Nor can the laureate's wife, Liu Xia, or his closest relatives be here with us. No medal or diploma will therefore be presented here today. This fact alone shows that the award was necessary and appropriate." The presentation ceremony also included a complete reading of Liu's "I Have No Enemies" speech, the final statement Liu had prepared for his 2009 trial but was not permitted to present to the court in its entirety. President Barack Obama, the 2009 Nobel Peace Prize laureate, issued a statement on the day of the ceremony. "Liu reminds us that human dignity also depends upon the advance of democracy, open society, and the rule of law," Obama emphasized. "The values he espouses are universal, his struggle is peaceful, and he should be released as soon as possible."

"

Liu has always insisted on nonviolence and rationality in his thoughts and actions, as reflected in his final statement to the Beijing court before serving his prison sentence. "What I demanded of myself was this: whether as a person or as a writer, I would lead a life of honesty, responsibility, and dignity.... Hatred can rot away at a person's intelligence and conscience."

"

Despite the setbacks he has suffered as an activist over the past two decades, Liu has maintained that democratic change is inevitable in China.

"I firmly believe that China's political progress will not stop, and I, filled with optimism, look forward to the advent of a future free China," he said. "For there is no force that can put an end to the human quest for freedom, and China will in the end become a nation ruled by law, where human rights reign supreme." The international community has continued to support his cause, organizing protests on his behalf. Activists in Hong Kong marked the first anniversary of his conviction with a march outside the Chinese embassy, demonstrating Liu's contention that "the driving force for positive change within the Chinese political system does not come from the top, it comes from ordinary people." Harvard University Press plans to publish the first English-language compilation of his work in 2012.

MARRIAGE AND FAMILY

Liu married the poet and photographer Liu Xia in a modest ceremony in early 1996, just before he was sentenced to three years in a reeducation-through-labor camp. They were unable to legally document the marriage at first because Liu's household registration was in a different municipality. "Right after that he was put into a labor camp," Liu Xia told the *Observer*. "When I said I was his wife they would ask for the marriage certificate. So I couldn't see him for 18 months." In spite of these challenges, Liu Xia looks back on the experience with fondness. "I was very happy because once we were officially married I could visit him," she said. Liu and Liu Xia were both previously married. They initially met in college in 1982 and maintained a friendship based on their mutual love of poetry. They remained acquaintances until the 1990s when, following their divorces, they became a couple. "At the very beginning, we fell in love because of literature; he always liked my writing. And my cooking," Liu Xia stated in the *Observer*. With her husband behind bars, she misses the simple, everyday moments they shared together. "It's daily life I miss most; going to the market to shop for food and asking him what he would like. Just things like that," she said.

After Liu Xia met with her husband in prison to notify him of the 2010 Nobel honor, she was placed under house arrest in Beijing. This imprisonment has prompted condemnation by the international community since she has not been accused of a crime. In response to American criticism of her treatment by the Chinese government, authorities allowed her to eat a meal with her elderly parents in January 2011 while President Hu Jintao was visiting the United States. She is unable to communicate via telephone or the Internet and is under constant surveillance. Liu has described his wife as "a woman with a very strong sense of justice and responsibility." "She understands why I do this work," he added, "despite the fact it means she gets followed by the police."

Protestors continue to support Liu, as in this demonstration in Hong Kong in January 2011. The poster at right shows Liu with his wife in happier times.

Before being sent to prison to serve his 11-year sentence, Liu issued a public statement in which he expressed, through poetry, his enduring love for his wife."Your love is the sunlight that leaps over high walls and penetrates the iron bars of my prison window, stroking every inch of my skin, warming every cell of my body, allowing me to always keep peace, openness, and brightness in my heart, and filling every minute of my time in prison with meaning."

HOBBIES AND OTHER INTERESTS

Those close to Liu have cited his steadfast dedication to writing as one of his defining characteristics. They have described him as bookish, multilayered, and independent-minded, and they have identified his desire for complete freedom of expression as that which led him to political activism. "Actually he is less of a political figure to me than a passionate poet," explained one of his oldest friends, Liao Yiwu, in the *Guardian*. Liu still enjoys writing poems, according to his wife. Even when the prison warden took away his pen and paper, he continued to compose poetry and commit it to memory. He is fond of the writings of Franz Kafka and Fyodor Dostoevsky.

In prison, Liu reportedly shares a cell with five other inmates, has access to books published in China, and is allowed rare visits from his wife. For exercise, he runs for an hour a day. Despite his incarceration, he has remained remarkably optimistic, stressing ways in which conditions in the prison have improved. Friends have described him as being very courteous to others. He has always insisted on nonviolence and rationality in his thoughts and actions, as reflected in his final statement to the Beijing court before serving his prison sentence."What I demanded of myself was this: whether as a person or as a writer, I would lead a life of honesty, responsibility, and dignity.... Hatred can rot away at a person's intelligence and conscience."

SELECTED WRITINGS

Criticism of the Choice: Dialogues with Li Zehou, 1987 (nonfiction)
Aesthetic and Human Freedom, 1988 (doctoral thesis)
The Fog of Metaphysics, 1989 (nonfiction)
"The June 2nd Hunger Strike Declaration,"1989 (essay)
The Monologues of a Doomsday's Survivor, 1992 (memoir)
A Nation That Lies to Conscience, 2000 (political criticism)
Selection of Poems by Liu Xiaobo and Liu Xia, 2000 (poetry)
Future of Free China Exists in Civil Society, 2005 (political criticism)
Single-Blade Poisonous Sword: Criticism of Chinese Nationalism, 2005 (political criticism)
"The Internet Is God's Present to China,"2006 (essay)
"Authoritarianism in the Light of the Olympic Flame,"2008 (essay)
"I Have No Enemies: My Final Statement,"2009 (speech)

HONORS AND AWARDS

Hellman-Hammett Grant (Human Rights Watch): 1990,1996
Fondation de France Prize (Reporters without Borders): 2004, for defending freedom of the press
Hong Kong Human Rights Press Award (Hong Kong Journalists Association): 2004, 2005, 2006
Homo Homini Award (People in Need): 2008
PEN/Barbara Goldsmith Freedom to Write Award (PEN American Center): 2009
Alison Des Forges Award for Extraordinary Activism (Human Rights Watch): 2010
Hermann Kesten Award (PEN German Center): 2010
Nobel Peace Prize: 2010

FURTHER READING

Books

Encyclopedia of Modern China, 2009

Periodicals

Los Angeles Times, Dec. 10, 2008, p.A8; Dec. 11, 2010, p.A1
New York Review of Books, Jan. 15, 2009, p.54; May 28, 2009, p.45; Nov. 11, 2010, p.7
New York Times, Oct. 23, 2010, p.A21; Dec. 7, 2010, p.A6; Dec. 10, 2010, p.A1
Time, Oct. 25, 2010, p.1
Washington Post, Dec. 11, 2008, p.A18; Jan. 30, 2009, p.A18

Online Articles

http://www.bbc.co.uk
(BBC News,"Liu Xiaobo: 20 Years of Activism," Dec. 9, 2010)
http://www.earthtimes.org
(Earth Times,"Interview: Bio Author; Liu Xiaobo Is an Intellectual, Not a Leader," Dec. 8, 2010)
http://www.foreignpolicy.com
(Foreign Policy,"Why I'm Going to Oslo," Dec. 9, 2010)
http://www.hrw.org
(Human Rights Watch,"China: Retaliation for Signatories of Rights Charter," Dec. 10, 2008; "China: Q and A on Nobel Peace Prize Winner Liu Xiaobo," Oct. 8, 2010)
http://www.latimes.com
(Los Angeles Times,"Nobel Peace Prize Winner Liu Xiaobo: Inside the Heart of a Gentle 'Subversive,'" Oct. 9, 2010)
http://www.nybooks.com
(New York Review of Books: NYRblog,"The Trial of Liu Xiaobo: A Citizens' Manifesto and a Chinese Crackdown," Dec. 21, 2009; "What Beijing Fears Most," Jan. 25, 2010; "Jailed for Words: Nobel Laureate Liu Xiaobo," Oct. 11, 2010; "'A Turning Point in the Long Struggle': Chinese Citizens Defend Liu Xiaobo," Oct. 18, 2010; "At the Nobel Ceremony: Liu Xiaobo's Empty Chair," Dec. 13, 2010)
http://topics.nytimes.com
(New York Times,"Liu Xiaobo," multiple articles, various dates)
http://www.newsweek.com
(Newsweek,"All Eyes on the Prize," Oct. 8, 2010)
http://www.guardian.co.uk
(Observer,"My Dear Husband Liu Xiaobo, the Writer China Has Put Behind Bars," Feb. 28, 2010; Guardian,"Liu Xiaobo's Wife Under House Arrest," Oct. 11, 2010)
http://www.time.com
(Time,"Chinese Dissident Liu Xiaobo Wins Nobel Peace Prize," Oct. 8, 2010)

ADDRESS

Liu Xiaobo
c/o Larry Siems
Freedom to Write and International Programs Director
PEN American Center
588 Broadway, Suite 303
New York, NY 10012

WORLD WIDE WEB SITES

http://www.chinesepen.org/english
http://hrw.org
http://nobelprize.org
http://www.pen.org/china
http://www.charter08.eu

Monica Lozano 1956-

American Newspaper Publisher
Chief Executive Officer of *La Opinión,* the Largest Spanish-Language Daily Newspaper in the U.S., and ImpreMedia, the Largest Spanish-Language News Company in the U.S.

BIRTH

Monica Cecilia Lozano was born on July 21, 1956, in Los Angeles, California. Her mother, Marta Navarro Lozano, was a homemaker. Her father, Ignacio E. Lozano Jr., was the publisher of *La Opinión,* a Spanish-language newspaper. *La*

Opinión was founded in 1926 by his father (Lozano's grandfather), Ignacio E. Lozano Sr. Monica Lozano is the third of four children. She has an older sister, Leticia; an older brother, José; and a younger brother, Francisco.

YOUTH

Lozano grew up in Newport Beach, California. All of her grandparents came to the U.S. from Mexico, and her parents were the first generation born in the U.S. They emphasized the importance of the family's Mexican heritage and made sure that Lozano and her brothers and sister learned about Mexican culture. "We were always taught to really respect and enjoy and value our cultural background and never to forget," she explained."We weren't allowed to speak English at home. We just literally were not allowed to speak English at home.... Most parents at that time wanted their kids to succeed by not speaking Spanish. My parents wanted us to learn English, but were adamant that we not forget Spanish and where we came from and our roots and all of that. It was really important to them."

> *"We were always taught to really respect and enjoy and value our cultural background and never to forget," Lozano explained. "Most parents at that time wanted their kids to succeed by not speaking Spanish. My parents wanted us to learn English, but were adamant that we not forget Spanish and where we came from and our roots and all of that. It was really important to them."*

As a child, Lozano learned more about Mexican culture each summer when she visited her extended family in Mexico City. "We were sent to Mexico every year," she recalled. "We would spend our summers in Mexico with my grandmother and all of our cousins. We were the only ones that lived here in the States, so it was really important to maintain the family together." Lozano enjoyed spending time in Mexico. "I liked it much more than I liked it up here," she reminisced. "I had a lot of friends and we had a great life. There's something missing here in the U.S. that you get in a place like Mexico, where family really means family, and extended family really is extended family. You interact as part of a larger group. Here everything is so individualized that if you're going to succeed, you do it on your own, and you advance on your own. People are much more competitive. I just don't think I ever really liked it as much as I like the other."

A 1940 photo of a Los Angeles couple reading the newspaper founded by Lozano's grandfather, La Opinión, *which became the largest Spanish-language daily newspaper in the U.S.*

As she got older, Lozano began to realize that she lived in two different worlds—one with her parents in the U.S. and one with her extended family in Mexico. She began to struggle with her identity as she looked for a place to fit in. "You go through periods where you wonder who you really are," she mused. "You go to Mexico and you know you're not Mexican.... You come here and you think, well, this isn't quite right either. It's a phenomenon that I think happens to a lot of Chicano kids that are second or third generation, where you have a real desire to maintain your cultural heritage, but it's not quite one thing or the other."

Lozano also began to learn about Mexico's political environment at a very young age. Her grandfather, Ignacio E. Lozano Sr., had died before she was born, but his story was an important part of the family history. "My grandfather was a journalist, a famous, well-respected, well-known writer from Northern Mexico, who also left during the [Mexican] revolution, mostly because he was writing things against the government and was more sympathetic to the need for change in Mexico." The Mexican Revolution began in 1910, with violent civil war and political unrest that continued for many years. The worst of the revolution ended in 1920, although occasional fighting continued until 1929. During this time, those who spoke out against the Mexican government were forced either to leave the country or risk being jailed or killed for their opinions. Many Mexican citizens fled to the U.S. during these years.

After arriving in San Antonio, Texas, Ignacio E. Lozano Sr. created *El Diario La Prensa* in 1913. This was the first of the Spanish-language newspapers that would become his family's business for generations to come. His goal was to be the voice of the Mexican immigrant community in the U.S. In 1926, he moved to Los Angeles and founded the newspaper *La Opinión*. By this time, the Mexican government had banned him from returning to Mexico. "He wasn't allowed to go back to Mexico because of his political writings," Monica Lozano explained. "It wasn't that he was publishing in Mexico stuff they didn't want; they didn't like what he was publishing up here in the United States. He found that it was the only place where he could actually say what he needed to say."

For Monica Lozano, her grandfather's legacy meant that she grew up surrounded by family members and others who were passionate about Mexican culture, Mexico's future, and keeping Mexican immigrants informed about important issues in the U.S. and in Mexico that affected their lives. Her father, older brother, and older sister all worked at *La Opinión*. Her father was also active in U.S. politics, and served as the U.S. ambassador to El Salvador for one year. During that year, Lozano lived in El Salvador with her parents and her younger brother.

EDUCATION

For her first two years of high school, Lozano attended Marywood, a Catholic girls' school in the city of Orange, California. For her third and fourth years of high school, she attended Santa Catalina School, a Catholic girls' boarding school in Monterey, California. She graduated from high school in 1974.

After high school, Lozano enrolled in the University of Oregon. She was not interested in joining the family newspaper business at that time. Instead, she wanted to pursue a career in social work or education. At the University of Oregon, she studied sociology and political science. She also worked at the Women's Press newspaper. Lozano left the university in 1976 without graduating.

After leaving college, Lozano and a friend traveled extensively throughout Latin America. "The two of us literally started in northern Mexico and made it all the way down to the very tip of South America. When I came back from that trip, I moved to San Francisco and never went back to the university, unfortunately. I would say unfortunately because I think it was a mistake not to have at some point gone back."

While Lozano never returned to the University of Oregon or completed her bachelor's degree, she did enroll in classes at San Francisco City College, a two-year community college, and earned a degree in printing technology in 1981.

> *"You go through periods where you wonder who you really are," Lozano mused. "You go to Mexico and you know you're not Mexican.... You come here and you think, well, this isn't quite right either. It's a phenomenon that I think happens to a lot of Chicano kids that are second or third generation, where you have a real desire to maintain your cultural heritage, but it's not quite one thing or the other."*

CAREER HIGHLIGHTS

Over the course of her career, Lozano has become known as one of the most influential women in U.S. journalism. After working for many years at *La Opinión,* she eventually became the head of the ImpreMedia publishing company, which includes *La Opinión* as well as many other Spanish-language and Spanish-English publications and web sites. Though she inherited a successful, established publishing company when she took over leadership of ImpreMedia, Lozano herself is credited with expanding the family business by creating new publications and web sites. She has often commented that "you can't separate my success from my family," but her success was not automatically guaranteed. Her achievements came only as a result of her own hard work, both at ImpreMedia and during the earlier years she spent deciding whether she wanted to work in the family business at all.

Starting Out

Lozano grew up knowing that newspapers were her family's business. Her grandfather, Ignacio E. Lozano Sr., founded the newspapers; her father, Ignacio E. Lozano Jr., ran them after her grandfather's death; her brother, José Lozano, took over after her father retired; and her sister, Leticia Lozano, worked there as well. The whole family was deeply committed to continuing the work begun by Ignacio E. Lozano Sr. Monica Lozano knew that the newspapers were important, but she wasn't sure that the family business was the right career for her. "I liked *La Opinión* and I liked the idea of what *La Opinión* was doing, but I just wasn't quite convinced that this was going to be my life. I didn't want to follow in anybody's footsteps."

In 1977, after leaving college, Lozano decided to move to San Francisco, though she didn't know anyone there. She got a job at a large printing company and learned to operate a printing press. She also worked for various community newspapers. During this time, she realized that she wanted to help her community. In order to do that, she would need to use all of her skills including her knowledge of newspapers. Lozano became more interested in the newspaper publishing business and decided to learn everything she could about running a paper, including taking classes in printing technology at San Francisco City College.

Although she had set out to make her own way in the world, Lozano ended up back where she started—in the newspaper business. "I guess there is such a thing as having ink in your veins," she observed. In 1985, she moved back to Los Angeles and began working for *La Opinión*.

Working at *La Opinión*

In 1985, Lozano joined the staff of *La Opinión* as a managing editor. During this time, it was still unusual for women to work as journalists. And it was even more unusual for a woman to be in a management position. "I couldn't have done it without my family," she acknowledged. "Literally, I wouldn't be here without the support and the confidence of my family." Lozano had no real experience working for a large daily newspaper but explained that "they really opened the doors and asked me to come in, knowing full well that I didn't have sort of a traditional background and experience that you would find in most managing editors."

In addition to learning the responsibilities of her new job, Lozano also had to learn how to get along in a work environment that was not always friendly to women. In describing one of her early experiences at the newspaper, "I came in not just as the daughter of the owner, but one of the first women in the newsroom," she recalled. "And absolutely, those were the days when, you know, men had pictures of women all over their cubicles ... it was just, you know, an entirely different atmosphere and attitude. And the women in the newsroom, when I came in—because I came in, in the position as managing editor—the women in the newsroom immediately asked for a meeting ... and lo and behold, they felt harassed and uncomfortable in that environment. But it wasn't until there was a woman in the leadership position that they felt that they actually had an outlet where

Lozano in the newsroom of La Opinión, *celebrating with staff members after announcing that the newspaper had won a major journalism award.*

their voice not only would be heard, but we actually could do something about changing the culture in that newsroom.... One of the first things that I did was issue memos saying that there will not be any more photographs and there will not be any more whistling.... I mean, really having to say some of the most basic things about how people should treat each other in a work environment."

Lozano's other duties as managing editor included full responsibility for all of the newspaper's special supplements and public service work. She immediately began working on creating newspaper inserts that focused on topics of particular importance or interest to readers. Her first project of this kind focused on the Immigration Reform and Control Act, a major immigration law that passed in 1986. "*La Opinión* knew that it had to do an extraordinary job in informing the community about it. It was a possibility for millions of people to become legalized. They had opened the door and said, 'If you're illegal right now, you've got a couple of years to become legal, to come out of the shadows.' So we did a lot of work on this particular law. We ended up winning awards."

Another of Lozano's big projects in 1986 was the publication of a newspaper insert that focused on the growing threat of the AIDS virus within the

Hispanic community. In 1988, this special publication received an advocacy award from the Hispanic Coalition of AIDS as a life-saving, educational contribution to the community. The AIDS insert also received an award from the Inter-American Press Association.

Moving Up the Corporate Ladder

Lozano was named associate publisher of *La Opinión* in 1990. In this position, she continued to create new publications that contributed to the growth of the newspaper's circulation. She expanded the paper's focus beyond the Mexican immigrant community, to include the more diverse community of native speakers of Spanish from other parts of the world. Lozano also formed partnerships with other organizations in order to better inform the community about health, immigration, education, and other important issues. Under her leadership, *La Opinión* grew to become the largest and most influential Spanish-language publication in the U.S.

In the following years, Lozano continued to move up the corporate ladder. In 2000 she was named president and chief operating officer of *La Opinión* as well as vice president of its parent company, Lozano Communications. In 2004 she became publisher and chief executive officer of *La Opinión,* the top position at the paper.

Also in 2004, ImpreMedia was formed as the parent company of a range of publications, including *El Diario La Prensa,* the oldest Spanish-language daily newspaper in the U.S., founded in 1913 by Lozano's grandfather; and *La Opinión,* the largest Spanish-language daily newspaper in the U.S., founded in 1926 also by Lozano's grandfather. The goal of the new company was to create a national group of Latino media. ImpreMedia provides news and information online and in print format, with daily and weekly newspapers, monthly magazines, and web sites. In addition to *La Opinión* and *El Diario La Prensa,* national publications include the Spanish-language entertainment weekly *La Vibra* and the Spanish-English monthly magazine *Vista*. ImpreMedia also publishes local Spanish-language newspapers, including *El Mensajero* in San Francisco, *La Prensa* in central Florida, and *La Raza* in Chicago. The web site Impre.com has grown to be one of the top Spanish-language news sites in the U.S.

When ImpreMedia was created in 2004, Lozano was named senior vice president, overseeing the company's publishing group. In 2010, she became the company's chief executive officer. In that position she now oversees a collection of 27 Spanish-language and Spanish-English newspapers, magazines, and web sites.

Lozano in 2004, at a major moment in her career: her ascension to senior vice president of the new company ImpreMedia and simultaneously to publisher and CEO of La Opinión.

In addition to running a large publishing company, Lozano has served on the board of directors for major U.S. corporations, including Bank of America and the Walt Disney Company. She has also served on the board of directors for non-profit groups, including the California Health Care Foundation, the National Council of La Raza, and the Los Angeles County Museum of Art. She has received honorary degrees from several universities as well as a number of prestigious awards from national media, business, and community groups. In 2009, Lozano was named as a member of President Barack Obama's Economic Recovery Advisory Board, a group of business leaders who help the President decide how best to respond to the U.S. economic crisis.

Changing Perceptions

One of Lozano's lifelong goals has been to help people understand the importance and value of Spanish-language publications for readers in the U.S. She acknowledges that many people believe Spanish-language newspapers and magazines encourage immigrants to remain isolated and outside of American culture. But Lozano believes that is simply not true. "The way that we approach our content, is that we, in fact, are a tool for integration.... So, actually, the newspaper is used not as a way of keeping kids monolingual, but a way of teaching literacy that then allows them to transfer over to English. So it's really a tool towards learning English, and most people I don't think understand that."

Lozano feels strongly about the importance of educating readers, especially those who primarily speak Spanish. "As a group, we can have power if we are informed and educated.... I really believe in what I am doing," she explained. "If we were not to exist, you would have millions of people in L.A. who are uninformed and unable to participate. And which is worse? I think it's better for us to exist and to allow people, one, to continue their education through reading newspapers like ours, to be informed, to be able to make decisions, to participate in decision-making processes. We don't advocate staying in the Spanish language completely. We understand that it's important if you're going to be in this country and you're going to succeed and you're going to thrive and survive, you have to speak English, and we say that directly."

"I carry on a tradition that was established by my grandfather," Lozano said. "That mission was to serve the community, which, in that case, was primarily an immigrant population, primarily from Mexico, that needed a source of information about their issues and reflected their reality. Our community today is much more diverse and our scope of influence is much broader, but the core value stays intact."

Lozano is determined to change the way that Spanish-speaking immigrants are viewed by others. "The worst of it is to hear people say, 'Hispanics don't read.' It's a fallacy. It's absolutely false. I don't know where that came from ... because you can go into any Latin American country and newspapers are so prevalent. I mean, in Mexico City there's over 40 daily newspapers. Everybody reads." Lozano explained that this particular misconception is "one of the reasons why we've made the decision that we have to go bilingual. So for example, all of our editorials are published bilingually because if we have a statement, we want to make sure that it reaches the broadest audience possible."

A Family Legacy

Lozano may not have known right away that the newspaper business would become her life's work, but she is now committed to carrying on the family tradition. "I really love what I'm doing and think I'm good at it and

Lozano working at the White House on the Economic Recovery Advisory Board, alongside (from left) Mark T. Gallogly, Paul Volcker, President Barack Obama, and John Doerr.

think that the paper is doing something that's really valuable," Lozano said. "I know I carry on a tradition that was established by my grandfather.... That mission was to serve the community, which, in that case, was primarily an immigrant population, primarily from Mexico, that needed a source of information about their issues and reflected their reality. Our community today is much more diverse and our scope of influence is much broader, but the core value stays intact."

Lozano's success has come from a combination of unique opportunities and her own dedication to community education and service. "I think I was very fortunate that the opportunity was available to me; clearly something like this is available to only a handful of people. But the fact that I've taken such advantage of it speaks more to me as an individual than the fact that it's just there," Lozano said. "If you are going to do it, you should be prepared to go all the way.

"I always say, one, you know, follow your passion and do what it is that you are most compelled to do, because life is too short to not do things that you absolutely love doing. And the other thing is around both perseverance and also determination.... You don't start at the top. You work your way up. And, you know, constantly just demanding more of yourself, making sure that you're working at the very highest level, and making sure that your reputation is intact as you move along the path of life. Because at the end of the day, that's what you carry with you and that's what people will remember about you. So just make sure, along the way, that you're working hard. When people turn around and say, you know, that woman is really good; I can depend on her—that's what you want them to say about you. You know, strong values: highly ethical, smart decision-making, you know, philosophy—that's what's important."

MARRIAGE AND FAMILY

Lozano married Marcelo Centanino in 1986. The couple had two children, Santiago, born in 1987, and Gabriela, born in 1989. The marriage ended in divorce. Lozano later married her second husband, David Ayala, a political scientist. They live in Los Angeles.

HONORS AND AWARDS

100 Most Influential Hispanic Women (*Hispanic Business*): 1987, 1992
Central American Refugee Center Award: 1988, for contribution to immigrant rights
Outstanding Woman of the Year Award (Mexican American Opportunities Foundation): 1989
Distinction in Media Excellence Award (March of Dimes): 1992, for special publication on pre-natal care
National Organization for Women Legal Defense and Education Fund Award (National Organization for Women): 1992
Hubert H. Humphrey Civil Rights Award (Leadership Conference on Civil Rights): 2006
Marketing y Medios Print Media All-Star of the Year (*Adweek*): 2007
Medallion of Excellence for Leadership and Community Service (Congressional Hispanic Caucus Institute): 2007
PODER-BCG Business Awards (*PODER* magazine and the Boston Consulting Group): 2008, for Excellence in Media
Best Latinos in Business (*Hispanic Magazine*): 2009

FURTHER READING

Books

Ruíz Vicki, and Virginia Sánchez Korrol. *Latinas in the United States: A Historical Encyclopedia,* Vol. 1, 2006

Periodicals

Hispanic Business, Apr. 2004, p.44
Los Angeles Times, May 26, 2010

Online Articles

http://findarticles.com/p/articles/mi_m0PCH/is_1_6/ai_n13661865/
(B Net, CBS Business Network,"Monica Lozano,"Feb-Mar. 2005)
http://www.npr.org
(NPR.org,"Latina Publishing Magnate Shares Wisdom from the Trade," July 28, 2010)
http://www.wpcf.org/oralhistory/loz.html
(Washington Press Club Foundation,"Interviews with Monica Lozano," 1993-1994)

ADDRESS

Monica Lozano
ImpreMedia
700 South Flower Street
Los Angeles, CA 90017

WORLD WIDE WEB SITE

http://www.impremedia.com

Jane Lubchenco 1947-

American Marine Ecologist and Environmental Scientist

First Woman to Serve as Administrator of the U.S. National Oceanic and Atmospheric Administration (NOAA)

BIRTH

Jane Lubchenco (pronounced loob-CHEN-ko) was born on December 4, 1947, in Denver, Colorado. Both of her parents were doctors: her father was a surgeon, and her mother was a pediatrician. Lubchenco has five younger sisters.

YOUTH

As a child growing up in Denver, Lubchenco enjoyed being outdoors. Family vacations were often spent camping and hiking in the Rocky Mountains. Lubchenco developed an early love of nature, particularly any opportunity to be in the water. She remembers sharing this enthusiasm with her sisters. "My five sisters and I were part fish," she recalled. "We'd seek water anywhere—lakes and rivers in Colorado, the ocean on family trips to Southern California. I remember my first ocean swim, the saltiness of it." Fishing was another one of her favorite pastimes. "I have fond memories of trout fishing with my father in Colorado mountain lakes and streams and, as a high school student, going salmon fishing with him on charter boats in Oregon and Washington."

"As a Colorado native, I was astounded to discover a wealth of life in oceans. It was a world filled with incredible diversity of forms and functions, from sea stars to lobsters to exotic small creatures.... I had never really appreciated until that summer just the immense diversity and the incredible beauty and the exotic nature of all the different species in the oceans."

— ” —

EDUCATION

Lubchenco's interest in nature and the environment led her to study biology at Colorado College. As part of her coursework, she participated in a summer program at the Marine Biological Laboratory in Woods Hole, Massachusetts. The Marine Biological Lab is an internationally known scientific research facility located just off the Atlantic Ocean on the southwestern tip of Cape Cod.

Lubchenco had visited the ocean before, but working at the Marine Biological Lab was her first opportunity to study ocean ecology. (Ecology is a branch of biology that focuses on studying communities of plants and animals and their relationship to their surroundings.) "As a Colorado native, I was astounded to discover a wealth of life in oceans. It was a world filled with incredible diversity of forms and functions, from sea stars to lobsters to exotic small creatures, many of whose daily rhythms were profoundly linked to the far away moon and its influence on the earth's tides." The experience made a great impact on Lubchenco. She explained, "I had never really appreciated until that summer just the immense diversity and the incredible beauty and the exotic nature of all the different species in the oceans."

Lubchenco earned a bachelor's degree in biology from Colorado College in 1969. She earned a master's degree in zoology from the University of Washington in 1971. (Zoology is a branch of biology that focuses on studying the unique characteristics of animals.) In 1975, Lubchenco completed her PhD (doctorate) in ecology at Harvard University. Her doctoral studies focused on the ecology of plants and animals that live in rocky coastal waters.

CAREER HIGHLIGHTS

Over the course of her long career, Lubchenco has become known for her deep understanding of ocean ecology. She is recognized as an expert in the relationship between oceans and climate change and the connection between the environment and human health and welfare. Her work is widely seen as both groundbreaking and extremely useful in furthering scientific understanding of oceans and marine life. She has traveled the world studying marine ecology in different areas, including the Arctic regions of Greenland and Alaska as well as the tropics of Central America. She has also studied sea life in the Mediterranean, Europe, China, New Zealand, coastal areas of North America, and many other places. She uses the results of her scientific research to educate people about the current conditions of the world's waterways and to make predictions about the future of oceans and sea life. Lubchenco is also known for her interest in creating practical solutions to problems like pollution and global warming. The Natural Resources Defense Council, an environmental protection group, called her "one of the best-known American voices for marine conservation."

Early in her career, Lubchenco balanced a number of different teaching and research positions. After earning her PhD in 1975, she became an assistant professor at Harvard. In 1978, she moved across the country to begin teaching marine biology at Oregon State University. Also in 1978, Lubchenco began working as a research associate with the Smithsonian Institution in Washington, DC, and as a science advisor for the Ocean Trust Foundation. During this time, her research focused primarily on evolutionary ecology (studying how plants and animals interact with the environment over time).

Understanding Climate Change

Through her research and work around the world, Lubchenco was able to see firsthand the damaging effects of human actions on oceans and marine life. She focused on evolutionary ecology, which compares current and previous environmental conditions and looks for differences between the

Lubchenco, a marine biologist, is shown working in the field.

past and present. By studying environmental changes over time, Lubchenco was one of the first scientists to show evidence that climate change was occurring. She observed and documented the significant environmental damage being done by global warming and pollution. Her studies exposed clear examples of the many ways in which humans have unintentionally caused harm to the environment.

As a result of her findings, Lubchenco realized that people needed to become better stewards of the earth's natural resources. Although she was publishing her studies within the scientific community, she wanted to bring her findings to a larger audience. She knew that further environmental damage could be prevented only through the involvement of government, industry, and the general public. Lubchenco set out to find ways to bring scientific information to the public in forms that would be easy for the average person to understand.

Lubchenco strongly believed that scientists have a responsibility to educate the public about research on important issues. "Science is more than just fascinating knowledge, it is also useful knowledge," she explained. "I believe passionately that science should inform our decisions." She saw a gap between the scientific community and the rest of the world, and she wanted to help bridge that gap. Lubchenco realized that scientific researchers were often unprepared to communicate well with non-scientists. To help scientists become better communicators, she founded the Leopold Leadership Program in 1998.

"

"Most Americans still believe that the oceans are so vast and bountiful that there is very little that we can do that would truly change them," Lubchenco commented. "The reality is that we are not just using oceans—we are using them up. If we truly want to be able to use them tomorrow, we have to do a better job of protecting them today."

"

The Leopold Leadership Program was designed to help environmental scientists bring their work to people outside the scientific and academic communities. Lubchenco's goal was to train researchers to talk to government leaders and the media, in the hope that science could inform public policy decisions and law-making. As she explained, "I am not suggesting that scientists should dictate what individuals or societies should do or not do. Rather, I emphasize that one of the most important roles of science is to inform, to provide information, so that decision-makers can take that information into consideration and understand the full ramifications of a course of action."

Teaching public communication skills to scientific researchers was a new idea at that time, and the Leopold Leadership Program was the first organization of its kind. "When we started the program, we were not at all sure that scientists, and the best scientists, would even apply to the program much less to be willing to invest two very intense weeks in learning new skills," Lubchenco recalled. "Much to our delight, and more importantly to the benefit of the nation, we have been overwhelmed by applications from the most outstanding scientists."

The Leopold Leadership Program has been successful in teaching scientists how to explain their work in ways that are both relevant and easy to understand. The program has been especially successful for topics related to global warming and climate change. Lubchenco sees these issues as particularly difficult for non-scientists to absorb. "Assessment of climate change is a good example of the problem that decision-makers face," she observed. "One hears conflicting opinions: on the one hand, 'global warming is happening,' on the other hand someone else says, 'oh no, that's not true.' It's very difficult for most folks to sort through all the conflicting opinions and complex evidence. In its zeal to be 'balanced,' the press often presents 'both sides' with equal credibility, despite the fact that the overwhelming majority of experts agree and are on one 'side.'"

In 2002, Lubchenco was honored for her work with the Leopold Leadership Program. She received the prestigious Heinz Award for the Environment. This award recognized her as one of the most respected and recognized ecologists in the country and praised her efforts to help scientists communicate more effectively. In presenting the award to Lubchenco, Heinz Family Philanthropies said, "She has shown that, while scientists should be excellent, pure and dispassionate, scientists should not sacrifice their right—and must not ignore their responsibility—to communicate their knowledge about how the earth is changing or to say what they believe will be the likely consequence of different policy options."

Moving into Government

By the mid-2000s, Lubchenco's reputation as an environmental expert was firmly in place, acknowledged by other scholars, academic institutions, and governmental agencies. Her experience had grown to include visiting professorships at universities in Chile, China, and New Zealand. She had become a member of the National Academy of Sciences, the American Philosophical Society, the American Academy of Arts and Sciences, the Royal Society, and

Lubchenco in a briefing for President Barack Obama in the situation room of the White House. Seated at the table (from left to right): Homeland Security secretary Janet Napolitano, National Incident commander Admiral Thad Allen, Environmental Protection Agency administrator Lisa P. Jackson, U.S. Coast Guard rear admiral Peter Neffenger, press secretary Robert Gibbs, interior secretary Ken Salazar, NOAA administrator Jane Lubchenco, energy secretary Steven Chu, and chief of staff Rahm Emanuel.

the Academy of Sciences for the Developing World, Europe, and Chile. She was a member of the board of directors for the National Science Board, the National Science Foundation, the Joint Oceans Commission Initiative, the Aspen Institute Arctic Commission, and the Council of Advisors for Google Ocean. She headed the Partnership for Interdisciplinary Studies of Coastal Oceans and was a scientific advisor to the U.S. Congress and Presidents George H.W. Bush, Bill Clinton, and George W. Bush. Lubchenco had become one of the most highly respected ecologists in the world.

Lubchenco's successful scientific career prompted President Barack Obama to nominate her for the position of administrator of the U.S. National Oceanic and Atmospheric Administration (NOAA) and U.S. under secretary of commerce for Oceans and Atmosphere. Congress confirmed her nomination in 2009, making Lubchenco the first woman to serve in this role.

NOAA's area of responsibility stretches from the ocean floor, to the upper reaches of the earth's atmosphere, and beyond to the surface of the sun. Its mission is to understand and predict changes in the earth's environment and to conserve and manage U.S. coastal and marine resources. NOAA protects, maintains, and restores the sustainability of U.S. oceans and the Great Lakes. NOAA is also the nation's primary source of information and research on oceans and the atmosphere, and it works to increase scientific understanding of climate change. The National Weather Service is part of NOAA and operates the nation's weather observation, forecasting, and severe weather early warning systems.

Lubchenco sees her new position as an extension of the work she started with the Leopold Leadership Program. "Being in this job has only reinforced the importance of communicating scientific information in a way that is understandable and relevant to the decisions being made, with concrete examples, and in as unequivocal a fashion as possible, while still remaining true to the nuances that are important," she remarked. "And I think all too many scientists assume that everybody knows what they know, and especially members of Congress, and members of the administration. And so it's critically important that more scientists become bilingual—able to speak the language of science, but also able to speak the language of lay people when talking to non-scientists."

In pursuit of her goal to make more environmental information available to the public, one of Lubchenco's first acts as the head of NOAA was to create the Climate Service. She described the Climate Service as a source of "trusted, timely, and accessible" climate information. "We are envisioning it as analogous to the National Weather Service," she said. "I believe it's an idea whose time has come." NOAA has enough information to make climate forecasts in the same way that the National Weather Service provides weather forecasts, according to Lubchenco. However, the Climate Service would be able to provide forecasts for a much longer future time frame. For example, "If you're building a wind farm, you would want to know not just where the winds have been good for the past 100 years, but where they're likely to be good the next 100 years," she explained. "So there are a number of new ways that climate is affecting our lives that if we had some reasonable forecasts for 20- to 30-year horizons, we could be doing a much better job of making decisions about land use, about water management, about crops, about a whole suite of different things."

Ocean "Dead Zones"

In addition to working on climate change, Lubchenco has also focused her work at NOAA on what she calls the "equally evil" problem of ocean acidification. Ocean acidification describes the result of excessive carbon diox-

NOAA was deeply involved in assessing the damage to natural resources after the 2010 BP oil spill in the Gulf of Mexico. Here, Lubchenco is shown on a survey off the coast of Mississippi taking samples of sea life.

ide in the air being absorbed by the ocean, resulting in a change to the chemical balance of the water. This process begins when pollution such as automobile exhaust creates more carbon dioxide in the air than can be removed by plants and trees. When carbon dioxide dissolves into the ocean, it produces an increase of hydrogen in the water. This in turn produces water that contains less oxygen, creating an aquatic environment that will not support sea life.

"We're changing the world in ways it's never been changed before, at faster rates and over larger scales, and we don't know the consequences. It's a massive experiment, and we don't know the outcome," Lubchenco claimed. "In the end, the decisions we make about the environment will be based on moral and ethical values. But those decisions will be much better decisions if they are in fact formed by the best possible science."

Low-oxygen water creates areas in the ocean known as "dead zones." Without enough oxygen, plants and sea creatures suffocate and die. As Lubchenco explained, "The oceans are indeed becoming more acidic, as a result of absorbing carbon dioxide from the atmosphere, and that acidity represents a very real threat to much of the life in oceans, ranging from the smallest microscopic plants, to coral reefs, to things that form shells—mussels, oysters, clams—but even things like lobsters and crabs. We've only begun to scratch the surface in terms of really understanding the full range of the impacts of ocean acidifications, and it also affects physiology, not just the making of shells and skeletons."

Lubchenco believes education is the first step in protecting the ocean from further acidification. "I think that oceans in general for many people are still out of sight, out of mind, and there is a lack of appreciation for how important the ocean is in the whole climate system, how important it is to people's everyday lives, and what the real risk is." Lubchenco hopes that NOAA can help to make more people aware of this unintended side effect of modern lifestyles. "When you think about the fact that half of Americans live in the coastal areas and the other half often goes there to play, we begin to appreciate the connectedness between the land and the ocean, and our lives and livelihoods and the environmental changes that are affecting the oceans and the land.

"Most Americans still believe that the oceans are so vast and bountiful that there is very little that we can do that would truly change them. The reality is that we are not just using oceans—we are using them up. If we truly want to be able to use them tomorrow, we have to do a better job of protecting them today," Lubchenco said. "The bottom line is, we're just dumping too many things into the ocean and we're taking too much out." For this reason, another of her main NOAA projects is the creation of marine reserves. A marine reserve is an aquatic version of the national parks and wilderness conservation areas that have been established on land. Marine reserves create "no take" areas in the ocean. In these areas, no fishing, mining, drilling, or dumping is allowed. Successful marine reserves have been maintained around the world for many years, but they are still relatively new in the U.S. "These fully protected marine reserves have been shown quite definitely to be extremely powerful in protecting habitat, in protecting biodiversity, and protecting the essential services provided by marine ecosystems," she argued. "And in some cases, they are also helping to replenish depleted fisheries. At present, far less than 1 percent of U.S. water is fully protected." Through NOAA, Lubchenco plans to expand the number of marine reserves that exist in U.S. waters.

Lubchenco believes marine reserves are one way to start reversing the damage done to the environment. "Because we are capable of understanding what we're doing, it's appropriate for us to take stock of these changes and to ask what other choices we have," she explained. "If you asked most people how they depend on nature, they will focus on the things that we get—the food, the fiber, medicines, genes. But most people are unaware of the fact that ecosystems also provide services.... For example, forests provide flood control. They absorb water. They keep the water from just gushing downslope and causing floods.... The services by and large are outside our economic valuation system. We don't buy and sell and trade them. They're just there. We've always taken them for granted."

Looking to the Future

As she has done throughout her career, Lubchenco continues to look to science to provide solutions for critical environmental problems. In her role as head of NOAA, she works to find practical ways to repair environmental damage and prevent further damage from being done. She prefers a balance of short- and long-term actions because she believes immediate changes provide people with a much-needed sense of confidence and hope for the future. "We're changing the world in ways it's never been changed before, at faster rates and over larger scales, and we don't know the consequences. It's a massive experiment, and we don't know the outcome,"

Lubchenco on an airboat tour of the Delta National Wildlife Refuge in Louisiana and other areas affected by the 2010 BP oil spill.

Lubchenco said."In the end, the decisions we make about the environment will be based on moral and ethical values. But those decisions will be much better decisions if they are in fact formed by the best possible science."

"I think that what most members of the public are interested in is ... will it affect me? Will it affect the things I care about? Can I do something about it?" But, she observed, "Nobody knows the definitive answers to these questions because we've never run this 'experiment' before. Human actions have inadvertently initiated a completely novel scenario. The real question is whether or not we wish to continue running this experiment."

MARRIAGE AND FAMILY

In 1971, Lubchenko married Bruce Menge, an ecologist and marine biology professor. They have two sons, Alexei, born in 1979, and Duncan, born in 1982.

HOBBIES AND OTHER INTERESTS

When she is not working, Lubchenco enjoys hiking, bird watching, traveling, dancing, and spending time with her family. She is interested in natural history and art and collecting ocean-inspired jewelry. Her favorite books include *Fragile Dominion* by Simon Levin, *Pine Island Paradox* by Kathleen Dean Moore, and *Arctic Dreams* by Barry Lopez. She loves being on or in the ocean and is happiest wading through mud and low tides, searching for marine life along the Pacific Ocean coastline.

HONORS AND AWARDS

Mercer Award (Ecological Society of America): 1979

Pew Scholar in Conservation and the Environment (Pew Charitable Trusts): 1992

MacArthur Fellowship (John D. and Catherine T. MacArthur Foundation): 1993

Heinz Award for the Environment (Heinz Family Philanthropies): 2002

Distinguished Service Award (Society for Conservation Biology): 2003

Nierenberg Award for Science in the Public Interest (Scripps Institution of Oceanography): 2003

Distinguished Scientist Award (American Institute of Biological Sciences): 2004

Environmental Law Institute Award: 2004

Public Understanding of Science and Technology Award (American Association for the Advancement of Science): 2005

Beijer Fellow of the Royal Swedish Academy of Sciences (Beijer Institute of Ecological Economics, Sweden): 2007

Zayed International Prize for the Environment (United Arab Emirates): 2008

Blue Planet Award: 2011, for substantial contributions to the understanding of biodiversity and marine ecology and clear demonstration to the world of the importance of the social responsibility of scientists

Heinz Award for the Environment: 2011, for her role in broadening awareness of the importance of biological sustainability to the future of humanity, her efforts to raise the visibility of ocean issues, her commitment to opening the lines of communication between scientists and citizens, and her pioneering concept of the social contract that exists between science and society

FURTHER READING

Periodicals

Christian Science Monitor, Aug. 15, 1997, p.10; May 3, 2001, p.18

Nature, Mar. 26, 2009

New York Times, Dec. 23, 2008, p.3; Apr. 11, 2009, p.16

OnEarth, Summer 2007, p.8

Smithsonian, Apr. 2010, p.25

Online Articles

http://www.heinzawards.net
(Heinz Awards,"Jane Lubchenco," undated)
http://www.nasonline.org
(National Academy of Sciences,"InterViews: Jane Lubchenco,"2004)
http://www.nytimes.com/2009/03/24/science/earth/24prof.html
(New York Times,"NOAA Chief Believes in Science as Social Contract," Mar. 24, 2009)
http://www.npr.org
(NPR,"NOAA Head Jane Lubchenco on Ocean Policy,"Mar. 27, 2009)
http://www.open-spaces.com
(Open Spaces,"Earth's Unruly Tenant,"Aug. 10, 2010)
http://e360.yale.edu
(Yale Environment 360,"NOAA's New Chief on Restoring Science to U.S. Climate Policy,"July 9, 2009)

ADDRESS

Jane Lubchenco
National Oceanic and Atmospheric Administration (NOAA)
1401 Constitution Ave. NW
Washington, DC 20230

WORLD WIDE WEB SITE

http://www.noaa.gov

Mike Lupica 1952-

American Journalist and Author
Nationally Syndicated Sports Columnist, TV Sports Commentator, and Author of Popular Novels for Young Adults

BIRTH

Michael Thomas Lupica (pronounced LOO-pik-uh) was born on May 11, 1952, in Oneida, New York.

YOUTH

Lupica grew up in Nashua, New Hampshire. His father was an enthusiastic sports fan who shared his love of sports with his son. From a very young age, Lupica was enthralled with all aspects of sports. He and his father kept track of all kinds of statistics and scores and monitored the performances of professional teams and individual players. Sometimes the games they followed ran late into the evening, past Lupica's bedtime. Then his father would write notes about what happened after Lupica went to sleep. He would leave the notes for Lupica to read the next morning, so Lupica would always know right away what had happened in sports the night before.

> *"I always tell anyone that wants to write, if there is a school paper, it is the greatest training ground in the world, because you would never want to embarrass yourself in front of your friends," Lupica recalled. "If your friends are reading your stuff, you've got to make it as good as you can."*

Even as a child, Lupica knew he wanted to be a writer. He wanted to write about sports for a big newspaper, and maybe have his own sports column one day. And he also knew that he wanted to write books. Lupica started writing mystery stories when he was ten years old.

Lupica's first journalism experience was writing about sports for his high school newspaper. This was good writing practice, and it also led to his first paying job as a writer. "When I was in high school, I started writing for my school paper," he recalled. "I always tell anyone that wants to write, if there is a school paper, it is the greatest training ground in the world, because you would never want to embarrass yourself in front of your friends. If your friends are reading your stuff, you've got to make it as good as you can. Then I started covering my high school sports teams for my newspaper up in Nashua, New Hampshire—the *Nashua Telegraph*. I got five dollars a story, and I thought I was the richest guy in the world."

Lupica's love of sports wasn't limited to writing about it. In baseball, he played second base. He was also a point guard on his high school basketball team. "I think I still hold the New Hampshire high school record—I broke my glasses 14 times in my senior year." He also played golf and was a member of his high school cross country running team.

EDUCATION

By the time Lupica enrolled in Boston College, he was committed to a career as a writer. "I was writing for three school newspapers and working nights at the *Boston Globe,*" he mentioned. "So I had clearly decided that this was what I wanted to do." During that time, Lupica also worked for several area newspapers. From 1970 to 1974, he was a sports correspondent for the *Boston Globe,* a large daily newspaper. From 1971 to 1975, he wrote a column for the *Boston Phoenix,* an arts and entertainment newsweekly, and sold some feature articles to the *Washington Star* daily newspaper in Washington, DC. Lupica graduated from Boston College in 1974.

CAREER HIGHLIGHTS

With a sports writing career spanning more than 30 years, Lupica has become one of the most well-known sports personalities in the U.S. His columns in the *New York Daily News* are reprinted in newspapers around the country. He is an anchor on "The Sports Reporters" talk show on ESPN and previously hosted "The Mike Lupica Show" on ESPN2. Lupica's blunt style and frequent rants about professional sports earned him the nickname "The Lip" and a reputation for being outspoken and unafraid to share his opinions. He doesn't mind if people agree with him or not. He explained that his reputation is "very liberating. I absolutely don't care what people think."

In addition to his career in sports journalism, Lupica is also the author of many books. He has written or contributed to a number of best-selling nonfiction books and has published a growing collection of popular novels for young adults. He manages these parallel careers by continuing to write his newspaper sports columns and appear on TV sports shows while working on his novels at the same time. Lupica has said that his successful career as both a sports columnist and an author is the fulfillment of the goal he set for himself in childhood.

Early Jobs

Although Lupica got his first paying job as a sports writer while he was still in high school, his professional career began after he graduated from college. In 1975, he began his first full-time job in sports journalism at the *New York Post* newspaper. There he was responsible for reporting on the NBA, particularly the New York Knicks basketball team. Lupica covered basketball for the *New York Post* for only a short time before he moved to the *New York Daily News* in 1977. At the *New York Daily News,* he became the youngest columnist ever to work at a major New York newspaper.

While continuing to write for the *New York Daily News,* Lupica also contributed stories to many different magazines. His writing appeared in many publications, including *World Tennis, Sport, Tennis, Golf Digest, Sports Illus-*

4 STAR ★★★★ FINAL

SUBWAY SERIES

32-PAGE SECTION WRAPS MAIN PAPER

DAILY NEWS

50¢ www.nydailynews.com NEW YORK'S HOMETOWN NEWSPAPER Friday, October 27, 2000

THE LONGEST SEASON

Mike Lupica on Joe Torre's incredible year – and his future

SEE PAGES 4-5 IN WRAP

LINDA CATAFFO DAILY NEWS

As a sports journalist, Lupica has worked at the New York Daily News *since 1977.*

trated, Men's Journal, Parade, and *ESPN: The Magazine*. He created *Esquire* magazine's column "The Sporting Life" and wrote there for ten years.

During these years, Lupica brought his particular brand of sports journalism to television. He was a frequent guest on the TV news programs

"MacNeil-Lehrer NewsHour" and "Good Morning America." In 1982, he was a sports journalist for ESPN and also began appearing as a panelist on "The Sports Reporters." From 1982 to 1984 he was a sports reporter on the "CBS Morning News" program. Around this time, Lupica tried sports radio broadcasting, hosting a sports talk show on WNBC Radio. This lasted only a short time because he found that he really didn't care for the job. He later explained, "The function talk radio really seems to fulfill, is it's a place for people to [complain] and people will listen to them. It's anger 24 hours a day."

Becoming an Author

After working as a sports journalist for newspapers and TV for several years, Lupica began writing books as well. In the 1980s, he published three mystery novels for adults: *Dead Air* (1986), *Extra Credits* (1988), and *Limited Partner* (1990). All three books feature Peter Finley, an investigative reporter for a New York City cable TV station. In each book, Finley finds himself immersed in an investigation into murder where only he can find the truth. His first book, *Dead Air,* was nominated for an Edgar Allan Poe Award for Best First Mystery; Lupica later wrote a screenplay based on *Dead Air* that became the CBS TV movie *Money, Power, Murder.*

Lupica also published several non-fiction books related to sports journalism. He co-wrote autobiographies with baseball player Reggie Jackson (*Reggie: The Autobiography,* 1984) and NFL football coach Bill Parcells (*Parcells: Autobiography of the Biggest Giant of Them All,* 1987). He also collaborated with noted author and screenwriter William Goldman on *Wait 'Till Next Year: The Story of a Season When What Should've Happened Didn't, and What Could've Gone Wrong Did* (1988), a look at one year in New York City sports. He reprinted several of his most popular pieces in the 1988 book *Shooting from the Lip: Essays, Columns, Quips, and Gripes in the Grand Tradition of Dyspeptic Sports Writing.* In 1996, Lupica published the book *Mad as Hell: How Sports Got Away from the Fans—And How We Get It Back.* This nonfiction book presents his criticism of the professional sports industry. In writing about the complaints of many die-hard sports fans, he attacks such problems as greedy team owners, overpaid players, and the high price of tickets for live sporting events. A *Booklist* reviewer declared that disgruntled sports fans "will enjoy sputtering angrily as they read this litany of wrongdoing."

Lupica's next sports-related non-fiction book was *Summer of '98: When Homers Flew, Records Fell, and Baseball Reclaimed America,* published in 1999. This book combined the dramatic story of the 1998 professional

Since 1982, Lupica has appeared regularly on the weekly ESPN program "The Sports Reporters," where several sports commentators discuss the week's news. He's shown here with (from left) Mitch Albom, Israel Gutierrez, and John Saunders.

baseball season with personal stories about Lupica and his young sons. During that season, he and his sons followed the ongoing competition between Mark McGwire and Sammy Sosa as the two star hitters raced to break the record for most home runs in one season."The book is about the home-run chase and about how baseball came into my sons' lives this summer … when the home runs were landing in our living room." *Publishers Weekly* called it"A feel-great book.… [Lupica] gives himself completely over to the beauty of baseball as both a game and as an agent of bonding between fathers and children."

Lupica soon combined his interest in writing novels with his love for sports in several new novels for adults. These books—set in the worlds of basketball, football, and baseball—provide an insider's view of professional sports. In *Jump* (1995), investigative attorney Mike DiMaggio must discover the truth when two professional basketball players are accused of rape. In *Bump and Run* (2000) Lupica introduced Jack Malloy, who unexpectedly inherits a professional football team when his father dies suddenly. In spite of his complete lack of experience, Malloy is determined to take his team to the Super Bowl. In *Full Court Press* (2001), talented Delilah "Dee" Gerard becomes the first woman to play in the NBA. Used as a marketing gimmick by the team owner and largely ignored by her teammates, Gerard also struggles with a vindictive sports writer intent on discovering scandals from her past. In *Wild Pitch* (2002), retired pitcher Charlie Stoddard returns for one last season on the mound, only to stir up conflict with his son—also a pitcher on the same team.

Lupica returned to the world of Jack Malloy with *Red Zone* (2003), a sequel to *Bump and Run.* Malloy has lost ownership of his team, but he continues to scheme to regain control and bring the team back on track, despite the interference of his twin sons. In *Too Far* (2004), former sports writer Ben Mitchell investigates the mysterious death of a high school basketball coach. When Mitchell uncovers what looks like evidence of violent hazing activities, he suddenly finds that there are some people who will do anything to prevent the truth from being revealed.

"Sports teaches kids about being on a team, being part of something greater than themselves if they play hard and well and unselfishly. If they can learn that, they can apply it to anything they do, in or out of sports, for the rest of their lives."

”

Writing for Young Adults

In 2004, Lupica published his first novel for young adult readers. *Travel Team* is the story of Danny Walker, who is 12 years old and in love with the game of basketball. Danny has natural talent and a drive to succeed, but finds that he is too short to qualify for the middle school basketball team. When Danny's father, a former professional basketball player, learns that his son didn't make the school team, he starts up a new team to give kids like Danny a chance to play. Danny's father turns out to be a highly competitive coach, and Danny struggles with the pros and cons of playing on his father's team. Ultimately Danny must decide how important basketball really is, and whether he wants to devote his life to the sport like his father did.

In writing *Travel Team,* Lupica drew on his own experiences as a youth basketball coach. "My middle son got cut from his seventh grade boys travel basketball team, along with another boy, for being too small. I started a team for all the kids that got cut. I hired a coach. We had a season. It turned out to be a tremendous experience, and that gave me the bare bones of the idea for *Travel Team.*"

After writing several books for adults, Lupica wrote Travel Team, *his first novel for young adults and the first of many books that have featured kids dealing with real-life issues within the context of stories about sports.*

Travel Team became the first of many novels written for young adults that have been widely praised for their deep knowledge of sports, interesting characters, believable family situations, and compelling stories. "Lupica has great respect for the boys struggling to deal with their own skills, their fathers, their teammates, and their coaches," Claire Rosser wrote in *Kliatt.* "All the details of basketball games and practices will be welcome to true basketball fans. It's such a relief to have a sports tale written by someone who truly understands the game—and Lupica knows how to create believable characters as well. An excellent sports story." That view was echoed in *Kirkus Reviews.* "[Lupica] has the knowledge of the game and the lean prose to make this a taut, realistic story not just about the game but about heart, character, and family. A winner."

Lupica's next young adult novel, *Heat* (2006), focuses on 12-year-old Michael and 17-year-old Carlos Arroyo, two Cuban-American brothers recently orphaned by their father's sudden death. In order to avoid being separated in foster care, the boys pretend that their father is still alive. They tell everyone that their father is visiting relatives in Miami so they can stay together in their apartment until Carlos turns 18. The plan seems to work until Michael is challenged by some of the other Little League coaches, who suspect that he is too old for Little League because of his strength and talent as a top-notch pitcher. Just when things seem to be falling apart, heroes emerge from unexpected places. "Lupica wrings plenty of genuine emotion from the melodramatic frame story ... by building characters who speak for themselves, not the author, and by enlivening the story with a teen version of street humor," raved Bill Ott in *Booklist.* "The dialogue crackles, and the rich cast of supporting characters—especially Michael's battery mate, catcher, and raconteur Manny—nearly steals the show. Top-notch entertainment."

In *Miracle on 49th Street* (2006), Lupica tells the story of 12-year-old Molly Parker, who loves basketball mostly because her father is Josh Cameron, star player for the Boston Celtics. Molly was raised in England by her mother, who never told Josh that he had a daughter. After her mother dies, Molly finds Josh and tells him that he is her father. The plot unfolds as Josh and Molly get to know each other and grow into their new relationship. "Lupica creates intriguing, complex characters in Molly, Sam, and Josh, and he paces his story well, with enough twists and cliff-hangers to keep the pages turning," Jeffrey A. French wrote in *School Library Journal.* "This is an entertaining work."

Lupica returned to the characters of *Travel Team* with the 2007 sequel *Summer Ball.* The story opens with Danny still waiting for his growth spurt as he sets off for summer basketball camp. Worrying that everyone at camp will be bigger and better than him, Danny quickly finds camp life complicated by a coach who seems to have a problem with him. Danny again questions whether he should just quit basketball for good. But then he discovers that there might be a reason why the coach doesn't like him, and it might have something to do with Danny's father. "*Summer Ball* is a great stand-alone novel," Sarah Sawtelle noted in a review for TeenReads.com. "With humor and fast action both on and off the court, this is a summer read not to be missed."

Published in 2008, *The Big Field* is a young adult baseball story starring 14-year-old Keith "Hutch" Hutchinson. Hutch plays second base and is the captain of his American Legion team. But the real star of the team is his friend Darryl "D-Will" Williams, a top shortstop. Hutch is a solid player, but knows he could be better with the help of his father, a former amateur baseball star. But his father's disappointment with his own failures prevents him from helping his son. Just as Hutch's team is about to make it to the state championships, Hutch finds out that his father has been training with Darryl instead of him. "Vivid descriptions of pivotal innings and plays, snappy dialogue, and realistic conflicts propel the characters and the story toward the state finals and a father-son breakthrough," reviewer Gerry Larson wrote in *School Library Journal*. "Baseball fans will revel in Lupica's exciting sports commentary and Hutch's competitive spirit and emotional highs and lows."

——— " ———

"Sports teaches kids about being on a team, being part of something greater than themselves if they play hard and well and unselfishly," Lupica argued. "If they can learn that, they can apply it to anything they do, in or out of sports, for the rest of their lives."

——— " ———

In *The Million Dollar Throw* (2009), 13-year-old Nate Brodie has finally saved up enough money to buy the autographed football he's wanted. But something completely unexpected comes along with the football—a chance to win a million dollars. All he has to do is throw a pass through a target at a New England Patriots game. Nate should be excited but instead, all he feels is pressure. His dad lost his job and the family is about to lose their home. Winning the prize money would make everything okay again. Except that Nate suddenly finds he's lost his talent for making pin-point passes. Will he be able to make the throw of a lifetime? A reviewer for *Horn*

Book said *The Million Dollar Throw* has "plenty of fast-paced football details for sports fans in this story propelled by the strength of family, friendship, and team."

In *The Batboy* (2010), Lupica tells the story of 14-year-old Brian Dudley, who has just landed his dream summer job: batboy for his favorite team, the Detroit Tigers. For Brian, the job means more than a chance to hang around with his baseball idols. Brian hopes to understand some things about his father, who chose baseball over Brian and his mother. As the summer progresses, Brian develops an unlikely friendship with Hank Bishop, a disgraced baseball player trying to rebuild his career. Brian and Hank each find what they were looking for, although not in the ways they expected. "Lupica is at the top of his game, crafting a crisp, fast-paced novel teeming with edge-of-the-seat baseball drama," reviewer Marilyn Taniguchi wrote in *School Library Journal*. "Though this novel will undoubtedly appeal to those who equate summer with baseball, it should also win over readers who appreciate finely crafted storytelling and engaging characters.

The "Comeback Kids" Series

In 2007, Lupica decided to begin writing the "Comeback Kids" series, a new series of sports novels aimed at slightly younger readers. The first book in the series was *Hot Hand*, the story of ten-year-old Billy and his life on and off the basketball court. Billy's life hasn't been so good since his parents divorced. His mother works long hours and takes a lot of business trips. His father moved out of the family home but still coaches Billy's basketball team and is as hard on Billy as ever. Billy's younger brother Ben has been growing more and more quiet since the divorce and doesn't seem interested in anything. To make matters worse, Ben is being bullied at school and Billy has to be the one to handle it. When the family is thrown into turmoil, Billy must be the one to find a solution that works for everyone.

Two-Minute Drill, another "Comeback Kids" book published in 2007, focuses on two sixth grade football players with completely different talents. Scott is a straight-A student, but is not very good at football. Chris is the star quarterback and the most popular kid in school, but is not very good at his schoolwork—dyslexia makes him a poor student. The two boys discover that they each have a secret, and they become friends as the story unfolds. In facing their own challenges, Scott and Chris both discover that the will to succeed is sometimes more important than natural ability.

Lupica published two more "Comeback Kids" books in 2008. In *Long Shot*, Pedro Morales is a model point guard. Always content with helping others

The Comeback Kids novels are geared to slightly younger readers but still focus on sports themes.

look great, Pedro's job on the basketball court is to set up his teammates to score. When Pedro decides to run for class president, he soon learns that he will be going up against Ned, the star forward and also the most popular boy in school. For once, Pedro wants to win something great for himself. But he learns the hard way that being a good teammate doesn't always mean that others will return the favor. *Safe at Home* tells the story of Nick Crandall, who feels like he doesn't belong anywhere. He certainly doesn't feel at home with his new foster parents. They are both college professors who know nothing about sports. Nick is a star athlete but not much of a student. He is good enough to make the varsity baseball team even though he's only 12 years old, but his teammates aren't interested in having a little kid for a catcher. Before everyone realizes he's in the wrong place, Nick wants to figure out how to prove that he belongs.

In 2010, Lupica published *Shoot-Out,* a Comeback Kids book that looks at what happens when a star player ends up on the worst team in the league. Jake loves soccer and had been a member of the championship team. When he finds himself playing for the last place team, he realizes that if he doesn't want to quit soccer, he has to learn to lose. Jake struggles to maintain a positive attitude while his team is trounced in every game. Ultimately, Jake's teammate Kevin shows him that good sportsmanship is equally important on and off the field.

According to reviewers, the "Comeback Kids" books feature many of the same characteristics that have made Lupica's books for older readers so compelling: fast-paced stories, interesting characters, meaty plots, and realistic sports action. "[*Shoot-Out* is] an enjoyable sports story with lots of action," Todd Morning wrote in *Booklist.* "*[Long Shot]* sends kids a message about the importance of cooperation and teamwork both on and off the court, without being preachy and didactic," Amy Joslyn wrote in *School Library Journal.* "This brisk story of friendship and football will be a huge hit with the target audience," a writer for *Kirkus Reviews* said about *Two-Minute Drill.*

Trying Something New

In 2010, Lupica published a book that was different from his earlier writings: *Hero,* his first young adult book that is not about sports. *Hero* imagines what happens when 14-year-old Zach Harriman begins to develop super powers. After his father's sudden death, Zach gradually discovers that he has new abilities. He can move from one place to another as fast as a text message travels. He can become invisible. He has incredible strength, sharpened senses, and a strange need to patrol New York City's Central Park at night. And he can fly. Zach doesn't understand these new powers or why he has them. Slowly he learns that it might have something to do with his father's death. Zach knew his dad had been a hero who saved America. What Zach didn't know was that his dad was a superhero, and now it's Zach's turn to take up the battle against evil."In a major departure from his YA sports fiction," Richard Luzer wrote in *School Library Journal,* "the popular Lupica opts for a high-concept, high-octane action thriller."A reviewer for *Publishers Weekly* offered another view, calling Hero"a moving tale of adolescent growth."

"All my books, at some point, are about the things that I think are the most important, which are friendship and loyalty and also the ability to get back up after you get knocked down a little," Lupica concluded."Anybody can get knocked down in life or in sports.... It's how you get back up that is a measure of your heart and your character and your spirit. So I hope people always take that message away from my books."

Lupica explained why he decided to write a non-sports book. "I always thought about what it would be like if I took a kid and gave him superpowers. Then, when my editor found out that I liked comic books, he asked me the eternal superhero question:'If you could fly or be invisible, which would you be?'I said fly and I thought flying would always win hands down, but I was surprised to find that when I asked different groups the answer always came out 50/50. So having a kid with both powers was my jumping off point for this book."

Lupica plans to continue his dual careers as a sports journalist and a novelist. He continues to appear as a commentator on TV sports shows and to write for the *New York Daily News.* There, his Sunday column "Shooting from the Lip" has become a staple of New York journalism, supplemented by his Monday column,"Mondays with Mike," and his web-only column, all known for their strong opinions, exclusive interviews, and insightful observations.

But Lupica also enjoys writing novels for young readers, and his next book, *The Underdogs* (due out in late 2011), focuses on a young football player. He has said that he likes writing sports fiction because"sports teaches kids about being on a team, being part of something greater than themselves if they play hard and well and unselfishly. If they can learn that, they can

Lupica reading his book Long Shot *to sixth graders from a New York City middle school.*

apply it to anything they do, in or out of sports, for the rest of their lives." However, he is not ruling out the possibility of writing more non-sports books. "All my books, at some point, are about the things that I think are the most important, which are friendship and loyalty and also the ability to get back up after you get knocked down a little," he concluded. "Anybody can get knocked down in life or in sports. That doesn't show anybody anything about you. But it's how you get back up that is a measure of your heart and your character and your spirit. So I hope people always take that message away from my books."

For young people who are interested in a writing career, Lupica's advice is to get started as soon as possible. "If you want to write, and that is your passion and dream, just write as much as you can," he stressed. "If there is a school paper, write for that. Keep a journal. Write observations about the world. The first time that you write a story that you are proud of and somebody wants to read it, you're a writer. Another way to get better as a writer is to read. There is still no microchip, technology, cable remote, iPod, or video game that can do what a good story does. It takes you to a world that you may have never inhabited on your own. That is more magic to me than anything that a computer can do."

HOBBIES AND OTHER INTERESTS

Lupica enjoys all sports, but his favorite is baseball. "There is nothing I like better than taking my kids and sitting in a ballpark on a nice day and eating popcorn and watching baseball." In his spare time, he likes to play tennis and golf. Lupica also coaches youth sports, including basketball, soccer, and Little League baseball. He claimed that he follows the coaching plan he learned from his friend Paul Westphal, a former NBA player and coach:

1. If you're open, shoot.
2. If somebody else is more open, pass him the ball and let him shoot.
3. Have fun.

"I tell the kids all the time, this ain't a job, this is playing ball with your buddies, and if you can't do it with a smile on your face, we're all wasting our time."

MARRIAGE AND FAMILY

Lupica married his wife Taylor in 1986. They have three sons, Christopher, Alex, and Zach, and one daughter, Hannah. Lupica lives with his family in New Canaan, Connecticut.

SELECTED WRITINGS

Young Adult Novels

Travel Team, 2004
Heat, 2006
Miracle on 49th Street, 2006
Summer Ball, 2007
The Big Field, 2008
Million Dollar Throw, 2009
The Batboy, 2010
Hero, 2010

Comeback Kids Novels

Hot Hand, 2007
Two-Minute Drill, 2007
Long Shot, 2008
Safe at Home, 2008
Shoot-Out, 2010

Other Writings

Reggie: The Autobiography, 1984 (with Reggie Jackson)
Dead Air, 1986
Parcells: Autobiography of the Biggest Giant of Them All, 1987 (with Bill Parcells)
Extra Credits, 1988
Shooting from the Lip: Essays, Columns, Quips, and Gripes in the Grand Tradition of Dyspeptic Sports Writing, 1988
Wait 'Till Next Year: The Story of a Season When What Should've Happened Didn't, and What Could've Gone Wrong Did, 1988 (with William Goldman)
Limited Partner, 1990
Jump, 1995
Mad as Hell: How Sports Got Away from the Fans—And How We Get It Back, 1996
Summer of '98: When Homers Flew, Records Fell, and Baseball Reclaimed America, 1999
Bump and Run, 2000
Full Court Press, 2001
Wild Pitch, 2002
Red Zone, 2003
Too Far, 2004

HONORS AND AWARDS

Jim Murray Award (National Football Foundation): 2003
New York Sportswriter of the Year (National Sportscasters and Sportwriters Association): 2010

FURTHER READING

Periodicals

Christian Science Monitor, May 13, 1999, p.18
Connecticut Post, May 29, 2007
Denver Post, Nov. 16, 2009, p.A17
South Florida Sun-Sentinel, June 6, 2006, p.E2
USA Today, Nov. 7, 2000, p.C3

Online Articles

http://www.huffingtonpost.com/mike-lupica/we-still-love-a-good-stor_b_352862.html
(Huffington Post, "We Still Love a Good Story," Nov. 11, 2009)
http://www.tampabay.com
(St. Petersburg Times/Tampa Bay.com, "Sportswriter Mike Lupica Writes Young Adult Novels with Message: Character Counts," Nov. 14, 2010)
http://www.teenreads.com/authors
(Teen Reads, "Author Profile: Mike Lupica," no date)
http://www.timeforkids.com
(Time for Kids, "Catching Up with Mike Lupica," May 7, 2010)

ADDRESS

Mike Lupica
Penguin Group USA
375 Hudson St.
New York, NY 10014

WORLD WIDE WEB SITE

http://www.mikelupicabooks.com

Charles Martinet 1955-

American Actor

Voice of Mario and Other Nintendo Characters

BIRTH

Charles Martinet was born on September 17, 1955, in San Jose, California. He has sometimes spelled his last name Martinee or Martinez in his acting credits.

YOUTH

Martinet's family moved to Spain when he was 12 years old. They later lived in France. As a result, he learned to speak both Spanish and French fluently. He also speaks a little Italian.

EDUCATION

Martinet attended the American School of Paris, located in the Parisian suburb of Saint-Cloud. As a young adult, his ambition was to become a lawyer. When he was about 20 years old, however, a friend convinced him to take a drama class. He loved it and immediately decided to drop out of college in order to pursue a professional acting career. He auditioned for, and won, an apprenticeship at the Berkeley Repertory Theater, a famous and respected community theater in California. After spending some time there, he went to England to study at the Drama Studio London. He then returned to California, where he continued acting. "My parents have always been incredibly supportive; they put me through college, then [I] left college and then they put me through drama school," Martinet acknowledged. "They helped me get started and it's been nothing but love and support."

"My parents have always been incredibly supportive; they put me through college, then [I] left college and then they put me through drama school," Martinet acknowledged. "They helped me get started and it's been nothing but love and support."

FIRST JOBS

Martinet was involved with some 75 plays in London and California. Among them were several plays written by William Shakespeare, a 16th-century playwright considered by many to be the world's greatest. Those acting jobs helped him years later: he used his experience playing one of the Shakespearean characters to inspire his work in video games.

Making Corporate Videos

Martinet's next career move was to become involved in the world of corporate videos. For the most part, these videos are never seen by the general public. Instead, they present information about a business or company to possible partners, customers, or clients. Corporate videos are an important business tool, and large companies may spend a lot of money producing them. They can be serious or humorous in tone. Martinet has appeared in more than 500 of these videos, many of them for major companies such as Apple Computers, Microsoft, and IBM. He sometimes filled the role of a serious narrator, while at other times, he played such characters as an engineer, a crazy scientist, a cowboy, or a geek. In addition, he portrayed these characters live at trade shows, where business people come to learn about other businesses.

CAREER HIGHLIGHTS

Audition of a Lifetime

One day in 1987, Martinet was relaxing at the beach when he got a message from a friend, urging him to go to an audition for a trade show. Martinet didn't really want to leave the beach, but he finally did go to the audition—arriving just as the crew was preparing to leave. "I said, 'Excuse me, can I please read for this?'" he remembered. "The producer looked at his watch, said, 'OK. You're an Italian plumber from Brooklyn and we've got this animation system, and we're not sure it's even going to work yet, and you'll have this stuff glued to your face and the cartoon character will move when you talk.'" Video games were still fairly new at the time, based mainly on simple movements and actions. The very idea of a game with a storyline was somewhat surprising to Martinet, and there was no picture of the character to inspire him.

"It's never been done before and in any case if it doesn't work you still gotta talk to people. So make up a video game, make up an accent and start talking to people," the producer told him. The actor's first idea was to use a stereotypical, gruff New York accent for the character, but the producer had told him the game was supposed to be appealing to all ages. He searched in his mind for a voice that would be more appropriate for young children, something softer and gentler. He had played an old Italian man named Gemio in Shakespeare's *The Taming of the Shrew,* and Gemio suddenly came back to him as he prepared to audition. Making the old man's voice younger and more energetic, he turned to the camera and started talking.

"I said, 'Hello, it's a-me, Mario! Okey dokey, let's make a pizza pie together! You a-gonna get some sauces. I'm-a gonna get some spaghetti. We're gonna put the spaghetti and the sauces into the pizza. Then we're gonna make lasagna. Then we're gonna make spaghetti and meatballs! Ooh, mama mia, I'm getting hungry!'" Martinet remembered. "I don't know what I said, but I talked and I talked for 30 minutes or longer, until I heard 'Cut! Stop! We have no more tape! Thank you. We'll be in touch.'" He didn't find that reassuring, because he knew that "we'll be in touch" often really means "you will not be called back" at auditions. In this case, however, Martinet's tape was such a standout that it was the only one sent to Nintendo for approval. He was soon hired to give life to the Mario character at the trade show.

Martinet voiced the character of Mario at trade shows for several years before technology advanced enough to allow voices in video games. The first game to feature Martinet as Mario was Super Mario 64 *in 1996.*

Origins of Mario

Mario had first appeared in an early video arcade game called *Donkey Kong,* created by Shigeru Miyamoto for the Nintendo company. (For more information on Miyamoto, see *Biography Today Scientists and Inventors,* Vol. 5.) *Donkey Kong* was the first game to have characters acting out a simple story, which had been developed before the technical aspects of the game. The plot had Donkey Kong, a huge ape, kidnapping a girl named Pauline. The third character was a carpenter who had to overcome various obstacles in order to rescue Pauline from Donkey Kong. His outstanding power was his ability to jump over gaps, and he had to do this repeatedly in order to foil Donkey Kong. The character was known as Jumpman, but he had the big hat, bushy mustache, and blue overalls that Mario still wears today.

Jumpman was so popular that Nintendo began developing a new game that would feature him. That game was *Mario Bros.,* and it was released in 1983. Jumpman now had a real name: Mario. It was chosen because of the character's resemblance to Mario Segale, the landlord of Nintendo's warehouse in Redmond, Washington. Mario had also been transformed from a carpenter to a plumber, and he had been given a brother named Luigi to help him defeat nasty creatures down in New York City's sewer system. In 1985, a sequel called *Super Mario Bros.* was released, and for many years it was the top-selling video game in the industry. *Super Mario Bros.* first saw Mario and Luigi battling against Bowser, navigating the Mushroom Kingdom, and trying to save Princess Peach—all of which became recurring elements in later updates of the *Mario Bros.* games.

"

Martinet has created hundreds of characters, but he says that Mario is definitely his favorite. "For me, it's a perfect marriage because Mario and I have so much in common—joy, fun, laughter, life adventure. I bring that aspect of myself to Mario. It seems to work."

"

Actor in a Box

Computer memory was limited in the early days of video games, so it wasn't possible to have Mario speak during his first years. At the trade show Martinet auditioned for, however, Nintendo was going to use advanced technology that would allow him to give life to Mario, while hiding

Martinet with Mario and Luigi, two of the Nintendo characters he voices.

in a soundproof box with a complex computer system. A mold was made of the actor's face, and a mask produced from the mold. Contact wires were glued and taped to his face and connected to the processing system.

When everything was in place, the system was supposed to translate Martinet's speech and facial expressions to an animated Mario appearing on a monitor a short distance away. Martinet would be able to see the people who were looking at the monitor, but they wouldn't be able to see him. He could have real-time conversations with them and it would seem exactly as if Mario was speaking to them. The people at Nintendo hoped that all the equipment would work correctly and hold up until the conclusion of the trade show. It was so hot in the box that the glue and tape on Martinet's face began to melt. The system kept working, however, and Martinet was a huge success as the voice and personality of Mario. He has continued to play Mario at trade shows for more than 20 years.

It was a major step forward for video games and for Martinet's career when technology advanced enough to allow Mario to speak a little more in his games. Martinet first provided the voice of Mario for a Nintendo game with *Super Mario 64*, which was first released in Japan on June 23, 1996. In addition to enhanced sound capability, *Super Mario 64* had 3-D graphics and became one of the world's best-selling video games. It is still ranked by many gamers as one of the best games of all time.

Voice of Nintendo

The Mario character went on to appear in more than 200 games produced by Nintendo, both in starring roles and minor parts, as the company continued to develop and use the newest technological innovations. Mario has appeared in virtually every gaming platform, from arcade games to Wii. Mario titles include *Mario Kart, Super Smash Bros., Super Mario Sunshine, Mario Golf, Mario Party,* and many more. The little plumber has become the symbol of the entire Nintendo company.

> *Martinet finds it amusing that millions of people around the world have heard his voice, but he can usually walk down the street completely unnoticed. "There is a certain level of wonderfulness that comes with being a celebrity without fame," he said.*

Every time he voices Mario, Martinet keeps the character light, positive, fun, and upbeat, no matter what challenges or enemies he has to face. Mario is known for his playful shouts of "Wa-hoo!" and "Mamma mia!" Martinet continues to be the voice of Mario in games and in real-time appearances, but he is also the voice of many other major Nintendo characters as well, including Mario's brother Luigi, Baby Mario, Mario's enemy Wario, Waluigi, Toadsworth, and others.

The process of developing a game from start to finish is a long one. Martinet's part in any new Mario game is very important, but in the overall picture, it doesn't take much time. Sometimes he is sent video of the game beforehand, so he can think about how he might like to have the character react to certain situations. At other times, he has no idea what the game will look like until it's time to record. In the first games he voiced, only very small sound bites could be used, but as technology advanced, Mario's personality and vocabulary has grown, too. A script is provided, but Martinet does a lot of improvising. In the end, the best takes are sent to Nintendo for final approval by Shigeru Miyamoto, who makes the ultimate choice about what is used.

Improved technology has drastically changed the experience of performing as Mario, Wario, and other characters in real-time situations. Computers have become so much more powerful and efficient that Martinet no longer has to be cooped up in a hot, soundproofed box, or to have equipment taped or glued to his face. He does still travel and make live appearances, but now it is also possible for him to sit in his own home and give life to Mario and other Nintendo characters at locations that are thousands of miles away, and he often does this."I sit there in my little bunny shoes in the morning, and just talk with people at the Nintendo World Store, or anywhere in the world," he said.

Martinet feels the public loves Mario because the little plumber "loves life, loves adventure, jumps over challenges and finds a way to get through. He always moves forward in a positive way.

Life beyond Mario

Providing voices for Mario and his companions is certainly Martinet's best-known job, but he continues to do many others. He has supplied voices for many other video games, including those for companies competing with Nintendo. He can be heard in the "Carmen Sandiego" and "Star Wars" games, and in *Slave Zero, Uprising, Cel Damage, Space Quest 6: The Final Frontier,* and many others. He also lends his voice to educational software. In "The Cat in the Hat" educational software, Martinet plays the Cat and Yertle the Turtle. In the popular "Reader Rabbit" series, which helps children learn reading, math, and other skills, he plays Reader Rabbit in the English, French, and Spanish versions of the programs. He is also the voice of the Leapfrog Express line of educational toys, recognizable by his friendly invitation, "Ribbit ribbit, let's play!" More than 100 educational games and toys feature Martinet's voice.

Martinet has also done voice work for television and radio. He has played over 100 characters in animated features for Sony Wonderfilm and Hallmark Cartoons, including King Arthur, Moses, and Tarzan. He has also played small parts as a regular actor in the films *The Game* and *Nine Months,* as well as the television movie *The Last of His Tribe.* He has appeared in television programs, including "Nash Bridges" and "Midnight Caller."

Although he enjoys all kinds of acting and performing, Martinet says that voice acting is a special kind of fun. He finds it amusing that while millions of people around the world have heard his voice, he can usually walk

Mario and the gang have continued to appear in Nintendo games on each new gaming platform, including Wii.

down the street and be completely unnoticed. "There is a certain level of wonderfulness that comes with being a celebrity without fame," he said.

Martinet gets ideas for his characters by watching people, studying their movements and mannerisms, and listening to their speech patterns. He commented that voice acting requires good general health. "I try to take care of my whole body by keeping in shape," he explained. "I try to eat well and get a good night's sleep. It's important to drink lots of water and not a lot of dairy products because you want to keep your throat nice and clear. You also have to laugh and smile a lot and I don't scream too much because that really strains the vocal folds."

When all his work is taken into consideration, this versatile actor has created hundreds of characters, but he says that Mario is definitely his favorite.

"For me, it's a perfect marriage because Mario and I have so much in common—joy, fun, laughter, life adventure. I bring that aspect of myself to Mario. It seems to work." He feels the public loves Mario because the little plumber "loves life, loves adventure, jumps over challenges and finds a way to get through. He always moves forward in a positive way."

Mario may not be a very complex character, but even after more than 20 years, Martinet doesn't find it dull playing him. "I never get bored," he said. "It is so much fun to do and to see what new things are going to come out of the genius that is Mr. Miyamoto and the incredible team at Nintendo. Talking to fans and seeing their enthusiasm and the wonderful impact the games have on people will always bring me joy."

MAJOR INFLUENCES

Martinet says that one of his greatest inspirations in life is Mario himself. "He has a positive attitude to life and is never cynical. If I could be anyone it would be Mario."

HOBBIES AND OTHER INTERESTS

Martinet enjoys playing video games, and his favorites are those featuring Mario, especially *Mario Kart.* Some of his favorite actors are Robin Williams, Robert De Niro, and Colin Firth.

SELECTED CREDITS

Movies

Last of His Tribe, 1992 (TV movie)
Nine Months, 1995
The Game, 1997

Video Games

Space Quest 6: The Final Frontier, 1995
Super Mario Bros. 64, 1996
Mario Kart 64, 1996
Uprising, 1997
Mario Party, 1998
Mario Golf, 1999
Slave Zero, 1999
Mario Party 3, 2000
Cel Damage, 2001
Super Mario World, 2001
Super Mario Sunshine, 2002

Mario vs. Donkey Kong, 2004
Super Mario 64 DS, 2004
Mario Superstar Basketball, 2005
Mario Kart DS, 2005
Super Smash Bros. Brawl, 2008
Mario Kart Wii, 2008
Resonance of Fate, 2010
Super Mario Galaxy 2, 2010

FURTHER READING

Periodicals

Sunday Herald Sun (Melbourne, Australia), Oct. 13, 2002, p.F3

Online Articles

http://www.bbc.co.uk/newsbeat/10283772
(BBC Newsbeat,"Mamma Mia! It's the Voice of Mario!"June 11, 2010)
http://www.cubed3.com
(Cubed3,"Interview with Charles Martinet,"Dec. 7, 2003)
http://www.gamervision.com
(Gamervision,"Charles Martinet on Being the Voice of Mario,"June 2, 2010)
http://www.n-sider.com
(N-Sider,"Charles Martinet Down Under,"Nov. 14, 2002)
http://www.wii-kombo.com
(Wii Kombo, David Oxford,"Charles Martinet Celebrates 15 Years of Mario with Kombo,"Sep. 15, 2008)

ADDRESS

Charles Martinet
CAM Creative Service
603 Main Street
Sausalito, CA 94965-2318

WORLD WIDE WEB SITE

http://www.charlesmartinet.com

Bridgit Mendler 1992-

American Actress
Star of the Disney Channel TV Program "Good Luck Charlie"

BIRTH

Bridgit Claire Mendler was born on December 18, 1992, in Washington, DC. She has a brother, Nicolas, and a sister, Zoey.

YOUTH AND EDUCATION

In 2000, when Mendler was eight years old, the family moved to Mill Valley, California, which is near San Francis-

Mendler decided early on that she wanted to act. "I was finishing up one play that I was working on through the community theater program, and I came up to her and I said, 'Mommy, this is what I want to do!'" she recalled. "It seems like that was about right, because I've kept up with it."

co. Her family chose not to have a television for several years, so she and her siblings had to learn other ways to keep themselves entertained. "I liked hanging out with the other kids," she recalled. "I liked reading. I was crazy about the Harry Potter books." While she was in the second grade, she took part in a school play about mathematics, in the role of Princess Multiplication. She enjoyed the experience so much that she started attending drama camps and being involved with other local theater productions.

Mendler decided early on that she wanted to stick with acting. "My mom actually remembers, and I don't remember this," she said. "But I was finishing up one play that I was working on through the community theater program, and I came up to her and I said, 'Mommy, this is what I want to do!' I don't remember saying that, but apparently I said that. It seems like that was about right, because I've kept up with it."

Mendler has adapted her education to suit her growing career as an actor. She attends high school online through the Education Program for Gifted Youth at Stanford University.

FIRST JOBS

As a child, Mendler worked in many local theater productions in the San Francisco Bay Area. She eventually became the youngest performer ever in the San Francisco Fringe Festival, a respected theater festival that is held yearly.

Signing with a Talent Agent

Mendler's parents were very supportive of her acting ambitions, and by the time she was 11 years old, she had signed with a talent agent. She did voice acting for the animated film *The Legend of Buddha,* released in 2004. It told the story of the founder of Buddhism, from his youthful days through his quest for spiritual enlightenment. It was nominated for an Academy Award for best animated feature film. Following that, she played the part

Mendler (left) in a scene from The Clique.

of Thorn in the video game *Bone: The Great Cow Race,* which is based on the "Bone" series of graphic novels.

At age 13, Mendler started traveling to audition in Los Angeles, which was about 400 miles from her home. Because Los Angeles is the center of the film and entertainment industry, many of the most high-profile jobs are found there. In 2006, shortly after she began auditioning in Los Angeles, Mendler was chosen for a guest role on the daytime TV drama "General Hospital," a long-running and very popular soap opera that is seen nationally.

In 2007, Mendler played Pamela, a minor character in the film *Alice Upside Down,* which starred Alyson Stoner and featured Luke Perry. The story concerns Alice, a shy, adolescent girl whose mother has died. When her father moves with Alice and her brother to a new town, the girl feels even more isolated and out of place. She creates a vivid fantasy life for herself, which sometimes gets her into trouble. In addition to having a small on-screen part in the movie, Mendler also performed two songs for the soundtrack, "Free Spirit" and "Frog Prince Song."

In 2008, Mendler appeared as Kristen Gregory in the direct-to-DVD movie *The Clique.* Kristen is part of the self-named "Pretty Committee," a small group of the most popular and fashionable girls at the Octavian Country

Day School. Kristen, an athletic girl, has a secret. She attends Octavian on a scholarship, and her parents are very poor. The clique's leader, Massie, finds her own status at the school threatened when her parents' middle-class friends move into their guest house, bringing along their daughter Claire. The girls of the clique reject Claire at first, but as time passes, she proves to be a true friend. Claire finds out the truth about Kristen's family, but she does not tell the other "Pretty Committee" girls, who would immediately have rejected Kristen if they knew she was not wealthy.

CAREER HIGHLIGHTS

Like many young actors, Mendler hoped to work for Disney. The Disney studios are known for giving selected young actors a chance at huge success. Disney specializes in picking out young, inexperienced performers with potential and then giving them the training, experience, publicity, and opportunity to become famous. Britney Spears, Justin Timberlake, and Miley Cyrus all got their start with Disney. Mendler did a few auditions for Disney, including one for a part in the show "Sonny with a Chance," which went to Demi Lovato instead. Mendler began to get discouraged, but the producers at the Disney studio had really already noticed her. "Bridgit is a great example of … us finding somebody, knowing that we wanted to do business with her and then waiting to find the perfect role," stated Gary Marsh, chief creative officer for Disney Channels Worldwide.

First Appearances on the Disney Channel

Mendler got her first Disney role in 2008. In October 2008, she made a guest appearance on the premiere episode of the program "JONAS," a Disney program featuring the popular singing group the Jonas Brothers. In the show, the brothers played characters much like themselves, siblings who have formed a hit musical group. Mendler played Penny, a girl on whom Nick Jonas's character has a crush. Mendler not only acted in the program, she also had the chance to demonstrate her musical skills, playing a guitar and singing a duet with Nick Jonas. "I was pretty star struck, I'm not going to lie!" she recalled. Once she relaxed, however, she enjoyed working with the Jonas Brothers. "I think it was the first day on set that they brought me into the studio and I started recording the song. So I was a little intimidated but it was really fun," she remembered.

Just a couple of weeks after she finished work on "JONAS," Mendler began work on "Wizards of Waverly Place," a Disney program starring Selena Gomez, David Henrie, and Jake T. Austin as a trio of siblings who are all wizards-in-training. Their father is an ex-wizard, while their mother is a mortal.

Mendler playing a vampire in a scene from the Disney program "Wizards of Waverly Place," with David Henrie and Jake T. Austin.

In addition to needing to keep their magical heritage a secret from the world at large, the siblings have to compete with each other—only one can become the wizard of their generation, and the other two must eventually become mortal. Mendler worked on four episodes of the series initially, playing the part of Juliet Van Heusen, a vampire who is the love interest of Justin, the eldest of the young wizards. Unlike most vampires, Juliet has a soul, and she is considerably nicer than most vampires. She and Justin face the disapproval of their families because of their different backgrounds, but they remain committed to each other. Mendler later returned to the show and appeared in a second round of episodes, still playing the character of Juliet.

Mendler enjoyed working on the program. "I think that the writers on that show are really funny, so that's good," she commented. "The cast and the crew were incredibly welcoming to me, and I felt like I was part of the family when I was on the show."

In addition to her work for Disney, Mendler worked on other projects. She did voice acting again in the animated feature *Alvin and the Chipmunks: The Squeakquel,* supplying the voice of a minor character named Becca. She had a more significant role in the TV movie *Labor Pains,* starring Lindsay Lohan, first broadcast on the ABC Family Channel. Mendler played Emma, the younger sister of Lohan's character Thea Clayhill. Their parents have died, so Thea is the guardian of teenaged Emma. Feeling that she is about to be fired, Thea pretends to be pregnant, thereby gaining her employer's sympathy and holding on to the job that supports her and her sister. *Labor Pains* and *Alvin and the Chipmunks: The Squeakquel* were both released in 2009.

Filming a Pilot

While working on these other projects, Mendler had auditioned for a new show Disney was developing, originally titled "Love, Teddy." Many of Disney's programs include a fantastic element, such as a character's secret life, magical powers, or fabulous wealth. In contrast, this new show, "Love, Teddy," would be more along the lines of the classic TV comedies of the past, featuring a family facing everyday challenges. The people at Disney hoped it would be a program that parents would watch with their children.

The show revolves around two teenaged siblings who find themselves in charge of their infant sister when both of their parents must return to work full-time. Teddy and her older brother PJ cooperate with each other, but in addition to taking care of the baby, they also have to cope with their tween brother Gabe, who feels jealous and insecure about his place in the family. Teddy decides to record a video diary for her sister, with tips and wisdom for surviving in their family. The video segments close each episode, and the title "Love, Teddy" was a reference to the way Teddy ended each of her diary entries to her little sister, Charlie.

For Mendler, the process of auditioning for the show was long. "I was anxiously waiting by the phone for days and days at home," she remembered. "I went into the final audition and then they didn't let me know for, like, a week or two about if I got it or not. You kind of start to lose your confidence the longer [they don't get back to you]. By the end, I was like, 'oh my gosh, will they ever call? Will I know?' I was jumping up and down when I found out I got it."

About a month after finishing up her initial work on "Wizards of Waverly Place," Mendler shot the pilot episode for the program "Love, Teddy." A pilot is a test episode of a program that's being considered for production as a regular series. Depending on how well the pilot is received, the show may go into regular production, or it may be set aside.

"Good Luck Charlie"

By the time Mendler filmed her second batch of appearances on "Wizards of Waverly Place," Disney was ready to go ahead with regular production of "Love, Teddy," now named "Good Luck Charlie." The cast included Mendler as Teddy Duncan, Jason Dolley as PJ, Bradley Steven Perry as

Gabe, Mia Talerico as baby Charlie, and Eric Allan Kramer and Leigh-Allyn Baker as parents Bob and Amy. In addition to starring in the show, Mendler also sang the theme song.

"Teddy's great," Mendler said about her character. "I think in a lot of ways she's just your normal teen girl. She's interested in all the teen girl things. There's an episode where she's into a certain vampire craze; it's like the equivalent of *Twilight.* She's into boys and has her whole teen drama stuff. She's kind of a perfectionist. She likes things to go her way; she likes things to be done right." Reviewing the show for *Daily Variety,* Brian Lowry said that Mendler was "easily the best thing about the sprightly new sitcom 'Good Luck Charlie,' a surprisingly refreshing throwback to ABC's TGIF-style sitcoms."

"

"Teddy's great," Mendler said about her character. "I think in a lot of ways she's just your normal teen girl. She's interested in all the teen girl things. There's an episode where she's into a certain vampire craze; it's like the equivalent of Twilight. *She's into boys and has her whole teen drama stuff. She's kind of a perfectionist. She likes things to go her way; she likes things to be done right."*

"

Discussing Mendler and "Good Luck Charlie" on the web site Radio Free.com, Michael J. Lee wrote, "Any sentimentality in 'Charlie' is usually deftly trumped by a well-balanced moment of disarming humor." He noted that the show allows Mendler a chance to develop a more realistic character than the one she had played in "Wizards of Waverly Place" and called Teddy "a conscientious teen of the internet age who balances her responsibilities at home with the lightheartedness of adolescence." Mendler has said that she appreciates the underlying message in "Good Luck Charlie" that teenagers should take on some adult responsibilities. She's also happy that the message doesn't overpower the episodes' storylines, remaining in the background instead. In addition to the TV program, a movie version of "Good Luck Charlie" is being developed. *Good Luck Charlie, It's Christmas* is scheduled to premiere in December 2011.

Developing a Musical Career

Many of Disney's TV stars have gone on to have high-powered careers in the music business. Mendler already liked to sing and write songs when

Mendler with the cast of "Good Luck Charlie." The Duncan family (from left): Mendler (Teddy), Eric Allan Kramer (Bob), Bradley Steven Perry (Gabe), Mia Talerico (Charlie), Leigh-Allyn Baker (Amy), and Jason Dolley (PJ).

she signed a contract with the studio. "I do that for my own fun and so I don't think I'm doing it because I'm a part of Disney," she explained. "Hopefully at some point I'll be able to show people my actual songs, maybe put together an album."

Mendler has had several opportunities to demonstrate her singing. She recorded "When She Loved Me" from *Toy Story 2* for *DisneyMania7*, part of the series featuring music from the studio's music soundtracks. "I am happy with it. I thought it was a fun song to do and I hope that other people like it too." She also recorded "How to Believe," a song for the Disney DVD feature *Tinkerbell and the Great Fairy Rescue*. She recently signed with Hollywood Records and will begin work on her debut album.

Mendler's singing and acting skills are showcased in the 2011 Disney Channel TV movie *Lemonade Mouth,* based on the book by Mark Peter Hughes. Mendler played one of the lead characters, Olivia White, alongside Adam Hicks, who played Wen. Olivia, Wen, Mo, Charlie, and Stella are five high school students who get to know each other when they are all assigned to detention. Alone, they may feel like misfits, but as a group, they start up a rock band that gives them confidence and threatens their school's snobby elite. The music is a bit of a departure from standard Disney pop, with a blend of pop, rock 'n roll, and rap that features a slightly harder edge. The movie premiered in April 2011 to immediate success. At last count, Disney Channel had run the movie 16 times, making it the No. 1 movie for cable in total viewers. The movie was so successful that a sequel is being planned featuring Mendler and the other original actors.

Despite success in TV, movies, and music, Mendler doesn't take herself too seriously. She says her family helps to keep her down to earth. "I trip over everything … I'm a huge klutz," she said. "I'm not cool at all."

FAVORITE BOOKS AND TELEVISION

Mendler enjoys the TV shows "The Office" and "90210," calling the latter her "guilty pleasure." She enjoys "The Twilight Saga" series of books and describes herself as "Team Jacob." Her favorite actress is Natalie Portman.

HOBBIES AND OTHER INTERESTS

Mendler considers herself "a huge nerd. I love reading and math—and I'm really into nerdy dancing. In my book, there's no such thing as a wrong move." She loves music, whether writing it, performing, or just listening. "Every morning when I'm in the car going to work, we'll blast music," she said. "We just jam out. It's a great way to start the day because sometimes, you know, if it's gonna be a stressful day, it's nice to loosen up and have fun." She has a collection of vinyl records and enjoys playing them on her record player. She loves to document things on video and create her own music videos. Her favorite foods are sushi and chocolate.

SELECTED CREDITS

Television

"JONAS," 2009 (guest star)
Labor Pains, 2009 (TV movie)
"Wizards of Waverly Place," 2009-2010 (guest star)
"Good Luck Charlie," 2010-

Movies

The Legend of Buddha, 2004
Alice Upside Down, 2007
The Clique, 2008
Alvin and the Chipmunks: The Squeakquel, 2009

FURTHER READING

Periodicals

Billboard, Apr. 9, 2011, p.9
Girls' Life, Apr. 1, 2010, p.50

Online Articles

http://www.girlslife.com
(Girls' Life, "GL Set Visit: Hangin' with Good Luck Charlie's Bridgit Mendler," Apr. 2, 2010)
http://www.radiofree.com
(Radio Free, "Family Antics, Breakthrough Roles, and Wagon Rides: An Exclusive Interview with Bridgit Mendler," May 11, 2010)
http://tommy2.net
(Tommy2.net, "Interview: Bridgit Mendler," undated)

ADDRESS

Bridgit Mendler
Disney Studios
500 South Buena Vista Street
Burbank, CA 91506

WORLD WIDE WEB SITES

http://tv.disney.go.com/disneychannel/goodluckcharlie
http://www.facebook.com

Lea Michele 1986-

American Singer and Actress
Broadway Performer
Star of the Hit Television Series "Glee"

BIRTH

Lea Michele Sarfati was born on August 29, 1986, in the Bronx, New York. She is the only child of Marc and Edith Sarfati. Early in her stage career, she dropped the use of her parents' last name, and she continues to use "Lea Michele" as her professional name.

YOUTH

Michele spent her first years in the Bronx, a borough of New York City. Most of her extended family still lives there. Her father, who is Jewish, ran a delicatessen, and her mother, who is Italian-American, worked as a nurse. When Michele started school, her family decided that she would get a better education if they moved to Tenafly, New Jersey, not far from New York City.

"If you didn't have a nose job and money and if you weren't thin, you weren't cool, popular, beautiful," Michele said. "I didn't conform to what people thought was cool in high school. I did what I wanted to do, what I believed in."

Michele began getting parts in Broadway shows while she was still in elementary school. Her parents then began renting an apartment in New York City so the family would have a temporary home base, close to the theaters where she performed. "I had my life and school and place to live in New Jersey, but we also had a place to stay when I was doing whatever show that I was doing in the city. It was a pretty good deal!" she recalled.

EDUCATION

Michele juggled the commitments of her Broadway career and her education for several years. When she reached high school, she decided to put performing on hold. At Tenafly High School, she played volleyball and was a member of the debate team. It was a good school, but there was a lot of pressure to have a certain look. "If you didn't have a nose job and money and if you weren't thin, you weren't cool, popular, beautiful," she recalled. Michele wasn't bothered by the peer pressure, though. She already had a lot of experience of the world and plenty of confidence in herself. "I didn't conform to what people thought was cool in high school," she said. "I did what I wanted to do, what I believed in."

FIRST JOBS

Les Misérables

Michele's impressive career began with an impulsive decision, made when she was eight years old. A friend of hers was planning to go to an audition for a part in the Broadway musical *Les Misérables,* a musical set in Paris dur-

Michele's first role was in the Broadway production of Les Misérables.

ing the 1800s. The musical is based on the 1862 novel by French author Victor Hugo. Just before the audition, the friend's father became ill and wasn't able to drive her to the event, so Michele's parents took her instead. Michele went along with them. The audition process looked like so much fun that she decided to join in, although she hadn't prepared for it and had never sung for an audience. She had recently seen *Phantom of the Opera* on Broadway and had been singing along with a CD of the music from the show since then. When the time came for her to solo during the audition, she launched into "Angel of Music," a song from *Phantom of the Opera.* On the basis of her audition and other tryouts that followed, she was selected to play the part of Young Cosette in the Broadway production of *Les Misérables.*

In the play, Cosette is an orphan who is cared for by the main character, a fugitive named Jean Valjean. Through the course of the story, the character ages from a child to a young woman. Michele performed in the role in 1995 and 1996, until she outgrew it. She loved the experience of doing the show, and she was determined to continue with singing and acting. She didn't have long to wait for her next part.

In 1997, shortly after leaving the cast of *Les Misérables,* Michele accepted a new role with the original cast of the hit show *Ragtime. Ragtime* is based on a novel of the same title that was written by E.L. Doctorow. It is set during the early years of the 20th century and tells the stories of three New York families: one white, one Jewish, and one African American. The central figure is Coalhouse Walker Jr., a ragtime pianist. Famous real-life people from the era are characters in the play, including illusionist Harry Houdini and manufacturing pioneer Henry Ford. Though the part played by Michele in the show is important, the character is known only as Little Girl. Michele appeared in the show in 1998 and 1999—she spent a year living in Toronto with her mother while the show played there, and another year with the show on Broadway.

Other Work in the Theater

In 1999 Michele became involved with an unusual show called *Spring Awakening.* At that point the play was still being developed in theater workshops and was not yet ready to be staged in major theaters. *Spring Awakening* is a rock-opera adaptation of a play by Frank Wedekind that was originally written in 1891. The story concerns troubled teenagers in a repressive German town. Michele played the part of Wendla, a girl who becomes pregnant. The spoken parts of the script use old-fashioned speech appropriate to the time of the original play, but the music is very contemporary—when the characters express their rage, compassion, and other emotions in song, the music is modern, edgy rock.

Michele appeared on Broadway in Ragtime *when she was 12 in the role of Little Girl.*

Despite her ongoing involvement with *Spring Awakening,* Michele limited her theater work during high school. After her graduation, she was accepted to New York University. At the same time, she was asked to join the cast of another major Broadway production, the 35th anniversary revival of the musical *Fiddler on the Roof.* First produced on Broadway in 1964, *Fiddler on the Roof* continued its original run for eight years, which at the time made it Broadway's longest-running show. The story is set in a Jewish village in Russia in 1905, at a time when society was changing rapidly. The central character, Tevye, is the father of five daughters. He struggles to hold onto the traditions of his culture, but when his daughters are old enough to marry, they challenge him with their unconventional choices. The play remains very popular both for its lively music and its affectionate depiction of a bygone way of life. After thinking seriously about her decision, Michele chose to join the cast of the revival of *Fiddler on the Roof* rather than enroll in college.

"When *Fiddler* came it was a big deciding point in my life," Michele remembered. "I was just about to graduate and head to college so it was a real deciding factor for me—which way is your life going to go? The college route and act a little bit on the side and major in law or something or are you just going to really give yourself to this? And that's what I decided to do. When I graduated I got an apartment in the city and I decided to not go to NYU and I've been working from then on." Michele was with the cast of *Fiddler* from 2004 to 2006, playing the parts of Tevye's daughters Chava and Shprintze.

After leaving *Fiddler,* Michele faced another tough decision. *Spring Awakening* was ready to open on Broadway, and she was asked to play Wendla. She had also been offered the part of Eponine in *Les Misérables,* a role she had wanted for years. Due to her long involvement with *Spring Awakening,* she chose to stay with that show and appeared as Wendla from 2006 to 2008. Reviewers praised her work, and she was nominated for a Drama Desk Award for Outstanding Actress in a Musical in 2007.

Looking back on her extensive stage career, Michele said that one of the most important things she has learned is how to maintain her voice and health under the demands of a grueling schedule. "When you can do eight shows a week for a year, two years, or however long you're in a show, you can pretty much do anything," she said.

CAREER HIGHLIGHTS

"Glee"

While appearing in *Spring Awakening,* Michele met Ryan Murphy, a writer, director, and producer for television and film. His work includes "Popular," a TV series about the popular and unpopular cliques at a high school, and particularly two girls, one from each group; and "Nip/Tuck," a dark TV series about a plastic surgery center and the two doctors who run it. When Michele later heard that Murphy was working to develop "Glee," a program about a high school choir, she knew she wanted to be part of it. "The minute I read the script, already being a fan of Ryan Murphy, I was

Members of the cast of "Glee."

so excited to get the opportunity to audition," she said. "I immediately started fighting and making sure that I was able to get in. Like, every day I would call [my agent] and be like, 'When am I going in for "Glee"? When am I going in for "Glee"? Make sure you stay on top of this project!'"

After successfully making it through the first two rounds of auditions, Michele was on her way to the final call when she was involved in a fairly serious car accident. Desperate to get her chance at the role of Rachel, she ran on foot the rest of the way to the audition. "I had to leave the smoking car on the street. I had glass in my hair and nicks all over my body," she remembered. She felt that kind of fanatical determination was something that Rachel, her character, would have shown in pursuit of a part. It was only much later, after she had been cast as Rachel, that Michele learned Murphy had written the part with her in mind.

Comedy, Drama, and Music

"Glee" is funny, dramatic, and full of music. The hour-long program draws on the appeal of movies and TV programs like *High School Musical* and "American Idol," but it has a self-mocking twist that makes it unique. The show is set at William McKinley High School in Lima, Ohio. The plot turns on the rivalry between the school's unpopular and popular groups as embodied by the school's glee club or "show choir," which is called New Directions, and the championship cheerleading squad, known as the Cheerios, as well as the other school athletes. New Directions is sponsored by the idealistic Spanish teacher, Mr. Schuester (played by Matthew Morrison). He fondly remembers his own days in the choir and wants to transform the underdog and geeky singing group into something wonderful. Schuester's rival is Sue Sylvester (played by Jane Lynch), the aggressive, humorless coach of the Cheerios. She is horrified when Mr. Schuester convinces Finn (played by Cory Monteith), one of the school's top athletes and most popular students, to join the choir—and even more horrified when he begins to date Rachel.

Michele plays Rachel Barry, a member of the glee club, a talented, hard-driving young woman who is certain that stardom is her destiny. In fact, every time she signs her name, she puts a gold star after it to symbolize her inborn stardom and her ambitions. Rachel definitely wants fame more than anything else, but she is also insecure and desperately wants to be liked. Instead, she is frequently the target of bullying by the more popular students at the school. Michele knows that Rachel has some annoying traits, but she understands her very well. Of "Glee," she said, "I think it's what we need on TV—a show that is filled with heart and love, that is funny. It sends an amazing message to kids about the arts and being who you are."

"I think it's what we need on TV—a show that is filled with heart and love, that is funny," Michele said about "Glee." "It sends an amazing message to kids about the arts and being who you are."

"Glee" holds the attention of audiences in part because of its engaging storylines, focusing on the ups and downs of the characters' personal lives. The core of the show, however, is music. In each episode, several musical numbers are featured. These are sometimes woven into the plot as songs being performed or rehearsed by New Directions, while at other times they are presented as spontaneous moments when the characters sing and dance to express their emotions. The music featured on the show comes from a variety of sources and time periods. It has included songs originally recorded by such classic rock groups as Journey, Kiss, and Queen, as well as some made famous by such contemporary performers as Beyoncé, Lady Gaga, Britney Spears, and Kanye West.

Gleeks Take "Glee" to the Top

Michele with Cory Monteith, who plays her boyfriend, Finn.

"Glee" was introduced to television viewers in three stages. A sneak peek at the show was aired after the May 2009 finale of the "American Idol" talent competition. Next, 12 episodes of the show were aired on the Fox network from September through December that year. A four-month break followed, then nine new episodes of "Glee" began broadcasting in April 2010. The show ended its first season in June 2010, followed by a second season from 2010 to 2011.

The show's fan base grew rapidly, with loyal viewers calling themselves "Gleeks." Gleeks not only love the music and melodrama of their favorite show, they also take to heart the underlying message that everyone should have respect for themselves and for others, especially those who are different. The show's message of tolerance has taken on special resonance in the story lines about characters who are gay, disabled, or bullied.

The show soon became a cultural phenomenon whose popularity extended beyond television. Recordings of the music, released on iTunes as soon as each episode aired, regularly became bestsellers, with more than 33 million downloads and two platinum and three gold albums. Fans posted tribute videos on YouTube and formed "Glee" clubs on Facebook. When the show's producers created the concert tour "Glee Live! In Concert!" it sold out a total of 13 shows in 2010 and 22 shows in 2011. A blockbuster 3D movie of the concert tour was released in 2011, as well as the debut of the reality TV series "The Glee Project," in which contestants compete to appear on "Glee."

"Glee" has been recognized and rewarded with an impressive array of honors and awards, including a Peabody Award, given annually for excellence in electronic media; three Golden Globe Awards, including the award for Best Television Series-Comedy or Musical; four Emmy Awards; and two

"Glee" does Lady Gaga.

Grammy Award nominations. That type of acclaim was reinforced by critics as well. "Bold story lines, witty writing, and Michele's knock-down-drag-out voice" are among the show's strongest points, according to Christina Kinon in the *New York Daily News*. Writing in *USA Today*, Robert Bianco said, "There have been few shows as rousing, promising, perplexing, and potentially heartbreaking as this high school musical comedy. . . . When "Glee" is at its singing, dancing, comic best (and it often is), the effect can be sheer bliss." In his opinion, one of the highlights of the show's first season was when Michele's "driven and yet somehow endearing Rachel is tearing into a first-rate version of Rihanna's 'Take a Bow.'" Another reviewer, Domonic Botto of the *St. Petersburg Times*, also noted that moment. "Lea Michele better 'Take a Bow' after belting out Rihanna's single," Botto wrote. "Her voice is stunning." Reviewing the show for *Daily Variety*, Andrew Barker compared her to superstar Barbra Streisand, a powerful singer and actress. "Broadway-tested Lea Michele revealed herself as the most obvious pro, performing snippets of Streisand with power and presence."

For Michele, the comparison to Streisand was a welcome one. Michele does not fit into the Hollywood stereotype of a blue-eyed blond starlet, and she hopes her looks will make her a role model for other girls like her. "I remember looking up to Barbra Streisand, and thinking, 'Finally, someone who has a Jewish nose, who didn't get a nose job,'" Michele has said. "I love me and my body and my Jewish nose. If that is inspiring and can give young girls a sense of confidence, that's great."

Despite all the accolades, many say Michele is a pleasure to work with. According to cast member Jenna Ushkowitz, who plays Tina, "[Michele] always has everything down before she comes to the set, her lines and her songs. She's a perfectionist in every way." Ryan Murphy also praised Michele's attitude. "Lea is the sweetest, most professional girl," he observed. "She's incredibly kind and she's always on time and she's always with her cast, hanging out. They're all close."

HOME AND FAMILY

Parents of children in show business are often seen as pushy and troublesome. Michele said her parents didn't fit that mold. "Over the years, you can ask just about anybody in the business, they were the coolest parents to work with. They really helped me in getting jobs because they had such a great reputation of being cool parents in a world of crazy [ones]."

Michele now divides her time between New York City and Los Angeles, California, where "Glee" is filmed. After signing on with "Glee," she tried to make a new life for herself in Los Angeles, but she soon realized New York would always be her home. "Los Angeles is my work base," she said. "I'm very comfortable out there and have a safe group of people that I trust. And then I come home.... I work, work, work out there and then I come [to New York]. I see shows and hang out with my family and I recharge." Michele has shared a home with Dianne Argonne, who plays Quinn, another "Glee" character. She is dating Theo Stockman, a Broadway actor.

FAVORITE MUSIC

Michele likes all kinds of music, including classic rock, such as Queen, The Who, and Journey; Broadway show tunes; Celine Dion; Alanis Morrisette; Barbra Streisand; and Dolly Parton.

HOBBIES AND OTHER INTERESTS

When not working, Michele likes to relax by watching television and movies, getting pizza with friends, doing yoga, hiking, and exercising. She is a vegetarian and a spokesperson for PETA (People for the Ethical Treatment of Animals). She has two cats, Sheila and Claude.

ACTING CREDITS

Broadway Plays

Les Misérables, 1995-96
Ragtime, 1998-99

Fiddler on the Roof, 2004-06
Spring Awakening, 2006-08

Television

"Glee,"2009-

HONORS AND AWARDS

Satellite Award: 2009, for Best Actress in a Series, Comedy or Musical
Screen Actors Guild Award: 2010, for Performance by an Ensemble in a Comedy Series (shared with the cast of"Glee")

FURTHER READING

Periodicals

Billboard, May 8, 2010, p.16
Cleo, Jan. 1, 2011
Daily Variety, May 24, 2010, p.2
Entertainment Weekly, May 22, 2009, p.48; Sep. 18, 2009, p.76
Glamour, Oct. 2010, p.268
Marie Claire, May 2011, p.144
New York Times, Apr. 11, 2010, p.19; May 31, 2010, p.C1; July 26, 2011, p.C3
Teen Vogue, Dec. 2010, p.136
USA Today, May 10, 2010, p.D1
Vanity Fair, Jan. 2010, p.42
Washington Post, Sep. 6, 2009, p.E3

Online Articles

www.broadwayworld.com
(Broadway World,"Spring [Awakening] Fever: An Interview with Lea Michele,"Jan. 23, 2007)
www.playbill.com
(Playbill, Interview with Lea Michele, Nov. 24, 2006)

ADDRESS

Lea Michele
"Glee"
Fox Broadcasting Publicity Dept.
PO Box 900
Beverly Hills, CA 90213-0900

WORLD WIDE WEB SITE

http://www.fox.com/glee

Janelle Monáe 1985-

American Singer and Songwriter
Creator of *Metropolis—The Chase* and *The ArchAndroid*

BIRTH

Janelle Monáe Robinson was born on December 1, 1985, in Kansas City, Kansas. Her father worked as a sanitation truck driver, and her mother worked as a janitor. Her parents later split up, and her stepfather worked for the U.S. Postal Service.

YOUTH

Monáe grew up in a low-income, working-class community in Kansas City. Her father was a drug addict, which deeply affected her childhood. "Though there were plenty of good days, it really damaged my family. There were times when mentally I had to create my own world," she recalled. "There was a lot of confusion and nonsense where I grew up, so I reacted by creating my own little world. I began to see how music could change lives, and I began to dream about a world where every day was like anime and Broadway, where music fell from the sky and anything could happen."

———— " ————

"I actually decided what I wanted to do very early on in life," Monáe recalled. "In fact, when I was about nine years old I had a meeting with my family, told them what my plans were, and asked them to get on board.... And they've been very supportive ever since."

Music was a big part of Monáe's early life, much of it from the family's involvement at church. "My father's side are very musically inclined, his mother—my grandmother—played the organ, and my cousins would sing raw gospel—a kind of James Brown sound," she recalled. "And then the other side was classically trained, beautiful operatic voices. So I would jump back and forth between those sides of my family.... They were very encouraging of me, when I told them what I wanted to do." With this type of background, it was perhaps no surprise that Monáe became interested in singing, dancing, writing, and musical theater. "I actually decided what I wanted to do very early on in life. In fact, when I was about nine years old I had a meeting with my family, told them what my plans were, and asked them to get on board.... And they've been very supportive ever since."

Monáe was a member of the local Coterie Theatre and participated in their Young Playwrights' Round Table. When she was around 11 or 12 years old, she wrote her first play, about a boy and a girl who fall in love with a plant. "I was infatuated with photosynthesis," Monáe explained. (Photosynthesis is the process that plants use to get energy from sunlight.)

EDUCATION

Monáe's love of performing arts continued throughout high school. She was a member of an a capella choir, a type of singing group that performs without musical accompaniment. She also performed in her school's musical theater productions of *Cinderella* and *The Wiz.*

An early shot of Monáe with Scar, Big Boi, and André 3000 from Outkast.

Even though she participated in many of the arts programs offered in her community, Monáe began to feel limited by the lack of performing arts opportunities in Kansas City. "A lot of the people that I was hanging out with didn't really have a lot of goals. And I felt myself ending up walking dead, and so that's when I realized that I could actually go away and show that just because you come from a small little town in Kansas, [in] the poorest county, that you definitely have a choice."

Monáe was awarded a scholarship to the prestigious American Musical and Dramatic Academy in New York City. As soon as she graduated from high school, she moved to New York and began studying musical theater. But after two years at the Academy, Monáe once again began to feel that her creativity was being limited. She wanted to write her own stories and create her own characters, but the Academy's formal program of study did not allow students to perform their own original work. "School in New York honed my craft even further," she said. "It taught me different techniques, but it also taught me that I don't want to just be another musical-theater student auditioning for Broadway plays and getting roles thousands of people have already played. I want to create my own roles, my own musicals.... Going to school helped me realize I have a hunger for creating." She left the Academy in 2004 without completing the program.

CAREER HIGHLIGHTS

After leaving school, Monáe decided that she wanted to travel. On a whim, she bought a ticket for a flight to the Netherlands, a country in Northern Europe that is also known as Holland. The plane made a stop in Atlanta, Georgia, before continuing on to Europe. Monáe impulsively decided to get off the plane and stay in Atlanta. "I had an intuition about Atlanta," she explained. "I knew that really creative people like Outkast had come from here, so my subconscious was telling me that I should stay. I felt like this could be a place where I could start my own movement."

Monáe soon joined a band and began touring, playing at local colleges and small bars. Around this time, she formed the Wondaland Arts Society with a group of fellow artists in Atlanta. Wondaland is a cooperative arts organization that helps new artists to produce their work outside of the traditional music industry. Wondaland includes an independent record label and other resources that connect music with literature, theater, dance, and performance art. "The Wondaland Arts Society was created [to come up with] a different blueprint for aspiring artists," Monáe stressed. "We were going back and forth, talking to labels, and I just felt like they were really out of touch with where the people were, what they wanted to hear, and where music was headed. So I got connected with a collective of individuals who had the same goals as mine." With Wondaland, Monáe produced a demo CD of her music and began selling it on her own.

The First Big Break

In 2005, Monáe performed at the opening night party for a new Atlanta restaurant owned by rapper and record producer Sean "Diddy" Combs. Antwan "Big Boi" Patton of the hip-hop duo Outkast was in the audience that night, and he was impressed by her performance. Patton and Monáe soon began working together. Two of her songs were included on Patton's compilation CD *Got Purp? Vol. 2,* including the track "Lettin' Go." This was Monáe's first national release. She continued to collaborate with Outkast in 2006, appearing in the music video for the track "Morris Brown" and contributing to their album *Idlewild,* a soundtrack for the movie musical of the same name, set in a nightclub in the South during the Prohibition era. (For more information on Outkast, see *Biography Today*, Sep. 2004.)

Metropolis—The Chase

In 2007, Monáe released her debut extended play recording *Metropolis—The Chase.* She conceived it as a concept album, meaning that the music tells a story, with each song being like a chapter in a book. The story of *Me-*

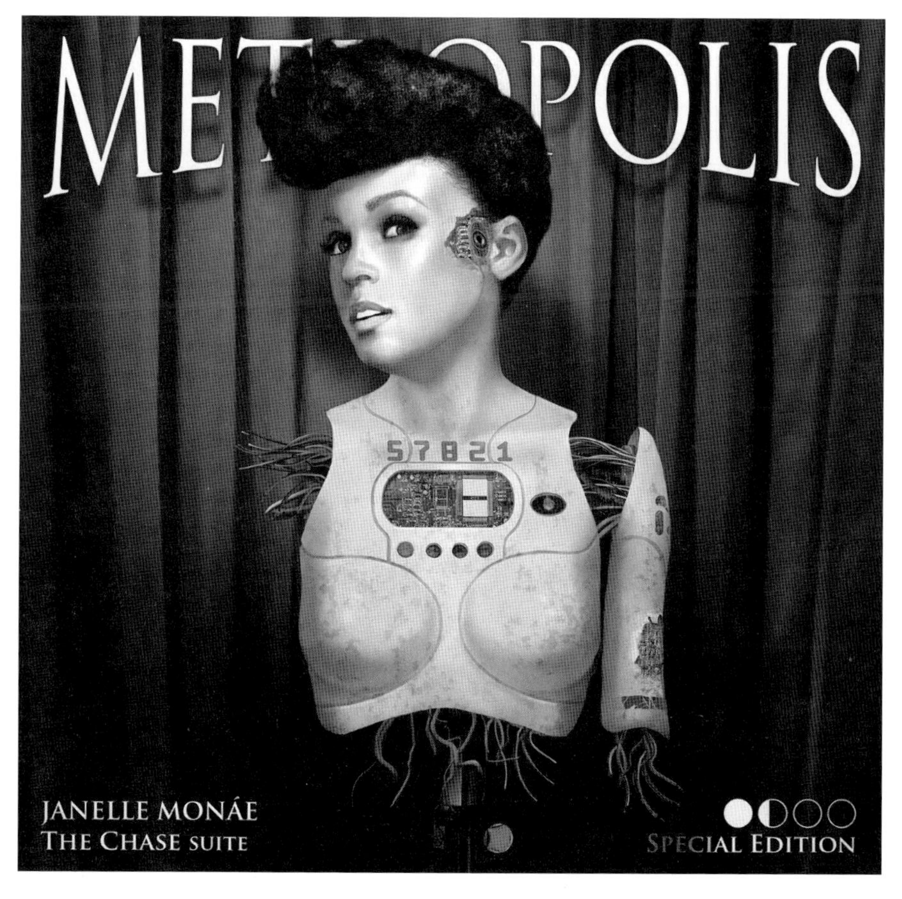

Monáe as the android Cindi Mayweather.

tropolis—The Chase takes place in the year 2719. An android (a robot designed to look and act like a human) named Cindi Mayweather is in trouble because she has broken the law by falling in love with a human. Cindi is on the run, trying to escape disassembly—the death sentence for androids. Her story unfolds through the music, a blend of hip-hop, rock, soul, and rhythm and blues that the *Boston Globe* called "futuristic" and "very much the singular product of [Monáe's] imagination."

In creating the story of Cindi Mayweather, Monáe was inspired by the 1920s black-and-white silent movie *Metropolis,* a classic film created by Fritz Lang. This movie tells the story of a future in which the wealthiest business people live in a luxurious city in the clouds. The workers who keep the city running are forced to live underground in terrible conditions. One day, the son of a rich city-dweller discovers the worker community.

Horrified, he becomes determined to free the workers and create a bridge between the two separate worlds. "I'm a huge fan of science fiction, and *Metropolis* is the godfather of the genre," Monáe explained.

For Monáe, the movie *Metropolis* was a powerful story about the "constant struggle between the haves and the have-nots, the 'other.' Androids will be the new other." With *Metropolis—The Chase,* Monáe imagined a future time when humans and androids live side by side. "The android is always looked at as the other, the same way that blacks, foreigners, and homosexuals are looked at as the other," she suggested. "I wanted people to prepare for a time when we all have to get along with androids. Will we hate them? Be afraid of them?" Monáe intended *Metropolis—The Chase* to be the first in a four-part series about Cindi Mayweather. She envisioned the complete series as a musical science fiction adventure.

The creativity and innovative style of *Metropolis—The Chase* once again caught the attention of Sean "Diddy" Combs. In 2008, he signed a record distribution contract with Monáe and produced a repackaged special edition of *Metropolis—The Chase* that included several new tracks. Her international career was launched when the track "Many Moons" was nominated in 2009 for a Grammy Award for Best Urban/Alternative Performance. Combs has praised her in many different interviews. "Janelle Monáe is one of the most important signings of my career," he contended. "There is no doubt in my mind that Janelle is the kind of artist that changes the game. She is a true visionary, with an original sound and a mesmerizing presence. I can't wait to watch her future unfold."

The ArchAndroid

In 2010, Monáe released *The ArchAndroid,* containing the second and third parts of the Cindi Mayweather story. This recording tells the story of Cindi's mission to free the citizens of Metropolis from the Great Divide, a secret society that has been using time travel to suppress freedom and love throughout the ages. "Musically, *The ArchAndroid* is an epic James Bond film in outer space," she declared. "In terms of influence, it encompasses all the things I love—scores for films like *Goldfinger* mixed with albums like Stevie Wonder's *Music of My Mind* and David Bowie's *Ziggy Stardust,* along with experimental hip-hop stuff like Outkast's *Stankonia.*"

Monáe worked in collaboration with many other artists to create *The ArchAndroid.* The record includes contributions from Outkast, self-described "punk prophets" Deep Cotton, poet Saul Williams, the Emory University Symphony Orchestra, and the dance-punk troupe Of Montreal.

Monáe's headpiece is said to evoke imagery from the movie Metropolis.

Monáe described the process of creating *The ArchAndroid* as very intense. "The music would sometimes wake us up in our sleep. We'd record melodies on our phones. Sometimes we'd stay up for days at a time just writing this music. The story and visions coming to us were so great that we wanted this music to capture everything we were feeling inside," Monáe explained. "In terms of writing the music, we wanted the story to be very compelling, but we also wanted to make sure the journey we're taking people on makes them feel like they're watching one big 'emotion picture.'"

The ArchAndroid enjoyed rave reviews from music critics, including these comments from Jody Rosen in *Rolling Stone*: "[*The ArchAndroid*] is so ambitious, so freighted with sounds and ideas and allusions, it threatens at times to sink under its own weight," she acknowledged. "But on ferocious songs like 'Come Alive' and the manic neojump blues 'Tightrope' (featuring

Big Boi), Monáe's charisma and energy are so forceful that the jumble makes perfect sense. Whoever else—whatever else—Janelle Monáe is, she's a star." Jon Pareles offered similar comments in the *New York Times.* "This sci-fi concept album brims over with Ms. Monáe's ambitions: singing, rapping, flirting, fighting for change, and absorbing—for starters—funk, psychedelia, hip-hop, and show tunes. It's a tour de force; even the misfires are promising." Writing in the *Chicago Tribune,* Greg Kot observed that "A star is born."

Becoming Famous

Monáe's reputation began to grow after the release of *The ArchAndroid.* The continued support of music industry giants like Combs and Patton helped introduce Monáe to new audiences around the world. In 2010, she won the Soul Train Centric Award and the Rhythm & Soul Music Vanguard Award, and *The ArchAndroid* was nominated for Best R&B Album in the 2010 Teen Choice Awards. The honors continued in 2011, with Grammy nominations for Best Contemporary R&B Album for *The ArchAndroid* and Best Urban/Alternative Performance for "Tightrope." Monáe was named one of the 2011 *Essence* Black Women in Music honorees by *Essence* magazine, which called her a "remarkable creative force and a passionately talented young performer." She was also honored as one of the 2011 TheGrio's 100 History Makers in the Making.

In the midst of all the praise and attention, Monáe has managed to remain modest and focused on her career. "As an artist it's very important to always keep my balance and not get too high or too low about things. Even when I'm getting lots of positive reinforcement, to remain calm and enjoy the journey," she observed. "This is just the beginning of my career so to be recognized at such an early stage just gives me more encouragement and hopefully I can open up doors for more young girls."

"It means a lot that I'm not just looked at as an underground artist, that I'm being respected on a different level," Monáe continued. "I want to be looked at as a leader and a business woman. I really feel that music and artists have a huge influence in the way we think. My goal is to help bring as many people as I possibly can together with my music."

MAJOR INFLUENCES

Monáe's distinctive personal style has gotten as much attention as her music. Her trademark tuxedo and stylized fashion sense were inspired by singer and actress Marlene Dietrich, actress Katharine Hepburn, and her own parents."I grew up in a working-class family. My mother was a janitor, my father drove trash trucks, and my step-father still works for the post office. So, because I feel very connected to the working class, I do pay homage to them by wearing a black-and-white uniform every time I perform and whenever I'm out and about. Because I still consider what I do as work, even if it is very much work that I enjoy.... I mean, to me I make music for the people—to uplift them, to motivate them, and to be a beacon of hope for them.... I basically represent for individuals who are gonna turn nothing into something."

"With regards to the way that I dress, to the things that come out of my mouth, I'm really trying to give a different perspective," Monáe explained. "And I think there are a lot of young girls out there who are like me." She continued, "I don't believe in menswear and women's wear. I just like what I like and I want to be respected as an individual. I think it's time for someone to help redefine what a woman can wear, how she can dress and wear her hair. There are lots of young girls right now who are dealing with identity crises and unsure if they should be who they are. I always say embrace those things that make you unique and use them as super powers. Being a woman can be defined in so many ways. You don't have to wear dresses or heels. Why, in order to be successful, should we follow the same blueprint of playing the doll or the sexy vixen? If I had to fit in, part of the real me is just being erased because I am being a mimic. Every day I still feel like we are fighting against conformity."

"Because I feel very connected to the working class, I do pay homage to them by wearing a black-and-white uniform every time I perform and whenever I'm out and about. Because I still consider what I do as work, even if it is very much work that I enjoy."

Monáe's music is influenced by a wide variety of artists spanning many decades. Among her favorites, she lists Judy Garland, Elvis Presley, James Brown, David Bowie, Anita Baker, The Monkees, Jimi Hendrix, Lauryn Hill, and Fela Kuti. She has also acknowledged the tremendous influence of her parents."I'm just thankful to have parents who have supported me since I've been two years old and who have never discouraged me not to sing or to be in every musical in middle school or high school," Monáe declared. "That means a lot to me because your parents are sometimes your biggest influ-

Monáe in her "uniform."

ences, and the fact that they have always been encouraging to me no matter what direction I go in means a lot. They want me to be free and fearless."

HOBBIES AND OTHER INTERESTS

Monáe volunteers as a mentor for Just Us Girls, an organization in Atlanta, Georgia, that works with inner-city girls who are interested in the performing arts.

SELECTED RECORDINGS

"Lettin' Go," 2005 (single)
Metropolis—The Chase Suite, 2007 (extended play)
Metropolis—The Chase Suite, Special Edition, 2008
The ArchAndroid, 2010

HONORS AND AWARDS

Centric Award (Soul Train): 2010
Vanguard Award (ASCAP Rhythm & Soul Music Awards): 2010
Essence Black Women in Music Honoree (*Essence*): 2011
TheGrio's 100 History Makers in the Making (TheGrio.com): 2011

FURTHER READING

Periodicals

Atlanta Journal-Constitution, May 18, 2010, p.D1
Crisis, Summer 2010, p.5
Ebony, Aug. 20, 2010, p.75
Essence, Feb. 9, 2011
Interview, May 1, 2009
Jet, Aug. 2, 2010
Los Angeles Times, June 20, 2010, p.E1
Mother Jones, Nov.-Dec. 2010, p.68
New York, May 24, 2010
Rolling Stone, Dec. 11, 2008, p.76
Sojourners, Sep./Oct. 2010, p.41
USA Today, Oct. 22, 2010

Online Articles

http://atlanticrecords.com
(Atlantic Records, "Countdown to the Grammys: Janelle Monáe," Jan. 31, 2011)

http://www.bluesandsoul.com
(Blues & Soul,"Janelle Monáe: Funky Sensation," undated)
http://www.thegrio.com/black-history/thegrios-100/2011-janelle-Monáe.php
(The Grio,"The Grio's 100: Janelle Monáe, Of-the-Moment Artist with Timeless Appeal,"Feb. 22, 2011)
http://www.lilithfair.com/artists/janelle-Monáe
(Lilith Fair,"Janelle Monáe,"2010)
http://www.papermag.com
(Paper Mag,"I Am, I Be,"June 29, 2009)

ADDRESS

Janelle Monáe
Atlantic Record Group
1290 Avenue of the Americas
New York, NY 10104

WORLD WIDE WEB SITE

http://www.jmonae.com

Melanie Oudin 1991-

American Professional Tennis Player
WTA Tour Newcomer of the Year in 2009

BIRTH

Melanie Oudin (pronounced ooh-DAN) was born on September 23, 1991, in Marietta, Georgia. Her father, John Oudin, works in software sales and marketing. Her mother, Leslie (Robertson) Oudin, played college tennis at the University of Georgia. Melanie has a fraternal twin sister, Katherine, who was born one minute before her. "We don't even look like sisters," Melanie noted. "I've got blond hair and bluish-green eyes and she's got brown hair and brown eyes." She also has a younger sister, Christina.

YOUTH

Melanie grew up in the West Cobb subdivision of Marietta, on the outskirts of Atlanta. She was an active girl who spent a lot of time outside playing four square, badminton, soccer, and other sports. She and her twin sister took up tennis at age seven at the suggestion of their grandmother, Joan Robertson. A longtime member of the Atlanta Lawn Tennis Association, Robertson promised to teach her granddaughters the game—as long as they agreed to come to the courts first thing in the morning. "I said, 'You need to be out there by 7:30,'" Robertson recalled. "Sure enough, [Melanie] would come trotting down those stairs in that little white hat."

"Melanie fell in love with tennis right away. Although both she and her sister Katherine showed talent, Melanie's dedication to the game went far deeper than her sister's. "We used to hit against the garage door," Katherine remembered. "I would get tired and she would just stay out there and keep hitting balls over and over.""

Melanie fell in love with tennis right away. She would cry whenever it rained, because that meant her morning tennis lesson would be canceled. Although both she and Katherine showed talent, Melanie's dedication to the game went far deeper than her sister's. "We used to hit against the garage door," Katherine remembered. "I would get tired and she would just stay out there and keep hitting balls over and over."

When Melanie was nine, she began working with Coach Brian de Villiers at the Racquet Club of the South (RCS Academy) in Norcross, Georgia. He made her get up early, eat healthy foods, do tough conditioning workouts, and play matches against older opponents. But de Villiers soon found that Melanie's intensity matched his own. "When they're that young, you never really know if they have the tools," he explained. "But for a nine-, ten-year-old she was very focused. And she hated to lose."

In 2004, at the age of 12, Melanie won the state of Georgia's junior singles tennis title for girls 14 and under. In addition, she and Katherine were runners up for the state title in doubles that year. By 2006, when Melanie

Oudin in 2008, in her first season on the women's professional tour.

turned 14, the U.S. Tennis Association ranked her as the top girl her age in the country.

EDUCATION

Around that time, Melanie and her parents made an important decision about her education. Melanie had attended Eastside Christian School in Marietta through the sixth grade. But once she began traveling around the country to compete in tournaments, she found it very difficult to juggle the responsibilities of school and tennis. "A lot of times she had to turn in homework before she left, so we'd be up late trying to finish it," her mother remembered, "and then we'd get to the tournament and she was exhausted."

Before the start of seventh grade, Melanie convinced her parents to allow her to home-school so that she could devote more time to tennis. She enrolled in an online education program called Keystone School, which gave her the flexible schedule she needed to travel and to practice five hours per day. On a typical day, Melanie did school work in the morning from 8:00 to 11:00, played tennis all afternoon, came home for dinner with her family in the evening, then did a couple more hours of school work before bed. "Not seeing my friends as much, that's been tough, and I'll be missing out on high school, but I'm willing to give it up to go pro," she stated.

Unwilling to make that kind of sacrifice, her twin sister stayed in school and eventually became the top girls' singles player on her high school team. "Melanie will stay on the tennis court all day and night," Katherine noted. "Tennis, it gets me in shape, it's a hobby, and I want to get a college scholarship. But Melanie loves tennis more than I have seen anyone."

CAREER HIGHLIGHTS

Turning Pro

In 2006 Oudin joined the International Tennis Federation (ITF) Junior Circuit, the world's premiere series of tennis tournaments for players under the age of 18. After learning the ropes as a 15-year-old, she emerged as one of the most dominant players on the tour in late 2007. Oudin claimed her first ITF junior tournament title in September of that year. Then she went on to win 27 consecutive matches and four more titles before finally losing in the girls' 18-and-under singles final in December. "It was like I didn't know how to lose. I'd be down a set, a break, and still be confident I could come back and win," she related. "It's always been about confidence, about believing in myself."

TENNIS FACTS

The professional women's tour consists of a series of tournaments over the course of the year. Each tennis tournament is organized in rounds of competition. Winning players advance to the next round, while losing players are eliminated. Most tournaments consist of three or four preliminary rounds, followed by quarterfinals (featuring eight players), semifinals (four players), and finals (two players). The player who wins the final match is the tournament champion and claims the title.

A player wins a match by defeating her opponent in 2 of 3 sets, with each set including multiple games. The first player to win 6 games usually wins the set, but if the margin of victory is less than 2 games, the set is decided by a tie-breaker. Shorthand notation is often used to show the score of a tennis match. For example, 5-7, 6-4, 6-3 means that the player in question lost the first set in a tie-breaker, then came back to win the next two sets by scores of 6 games to 4 and 6 games to 3.

Over the course of her remarkable winning streak, Oudin's world junior ranking jumped from number 90 to number 2. She became the only American girl to be ranked in the top 25. In February 2008 Oudin decided to turn professional and join the Sony-Ericsson Women's Tennis Association (WTA) Tour. "I think she's ready for the next step," de Villiers declared. Although the move meant that Oudin gave up her eligibility to play tennis in college, it also allowed her to begin earning prize money in both WTA and ITF professional tournaments. Since the WTA had age-eligibility rules that limited the number of tour events she could enter until she turned 18, Oudin also continued to play in some junior tournaments.

Shortly after turning pro, Oudin reached the finals of an ITF professional tournament at the $25,000 Fort Walton Beach in Florida. She captured her first ITF title in July at the $50,000 Lexington in Kentucky. Oudin chose to play in the junior division at the WTA Tour's four "major" tournaments (the Australian Open, the French Open, Wimbledon in England, and the U.S. Open), which are collectively known as the Grand Slam of professional tennis. Although she was the top-seeded junior player at the French Open, she lost in the quarterfinals. The U.S. Open in September 2008 marked the final junior tournament of her career. By the end of her first year as a pro, Oudin had increased her world ranking from 373 to 177.

At Wimbledon in 2009, Oudin defeated sixth-ranked Jelena Jankovic in the third round, her first victory over a top-10 player.

Making Her Move

As the 2009 WTA season got underway, Oudin felt ready to take on the big names in women's tennis. She especially hoped to play well in the Grand Slam tournaments and improve her world ranking. "This is the year I need to make my move. I know that," she stated. "This is the year I need to do something, make a name for myself. I know there are so many things in my game that I can improve. I'm looking forward to the places I can go."

Although Oudin made an early exit at the Australian Open and French Open, she made a splash at Wimbledon. After fighting her way through the qualifying rounds to reach the main draw of 64 players, she pulled off three consecutive upsets over higher-ranked opponents. Oudin chalked up her first victory over a player ranked among the top 10 in the world by defeating sixth-seeded Jelena Jankovic in the third round. Jankovic was so shocked that she could not manage to be gracious in defeat. She claimed that she felt ill during the match and insisted that Oudin "cannot hurt you with anything. She doesn't have any weapons." Unfortunately, Oudin's impressive run ended in the fourth round, when she lost to 11th-seeded Agnieszka Radwanska.

Oudin's success at Wimbledon gave her a boost in confidence going into the most-watched event in professional tennis, the U.S. Open in New York City. As the prestigious tournament approached, the Adidas shoe company invited Oudin to design her own sneaker to wear on the court. With the help of her boyfriend, Austin Smith—an up-and-coming young tennis player whom she met at the Racquet Club of the South—Oudin used the Adidas website to create a distinctive, bright pink and yellow design. But then she struggled to come up with an appropriate phrase or slogan to put on the personalized nameplate on the heel of the shoe. Smith suggested "Believe," and Oudin decided that it was perfect. "For me, it's all about that," she explained. "It's believing that I can beat these girls."

Believing in Herself

Armed with ever-increasing self-confidence, Oudin went on a tear at the 2009 U.S. Open at Arthur Ashe Stadium. Once she worked her way through the qualifying rounds to reach the main draw, she upset four highly ranked Russian players in a row. Oudin's first-round victory came against Anastasia Pavlyuchenkova. Next she faced fourth-seeded Elena Dementieva, a former world number one player who had captured the gold medal in women's singles at the 2008 Olympic Games. Oudin overcame sweltering heat, a thigh injury, and the pressure of playing in front of 23,000 fans to win her second-round match by a score of 5-7, 6-4, 6-3.

"Elena was the highest-ranked player I've ever played, so it was a big deal today," Oudin said afterward. "I was just happy to be out there, and I'm glad I won."

In the third round, Oudin faced 2006 U.S. Open champion Maria Sharapova. (For more information on Sharapova, see *Biography Today,* September 2005.) Although Sharapova was only seeded number 29 because she was coming back from an injury, the towering Russian remained one of the hardest hitters in women's tennis. Few people gave Oudin any chance of winning. But after dropping the first set, the young American surged back and took control of the match. With the incredulous crowd squarely behind her, Oudin advanced by a score of 3-6, 6-4, 7-5. "I just kept fighting as hard as I could," she said afterward. "I think the biggest weapon can be mental toughness. It doesn't have to be a stroke or a shot or anything like that. If you're mentally tough out there, then you can beat anyone."

"I just kept fighting as hard as I could," Oudin said after beating Maria Sharapova at the U.S. Open. "I think the biggest weapon can be mental toughness. It doesn't have to be a stroke or a shot or anything like that. If you're mentally tough out there, then you can beat anyone."

By the time Oudin defeated 13th seed Nadia Petrova in the fourth round, she had emerged as the Cinderella story of the tournament. The young, inexperienced, relatively unknown player with "Believe" on her shoes inspired tennis fans across the country with her spirit and determination. For Oudin, becoming the youngest American to reach the quarterfinals of a Grand Slam tournament in a decade was like a dream come true. "Walking onto Arthur Ashe, I felt like I'd done it a thousand times, like I belonged there," she related. "Seeing the whole crowd clapping for me, that's what I worked for—that specific moment."

Unfortunately, Oudin's fairytale march through the U.S. Open ended in a quarterfinal loss to Caroline Wozniacki of Denmark. Oudin's confidence faded as she committed 43 unforced errors in the match, and she was eliminated 6-2, 6-2. "It was a deflating end to a heady 10 days for Oudin, who has quickly turned her winning combination of wide-eyed charm and steely-eyed competitive fire into a considerable following, emerging from relative obscurity to play four straight matches on the largest show court in

During the 2009 U.S. Open, Oudin defeated Maria Sharapova 3-6, 6-4, 7-5, but then lost in the quarterfinals to Caroline Wozniacki 6-2, 6-2.

Grand Slam tennis," Christopher Clarey wrote in the *New York Times.* Although Oudin was disappointed to be knocked out of the tournament, she looked back on the experience with pride. "I had a great run in this tournament," she noted. "The whole experience I had will take me a long way." She was also pleased to see her world ranking jump from number 70 to a career-high 44.

Coping with Fame

Oudin's gutsy underdog victories and poise on the court made her a huge fan favorite during the U.S. Open. She was surprised when people started stopping her on the streets and asking for her autograph. "These past two weeks have been really different for me," Oudin acknowledged. "I've gone from being just a normal tennis player to almost everyone in the United States knowing who I am now."

Oudin's instant popularity generated a great deal of media attention. She gave interviews on a number of television programs, including "The Today Show," "The Ellen DeGeneres Show," and "Late Night with Conan O'Brien." She also did photo shoots for magazines and received several new endorsement offers. At times Oudin found the attention somewhat overwhelming. "There's just so much that I didn't know, like photos and media and press conferences and appearances and sponsors," she noted. "I was like, 'How can it possibly be this much not about the tennis?' But I think if it happened again I would be 100 percent ready for it. I'm finally starting to reach my goals, so it's definitely worth it."

"If you work as hard as you possibly can, you can make things happen," Oudin declared. "I'm hoping I'll be a great tennis player one day. Get to the top of the rankings. I hope if I keep working so hard that I'll make that."

A few days after Oudin was knocked out of the U.S. Open, though, she experienced the downside of fame. Many people had noticed that when both of her parents attended her matches, they always sat separately. It turned out that John Oudin had filed for divorce several months earlier. The website SI.com published the couple's divorce papers, which alleged that Leslie Oudin had an affair with their daughter's longtime coach, Brian de Villiers. Melanie and her family struggled to deal with the shock and embarrassment of having such private information become public knowledge. "It was hard for everybody," she stated. "I didn't comprehend that happening at all, because for me it's always been about the tennis. But it was good for me to go through because now I know it comes with it."

Working Hard to Reach the Top

Thanks to her inspiring performance at the U.S. Open, Oudin received the WTA's Newcomer of the Year Award for 2009. She earned a total of $350,000 in prize money and became the third-highest ranked American woman after Venus and Serena Williams. Oudin's standing gave her the opportunity to represent the United States as a member of the Fed Cup team in 2009. The Fed Cup is a prestigious international team tennis tournament for women. Each country selects some of its top players to compete in a round-robin format, with several best-of-five match rounds, or "ties," held throughout the year.

In her first career Fed Cup tie, Oudin earned a key victory against Betina Jozami of Argentina to help the United States advance. "I'm thinking, 'If I lose, the United States loses,'" she said. "Basically, it's up to me, and that's a lot of pressure." Oudin and her teammates made it all the way to the Fed Cup finals in November 2009, playing against Italy for the championship. Unfortunately, Oudin lost both of her singles matches against Italy, and the U.S. team went down in defeat. Oudin returned to Fed Cup competition in early 2010 and won both of her matches to help the United States beat France. She made another strong showing against Russia in the semifinals, going 1-1 in match play to contribute to a 3-2 U.S. victory in the tie. That led to a repeat of the 2009 finals, with the U.S. team playing against Italy in the 2010 Fed Cup finals. While Oudin won both of her singles matches, the U.S. was defeated by Italy for the second year in a row.

Oudin also continued to show promise on the WTA Tour. She made it to the semifinals of a WTA tournament for the first time in Paris in February 2010, which helped her world ranking reach a career-high 31 in April. Oudin did not perform up to her expectations in the first three Grand Slam events of 2010. She was knocked out in the first round of the Australian Open and the French Open, and she lost in the second round at Wimbledon. Still, Oudin hoped to recapture the magic at the U.S. Open, trying to repeat her unexpected but memorable run in 2009, in which she defeated a string of towering Russian players. She defeated Olga Savchuk 6-3, 6-0 in the first round, then faced Alona Bondarenko in the second round. Oudin was cheered by the hometown crowd, but unfortunately her play proved erratic and full of errors, and she lost to Bondarenko 6-2, 7-5.

The 2011 season had both highs and lows. The high point came in September at the U.S. Open, where she and her partner, Jack Sock, took first in mixed doubles. It was an exciting tournament for the pair. In the opening round they came back from match point down against Vladimira Uhlirova and Filip Polasek, and in the second round they beat defending champions and top seeds Liezel Huger and Bob Bryan. In the finals, Oudin and Sock beat eighth-seeded Gisela Dulko and Eduardo Schwank 7-6 (4), 4-6, (10-8) to win their first Grand Slam title. "It's really cool. We just kind of can't believe we actually won a Grand Slam," Oudin said. "Especially because we didn't even know if we were going to be able to play mixed doubles here because we didn't know if we would get a wild card. . . . We're just really

Oudin with her Fed Cup teammates. From left: Oudin, Alexa Glatch, Liezel Huber, and Bethanie Mattek-Sands.

excited." Unfortunately, the rest of the season was a bit of a disappointment. Oudin did not do very well in singles events; at most tournaments she fell in the first or second round, and she reached the quarterfinals only once, in April at Fes, Morocco. Her disappointing play extended to the 2011 Fed Cup also. She lost twice in the quarterfinals, in which the U.S. was defeated 4-1 by Belgium, and then lost twice again in the playoff round, in which the U.S. was defeated 5-0 by Germany.

The 2011 season may not have lived up to Oudin's hopes, but she fully intended to keep moving forward. "If you work as hard as you possibly can, you can make things happen," she declared. "I'm hoping I'll be a great tennis player one day. Get to the top of the rankings. I hope if I keep working so hard that I'll make that."

MAJOR INFLUENCES

Oudin's route to the top of women's tennis is made more difficult by her physical size. At 5 feet, 6 inches tall, she is shorter than most of the best players in the world. The average height of the top 10 players on the WTA Tour in 2009 was 5′10″. Exceptionally tall players like Maria Sharapova at 6′2″ and Venus Williams at 6′1″ have significant advantages over Oudin, including a longer reach and a more powerful serve.

In order to compete with much taller opponents, Oudin patterned her game after another 5'6" player, Justine Henin of Belgium. Henin's career achievements include 43 WTA singles titles, 7 Grand Slam championships, and a gold medal in women's singles at the 2004 Olympic Games. Like Henin, Oudin excels on the court with speed, agility, and footwork. She also boasts a strong forehand shot and outstanding conditioning. These attributes—along with the belief that she can hold her own against anyone—give her the ability to control points against bigger, more aggressive players. "One of the strengths of my game is my footwork and I'm quick," she explained. "Those were Henin's biggest strengths against stronger girls, along with having a lot of variety and being strong at the net. Using all kinds of shots. I really like that part of her game. That's what I'm trying to work on."

HOME AND FAMILY

Oudin continues to live in Marietta, Georgia, in the same house where she grew up. "I have no plans to move out of my parents' house," she said.

HOBBIES AND OTHER INTERESTS

Oudin has insisted that her success on the tennis court has not changed her life much. She still enjoys hanging out with her friends, shopping, going to the movies, and playing games with her family. She points out that she still drives the same car and wears the same clothes as before. "Just because I have won some prize money, I am not going to buy things just because I can," she noted. "I would rather save it and keep working and buy something I really want someday."

HONORS AND AWARDS

Fed Cup by BNP Paribas Heart Award: 2009
WTA Tour Newcomer of the Year: 2009

FURTHER READING

Periodicals

Atlanta, Dec. 2009, p.90
Atlanta Journal-Constitution, July 20, 2006, p.C1; Dec. 14, 2007, p.D8; June 28, 2009, p.C1; Sep. 13, 2009, p.A1
New York Times, Mar. 11, 2009, p.L1; Sep. 4, 2009, p.B10; Sep. 11, 2009, p.B11; Sep. 6, 2010, p.L6; Feb. 8, 2010, p.D11
Tennis, Mar. 2010, p.28
USA Today, Sep. 4, 2009, p.C2; Sep. 11, 2009, p.C7; May 25, 2010

Online Articles

http://espn.go.com
(ESPN, "A New Take on Melanie Oudin's Magical Summer," Sep. 2, 2011)
http://sports.espn.go.com
(ESPN Magazine, "Next Athlete: Melanie Oudin," May 15, 2008; "Oudin a Welcome Addition for U.S. Tennis," Feb. 24, 2009; "Oudin's Mettle Made Her Fan Favorite," Sep. 9, 2009; "Melanie Oudin-Jack Sock Win Title," Sep. 10, 2011)
http://straightsets.blogs.nytimes.com
(New York Times, "In Mixed Doubles, A Title for the Americans," Sep. 10, 2011)
http://topics.nytimes.com
(New York Times, "Melanie Oudin," multiple articles, various dates)
http://sportsillustrated.cnn.com
(Sports Illustrated, "Q&A with Melanie Oudin," Aug. 13, 2009)
http://topics.wsj.com/index.html
(Wall Street Journal, "Melanie Oudin," multiple articles, various dates)

ADDRESS

Melanie Oudin
Sony Ericsson WTA Tour
One Progress Plaza, Suite 1500
St. Petersburg, FL 33701

WORLD WIDE WEB SITES

http://melanieoudin.com
http://www.wtatour.com
http://www.itftennis.com/womens/players
http://www.usta.com
http://www.usopen.com

Sarah Palin 1964-

American Politician and Political Commentator
Former Governor of Alaska
2008 Republican Candidate for Vice President

BIRTH

Sarah Palin was born Sarah Louise Heath on February 11, 1964, in Sandpoint, Idaho, the daughter of Chuck and Sally Heath. Both of her parents were involved in education, her father working as a teacher and her mother as a school secretary. She is the third of four children in her family, with two sisters, Heather and Molly, and one brother, Chuck Jr.

YOUTH

Shortly after Palin was born, her parents made a decision that had a huge effect on her life. They decided to move to Alaska, arriving in the town of Skagway when Sarah was just three months old. The family later moved to Eagle River before settling in Wasilla, about 45 miles northeast of Anchorage, the state's largest city. Wasilla was a small and somewhat remote town during the years that Palin grew up, having a population of just 400 in 1970. The community is surrounded by the scenic beauty that Alaska is known for, and Palin got to know it very well through the influence of her father. Chuck Heath worked as a science teacher in the Wasilla schools, and he had a deep interest in the natural world. Like many in Alaska, he was an avid hunter, and the bear, moose, birds, and other animals that he claimed on his excursions formed a big part of the family's food supply. He introduced his children to hunting early on, and by age 10, Palin was bringing home rabbits and ptarmigan (a type of game bird) to add to the menu. In one memorable incident when she was 14 years old, she helped her father field dress a moose he had shot, lifting the massive, 100-pound legs of the animal so that her father could cut up the meat for freezing.

In all of her pursuits, Palin learned to work hard, a lesson that her father stressed repeatedly. "I just pushed her and pushed her," he said. "My philosophy was no pain, no gain, and pay your dues, and the kid never argued with me." Their family rejected the traditional idea that daughters shouldn't take part in strenuous activities. "I was raised in a family where, you know, gender wasn't going to be an issue," Palin explained. "The girls did what the boys did."

Palin and her family spent very little time watching television, so she entertained herself by reading and playing sports, and there were also many chores to be done. In all of her pursuits, she learned to work hard, a lesson that her father stressed repeatedly. "I just pushed her and pushed her," he said. "My philosophy was no pain, no gain, and pay your dues, and the kid never argued with me." Their family rejected the traditional idea that daughters shouldn't take part in strenuous activities. "I was raised in a family where, you know, gender wasn't going to be an issue," Palin explained. "The girls did what the boys did."

Sarah Palin, right, with her sister Molly.

If Chuck Heath helped his children to appreciate the wonders of the earth, their mother, Sally Heath, focused their attention in a different direction. Sarah and her siblings were all baptized in the Catholic church as infants. After settling in Alaska, their mother began taking them to a local evangelical church, the Wasilla Assembly of God. In that denomination, members are baptized after they knowingly accept Christ as their savior, rather than as infants, and Palin underwent this rite at age 12. Palin's faith remained strong as she grew older, as was clear from the religious quote that accompanied her high school yearbook entry: "He is the Light and in the Light there is Life."

While religion was a constant in her life, political issues were not. "My family wasn't political, and certainly not obsessively partisan," Palin recalled. Her mother confirmed in the *New York Times* that "[Sarah] didn't talk about politics or getting into politics" during her youth. She did show an early interest in current events, however, particularly the Watergate scandal that ended the presidency of Richard Nixon in 1974, when Palin was 10 years old.

EDUCATION

A student in the local public schools, Palin graduated from Wasilla High in 1982. While she did well enough in academics to later earn admission to

Playing basketball for the Wasilla High School Warriors, Palin (# 22) earned the nickname "Sarah Barracuda" for her hard-nosed play.

college, she seemed to have been more profoundly influenced by her experiences as an athlete. She was a member of the school cross country, softball, and basketball teams, and it was on the basketball court that she got her first taste of public notoriety. By her senior year, her hard-nosed play as point guard for the Wasilla Warriors earned her the nickname "Sarah Barracuda," and she and her teammates battled their way into the state playoffs. "She was a little floor general," remembers her teammate, Michelle Kohinka. "She didn't score a lot, but she was a scrappy defender and was always the first to the loose balls." Palin suffered a serious ankle injury just before the state tournament but still hobbled onto the floor in the final minutes of the championship game and sank a key free throw that helped secure the state title. "I know this sounds hokey, but basketball was a life-changing experience for me," she later noted. "It's all about setting a goal, about discipline, teamwork, and then success."

After earning her diploma, Palin opted to attend college outside of Alaska. She and several friends initially headed to Hawaii, where Palin attended Hawaii Pacific College and, according to some sources, also enrolled at the

University of Hawaii. Deciding that "perpetual sunshine isn't necessarily conducive to serious academics for 18-year-old Alaska girls," she next studied in Idaho, taking classes at North Idaho College and the University of Idaho. She also spent a semester at Matanuska-Susitna College in Alaska before returning to the University of Idaho. She graduated in 1987 from Idaho with a major in journalism and a minor in political science.

Palin paid her own way through college and was able to cover some of her bills by taking part in beauty contests. She was chosen as Miss Wasilla in 1984 and went on to compete for Miss Alaska, where she finished as second runner-up and was awarded the title of Miss Congeniality. Her success covered several years of tuition, but Palin has admitted that she was uncomfortable with some aspects of being a beauty queen. "They made us line up in bathing suits and turn our backs so the male judges could look at our butts," she recalled. "I couldn't believe it."

FIRST JOBS

As a teenager and young adult, Palin worked at a variety of jobs, including cleaning offices, waiting tables, and processing seafood. Interested in a career in sports journalism, she interned in the sports departments at several television stations and later obtained a part-time position at KTUU in Anchorage, serving as a fill-in sports anchor for the station's newscasts.

HOME AND FAMILY

Throughout her political career, Palin's image has been closely linked to her family life. Her experiences as a wife and mother began in 1988, when she married her high school sweetheart, Todd Palin, who makes his living in commercial fishing and as an oil worker on Alaska's North Slope. He is also an avid competitor in snowmobile races and is a four-time winner of Alaska's prestigious Iron Dog competition. After marrying, the couple settled in Wasilla, where they continue to live and where their first child, Track, was born in 1989. Over the years, the household has grown to include three daughters, Bristol, Willow, and Piper, and a second son, Trig. All of the Palin children were raised while their mother held public office.

The arrival of Trig, the youngest child, in April 2008 proved an especially important moment for the family. The baby was diagnosed with Down syndrome before birth, and Palin has frequently spoken of her experiences in raising a child with special needs and her support for other parents who share that role. The birth itself has become part of her "supermom" legend. She went into labor when she was in Texas to address a conference but went ahead with her speech and then flew home to Alaska before delivering the child.

A 2007 family photo. Palin is in the center, with son Track and husband Todd in back; daughters Willow, Piper, and Bristol are in front. Baby Trig is not shown here.

While campaigning for office, Palin has portrayed herself as a normal "hockey mom" who understands the difficulties faced by families. She has bristled at those who have suggested that her responsibilities to her family would prevent her from doing an effective job as an elected official. Instead, she has argued that her duties in raising children have made her a better leader. "There's no better training ground for politics than motherhood," she said. "You have to be judge and jury in conflicts. You have to figure out a budget and how to prioritize. To be a mom you have to have more time management [skills] than any other CEO." In recent years, her family life has also given her experience in managing controversial situations. In 2008, her daughter Bristol, then 17 years old, became an unwed mother, with the pregnancy emerging as a sensational story in the midst of the presidential election. Bristol's on-again, off-again relationship with the baby's father, Levi Johnston, has been a continuing source of media attention in the years since. At times, Johnston has made negative statements about Sarah Palin, and he caused a further stir by posing for *Playgirl* magazine in 2010.

CAREER HIGHLIGHTS

Sarah Palin made her debut as a political candidate in 1992, at the age of 28, when she was elected to the Wasilla City Council. She had been recruited to run by a local citizens group, and her decision to enter public service surprised many people who knew her. Palin's political views and aspirations did not develop overnight, however. She had joined the Republican Party at age 18, inspired by the actions of President Ronald Reagan, her foremost political hero. Not surprisingly, much of her philosophy of government is based on ideas championed by Reagan, including his belief in low taxes, limited government, and a strong military. In addition, Palin has taken a conservative stance on social issues and has been particularly outspoken in her opposition to abortion and her support for the right to bear arms.

"There's no better training ground for politics than motherhood," Palin has said. "You have to be judge and jury in conflicts. You have to figure out a budget and how to prioritize. To be a mom you have to have more time management [skills] than any other CEO."

”

By the early 1990s, when Palin first took office, her once-tiny hometown had become a small city of 5,000 people. She focused on helping Wasilla manage its growth, supporting new sales taxes to increase city services while also favoring measures to promote local businesses. She was elected to a second term on the city council in 1995. She ran for mayor the following year, challenging the incumbent, who had already served three terms in that office. Setting the tone for many of her later races, Palin presented herself as a social conservative with a strong religious background, even though such issues had rarely figured in previous Wasilla elections. She also benefited from the support of some key members of the state Republican Party, who viewed her as a candidate with great potential. When she defeated her opponent by 211 votes, the 32-year-old candidate was the youngest person ever elected as Wasilla's mayor.

Palin served two terms as mayor, winning reelection in 1999. The job provided her with valuable administrative experience, but it also made her the target of criticism. After taking office, she demanded the resignation of several city officials, claiming that they were not supporting her programs. Critics charged that Palin was being vindictive because all those she sought to terminate had backed her opponent in the election. The mayor was also accused of being in favor of censorship after asking the librarian about her views on banning books, though Palin has denied that she was ever in favor of such measures.

Palin in her office as mayor of Wasilla.

Entering State Politics

Because of Wasilla's term-limit law, Palin was prevented from seeking re-election as the city's mayor in 2002. Deciding to continue her political career, she became a candidate for lieutenant governor of Alaska, the state's second highest executive office. She failed to attain widespread support in the primary election, however, and finished second in the balloting. Despite this setback, she threw herself into campaigning on behalf of the Republican candidate for governor, Frank Murkowski, who won the office in the November 2002 election. Murkowski rewarded Palin's support by appointing her as one of the three members of the Alaska Oil and Gas Conservation Commission (AOGCC), which regulates the state's petroleum reserves. This gave her input on Alaska's huge petroleum industry, which provides as much as 90 percent of the state's tax revenues. Because oil and gas are so essential to the state's economy, large energy companies exert a great deal of influence on the political process. Numerous Alaska officials have been accused of having corrupt dealings with "big oil," and Palin soon found herself in the middle of one of those scandals.

Palin learned that another member of the commission, Randy Ruedrich, was engaging in a number of questionable actions with members of the oil industry. She informed Governor Murkowski of these allegations, but he was slow to take action. Ruedrich ultimately resigned, but the scandal cast suspicion on all the commissioners, Palin included. Prevented from speaking publicly about the matter while she was a commissioner, she decided she could no longer continue her work. In January 2004, she resigned from the AOGCC after less than a year on the job. Palin was able to turn the situation to her advantage, however, when she told journalists what she knew about Ruedrich's actions. She later filed an ethics complaint against one of the governor's aides, who was also forced to resign, further enhancing her reputation as a reformer seeking to end corruption. That image became the centerpiece of her next political quest.

In October 2005, Palin announced herself as a candidate for the governor of Alaska, challenging Murkowski, who was seeking reelection. Her focus on fighting corruption proved very popular in the 2006 election. In addition to the events involving the AOGCC and Murkowski's staff, numerous other political scandals were rocking Alaska politics, with the FBI investigating alleged wrongdoing by a range of elected officials. In that atmosphere, Palin's promise to clean up government caught the attention of voters. Moreover, her relative lack of political experience became an asset, as she was able to present herself as a new breed of leader who had not become entangled in questionable dealings. In the Republican primary, she won the showdown with Murkowski to become her party's nominee, and in the November 2006 general election, she topped her Democratic opponent as well as four other candidates. She was the first woman to become the state's governor and, at age 42, she was the youngest person ever to win the office.

"

When Palin was elected governor, she sold the governor's private jet, reduced the size of her security detail, and fired the chef at the governor's mansion. "I don't want [my family] thinking when I'm done being governor that it's normal to have a chef," she said. "It's OK for them to have macaroni and cheese."

"

A New Breed of Governor

In keeping with her image as a down-to-earth public servant intent on serving the public, Palin sold the governor's private jet, reduced the size of her security detail, and fired the chef at the governor's mansion. "I

Palin addressing a press conference while governor of Alaska.

don't want [my family] thinking when I'm done being governor that it's normal to have a chef," she said. "It's OK for them to have macaroni and cheese." Her determination to end old practices went far beyond her personal behavior, however. Following through on her promise to clean up the corruption that plagued Alaska politics, she crafted an ethics reform bill that she described as "a rawhide-tough package of measures meant to pry state government away from special interests and put it back on the side of the people." Many of her proposals were later passed by state lawmakers, and the ethics law is viewed as one of her major accomplishments as governor.

Another focus was energy policy. Like many other conservatives, Palin has argued that oil and gas companies should be given greater access to the petroleum reserves of the U.S., including those that lie beneath such sensitive ecological areas as Alaska's Arctic National Wildlife Refuge. Her position on this issue was welcomed by the energy companies, but Palin took a tougher stance against big oil in other matters. Arguing that the state had been too generous in its dealings with petroleum producers, she convinced the legislature to enact higher taxes on oil company profits and to create strict requirements regarding the construction of an important new natural gas pipeline. The pipeline legislation may someday bring financial benefits to the state's citizens, but the measure has discouraged many large energy corporations from participating in the venture. As of 2011, planning for regulatory approvals, permits, engineering, and construction is ongoing, with construction expected to begin in about 2015.

Governor Palin's efforts proved popular with Alaska's citizens, and her approval rating reached as high as 90 percent during her first two years in office. Nevertheless, she was an unknown figure to most U.S. citizens outside of Alaska until the summer of 2008. Then, with one announcement, everything changed.

The Maverick Running Mate

In summer 2008, the country was in the middle of a presidential campaign, with Senator John McCain as the nominee from the Republican Party and Senator Barack Obama as the nominee from the Democratic Party. (For more information on McCain, see *Biography Today,* April 2000; for more information on Obama, see *Biography Today,* January 2007.) On August 29, Senator McCain stepped to a microphone at a rally in Dayton, Ohio, and presented Governor Sarah Palin as his vice presidential running mate in his quest to become the next president.

Palin's selection took nearly everyone by surprise and immediately shook up the presidential campaign. Within hours, she became a nationwide celebrity, a role she had almost no time to prepare for. While she had been on McCain's list of possible running mates for several months, she did not engage in detailed discussions about the job until two days prior to the Dayton announcement. Joining the presidential campaign was a sudden change of course in her life, but Palin later wrote that she was not shocked by the development. "I certainly didn't think, 'Well, of course this would happen.' But neither did I think, 'What an astonishing idea.' It seemed more comfortable than that, like a natural progression."

Others did not see the selection of Palin as quite so natural. Critics, particularly those who supported the Democratic cause, immediately focused on her lack of political experience and suggested that she was not qualified to be vice president. Most Republican supporters, on the other hand, were excited by the governor's presence on the ticket, believing that she fit well with McCain's image as a political maverick and hoping that she might convince more women to support the GOP. In addition, she received a warm welcome from the most conservative wing of the Republican Party, which approved of her Christian background and her views on such issues as abortion, oil drilling, and gun rights. Palin's arrival instantly energized McCain's campaign, which received $4.4 million dollars in donations in the 12 hours after her selection was announced and $10 million over the next several days.

Trials and Triumphs

Palin soon learned the down side of being in the national spotlight. Just three days after accepting McCain's offer, the press broke the story that her daughter, Bristol, was pregnant. In addition, the media took up the so-called Troopergate controversy. Some alleged that the governor forced the Alaska public safety commissioner to give up his job because Palin wanted him to fire her former brother-in-law, an Alaska state trooper, and the public safety commissioner refused. An official investigation later concluded that Palin had abused the power of her office during the incident but had done nothing illegal.

"Joining the presidential campaign was a sudden change in her life, but Palin wrote that she was not shocked by the development. "I certainly didn't think, 'Well, of course this would happen.' But neither did I think, 'What an astonishing idea.' It seemed more comfortable than that, like a natural progression.""

Palin's first major test came when she delivered her acceptance speech at the Republican National Convention, just a week after being announced as McCain's running mate. Appearing before thousands of conventioneers and a huge national television audience, she did not disappoint, demonstrating the sharp wit and down-to-earth language that would become her trademark during the campaign. Though her address had been crafted in advance with the help of a speechwriter, the most memorable line was Palin's own off-the-cuff remark about the power of determined mothers: "What is the difference between a hockey mom and a pit bull? … Lipstick!"

From the convention, Palin immediately hit the campaign trail, speaking at several rallies each day. She brought energy and life to a campaign that some observers felt was stagnating. Huge crowds began turning out to see her, and in those cases where she and McCain appeared together, it sometimes seemed that Palin was the bigger draw. As she had shown at the convention, she was an engaging speaker with the ability to rev up Republican crowds, but her gender and background also played an important part in her popularity. She was only the second woman to ever appear on a major party presidential ticket and the first since 1984, so she won the admiration of those who longed to see a female reach the highest levels of national executive power. Moreover, many voters identified with her as a

Palin appearing with her running mate, presidential candidate John McCain, at the 2008 Republican National Convention.

middle-class working mother, someone far removed from the wealthy and elite figures who often vied for the offices of president and vice president.

Palin's fame was fed by the attention she received from TV talk-show hosts and comedians, though their jokes often depicted the candidate in less-than-positive terms. This was especially true of comedian Tina Fey's portrayal of Palin on "Saturday Night Live," which became a public sensation. Closely resembling the governor and skilled at mimicking her manner of speaking, Fey played Palin as a bumbling politician who was in over head. For her part, Palin had a good sense of humor about the "Saturday Night Live" skits and even appeared on the show in October 2008.

Unanswered Questions

As many commentators noted, the attention swirling around Palin reflected the deep political divisions in the United States. To an even greater degree than most candidates, she inspired both great admiration and great opposition. Her detractors portrayed the governor as being too radically conservative, and they returned time and again to a central point: she lacked experience and knowledge and would be unprepared to act as president if McCain were unable to serve out his term. During her first month on the ticket, Palin had little opportunity to disprove these charges because the McCain campaign made a conscious decision to shield her from extensive contact with the media. Her seclusion came to an end in late September, when she completed a number of television interviews.

One interview in particular, a multipart discussion with Katie Couric, anchor of the CBS Evening News, proved to be a decisive moment in the campaign. On a number of different points in the interview, Palin seemed to be uninformed and was unable to hide her lack of knowledge under Couric's determined questioning. Queried about such important topics as foreign policy, Supreme Court rulings, and the nation's economic downturn, she could provide little specific information, offering only general campaign slogans or meandering answers that made little sense. The segment set off a firestorm of media commentary about Palin's abilities. In the *Los Angeles Times*, James Rainey described her performance as "rambling, marginally responsive, and even more adrift than during her network debut with ABC's Charles Gibson." CNN journalist Jack Cafferty took a tougher line, calling the Couric-Palin interview "one of the most pathetic pieces of tape I have ever seen from someone aspiring to one of the highest offices in this country."

Some of the criticism aimed at Palin in the weeks after the interview came from a surprising source—influential conservative columnists, who usually support Republican candidates. A number of them stated that Palin was hurting McCain's campaign, including a particularly blunt editorial by Kathleen Parker in the *National Review* that called for her to resign as McCain's running mate. "Palin's narrative is fun, inspiring and all-American in that frontier way we seem to admire," Parker wrote. "When Palin first emerged as John McCain's running mate, I confess I was delighted. She was … a refreshing feminist of a different order who personified the modern successful working mother. Palin didn't make a mess cracking the glass ceiling. She simply glided through it. It was fun while it lasted. Palin's recent interviews with Charles Gibson, Sean Hannity, and now Katie Couric have all revealed an attractive, earnest, confident candidate. Who Is Clearly Out Of Her League." In the midst of these attacks, Palin was able to recover some credibility by delivering a strong performance in her vice presidential debate with Senator Joe Biden. She still suffered from a general lack of support among potential voters, however. A *New York Times*/CBS News poll conducted shortly before the election showed that 59 percent of those polled felt she was not prepared for the job of vice president.

On election day in November, the Obama/Biden ticket triumphed, and Palin looked on as McCain delivered his concession speech in Arizona.

Palin enjoying some time outdoors with her daughter, Piper, while fishing at their family fishing site.

Many observers blamed Palin for the defeat, even though there were certainly many other elements that hampered the senator's quest for the White House. With the race over, Palin returned to Alaska and her duties as governor, believing, as she later wrote, that "everything would go back to the way it was before." She soon found that, in her case, "going back" was not an option.

Turmoil, Fame, and Resignation

Though she was a member of the losing ticket, Palin's celebrity did not fade in the months after the campaign, and this had both positive and negative effects on her political career. On the negative side, she had to grapple with a wave of lawsuits that charged her with ethical wrongdoing. Most of these accusations were for trivial matters and were lodged by individuals who sought to discredit the governor and diminish her national stature. All of the complaints were eventually dismissed. Nonetheless, Palin and her staff were forced to spend time dealing with each of the charges because of the requirements of the ethics reform law that the governor had helped enact several years earlier. "We spend most of our day, my staff, a lot of the members of the Department of Law, and myself dealing with things that have nothing to do with policy or governance," Palin noted. Moreover, she had to personally foot the bill for her legal defense in the ethics cases, and the costs quickly escalated. Her work as governor was also hampered by a huge number of requests filed under Alaska's Freedom of Information Act (FOIA), which requires the government to provide copies of official information to those who request it. Most of these FOIA inquiries were focused on Palin, and they forced her staff to expend a great deal of time and effort to collect and distribute the data in question.

"I knew early on that the smartest thing for me to do was to work hard, do the best that I can, make wise decisions based on good information in front of me. And then put my life ... on a path that could be dedicated to God and ask Him what I should do next. That will be the position I will be in as long as I'm on earth—that is, seeking the right path that God would have laid out for me."

On the other hand, the public's continued interest in the former vice president nominee made her one of the most prominent figures in the Republican Party. Calls for her to run for president in 2012 began almost as soon as the 2008 election ended. In March 2009 she formed her own political action committee, SarahPAC, which allowed her to raise money to promote causes and candidates of her choice. In addition, she became a vocal critic of President Obama, which made her sound increasingly like a candidate for office.

Speculation about Palin's political future became a popular topic for columnists, but few foresaw the event that took place on July 3, 2009. On that day, she called a press conference at her Wasilla home and announced that she was resigning as the governor of Alaska. In explaining her decision, she contended that the legal harassment she had been subjected to was costing the state huge amounts of money and preventing her from doing an effective job of governing. As a result, she would leave office and focus on other work. "My choice is to take a stand and effect change," she said in the speech, "not hit our heads against the wall and watch valuable state time and money, millions of your dollars, go down the drain."

Media Superstar and Tea Party Activist

There was speculation in some quarters that Palin had stepped down so that she could concentrate on running for president in 2012, while others argued that quitting her responsibilities as governor would destroy her

Palin appeared at the 2010 National Tea Party Convention, shown here, and worked with a number of Tea Party candidates in the 2010 elections for congress and state governors.

chances of ever attaining higher office. Palin herself refused direct comment about her political future, but she certainly did not fade quietly into the background. She began delivering speeches around the nation, and in fall 2009 she published her book *Going Rogue,* which became the top-selling nonfiction book of the year. In 2010 she followed that up with a second book, *America By Heart: Reflections on Family, Faith, and Flag.*

Palin also undertook several television projects beginning in early 2010, first appearing as a commentator on Fox News. She was named the host of that network's "Real American Stories," in which she planned to interview people to showcase their inspirational stories about overcoming adversity. Only one episode was filmed. In addition, she hosted "Sarah Palin's Alaska," an eight-part reality series for the TLC network in which members of the Palin family shared some of their favorite outdoor settings and activities, including salmon fishing, camping, and hiking on glaciers. Despite decent ratings, the show wasn't renewed. Through these various television projects, Palin continued to attract the attention of the national media.

The 2010 elections for congress and for state governors provided Palin with an opportunity to demonstrate her political influence. In the Republican primary races held around the country, she endorsed a number of candidates, and her celebrity and ability to raise money for those she favored became major factors in the races. While not all of Palin's picks won their primaries, a fair number of them did, which further enhanced her image. In many cases, she aligned herself with figures from the "Tea Party," a new conservative political movement that favors small government, lower taxes, and a balanced budget. Palin spoke at the 2010 National Tea Party Convention, declaring that "this party that we call the Tea Party ... is the future of politics in America." Palin also allied herself with several female candidates and coined the term "mama grizzlies" to describe women who were willing to fiercely defend conservative values.

Next Steps

As the contest for the next presidential race began to heat up in 2011, many questioned whether Palin planned to enter the race. Campaigning for president usually starts more than a year before the election, which will be held in November 2012. Typically, interested politicians from each political party declare their candidacy and then spend much of a year trying to earn the nomination to become the nominee at the party's political convention, held in late summer, followed by the general election in November. During the year or so before the election, before the nominees are chosen, candidates work on their campaigns: hiring staff and organizing a national campaign network; developing policy statements on issues; traveling around the country to speak to voters, especially in key battleground states; recruiting supporters; and appearing on TV political debates.

But Palin did not act like a typical candidate throughout much of 2011, according to political observers. For example, she and her family took a family vacation that summer, making speeches at national landmarks and traveling around the country on a bus emblazoned with patriotic images and words—but she claimed it was not a campaign trip. She traveled to some key states and gave speeches on political and economic issues—but she continued to position herself as an outsider who was not part of the political establishment. That seeming contradiction between her actions and her words kept many people guessing about her intentions.

In October 2011, after months of speculation, Palin announced that she would not seek the Republican nomination for president in the 2012 election. "After much prayer and serious consideration, I have decided that I will not be seeking the 2012 GOP nomination for president of the United States," she said. "I believe I can be more effective and I can be more aggressive in this mission in a supportive role of getting the right people elected." She planned to use her political influence to help elect state governors, U.S. senators and representatives, and the next president. Her comments suggested that she planned to play a major role in shaping American politics. Among conservative Republicans, political observers suggested, Palin has many ardent supporters who hoped she would run and who will be eager to hear her opinions; but observers also suggested that her influence on the larger political stage is significantly less profound, and may diminish over time. "The question now is what role she hopes to play going forward—and whether she can remain a politician capable of broadly influencing the direction of her party, the conservative movement, or the national debate," Dan Balz wrote in the *Washington Post.* "On that, opinions were mixed."

As she has continued her political saga, Palin has remained a polarizing figure who has both strong supporters and strident critics. But she has not let that detract from her sense of what to do. "I knew early on that the smartest thing for me to do was to work hard, do the best that I can, make wise decisions based on good information in front of me. And then put my life … on a path that could be dedicated to God and ask Him what I should do next," she declared. "That will be the position I will be in as long as I'm on earth—that is, seeking the right path that God would have laid out for me."

SELECTED CREDITS

Writings

Going Rogue: An American Life, 2009
America By Heart: Reflections on Family, Faith, and Flag, 2010

Television

"Fox News," 2010 (commentator)
"Real American Stories," 2010 (host)
"Sarah Palin's Alaska," 2010 (host)

FURTHER READING

Periodicals

American Spectator, Apr. 2010
Current Biography Yearbook, 2009
New York Times, Oct. 29, 2006; Aug. 30, 2008; Oct. 24, 2008; July 13, 2009; Apr. 4, 2010; Sep. 9, 2011
New Yorker, Sep. 22, 2008; Dec. 7, 2009, p.84; Apr. 25, 2010

Newsweek, Sep. 8, 2008, p.24; Sep. 15, 2008; June 21, 2010, p.32; May 9, 2011, p.26; July 18, 2011, p.32
People, Sep. 22, 2008; Nov. 30, 2009
Time, Aug. 29, 2008; Sep. 22, 2008; Oct. 20, 2008; Nov. 17, 2008; Dec. 29, 2008; July 20, 2009; Dec. 13, 2010
Washington Post, Oct. 2, 2008

Online Articles

http://spectator.org/topics
(American Spectator,"Sarah Palin," multiple articles, various dates)
http://www.nationalreview.com
(National Review Online,"Palin Problem," Sep. 26, 2008)
http://topics.nytimes.com
(New York Times,"Sarah Palin," multiple articles, various dates)
http://www.newyorker.com
(New Yorker,"The State of Sarah Palin: The Peculiar Political Landscape of the Vice-Presidential Hopeful," Sep. 22, 2008)
http://www.newsweek.com/topics.html
(Newsweek,"Sarah Palin," multiple articles, various dates)
http://www.time.com/time/topics
(Time,"Sarah Palin," multiple articles, various dates)
http://content.usatoday.com/topics/index
(USA Today,"Sarah Palin," multiple articles, various dates)
http://topics.wsj.com/index.html
(Wall Street Journal,"Sarah Palin," multiple articles, various dates)
http://www.whorunsgov.com/Profiles/Sarah_Palin
(Who Runs Gov/Washington Post,"Profile: Sarah Palin," no date)

ADDRESS

Sarah Palin
Author Mail, 11th Floor
HarperCollins Publishers
10 East 53rd Street
New York, NY 10022

WORLD WIDE WEB SITE

http://www.facebook.com/sarahpalin

Aaron Rodgers 1983-

American Professional Football Player with the Green Bay Packers
Most Valuable Player of the 2011 Super Bowl

BIRTH

Aaron Rodgers was born on December 2, 1983, in Chico, California. His parents are Darla and Ed Rodgers, who played college football at Chico State and also played semipro football for the Twin City Cougars of Marysville, California. He later became a chiropractor. Aaron has one older brother, Luke, and one younger brother, Jordan.

YOUTH AND EDUCATION

Rodgers was raised in Chico, a small city of fewer than 100,000 people located about 90 miles northeast of Sacramento. Even as a small child he showed an unusual interest in football. According to his parents, he used to watch entire football games on television when he was only two years old. He stared at the flickering images on the screen for hours at a time, barely moving a muscle.

When Rodgers entered kindergarten, his teacher reported that he often spent time before recess drawing diagrams of football plays to use out on the playground. As he grew older, he played countless games of football with his dad, his older brother, or his friends out in the family backyard. In these games, Rodgers often pretended that he was his childhood hero, San Francisco 49ers quarterback Joe Montana. This loyalty to Montana lasted for years. Even after he became a star quarterback at the University of California, Rodgers liked to wear a Joe Montana T-shirt under his game jersey.

> *According to his father, "Aaron has always had this interesting combination of being really humble and extremely confident."*

By the time Rodgers entered Pleasant Valley High School in Chico, he was known all around the neighborhood not only for his love for football, but also for his ability to throw the ball. He spent many hours honing his accuracy by tossing a football through a backyard tire swing, and he sometimes entertained his friends by making trick throws. One of his favorite tricks was to stand in a neighbor's front yard, then throw the football over the three-story house so that it would land directly in their backyard swimming pool. "I never worried about him breaking a window," recalled the owner of the house, "because he was always so darn accurate."

Like many other youngsters, Rodgers was small when he was young, and it took a while for his body to fill out. When he was a freshman, recalled Pleasant Valley principal John Shepherd, Rodgers "was all ears and feet." With each passing year of high school, though, he packed on a few more pounds of muscle. By his junior year, he had developed all the physical tools to be a successful high school quarterback.

People around Rodgers, though, were more impressed by other qualities. Teachers at Pleasant Valley recalled that he possessed natural leadership abilities and a maturity beyond his years. "I know I sound cliché," said

Shepherd, "but I don't know how to recommend him any higher than to say that as my kids grow up, I hope they have the same characteristics and attributes as Aaron." Another key factor in his success on the football field was his certainty that he could lead his team to victory in any game. As his father said, "Aaron has always had this interesting combination of being really humble and extremely confident."

As Pleasant Valley's starting quarterback, Rodgers passed for a total of 4,419 yards during his junior and senior seasons. In both the 2000 and 2001 seasons he also was named to the area's "all-sectional" team. To the surprise and disappointment of Rodgers and his family, however, his stellar high school performance was ignored by the big college football programs in California and around the country. Since Chico and the surrounding region were not known for high school football talent, college football scouts never dropped in to see him play. As a result, Rodgers did not receive a single scholarship offer from a Division I school when he graduated in 2001.

When Rodgers was passed over by the big college programs, he decided to launch his college football career at a nearby community college (or junior college). At these schools, students can obtain an Associate Degree, usually a two-year program. He enrolled at Butte College in Oroville, a town located about a dozen miles south of Chico. Rodgers attended school and played football there for one season before being recruited by the University of California at Berkeley (Cal). He attended Cal for two years before dropping out to join the NFL.

CAREER HIGHLIGHTS

NCAA—Butte College Roadrunners

When Rodgers enrolled at Butte College, it did not take long for the head football coach, Craig Rigsbee, to realize that a top-notch quarterback prospect had fallen into his lap. "He had grown to about 200 pounds," recalled Rigsbee, "and that first day of practice, that was the real defining moment. Aaron sprinted right, planted, and threw about 50 yards on a dime to the left. I looked over at my offensive coordinator and we just went, 'Wow. Where did that come from?'"

Rodgers secured the starting quarterback job, and in the 2002 season he led the Butte College Roadrunners to 10 victories in 11 games, a NorCal Conference championship, and a number two ranking among junior college (JUCO) programs across the nation. Rodgers accounted for 35 touchdowns on the season, throwing for 28 scores and running the ball into the

Rodgers during a Cal Bears victory over the USC Trojans, 2003.

end zone himself for another 7 touchdowns. Even more amazing, he threw only 4 interceptions on the season.

NCAA—University of California Golden Bears

At that point, Rodgers's football career took a dramatic turn. About 150 miles to the south of the Butte campus, the head coach of the University of California Golden Bears received some Butte game film from the 2002 season. The coach, Jeff Tedford, had requested the film because he had heard reports that one of Butte's other players might be worthy of a scholarship offer. As he watched the film, however, Tedford was stunned to see an unknown quarterback zinging passes effortlessly all over the field. Tedford promptly made a trip up to Oroville to see Rodgers throw in person. A private workout was arranged, and Tedford watched Rodgers execute various passing drills for about 25 minutes. He then turned to Rigsbee and declared,"this is the best junior college quarterback I've ever seen, and he's going to be an NFL player some day." Rigsbee asked him if he really thought so. "No," Tedford replied."I know so."

The University of California (known as Cal) quickly offered Rodgers a scholarship, which he happily accepted. Rodgers said his goodbyes to a proud Rigsbee and the rest of the Butte coaches and players, then transferred down to the Cal campus at Berkeley in early 2003. Hampered by a knee injury suffered in summer workouts, he narrowly lost the competition to be Cal's starting quarterback for the start of the 2003 season. When the team stumbled in its first few games, however, Tedford turned to Rodgers in hopes that he could give the Bears a lift. Rodgers started the fifth game of the season, and he kept the spot for the rest of the season. He posted a 7-3 record as a starter and led the Bears to a wild 52-49 victory over the Virginia Tech Hokies in the season-ending Insight Bowl. Rodgers threw for a career-best 394 yards in the bowl game, which marked Cal's first bowl appearance since 1996. His totals for the season included 2,903 yards passing, 19 touchdown passes, and only 5 interceptions.

This promising debut by Rodgers made Cal fans very excited about the 2004 season. Tedford shared their hopeful perspective, but he admitted that he needed to keep a lid on his own expectations. "I had a hard time last year remembering [Rodgers] was only 19 years old and in his first season playing at that level," explained Tedford. "He just handles himself so well. If he keeps going in the direction he's headed, I think he can be as good as anyone."

As the 2004 season unfolded, Rodgers showed that his sophomore year was not a fluke. He captained a Cal offense that became one of the most feared in the entire country. Led by Rodgers, who passed for 24 touchdowns and 2,566 yards, the Golden Bears routinely racked up 40 or more points against opponents in their march to a Top Ten ranking for much of the year. The team's only regular-season blemish was a narrow 23-17 loss to the top-ranked University of Southern California Trojans in a game that saw Rodgers complete his first 23 passes, an NCAA record. The season ended on a sour note, however, when Rodgers and the Bears failed in their bid to claim a second straight bowl victory. Cal lost 45-31 in the Holiday Bowl to the Texas Tech Red Raiders.

After the 2004 season, Rodgers faced a difficult decision. He loved playing for Cal and wanted to earn a college degree. But scouts in the National Football League (NFL) had been extremely impressed by his junior year performance. Many of them predicted that if he decided to enter the upcoming NFL draft, he would be the first quarterback selected.

Rodgers admitted that his sudden emergence into the spotlight was "crazy," but he said that "going under the radar for a couple of years helped me … because it kept me humble and working hard. I take the attention in stride because I know it could be taken away in a second." In the end, he decided to leave Cal and begin his career in the NFL, where he had dreamed of playing since his kindergarten days.

NFL—Green Bay Packers

In the April 2005 draft Rodgers was not selected as quickly as most analysts had expected. In fact, 23 other players (including one quarterback, Alex Smith of Utah) were taken before the Green Bay Packers used the 24th pick of the first round to take Rodgers. Upon hearing the news, he told reporters that he was excited to join the Packers, one of the most historic franchises in the NFL.

Rodgers (right) with Packers' teammate, fellow quarterback, and NFL legend Brett Favre (left).

Green Bay is the only community-owned franchise in America's major professional sports leagues, and the town itself is far smaller than any other city with an NFL team. In addition, the Packers have a long and proud history on the gridiron. During the "golden age" of professional football of the 1950s and 1960s, the Packers were one of the league's most dominant teams. The club won the first two Super Bowls (in 1966 and 1967), and it added a third Super Bowl title in 1997 under the direction of superstar quarterback Brett Favre. This record of football glory has led the people of Green Bay to refer to their community as Titletown USA.

Rodgers also told reporters that he was looking forward to learning from Favre, who remained entrenched as the club's starting quarterback. Draft experts agreed that Rodgers was entering an ideal situation. At a time when many other rookie quarterbacks were being thrown into NFL action before they were ready, Rodgers would have an opportunity to study the Packers playbook, get to know his teammates, and learn from an NFL legend without any pressure.

Waiting for a Chance

As planned, Rodgers spent virtually all of his rookie season on the bench. He made brief appearances in only three games in the 2005 season, completing 9 of 16 passes for 65 yards with one interception. Rodgers was even less visible in 2006. He appeared in only two games before suffering a fractured foot that caused him to miss the second half of the season. As the 2007 season approached, the third-year quarterback from Cal remained virtually unknown in Green Bay outside the team locker room.

As the 2007 campaign progressed, Rodgers felt increasingly restless about backing up the veteran Favre. After three seasons, he felt that he had learned all he could on the practice field. Besides, Favre had never really developed into a mentor to Rodgers. "He wasn't mean to [Rodgers] or anything, but he just didn't help him like other vets helped younger players at other positions," recalled one member of the Packers organization. "You could tell he felt threatened [by the presence of the younger quarterback]."

Rodgers was very careful not to cause any problems on the team, however. He tried to remain patient, and he assured Head Coach Mike McCarthy that he knew that he would get a crack at leading the team when Favre, the oldest starting quarterback in the league, decided to retire. "I'm sure it was killing him inside, because he's such a competitor," said Cal Lyman, a former teammate at Cal. "Sitting on the sideline is the last thing he wanted to do, but Aaron is such a stand-up guy, so classy, he'd never let that on. Every time we talked about it, he'd say, 'Hey, my time will come, no problem.' And he'd say it with a wink."

Late in the 2007 season, Rodgers finally received an opportunity to play in a meaningful game. Green Bay was pitted against the Dallas Cowboys in a match-up of two 10-1 teams. The Cowboys roared out to a 17-point lead, then knocked Favre out of the game with an injury. At that point, Rodgers trotted into the game and nearly engineered a remarkable comeback victory in front of a hostile Dallas crowd. By the final gun, the third-year signal caller had completed 18 of 26 passes for 201 yards and a touchdown against one of the best defenses in the NFL. The Packers lost the game, but Rodgers won a lot of respect from his teammates with his performance.

A Controversial Trade Opens the Door for Rodgers

The Packers posted a 13-3 record in 2007, and many NFL watchers thought that the team was Super Bowl-bound. In the NFC (National Football Conference) Championship Game, however, the Pack lost 23-20 in overtime to the New York Giants, who won the Super Bowl two weeks later against the AFC (American Football Conference) champion New England Patriots. The loss to the Giants deflated Packers fans, who were further demoralized in March 2008 when Favre announced his retirement.

Rodgers is tackled by linebacker Bradie James in a 2007 game against the Dallas Cowboys.

Favre's retirement made Rodgers the team's starting quarterback. Many Green Bay fans expressed skepticism about his ability to live up to Favre's legacy of great quarterback play. McCarthy and General Manager Ted Thompson, however, had watched Rodgers in practice and preseason play over the previous three years. They felt that he had all the tools to be a top quarterback, and they tried to assure the fan base that the team was in good hands.

Rodgers prepared all summer for the 2008 campaign. As training camp approached, however, Favre reconsidered his retirement decision. When he signaled that he wanted to return to the Packers for another season, McCarthy and Thompson told him that they had decided that it was time for Rodgers to take the helm. If Favre wanted to return to Green Bay, he would have to accept a back-up position. This decision did not sit well with Favre or Packers fans, who clamored for the return of the legendary number 4. But Thompson and McCarthy stuck by Rodgers, and just before the start of the 2008 season they traded Favre to the New York Jets.

The whole affair cast a dark cloud over Rodgers as he prepared for the season. At preseason training camp some Packer fans heckled him when he was out on the practice field and when he drove into the team parking lot in the morning."They missed Brett Favre,"Rodgers said."I understand that. But the little kids saying swear words to me, I didn't understand that."

In September 2008 Rodgers became the first quarterback other than Favre to start for the Packers in 16 years."I know the pressure that's going to be on me just following a legend," he admitted."I know my teammates have high expectations for my play, and so does the coaching staff and the personnel department. I know I'm expected to play at a high level, and I expect it as well."

Rodgers played well in his first season as an NFL starting quarterback. He showed off a strong and accurate passing arm, and he displayed a maturity and command of the huddle that impressed the Green Bay veterans. At season's end he ranked sixth in the entire NFL in passing, completing 63.6 percent of his passes for 4,038 yards, 28 touchdowns, and only 13 interceptions. Rodgers thus joined Kurt Warner as the only quarterbacks in NFL history to throw for more than 4,000 yards in their first year as a starter. But the Packers, saddled with a weak defense, only won 6 of their 16 games. As the losses piled up, Favre fans in Green Bay howled that Thompson and McCarthy had made a mistake in choosing Rodgers.

A Star in the Making

Much of this criticism subsided during the 2009 season. The fans became more accepting of Rodgers in part because of growing unhappiness with Favre. After one year in New York, Favre joined the Minnesota Vikings, one of the Packers' chief rivals. This decision to play quarterback for the hated Vikings angered many Green Bay fans, who saw the move as a betrayal.

An even bigger factor in Packers' fans acceptance of Rodgers, though, was his performance on the field. As the 2009 campaign rolled on, he displayed all of the qualities of a rising star. In addition to throwing for a personal record 4,434 yards, Rodgers completed an impressive 64.7 percent of his passes. He also fired 30 touchdown passes and ran for 5 more touchdowns, all while throwing only 7 interceptions for the entire season. He finished the season as the fourth-ranked passer in the NFL.

Best of all, Rodgers guided the Packers back into the playoffs with an 11-5 regular season record. In the first"wild card"round of the playoffs, though, the season ended in heartbreaking fashion. Teeing off against the Arizona Cardinals, Rodgers passed for a team-record 422 yards and four touchdowns. He also sent the game into overtime with a clutch touchdown toss in the final two minutes of regulation. But in the opening moments of overtime, he was hit while dropping back to pass and fumbled. An Arizona

Rodgers running for a touchdown against the Pittsburgh Steelers, 2009.

player recovered and ran the ball into the end zone for a game-winning touchdown.

The Arizona loss was tough for Rodgers to absorb. "I went back to my home in California and got away from it," he recalled. "I was able to start to digest the season and the good plays, the mistakes, things we need to clean up, and start to get a new hunger for the next year. Although you realize you're eight months away from anything, so that's tough because you want to get back out there."

When Rodgers returned to Green Bay to prepare for the 2010 season, he found that Favre's shadow was fading. Packer fans welcomed and encouraged him in a way that the young quarterback found very gratifying. "This is a community team, a team that means a lot to this area, this state. These people live and die for football," he said. "The game is the main talking point at the grocery store. When you don't win the Super Bowl, which hasn't happened here in a while, the off season is a really long one. It's not like this anywhere else. Talking to friends in the league, they enjoy their places, but a lot of them have other professional teams in the area, other stuff that's going on that's bigger than football. We're the only show in town."

Bringing another Title to Titletown USA

The 2010 regular season was challenging for the Packers. The team's defense was a talented one, the team's offense, guided by Rodgers, turned into one of the most explosive units in the NFL. But the team suffered a tremendous number of injuries over the course of the season. By season's end, 15 players were on injured reserve, meaning that they were done playing for the year. In addition, a number of other valuable players missed a game or two with injuries. Even Rodgers missed a game when he suffered a concussion.

As the Packers entered the home stretch of the regular season, the team found itself clawing just to qualify for the playoffs. With three games to go against tough opponents—the New England Patriots, New York Giants, and Chicago Bears—Packer players and fans knew that one more loss would knock them out of playoff contention. Led by Rodgers and the sturdy Pack defense, though, the team won all three games to sneak into the playoffs as the "six seed" in the NFC (six teams qualify for the playoffs in both the NFC and AFC, but the "five" and "six" seeds have to play an extra game against one another and do not get to host any games). Rodgers once again finished the season as one of the top-ranked quarterbacks in the league. He completed 65.7 percent of his passes for 3,922 yards, 28 touchdowns, and only 11 interceptions.

In the first round of the playoffs Green Bay traveled to Philadelphia and knocked off the Eagles by a 21-16 score. The Packers then moved on to Atlanta, where they shellacked the Falcons 48-21 behind a sparkling performance from Rodgers, who completed 31 of 36 passes for 366 yards and 3 touchdowns (he also added a rushing touchdown). The next week they faced off against the Bears in the NFC Championship Game for the right to play in Super Bowl XLV (45). The Packers built a big early lead, then hung on against a late rally to defeat Chicago by a 21-14 score.

The 2011 Super Bowl

Green Bay's opponent in Super Bowl XLV was the Pittsburgh Steelers, who entered the game with a stout defense, a rocket-armed quarterback of their own in Ben Roethlisberger, and an NFL-record six Super Bowl titles. Led by Rodgers's pinpoint passing, the Packers jumped out to a 21-3 lead. As the game wore on, however, key Green Bay players, including cornerback Charles Woodson and wide receiver Donald Driver, went to the sidelines with injuries. Pittsburgh fought back with big plays of its own, and by the middle of the fourth quarter the Packers were clinging to a narrow 28-25 lead.

Rodgers during the Packers' 31-25 win over the Pittsburgh Steelers in the 2011 Super Bowl. He was named MVP for his outstanding play.

Rodgers sensed that the game was slipping away from the Packers, but he kept his cool. With the Packers trapped deep in their own territory facing third down and 10 yards for a first down, Rodgers dropped back and fired a laser across the middle of the field to Greg Jennings, who advanced the ball into Steeler territory. The throw not only gave Green Bay a first down, it launched the Pack on a time-consuming drive deep into Pittsburgh's end of the field. "That one throw was all about the last three years of my career," Rodgers said after the game.

The drive ended with a field goal that made the score 31-25. Pittsburgh would now have to score a touchdown to win, since a field goal would not be enough to send the game into overtime. But the Steelers did not have enough time on the clock to mount a drive of their own. Instead, they could only call a series of desperate pass plays. Each pass fell harmlessly to the ground, and a few moments later the final gun sounded. Rodgers and his Packers teammates were Super Bowl champions.

To no one's surprise, Rodgers was named the most valuable player of the game. He had completed 24 of 39 passes for 304 yards and three touchdown strikes, despite several drops from his receivers. "We put this game on his shoulders," said McCarthy. In the locker room celebration afterwards, Rodgers expressed great satisfaction not only with the game, but also with his career in Green Bay. "The journey has been special," he said. "I'm not vindictive, but I'm blessed with a very good memory. You wait, you keep quiet, and you take advantage of an opportunity when it comes.... We've been through a lot together this season, and to be able to finish it off this way is incredible."

A Top NFL Quarterback for Years to Come

Green Bay fans now believe that they have the best quarterback in the NFL, and many coaches and analysts agree. "There are a lot of great quarterbacks," said Tedford. "But you take his athletic ability and the ability to manufacture plays, the things he's doing getting out of pressure and making things happen, along with the prototypical on-time throws and the decision making—I would take him over anybody else right now to lead my team."

Thompson believes that Rodgers's best years are still ahead of him, which is a scary thought for the rest of the NFL. "He is still growing, still getting better," he said. "I think people are going to write stories about him 10 years from now that he's pretty special. Even though he's done so much, he's sort of just getting started."

For his part, Rodgers has said that he would like to play for another decade or so. And when he's done, he remarked, "Hopefully the legacy I'll leave is one of somebody who was of high character, did things the right way, cared about his teammates, was coachable, and was good to the community he lived in."

HOME AND FAMILY

Rodgers is unmarried. He lives in Green Bay during the football season but visits his family and friends in Chico on a regular basis.

HOBBIES AND OTHER INTERESTS

Rodgers likes to golf and play the guitar, and he has participated in a number of charitable events. A big music fan, he started his own alternative rock label, Suspended Sunrise Recordings. In most ways, though, Rodgers prefers to be just "one of the guys." He admits that stardom "has opened some doors and allowed me to do some fun things—celebrity golf, the ESPYs, the Kentucky Derby—which is great. But at times I really enjoy the anonymity and being myself; I don't like having to be 'on' as Aaron Rodgers the quarterback."

HONORS AND AWARDS

NorCal (Northern California) Conference Most Valuable Player: 2003
All-Conference First Team (PAC-10 Conference): 2004
NFL Pro Bowl Selection: 2009
NFL Player of the Year (FedEx Air): 2010
Super Bowl XLV Most Valuable Player: 2011

FURTHER READING

Books

Hanrahan, Phil. *Life after Favre: A Season of Change with the Green Bay Packers,* 2009
Reischel, Rob. *Aaron Rodgers: Leader of the Pack,* 2011

Periodicals

Milwaukee Journal Sentinel, May 21, 2008
New York Times, Aug. 17, 2008, Sports, p.13; Jan. 10, 2011, Sports, p.2; Jan. 31, 2011, p.D1
San Francisco Chronicle, Oct. 27, 2004; Jan. 31, 2011, p.B1
San Jose (CA) Mercury News, Dec. 7, 2007; Feb. 4, 2011
Sporting News, Aug. 30, 2010, p.26; Feb. 14, 2011, p.58
Sports Illustrated, Mar. 31, 2008, p.30; July 7, 2008, p.48; Jan. 31, 2011, p.38; Feb. 14, 2011, p.32
Sports Illustrated Kids, Sep. 2009, p.20
USA Today, Aug. 23, 2004, p.C1; Aug. 11, 2006, p.C8; Jan. 20, 2011, p.C1

Online Articles

http://www.cbssports.com
(CBS Sports,"Rodgers No Longer Villain Who Forced Favre Out of Green Bay," February 3, 2011)
http://sports.espn.go.com
(ESPN,"Poised Aaron Rodgers Steadies Packers," February 7, 2011)

ADDRESS

Aaron Rodgers
Green Bay Packers
PO Box 10628
Green Bay, WI 54307-0628

WORLD WIDE WEB SITES

http://www.packers.com
http://www.nfl.com

Laurie Santos 1975-

American Scientist and Experimental Psychologist
Pioneering Researcher in the Shared Evolutionary Past of Humans and Monkeys

BIRTH

Laurie Renee Santos was born on August 19, 1975, in New Bedford, Massachusetts. Her mother, Marie, a high school guidance counselor, is descended from French-Canadians. Her father, Fred, a systems analyst, is descended from fishermen who came to New England generations ago from Cape Verde, a small island off the coast of Senegal, on the northwestern coast of Africa. Laurie has one brother, named Aaron.

YOUTH AND EDUCATION

As a child, Santos loved to write. When she was three years old, she wrote her first book, titled *The Cat and the Mouse*. Santos developed an early love for animals, like her mother. Marie Santos liked to rescue stray animals, so Laurie grew up surrounded by cats and dogs.

Santos attended New Bedford High School and graduated in 1993. She was a good student who did very well in school. Her favorite class was biology. "I had a fabulous high school biology teacher named Ms. Bonnie Ferreira who I still remember well even today," Santos recalled. "She gave me a love for the natural world. She was incredibly curious, funny, and a gift to her students."

"I had a fabulous high school biology teacher named Ms. Bonnie Ferreira who I still remember well even today," Santos recalled. "She gave me a love for the natural world. She was incredibly curious, funny, and a gift to her students."

Santos was accepted to Harvard University, where she intended to study law. Her plans changed when the pre-law class she needed to take was full. Santos explained, "I went to my freshman advisor very upset, you know, 'what am I going to do? I'm not going to be a lawyer.' And she said, 'Why don't you just take Introduction to Psychology? That's a good course for lawyers.' And then I took that course and it just stuck. And from there, I ended up taking more courses where I started thinking more about primates."

Becoming Interested in Primates

In her freshman year at Harvard, Santos volunteered for a position as a research assistant working with primates on an island reserve near Puerto Rico. She initially signed up for the job because the idea of field work seemed interesting. "But when I saw the monkeys, I got hooked," she recalled. "Watching them, you can't help but see that they have the same kinds of issues that we do. They play. You can see their social striving. You can see their battles, their caring. They want to make friends.... They care about their kids, and they want their friends to do well."

During that project, a pivotal experience motivated Santos to pursue a career working with primates. "One day I was alone on the beach and I picked out a nice spot to eat," she said. "A monkey came and sat beside me, and he had his monkey chow and was eating. We sat there together and I wondered what this monkey was thinking. Did he think the spot was beautiful? And how would I know that he did? That got me thinking about how they're a lot like us, but on the other hand so different. They're navigating these complicated motor situations, jumping from tree to tree, dealing with the stresses of new environments, and foraging. They do all of this minus language, minus the kind of social and cultural learning we humans have, yet they live, they mate, and they do some extremely complicated things, particularly in the social domain. How they achieve these same ends minus computers, BlackBerrys, or tape recorders is fascinating."

A capuchin monkey from the Yale Cognition Lab.

In 1997, Santos earned a Bachelor of Arts degree (BA) in psychology and biology from Harvard University and Radcliffe College, with a Certificate in Mind, Brain and Behavior. For graduate school, she continued studying at Harvard, earning a Master of Arts degree (MA) in psychology in 2001 and a doctoral degree, or doctorate (PhD), in psychology in 2003.

CAREER HIGHLIGHTS

In 2003, Santos took a position as associate professor of psychology at Yale University. At that time she also became the director of Yale's Comparative Cognition Laboratory. (Cognition is the process of thinking or knowing something.) Comparative cognition is a relatively new branch of psychology that studies the human brain by combining ideas from anthropology (the study of the origin and behavior of humans), cognitive science (the study of mental tasks and intelligence), and developmental psychology (the study of changes in behavior over an individual's lifetime).

Santos conducts experiments with monkeys and other primates to discover the behaviors and mental processes that humans share with monkeys. By identifying shared traits, she can then discover the traits that are uniquely human. "Our big goal is to understand how the human mind works … to explore what parts of human cognition are innate [natural]," Santos explained. "The more we learn about human cognition, the more we realize that much of the way we see the world and make decisions is controlled by lots of unconscious processes that are outside of our awareness."

Santos bases her research on the idea that the traits humans share with monkeys would have developed early in evolution in a common ancestor, and that uniquely human talents likely evolved after that split. "I want to know what makes humans tick, but if you're really interested in that question, it's actually kind of bad to study humans because they have too much stuff. You have too much education and culture and all that stuff, so we study primates to kind of strip away all that other stuff and actually look at humans in their more ancestral state, to try to get our evolutionary origins." To do her research, Santos conducts experiments with various primates at three different research facilities: the Comparative Cognition Lab, the Lemur Conservation Foundation Myakka City Reserve, and the Cayo Santiago Field Station.

At the Comparative Cognition Lab at Yale University, Santos studies a group of capuchin monkeys. She clarified that her lab is not a typical animal research facility. "I wanted to be able to set up a facility where the animals had a lot of space and could be comfortable," she remarked. "It's really exciting to have this large zoo enclosure, where we're able to have 10 of them housed really naturalistically—much different than the standard setup with cages."

At the Lemur Conservation Foundation Myakka City Reserve near Sarasota, Florida, Santos studies a variety of different lemurs, including ring-tailed lemurs, bamboo lemurs, mongoose lemurs, red-ruffed lemurs, and brown lemurs. "Lemurs are important to study because they're so distantly related to humans. If we see the same cognition in lemurs that we also see in macaques, capuchins, and chimpanzees, it allows us to learn more about how old that kind of cognition is. The other thing is that the lemurs developed in such a different environment on the island of Madagascar. So if we see the same kind of abilities in them, those abilities are probably widespread across primates."

At the Cayo Santiago Field Station on an island off the coast of Puerto Rico, Santos also works with rhesus macaques (monkeys). She explained that rhesus monkeys are "one of the best known and commonly used as a primate model."

Thinking Like a Monkey

Over the course of her career, Santos has achieved success by creating innovative experiments that demonstrate her uncanny knack for thinking like a monkey. Her studies focus on primates' natural behavioral tenden-

Santos with a rhesus monkey at the Cayo Santiago Field Station.

cies: to compete, to be sneaky, to deceive others, and to hoard items perceived as valuable. These behaviors are shared by humans, and so the outcomes of Santos's experiments can provide insight into the origin and evolution of certain actions and mental processes.

Santos created one of her best-known experiments with the help of an economist colleague. (Economists study individual and social behaviors related to money and other resources.) They wanted to see if monkeys could be taught to use money, which is a behavior usually considered to be uniquely human. Santos and her team designed an experiment that was intended to answer a series of questions. Could monkeys learn to use money? If so, what would they do with it? How would they behave and would there be any similarities to human behavior around money?

Santos set up an experiment that would explore these economic issues. "We did this by giving them little metal washers and teaching them that they could trade with human experimenters for food and the amazing thing was that they actually picked this up really quickly," she enthused. "We just then put them in a market. So they get a little wallet of tokens in the morning and they got to go into their enclosure and they had a choice of different experimenters who sold different foods at different prices....

What we found was really striking because in the spots where humans are very rational, where they obey all of the economists' models, the monkey did the same.... So if apples go on sale today, the monkeys would buy more apples. And they do it in a way that all the economic math would predict almost perfectly."

A variation in this experiment was designed to find out if monkeys could understand more subtle concepts about the value of money. Santos created the experiment to observe the monkeys' response to an unexpected outcome in a sales transaction. In this variation, two salespeople offer apple pieces. One appears to offer one piece of apple, but when the monkey pays him, the experimenter gives him an extra piece of apple. When buying from that vendor, the monkeys get two pieces of apple. Meanwhile, the other salesperson holds three pieces of apple, but when the monkey pays him, he takes one away and gives the monkey only two pieces. In this case, the monkey sees the loss of one piece of apple. Santos explained, "The important thing is that, on average, the monkeys get two pieces of apple from both experimenters. So in practice they shouldn't care and should trade randomly, but that's not what we see. The monkeys prefer to trade with the experimenter who's giving them the bonuses and avoid the experimenter who's giving them the losses."

"When I saw the monkeys, I got hooked," Santos recalled. "Watching them, you can't help but see that they have the same kinds of issues that we do. They play. You can see their social striving. You can see their battles, their caring. They want to make friends.... They care about their kids, and they want their friends to do well."

One particularly noteworthy outcome of the money experiment was that monkeys sometimes tried to cheat the human food sellers. Santos and her team observed that occasionally a monkey would buy an apple and take a bite out of it. Then the monkey would present the unbitten side of the apple to the vendor and try to get a refund. Monkeys also tried to buy food using counterfeit money, such as slices of cucumber instead of the metal washers they had been given.

Another of Santos's experiments involves observing the behavior of monkeys that have the opportunity to steal food. Santos created a simple experiment that she and her team of researchers have performed hundreds of times. Two identically dressed researchers approach a monkey that is paying attention to them. A third researcher, acting as an observer, calls out instructions to make sure that both of the active researchers do everything in unison. At the same time, both researchers show the monkey a grape, place the grape on a plate, and put the plate on the ground. When the grapes are on the ground, one researcher turns her back to the monkey. The other stays facing the monkey, and they wait. "Consistently the monkeys steal the food from the guy who's facing away. Even without training, they realize that when eyes are pointed at them, it's probably not a good idea to do it. But as soon as eyes are turned away, all bets are off," Santos explained. "We actually were able to film the experiment successfully and even photographed another one. It was amazing how fast the monkeys would make their decision to go for the grape … but each monkey would look up at the experimenter's back all the way to the grape before hightailing it back to the bush with treat in hand."

Santos described another experiment that focuses on the monkeys' perception of sound. "We have a single experimenter who has two boxes. One is covered in jingle bells, so when it moves it makes a lot of noise. The other one looks the same because it's covered in jingle bells, but we've taken the balls out of all the bells, so the monkey can hear that when the experimenter puts food in the box it's not making any sound," Santos related. "So when the experimenter freezes and looks away, the question is, which box does the monkey steal from? What we find is that they sneak over and take food out of the quiet box and avoid stealing things from the box they know is noisy."

Finding Meaning in Animal Behavior

Although her experiments have produced consistent results over time, Santos acknowledges that the meaning of those results is still unclear. "The real question is this: Are the monkeys just good at reading our behavior? 'Oh, she's turned away now.' Or are they thinking about our perceptions, mainly, 'She can't see now.' And this is still a question of much controversy in the field." This subtle difference is critical to interpreting the outcome of the experiments.

After years of research in the lab and in the field, Santos has concluded that primates are capable of understanding what others are thinking by reading social cues and body language. "They obviously can't verbally reason things out, but their choices are extremely similar to the ones humans make. So in that sense, I think they have to be reasoning." It is impossible to know for certain what goes on in a monkey's mind, but Santos uses established scientific measures to form her conclusions. "In terms of how they think, we use the same measures that we use in humans, and our

Santos with a lemur at the Lemur Conservation Foundation Myakka City Reserve.

studies suggest primates are reasoning about things they can't see and interpreting mental states. Just a few years ago, we didn't think primates could do this. Animals' mental lives are richer than we used to think."

"The hope is that seeing more of ourselves in them will help us treat them more humanely and work to conserve them and their habitats in future generations. Our experiments suggest that these primates can understand our intentions. Can they morally reason about what we do? Can they understand someone's intent to hurt them? When we get the full package of how they pay attention to the world, it might end up informing how we treat them."

Santos is still near the beginning of her career, but already her research has been called groundbreaking. Her work has been described by fellow Yale professor Paul Bloom as "excellent in just about every conceivable way—it is theoretically deep, methodologically precise, and addresses some of the most significant questions in psychology." Writing in *Discover* magazine, Linda Marsa praised Santos for providing "an unparalleled glimpse into our evolutionary past." In 2007, Santos was named as one of *Popular Science* magazine's Brilliant Ten young scientists in the U.S.

For young people interested in a career in science, Santos believes there are many important questions still to be explored."Be curious! There are so many open problems in the world that you can answer yourself with a little ingenuity and the scientific method," she said. "My advice is to find what you really love doing and thinking about, and find a way to do that for your career."

HOBBIES AND OTHER INTERESTS

Santos's hobby is taking photographs of animals' feet. While on a research trip early in her career, she took some pictures of monkey hands and feet. Since then, her collection has grown to include photos of giraffes, tortoises, rhinos, and other animals. Her favorite image is a picture of a monkey's hands wrapped around a tree, with details that clearly show the shared evolution of humans and primates.

HONORS AND AWARDS

Baccalaureate Award (Ford Foundation): 1996
Brilliant Ten (*Popular Science*): 2007
Stanton Prize (Society for Philosophy and Psychology): 2008

FURTHER READING

Periodicals

Christian Century, Dec. 16, 2008, p.9
Chronicle of Higher Education, Nov. 16, 2001
Discover, Nov. 2008
New York Times, June 5, 2005
Popular Science, Oct. 3, 2007
Science News, Mar. 12, 2007, p.163
Smithsonian, Oct. 2007; Jan. 2008, p.58

Online Articles

http://abcnews.go.com
(ABC News,"Monkeys Steal When No One's Looking,"Mar. 23, 2005)
http://bigthink.com/lauriesantos
(Big Think,"Laurie Santos,"June 9, 2010)
http://discovermagazine.com
(Discover,"The Monkey Whisperer Learns the Secrets of Primate Economics,"Oct. 13, 2008)
http://www.pbs.org/wgbh/nova/secretlife
(PBS,"The Secret Life of Scientists and Engineers: Laurie Santos—Experimental Psychologist,"Mar. 17, 2010)

http://www.popsci.com
(Popular Science,"The Monkey Economist," Oct. 3, 2007)
http://www.southcoasttoday.com
(South Coast Today,"Students Gain Insight Into Darwin's Theory," Feb. 16, 2010)

Videos

http://www.pbs.org/wgbh/nova/secretlife
(PBS,"The Secret Life of Scientists and Engineers," 2009)
http://www.pbs.org/wnet/humanspark
(PBS,"The Human Spark: So Human, So Chimp," Jan. 3, 2010)

ADDRESS

Dr. Laurie Santos
Yale University
Department of Psychology
Box 208205
New Haven, CT 06520

WORLD WIDE WEB SITE

http://www.yale.edu/monkeylab

Ryan Sheckler 1989-

American Skateboarder
Youngest-Ever Gold Medal Winner at the X Games

BIRTH

Ryan Allen Sheckler was born on December 30, 1989, in La Palma, California, a small city in the greater Los Angeles area. He was the first of three sons born to Gretchen, who managed a dental office, and Randall (Randy) Sheckler, a mechanical engineer and entrepreneur. His brother Shane was born when he was two, and his brother Kane when he was nine. The brothers grew up in San Clemente, California, a coastal city midway between Los Angeles and San Diego.

YOUTH

Sheckler was a very active child, and he first tried to ride a skateboard at 18 months of age. He had spied his father's skateboard in the garage and ended up riding it on one knee, like a surfboard. When he was young, he said, "Everywhere we went, that was the first thing that came out of the car with me. If we went to the park, I didn't want to play in the sandbox, I just wanted to ride that board." He received his own skateboard at age four and soon learned to perform an ollie, a basic skateboarding trick where the rider pops the tail of the board on the ground to make it jump, then levels the board in the air to land on all four wheels. From that point on, he obsessed over learning new tricks. When he was trying to master the kickflip—an ollie where the board rotates lengthwise before landing—his mother limited him to 100 attempts per day. It took him a year of practicing, but he finally mastered the trick.

When he was young, Sheckler said, "Everywhere we went, that was the first thing that came out of the car with me. If we went to the park, I didn't want to play in the sandbox, I just wanted to ride that board."

When Sheckler was seven, his father rewarded his devoted practice by building a small training ramp in the family's backyard. There were six skate parks near the family's home, including one used by skateboarding pioneer Tony Hawk. (For more information about Hawk, see *Biography Today,* Apr. 2001.) But Sheckler's family built their own, and their "park" eventually grew to include the rails, platforms, and ramps he needed to develop his skills. At age seven, he began competing in the California Amateur Skateboard League, winning every contest he entered during his first year, including the first of five consecutive state championships. Not long after, his mother quit her job to become his manager, scheduling family vacations so that her son could compete around the country. By the time Sheckler was 10, he was attracting sponsors like Oakley sunglasses, Etnies shoes, and Volcom clothes. He frequently finished in the top three at events like the Vans Warped Tour, sometimes even against professionals. By the time he was 13, it was clear Sheckler was ready to compete with the best, and he turned pro in 2003.

EDUCATION

As a professional skateboarder touring the world, Sheckler had little time for school. He was home schooled until he took a brief break from full-time competition to spend his freshman year at San Clemente High School, where he joined the wrestling team. After a year, however, the family decided that he was hurting his career by not competing widely, so he finished his education at Futures Halstrom High School in Mission Viejo, a school for independent study designed for serious young athletes and artists. He attended one-on-one classes twice a week and studied at home or on tour the rest of the time.

CAREER HIGHLIGHTS

Turning Pro

Sheckler's performance in 2003, his first season, soon justified his decision to turn pro. He competed in the park or street divisions of competitions, where skaters are judged on how they navigate a course and perform tricks on and around a series of obstacles. These obstacles could include ramps, boxes, rails, and walls; park competitions had taller ramps and walls, like a skate park, while street competitions were designed more like a real street. Sheckler earned a second place at the Scandinavian Open, then won the Vans Slam City Jam in Vancouver, making him the youngest skateboarder ever to win a professional event. He proved his success wasn't a fluke with additional first place finishes at the Gravity Games and the New Jersey Triple Crown. Two of his wins that year were in the Vans Triple Crown series, and a ninth-place finish in the final competition gave him the overall series title in the street division.

For competitors in action sports like skateboarding and motocross, the annual X Games, sponsored by cable sports network ESPN, is one of the most important competitions in their sport. Sheckler competed in his first X Games in 2003, entering the skateboard park event. He was the only competitor to land every trick he attempted, and he walked away with the gold medal. At 13, he was the youngest competitor ever to win an X Games event, a feat that landed him in the *Guinness Book of World Records.* He later attributed his success to a need to prove himself: "I turned pro that year and was really motivated to win everything I entered." Winning the X Games medal, he added, "changed everything. It changed the way I looked at skating because I knew I could hang with the big boys and I could skate." His successes over the year also earned him enough points to be named the year's overall street champion by the World Cup of Skateboarding.

Sheckler also grabbed attention early in his career by creating a signature move. Called the "Shecklair," the move was a kickflip where he grabbed the board between his feet (a move called an indy), but with his legs extended.

Sheckler competed in the X Games for the first time in 2003, when he was 13 years old, and won the gold medal in the park event.

His flair and his early success led to more opportunities. He went on tour with Tony Hawk and was featured in the skating star's video game *Underground 2.* He also got his first real movie work with a small role in the 2003 film *Grind.* Sheckler had been in a movie before, in the 2001 release *MVP: Most Vertical Primate,* in which he worked as a stunt double for a skateboarding monkey."I thought it was gonna be cool but it turned out kind of stupid," he recalled about having to skate in a monkey suit. In the skating film *Grind,* Sheckler had a small role as a young skateboarder, showing off some of his moves.

Dominating the First Dew Tour

During the 2004 season, Sheckler curbed his competition schedule, skipping everything but major events so he could attend high school like a regular kid. Unlike regular kids, he was earning six figures in competitions, collecting gifts from his sponsors, and being featured on an episode of MTV's "Cribs." He also began performing in skateboarding videos, contributing to Digital Skateboards' *Everyday* video and Almost Skateboards' video *Round Three.* At competitions before the school year started, Sheckler earned a first place at the Vancouver stop of the Vans Triple Crown and a bronze in street at the Gravity Games. Combined with a ninth-place finish in street at the X Games, he placed second overall in the World Cup of Skateboarding street series.

Sheckler returned to full-time competition in the 2005 season, the first year for the Dew Action Sports Tour (AST), a series of five skateboard and motocross competitions. He won the first two events, placed second at the third, and clinched the Dew Cup for street skateboarding by winning the fourth stop. He placed third at the last event, giving him more points than any athlete in any event, earning him the title of Action Sports Tour Athlete of the Year. Besides a bonus of $100,000, Sheckler earned a new Toyota Tacoma truck. At 15, he wasn't even old enough to drive. The victories also earned him another overall street championship from the World Cup of Skateboarding. That year he also made a cameo appearance as himself in the skateboarding movie *Dishdogz.*

The skater kept competing during the 2006 season, earning his second consecutive Dew Cup for park skateboarding. After winning the first stop on the tour, he showed his toughness by competing in the second event only two weeks after severely burning his foot on a hot grill during a beach barbeque. He went on to win the third and fourth Dew AST events and clinched the overall championship with a second-place finish in the final event. He also placed second at the X Games and was awarded Arby's Action Sports Awards for Skateboarder and Athlete of the Year. In 2006 he went on tour again with skateboarding legend Hawk, who told *USA Today* that Sheckler was "arguably one of the best all-around skaters today, probably the best. In terms of versatility, he's the best guy anywhere, and he's only 16." At 16, Sheckler already had a signature sneaker with Etnies, as well as his personal brands of Volcom jeans and eyewear for Oakley. The latter company featured him on its skateboarding video *Our Life* in 2006.

Sheckler won the Dew Cup in 2005, 2006, and 2007 (shown here)— the first skater to win it three years in a row.

The following season Sheckler again made history by becoming the first skater to win the Dew Action Sports Tour championship three years in a row. He won three events and placed second in the other two competitions, running away with the skate park title with 450 out of a possible 500 points. He also placed fourth at the street event at the 2007 X Games. As a teenager, Sheckler was living a life other kids could only dream about: traveling the world to competitions, attending celebrity parties and events like the MTV Video Awards, and earning a considerable income, as well as loads of free gifts from sponsors. "A part of me relates to kids my age, a part of me doesn't," he noted. "I'm not complaining about my life, but it definitely gets to me when I want to go to the beach. But then, I also want to travel and do all these cool things I get to do. It kind of clashes a little bit, but it's not something I can't handle."

Starring in a Hit Reality TV Show

Executives at MTV were intrigued with Sheckler's hectic lifestyle, and they asked to make a reality show out of his life. "Life of Ryan" debuted in fall 2007 and became MTV's best-rated new series that season, with 41 million viewers watching its eight episodes. While viewers were treated to glimpses of Sheckler traveling and competing, they mostly saw him dealing with the same issues other teens face: finding a girlfriend, managing his friendships, and, most prominently, dealing with his parents' recent divorce. "After years of commoners' showboating, here comes a showboat who wants to be common," critic Ned Martel noted in the *New York Times.* The reviewer added that the reality show was worth watching because Sheckler "is good at something and still manages to be humble yet charismatic, ambitious yet magnanimous, hard-working yet fun-loving."

Skateboarding legend Tony Hawk said that Sheckler is "arguably one of the best all-around skaters today, probably the best. In terms of versatility, he's the best guy anywhere, and he's only 16."

"Life of Ryan" continued for 21 more episodes over two seasons; Sheckler cut the third season short after six episodes because he felt it was taking away from his skateboarding. After his show took off, he got criticism from some skaters for "selling out" and taking skateboarding into the mainstream. He became one of the few skateboarding stars to appear in ads for non-skating products, including Axe body spray and Panasonic electronics, and some critics believed he was harming the sport by dulling its edge. Sheckler took the criticism in stride: "All I can do is focus on the positives, man.... Skating is a blessing and that's all I want to do. People can say what they want. I don't think negative anymore. It's too hard. Positivity will take you way further." The show brought plenty of positives to his life, including lots of fans who were new to skateboarding. Groups of screaming teenage girls became a common sight at his competitions.

Sheckler continued winning titles during the 2008 season. He picked up wins in the first and third events on the Dew Tour, as well as a second place at the fourth event; non-podium finishes in the other two events meant he finished third overall in skate park. He bounced back by earning his second X Games gold medal in 2008, placing first in street skateboarding despite competing with a broken elbow. He counted his first place at *Thrasher* magazine's Bust or Bail contest, in which competitors worked a rail on a set of 17 stairs, as one of his best victories. In 2008 he also worked on a video for sponsor Red Bull with his skateboarding friends and idols, arranging many of the film's events and taking the group to sites in Dubai and Australia. That year he also began branching out with an apparel line, helping to design his own shoe for Etnies and expanding his clothing line. He partnered with department store JC Penney to release a whole line of casual wear, called RS by Sheckler. He helped design the line, which included jeans, T-shirts, shorts, and hoodies.

Sheckler in his trophy room, in a scene from the MTV reality show "Life of Ryan."

In 2008, Sheckler created the Sheckler Foundation with his brothers to give back to the community. They sponsored an annual golf tournament, the Sheckler Foundation Celebrity Skins Classic, to raise money for a variety of causes. They partnered with several other charities, including the Make-A-Wish Foundation and groups supporting research into autism and spinal cord injuries. Other partners included a group that provided funds to help injured action athletes and the Rob Dyrdek Foundation, which helped promote skateboarding, especially to kids in underprivileged communities. "I feel really blessed to be involved in those things," Sheckler said. "I feel like I am supposed to give back. I have a responsibility to do more than just skateboard and sit around."

Coming Back from Injury

Sheckler had reconstructive surgery on his elbow in 2009, then returned to competition. He took first in the Skate Open ISF Skateboarding World Championships, the first event in the Dew Tour. At that year's X Games, however, he broke his foot during one of his runs, forcing him to sit out the rest of the season. Getting hurt has been part of being a professional skater, and over the course of his career Sheckler has also suffered a fractured foot, broken elbows (five times), and concussions (three times). "I got all these other scars from skating, but it's my life, dude," he said. "I absolutely love it. I am always hurt but what are you going to do? I have to skate."The foot injury kept him out of action for five months, but he kept busy with his growing acting career. He appeared in the 2009 film *Street Dreams* as the rival and friend of a young man trying to make it as a pro skater.

Sheckler took his first non-skating acting role with the 2010 comedy *The Tooth Fairy,* which starred Dwayne "The Rock" Johnson. Sheckler played Mick, a hockey player and teammate of Johnson's character, who is transformed into a tooth fairy. For the role, Sheckler learned to ice skate so he could perform all but the worst falls in his scenes. The experience was interesting enough that he said he would be open to other non-skateboarding acting roles: "I'll always have my skate life, but I absolutely like the fun of making movies."

After spending long months away from skating, Sheckler was eager to return. "I think that coming back into skateboarding is going to feel like the best thing that's ever happened to me," he remarked. He rejoined the Dew Tour, now consisting of four events, for the 2010 season. He followed a second-place finish at the first stop with two thirds and a fourth, ending up second overall on the Tour. At the X Games that summer he earned his third gold medal, clinching the skateboard street event with a near-perfect run. He also participated in the first season of skateboard entrepreneur Rob Dyrdek's Street League DC Pro Tour, a new series of competitions designed to feature the best skateboarders competing for a record $1.2 million in prize money. The new format instantly scored tricks as riders navigated the course, allowing riders and fans to see the success of each trick. Although Sheckler's best finish at the three events was only a fourth place, he did notch the highest scoring single trick of the series.

Competing against the best skaters appealed to him, Sheckler said. "I like the competition because it keeps me mentally focused on something besides learning a trick or linking tricks together. I'm always trying to figure out ways to one up everyone and that's what I love about competitions. I love challenging myself and pushing the envelope." He maintained good relationships with his fellow skaters, however, and felt honored when he was asked to join the skating team of Plan B skateboards. He toured with skaters like multiple X Games winner Paul Rodriguez and video stars Torey Pudwill and P. J. Ladd, and collaborated on the Plan B video *Superfuture.* "You know, we're competitors but we're all friends—really good friends—so ... it's nice to be in a place where it feels like we can all respect each other and respect what we're doing and respect mutual accomplishments," he explained.

Sheckler was surprised in 2010 when he won the Kids' Choice Award for favorite male athlete over basketball stars Kobe Bryant and LeBron James

After a tough injury in 2009, Sheckler came back and earned a gold medal in the street event at the 2010 X Games.

and snowboarder/skateboarder Shaun White. He attributed his growing popularity and continuing success to hard work. "People think this life was just handed to me. But I started from ground zero like everybody else," he said. "I have been doing tricks since I was six years old. I was focused and determined from that long ago. That's why I am where I am." He credited his family and his Christian faith for keeping him grounded and away from potential troubles with drinking or drugs. "I always skated for myself and just wanted to be good for myself," he explained. "Any pressure is only me wanting to succeed and pushing myself to do so."

With the Street League Tour offering revenue sharing to participating skaters, Sheckler decided to continue with that tour in 2011, even though it meant he might have to give up other tournaments. He placed fourth in the first event, then fifth in the second event. In the tour's third event, he moved up to take second, narrowly losing to Nyjah Huston, who won the first three events. But the final event of the season proved to be a disappointment, as Sheckler placed ninth in the initial section and was eliminated. At the 2011 X Games, where he was the defending champ, Sheckler put together an incredible run but came in third and took the bronze, losing to Nyjah Huston in first and Luan Oliveira in second. Some observers commented on the age discrepancy between the veteran Sheckler and the two younger skaters, noting especially that Huston was just 16 years old. As Colin Bane wrote for ESPN.com, "Call it a changing of the guard: at 21, Sheckler (who holds the distinction of once being the youngest athlete ever to win X Games gold as a 13-year-old in 2003) was the oldest skater on today's podium."

Sheckler continues to push himself as an athlete. He has begun working with a personal trainer to keep himself fit for competition, improving his stamina by biking or swimming nearly every day. A sponsor helped him build his own private two-story skate park for practicing his skating skills. He knows he can't skate forever, and he's thought about staying involved in the business side of skating after he retires. But for now, he has goals he still wants to achieve in the sport. He said his dream accomplishment would be earning *Thrasher* magazine's Skater of the Year, an award that is voted on by skateboarding's most hard-core fans. He thought he had the potential to achieve this goal, even if it took years. "I still don't know my boundaries," he acknowledged, "and I've been skating professionally since I was 13." Sheckler was once asked how he will know he's reached his ultimate goal—to be one of the best skaters ever. "I want to make a huge contribution to skateboarding," he replied. "The only way I will know that I have achieved legendary status is when my peers say I have. There is no other way."

HOME AND FAMILY

When Sheckler turned 18, he bought his own house and began living on his own. His house was close to both parents in San Clemente, California, so he could spend as much time as possible with his younger brothers and friends. In 2010 he got his first pet, a little dog he named Dollar.

HOBBIES AND OTHER INTERESTS

Away from skateboarding, Sheckler enjoys other action sports, including surfing, snowboarding, and riding dirt bikes. He also enjoys music and movies. In addition to his work with the Sheckler Foundation, the skater is quick to get involved in other charitable activities. He has skated with sick children for the Make-A-Wish Foundation, and in 2008 he donated his Range Rover to be auctioned for the Children's Cancer Research Fund, raising almost $200,000.

SELECTED CREDITS

Television

"Life of Ryan," 2007-08

Skateboarding Videos

Everyday, 2004
Round Three, 2004
Our Life, 2006
Tony Hawk's Secret Skatepark Tour, Vol. 2, 2006
Slaughter at the Opera, 2008

Movies

MVP: Most Vertical Primate, 2001 (stunt double)
Grind, 2003
Dishdogz, 2005 (as himself)
Street Dreams, 2009
The Tooth Fairy, 2010

HONORS AND AWARDS

Vans Triple Crown Overall Street Champion: 2003
Gold Medal in Skateboard Park (Summer X Games): 2003
Overall Street Champion (World Cup of Skateboarding): 2003 and 2005
Athlete of the Year (Dew Action Sports Tour): 2005
Dew Cup in Skateboard Park (Dew Action Sports Tour): 2005, 2006, 2007
Skateboarder and Athlete of the Year (Arby's Action Sports Awards): 2006

Gold Medal in Skateboard Street (Summer X Games): 2008, 2010
Kids' Choice Award (Nickelodeon): 2010, for Favorite Male Athlete
Teen Choice Award: 2010, for Choice Action Sports Athlete

FURTHER READING

Books

Nicholas, Kimberly, *Ryan Sheckler: The Real Life of a Hot Skater,* 2008

Periodicals

Denver Post, July 8, 2005, p.D10
Los Angeles Times, Oct. 5, 2000, p.1; July 20, 2004, p.D1; Oct. 14, 2006, p.D10
Miami Herald, Oct. 16, 2006
New York Times, Sep. 20, 2006, p.A1; Jan. 22, 2008, p.8
Sports Illustrated for Kids, Jan. 2004, p.52; Aug. 2008, p.18
Thrasher, Apr. 2004, p.156
Transworld Skateboarding, Aug. 2006, p.146; Apr. 2008, p.156; June 2010, p.126
USA Today, July 10, 2006, p.C12; July 2, 2008, p.C2

Online Articles

http://espn.go.com/action
(ESPN, "Just Another Lonely Millionaire Skateboarder," July 16, 2008; "Catching up with Ryan Sheckler," Dec. 9, 2009; "Candid Conversation: Ryan Sheckler," Jan. 21, 2010; "Checking in with Ryan Sheckler," May 19, 2010; "A League of Their Own," June 3, 2010; "Ryan Sheckler Juggles Skateboarding, His Fans," July 30, 2011)
http://sportsillustrated.cnn.com
(Sports Illustrated, "Q&A with Ryan Sheckler," Aug. 1, 2009)

ADDRESS

Ryan Sheckler
Ryan Sheckler, Inc.
111 Del Cabo
San Clemente, CA 92673

WORLD WIDE WEB SITES

http://www.ryansheckler.com
http://www.espn.go.com/action

Esperanza Spalding 1984-

American Bass Player and Jazz Musician
Winner of the 2011 Grammy Award for Best New Artist

BIRTH

Esperanza Spalding, whose name means "hope" in Spanish, was born on October 18, 1984, in Portland, Oregon. Her family comes from African-American, Asian, Native-American, Welsh, and Hispanic ancestry. She grew up with her mother and older brother in the lower-middle-class neighborhood of King, just outside of Portland. Her mother worked many part-time jobs in order to pay the bills.

YOUTH

Growing Up in King

Spalding spent her childhood in King. When she was very young, two rival gangs, the Crips and Bloods, moved to the Portland area from California and began fighting over the local drug trade. Spalding started sleeping on the floor in case stray bullets came through her bedroom window. Eventually her mother moved the family across town, but they were never quite able to get away from violence.

"I grew up with an incredibly loving and supportive family that gave me the impression there were a lot of options for me out there," Spalding recalled. "[My mother] took the time to ensure that my brother and I got a good education and were being fed with love. She had the endurance and willingness to push through, work hard, and provide for her family."

Spalding was never involved in gang violence herself, but she did have trouble behaving while she lived in King. She called her neighborhood a ghetto and pretty scary. "In Oregon, I got into so much trouble." she confessed. "I was a fool." She made it a point to learn from the mistakes she made growing up.

Little information is available about Spalding's father, who was not part of the family when she was growing up. Money was tight, and her mother needed to have several jobs to pay the bills and have enough money for food. Throughout Spalding's childhood, her mother worked as a carpenter, security guard, dishwasher, and daycare worker. Still, there never seemed to be enough money. The family came close to homelessness. Once, they even had to live in a friend's attic. Despite these problems, Spalding has only warm things to say about her upbringing. "I grew up with an incredibly loving and supportive family that gave me the impression there were a lot of options for me out there," she recalled. "[My mother] took the time to ensure that my brother and I got a good education and were being fed with love. She had the endurance and willingness to push through, work hard, and provide for her family."

Music in Her Home

Despite the difficulties with money, Spalding's mother made sure that life at home was full of joy, which meant it was full of music. Listening to her mother play the piano and sing was one of the reasons Spalding became interested in becoming a musician. "Mom used to make a song for everything," she claimed. Her mother would often sing, either in English or Spanish, to wake Spalding and her brother in the morning.

An early shot of Spalding.

Spalding's mother had gone to college to become a jazz guitarist and continued taking classes while her kids were growing up, and she was the first to notice her daughter's musical gifts. Once, when Spalding was four years old, she listened to her mother play the piano. Her mom was struggling with a difficult piece of music written by the classical music composer Ludwig von Beethoven. Spalding went over to the bench, sat down beside her mother, and began playing the song by ear. From there, she learned to create her own songs on the piano. She would write the melody, her mother told the *New Yorker* magazine, then "she'd arrange it in every style of music you could imagine, from bluegrass to classical to jazz. She'd call me over, and say, 'Look, I can play it this way. And I can play it this way, and then I can play it this way and this way.'"

Around the same time, Spalding was watching "Mr. Rogers' Neighborhood," where she saw a performance by the famous cello player Yo Yo Ma. She looked at her mother and said, "What is that thing making that sound? I want to play that!" Her mother could not afford a cello, but the community band program had a violin to offer Spalding for free. She played that for 10 years, joining the local Chamber Musical Society of Oregon, a nonprofit program with a children's chamber orchestra. She became the orchestra's concertmaster, or lead violinist, by age 15.

EDUCATION

Spalding's education was unusual, especially because she was in charge of it herself for three years, from fifth to eighth grades, when she was homeschooled. There were a few reasons she was homeschooled: she had a poor immune system, often making her sick and unable to attend school in a classroom, and her mother disapproved of many of the teaching methods and lessons in public schools. However, because of her mother's busy work schedule, she didn't have much time for one-on-one lessons. As a result, Spalding taught herself during those years, borrowing books from the library in order to learn the necessary material. She was even responsible for taking state-administered tests in order for her homeschooled education to be legal.

Back to the Classroom

Spalding enjoyed homeschooling, but it did not last. When she was 14, she accepted a full scholarship to Northwest Academy, a private school in Portland. Even though she was happy to continue learning, she found it difficult to enjoy classes, since it was a much more rigid system than she was used to.

"I remember distinctly," Spalding said, "the first thing you notice [about a bass] is the vibration is so powerful, particularly compared to a violin—or any other instrument. I felt it resonating through my whole system. I said, 'Wow. This is pretty hip.'"

At Northwest Academy, Spalding developed a passion for the standup bass. She was walking through the halls one day, skipping class, when she looked into the band room and saw a standup bass. She couldn't help but go in and see what it sounded like. "I remember distinctly," she said, "the first thing you notice [about a bass] is the vibration is so powerful, particularly compared to a violin—or any other instrument. I felt it resonating through my whole system. I said, 'Wow. This is pretty hip.' And I just kept noodling around." As she was playing, the band teacher walked in. Instead of being upset that Spalding was in the band room when she wasn't supposed to be, he taught her a bass line, which is a single rhythm played to back up a melody.

At age 15, Spalding could play the piano, oboe, clarinet, guitar, and violin. Still, it was when she began focusing on the bass that she found a real passion for an instrument—she knew that was the instrument she wanted her career to revolve around. From that point on, Spalding was a bassist.

Knowing that she wanted to play the bass was one thing; finding the perfect bass to play was another. Spalding bought her bass from a man who could no longer play because of tendonitis, or inflamed tendons in his hand. It stands at 5'6", just taller than Spalding, and it was made in France or Germany at least 200 years ago. When she bought it, the back was ready to fall off, the front was cracked, and glue was holding it together in about four places. Spalding's mother took out a loan to help pay for repairs, and the bass is perfect now.

College Years

When she was 15, Spalding dropped out of high school and earned her GED, which is the equivalent of a high school diploma. She then attended Portland State University, where she spent a year in the conservatory program and was the youngest bassist in the program. At 17, when most people are juniors in high school, Spalding got a full scholarship to Berklee College of Music, a college in Boston with an excellent music program. She took classes in arranging music, composition, vocal performance, and music from different musical styles. For her senior project, she led her own band and made a record that later became her first album, *Junjo*. She graduated with a music degree in 2005, when she was 20.

After graduating from Berklee, Spalding was asked to stay on as a teacher. At 20 years old, she was the second-youngest faculty member in the history of the college. She developed two courses: one on singing and playing, the other on harmony and music theory. She taught at Berklee for three years.

CAREER HIGHLIGHTS

Becoming a Performer

Spalding's career in music started early; in fact, she started getting musical jobs, or gigs, in high school. She played with an indie rock/pop band called Noise for Pretend, writing lyrics, composing music, and becoming the lead singer within a year. It was difficult to sing and play at the same time, Spalding said, especially since she had never sung professionally before. Getting more jobs with her bass was not difficult, however. During this time, her teen years, she was in about six bands at once. Because she was so involved in musical groups, Spalding got a lot of practice with the bass, which takes years to master. "You really have to practice very carefully to get to the point where you feel comfortable and at ease on it," she said.

Spalding learned the most about performing when she backed the R&B star Patti Austin on the "For Ella" tour while still a student at Berklee College. The tour celebrated the music of jazz singer Ella Fitzgerald, who performed between 1935 and 1993. Performing with Austin, Spalding was

Spalding with her bass.

able to tour Europe for three years, on and off. She said she learned how to accompany a singer and how to be on her game every night, even when she wasn't feeling her best. Working with Noise for Pretend and Patti Austin, along with others, helped Spalding develop into a quadruple threat: she could sing, play, compose, and arrange. These skills made it easy for her to work with a variety of artists in different styles.

Becoming a Recording Artist

Spalding's recording career began while she was still in college. She created her first album, *Junjo,* as part of a senior project for her music degree from Berklee. On *Junjo,* released in 2006, she plays the bass and sings while accompanied by a pianist and drummer. Because of her appreciation for different musical styles, she included the sounds of "world music," especially South American music, as well as American jazz. Spalding does not sing any songs with lyrics on *Junjo*. Instead, she scats, which means she sings rhythms and melodies without words, just sounds. Spalding earned fans in the jazz world, and the critics were impressed that someone so young could compose music so advanced. *Junjo* was the first step toward success for Spalding, and it opened the door for her to join the record label Heads Up International.

Spalding released her second album, *Esperanza,* in 2008. The album is full of her bass lines, which create a funky rhythm that accompanies her singing. A lot of the time, she would scat instead of sing, like she did on *Junjo*. However, this album does contain lyrics, which she sings in English, Spanish, or Portuguese. The album was sold around the world—the first time her music reached an audience outside of the United States—and it was a success. Esperanza spent 78 weeks on the *Billboard* charts, peaking at No. 2.

Critics especially praised her musical skill and the mix of jazz with music from other genres. "[*Esperanza* demonstrates] her talents as a virtuoso instrumentalist, gifted multi-lingual vocalist, and potent songwriter," Philip Booth wrote in *Bass Player* magazine. "She plays and sings on a jazz-rooted program marked by catchy if tricky melodies, pliable grooves informed by Latin, Brazilian, African, and bebop rhythms, and multiple bursts of ripping fingerboard work and scat singing." That assessment was later seconded by John Colapinto in the *New Yorker* magazine. "While the music was indisputably jazz, it suggested an almost bewildering array of influences—fusion, funk, soul, rhythm and blues, Brazilian samba and Cuban son, pop balladry, chanted vocalese—with lyrics sung in Spalding's three languages: English, Portuguese, and Spanish. An ebullient mash-up of sounds, styles, and tongues, the record seemed like something new—jazz for the iPod age."

In 2010, Spalding released her next album, *Chamber Music Society,* which combines her love for jazz and chamber music. This album was different from the music she had released in the past because it relied on the classical music training from her childhood, as Gail Mitchell explained in *Billboard* magazine. "That training provides the foundation for the musical prodigy's modernized take on chamber music: accenting the intuitive spontaneity of improvisation with string trio arrangements combining elements of jazz, folk, and world music." Spalding put together a group of musicians who played piano, drums, guitar, violin, and cello. The musicians played improvisational pieces, which means they made up a lot of the music while they performed. She presented the music in a classical chamber music style, which is more structured than her earlier work. The compositions on *Chamber Music Society* combine chamber music, jazz, folk, and musical sounds from other countries, and they also combine spontaneous improvisation with disciplined string arrangements. *Chamber Music Society* has spent 44 weeks on the *Billboard* charts to date, and the number is still climbing.

Shortly after the album's release, Spalding won the 2011 Grammy Award for Best New Artist. She was the first jazz artist ever to receive the award. Her win was one of the night's biggest surprises, since her competition included Justin Bieber, Drake, Florence and the Machine, and Mumford & Sons. After watching her win the award, spectators tweeted about Spalding for more than 18 hours straight. Her win certainly surprised many, but it also brought her to the attention of people who didn't know her music. "Spalding is one of those jigsaw pieces you never knew was missing from the world of music," wrote a reviewer from the *Guardian.* "Until she surprised everyone by winning the recent best newcomer Grammy that seemed destined for Justin Bieber, it never occurred to anyone that we needed a beautiful, enigmatic, singing double bassist who could sell Brazilian-tinged experimental jazz to a mainstream audience."

Fans in High Places

Spalding's music has been appreciated throughout the country by critics and by fans, as seen from her *Billboard* success, but it was also appreciated by a few of her personal heroes. She has played for President Barack Obama at his request three times, including at the 2010 Nobel Prize Ceremony in Norway. Spalding also has a fan in the pop sensation Prince, who personally asked her to play at the 2010 BET Awards Tribute. He also invited her to perform as the opening act for his "Welcome 2 America" tour in 2010.

Even Stevie Wonder, whom Spalding listened to while growing up, has said how much he admires her work. She performed with him at the White House in 2009. When she was in his dressing room to rehearse a

Chamber Music Society *combines some of the music Spalding loves most: jazz and chamber music.*

song they were going to play, "he completely weaved my song into the most incredibly rich, lush, exciting, different musical arrangement I've ever heard," Spalding confided. Listening to a musical hero play her song helped her realize how far she'd come.

"The danger in getting a lot of critical acclaim is that maybe you think you're further along than you really are," Spalding said. With all of her success, she has tried to stay grounded and keep her music genuine. While making a name for herself and finding her own sound, Spalding has strived to have the freedom, bravery, and confidence to develop a personal interpretation of what music should be. "Just like in literature or in screenplays," she explained, "people can take the same kind of ideas and the same themes like love or loss or war. The reason we find it interesting is not because of the content, it's because we get a new perspective on that subject that is familiar to all of us." That originality, for Spalding, is the key to her career. "Esperanza

Spalding may not be a mainstream-selling recording artist," Chanel Townsend wrote for BBC News,"but she definitely has the potential to be a significant creative force for many years to come. Many believe that, as her name'esperanza'says in Spanish, she is the'hope'for the future of jazz."

HOME AND FAMILY

Spalding is single. She has said that touring makes her too busy for romantic relationships, which limit the time she has for writing and practicing. She has two homes, a welcome change after growing up nearly homeless at some points. Spalding lives in New York City and Austin, Texas, and each city is an inspiration."In both those cities," she observed,"I can go out any night of the week and see people who are totally devoted to their craft and doing their thing and being themselves and not caring."

MAJOR INFLUENCES

Spalding's influences are as various as the types of music she plays, but her first and probably most important influence was her mother. Listening to her mom practice the piano and sing was a major reason Spalding took music seriously from an early age, and hearing her mother sing in Spanish encouraged Spalding to incorporate Spanish lyrics into her songs. She also sings in Portuguese since taking classes while visiting Brazil in her early 20s.

Spalding was influenced by famous musicians as well. Watching Yo Yo Ma, whom she saw on TV when she was four, helped her realize she wanted to play a stringed instrument. When she began playing with the Chamber Music Society, she was influenced by the Russian composer Dmitri Shostakovich. She has also been inspired by Prince, Stevie Wonder, and Jimi Hendrix. Beyond music, she uses poetry to inspire her compositions. For example, the lyrics of Spalding's song"Little Fly" come from a William Blake poem that used to hang above her desk. Overall, she says her diverse cultural background— including Hispanic, Native American, and African influences—guides her music."I suppose invariably I draw from my cultural background," Spalding acknowledged."But, it isn't intentional, just like my way of expressing myself in the way I speak and my body language comes from my ethnic background, because those various influences molded and shaped how I communicate with others."

HOBBIES AND OTHER INTERESTS

Spalding hasn't had a lot of free time to develop hobbies. Keeping up with technology is certainly not a hobby of hers. Although she enjoys creating mixed playlists on her iPod with jazz, classical, and rap music, she doesn't own a television and her first cell phone was given to her by her manager

because she was so difficult to contact without one. Spalding enjoys more traditional forms of communication. "When you get a letter in the mail from somebody, that's the best feeling," she observed.

One hobby that Spalding does enjoy is shopping; she likes to visit vintage stores to shop for used clothing, especially before a show. Every show requires a new outfit and a new look. "You have to think about those YouTube videos," she admitted.

WORKS

Junjo, 2006
Esperanza, 2008
Chamber Music Society, 2010

HONORS AND AWARDS

Oprah's Ten Women on the Rise: 2010
Grammy Award: 2011, for Best New Artist

FURTHER READING

Periodicals

Bass Player, Dec. 2006, p. 21; June 2008, p.32
Billboard, Aug. 7, 2010, p.26

Los Angeles Times, Feb. 14, 2011, p.D7
Marie Claire, June 2011, p.132
New Yorker, Mar. 15, 2010, p.32
USA Today, Jan. 28, 2011, p. D2
Washington Post, Feb. 6, 2009, p.T7; Dec. 7, 2009, p.C9; Aug. 17, 2010, p.C3

Online Articles and Videos

http://www.bassmusicianmagazine.com
(Bass Musician Magazine,"Bass Musician Magazine Featuring Esperanza Spalding: August 2010 3rd Anniversary Issue,"Aug. 1, 2010)
http://www.bbc.co.uk
(BBC News,"Esperanza Spalding: Bright Young Hope of Jazz,"July 5, 2011)
http://www.berklee.edu
(Berklee College of Music,"Esperanza Spalding,"Apr. 2004)
http://www.concordmusicgroup.com
(Heads Up International,"About Esperanza Spalding,"2011)
http://http://topics.nytimes.com
(New York Times,"Esperanza Spalding,"multiple articles, various dates)
http://www.nytimes.com
(New York Times,"Up to Her Ears,"July 27, 2008)
http://www.npr.org
(NPR Music,"Esperanza Spalding,"undated)
http://www.people.com
(People,"Five Things to Know About Grammy Nominated Esperanza Spalding,"Dec. 14, 2010)
http://topics.wsj.com/index.html
(Wall Street Journal,"Esperanza Spalding,"multiple articles, various dates)

ADDRESS

Esperanza Spalding
Heads Up International
23307 Commerce Park Road
Cleveland, OH 44122

WORLD WIDE WEBSITE

http://www.esperanzaspalding.com

Mark Zuckerberg 1984-

American Computer Programmer and Business Leader
Founder and CEO of Facebook

BIRTH

Mark Elliot Zuckerberg was born on May 14, 1984, in White Plains, New York. He grew up in Dobbs Ferry, a suburb of New York City in Westchester County. His father, Edward, is a dentist, known to the community as "painless Dr. Z." His mother, Karen, practiced psychiatry before leaving the profession to manage her husband's dental office, which is attached to the basement of the family's hilltop house. The second of four children, Mark has three sisters. His older sister, Randi, is head of consumer marketing and social-good initiatives for Facebook. His younger sisters, Donna and Arielle, are students.

YOUTH

Zuckerberg grew up in a supportive, well-educated family. "Education has always been important to me and my family," he stressed. "Growing up, my parents emphasized the importance of learning and academic success." In an interview with *Time*, Mark's father praised his son's natural gift for mathematics and science and solid academic performance. He also acknowledged that Mark was "strong-willed and relentless. For some kids, their questions could be answered with a simple *yes* or *no*. For Mark, if he asked for something, yes by itself would work, but no required much more. If you were going to say no to him, you had better be prepared with a strong argument backed by facts, experiences, logic, reasons. We envisioned him becoming a lawyer one day, with a near 100% success rate of convincing juries."

"

Zuckerberg grew up in a supportive, well-educated family. "Education has always been important to me and my family," he stressed. "Growing up, my parents emphasized the importance of learning and academic success."

"

Zuckerberg was exposed to computers at an early age, prompting a lifelong interest in technology. His father purchased computers for his office as early as 1985 and often had the latest high-tech gadgets, such as the Atari 800 system, which came with a disc for Atari BASIC programming. "I just liked making things," Zuckerberg explained. "Then I figured out I could make more things if I learned to program." He had a computer tutor, David Newman—a software developer who came to the house once a week—when he was 11. "He was a prodigy," Newman explained in the *New Yorker*. "Sometimes it was tough to stay ahead of him." Around the same time, Zuckerberg took a computer course at nearby Mercy College and read *C++ for Dummies*. One of his first software developments was an instant messaging program he wrote in 1996 for his father's office. The program, which he named "ZuckNet," allowed the receptionist to send a message to Dr. Zuckerberg on his home computer to inform him of a patient's arrival.

The Zuckerberg siblings have fond memories of growing up, such as the time they made a feature-length *Star Wars* movie parody, *The Star Wars*

Sill-ogy, over winter break. Mark starred as Luke Skywalker. In fact, he was such a fan of the George Lucas films that he had a *Star Wars* theme at his bar mitzvah, a Jewish ceremony celebrating a boy's 13th birthday and coming of age. In addition, he and his siblings enjoyed playing pranks on their parents. On New Year's Eve 1999, their parents were concerned about the Y2K bug, a potential problem in computer programs that many feared would lead to serious software and hardware failures around the globe. At midnight, the siblings shut off the power in their home, sending their parents into a momentary panic. Zuckerberg also played a harmless trick on his sister Donna, rigging her computer to count down to self-destruction in"5-4-3-2-1"seconds.

Aside from practical jokes, Zuckerberg spent his time outside of school writing computer versions of popular board games, including a Monopoly game set at his middle school and the game of Risk set in Roman times. He also created his own original games."I had a bunch of friends who were artists. They'd come over, draw stuff, and I'd build a game out of it,"he said.

EDUCATION

At Ardsley High School in Ardsley, New York, Zuckerberg enjoyed studying the classical Greek and Latin. In 11th grade, however, he transferred to Phillips Exeter Academy, a private boarding school in New Hampshire, for its advanced math and computer courses. There he won prizes in math, astronomy, physics, and classical languages. He was also captain of the fencing team. On his college application, he listed proficiency in Latin, Hebrew, French, and ancient Greek.

For his senior-year independent project, he and his roommate Adam D'Angelo created Synapse, a media player that searched for and recommended songs based on the musical preferences of the listener."It learned your listening patterns by figuring out how much you like each song at a given point and time, and which songs you tend to listen to around each other,"he explained. Zuckerberg and D'Angelo posted a plug-in version of Synapse Media Player on the Internet for free, attracting the attention of AOL and Microsoft, which expressed interest in the program and the young designers behind it."Some companies offered us right off the bat up to one million, and then we got another offer that was like two million,"he said. The friends decided not to sell. As Mark explained,"I don't really like putting a price-tag on the stuff I do. That's just like not the point."They also turned down employment offers, choosing instead to pursue their college plans. Zuckerberg graduated from Phillips Exeter Academy in 2002.

Harvard University

In fall 2002 Zuckerberg entered Harvard University and joined the Jewish fraternity Alpha Epsilon Pi. To his fraternity brothers he was known by the nickname "Slayer," tracking down membership dues in his role as exchequer. A psychology major, he was particularly interested in the intersections between the human mind and computer science. As Lev Grossman reported in *Time*, "Whereas earlier entrepreneurs looked at the Internet and saw a network of computers, Zuckerberg saw a network of people." By his sophomore year, he was designing programs with a pronounced social component, such as Course Match, which helped students determine which classes to take based on the selections of their peers. Hundreds of Harvard students used it.

Zuckerberg's next project, however, proved more rebellious. In an eight-hour programming session in November 2003, he created Facemash, an online student directory that showed users photos of two people and invited users to select which was more attractive. The photos originally appeared in the printed "facebooks" maintained by each of Harvard's undergraduate houses. Zuckerberg obtained the photos by hacking into their networks or using the credentials of a friend to access the images. He sent the link to a few friends, and it became an underground sensation. In just four hours, Facemash attracted 450 visitors who voted on 22,000 photos. At that point, Harvard administrators blocked his Internet connection in response to student group complaints of sexism and racism, and the site crashed. He was brought in front of the school's disciplinary board and accused of unlawfully accessing Harvard's computer system, violating copyrights, and invading privacy. The board put him on disciplinary probation and sent him to see a counselor. He apologized to the campus women's groups, but maintained that he never meant to distribute the site to a wide audience, only to get the input of a few friends. "I understood that some parts were still a little sketchy and I wanted some more time to think about whether or not this was really appropriate to release to the Harvard community," he said shortly after the incident.

Later that semester Zuckerberg created a less controversial program to help him study for the final in his art history class. He posted online images of paintings they were studying and invited classmates to view them and add comments from their lecture notes under the artwork. "Within two hours, all the images were populated with notes. I did very well in that class. We all did," he remembered. He and his roommates in Suite H33, Kirkland House—Chris Hughes, Dustin Moskovitz, and Billy Olson—spent many hours talking about how people were using the web and new ways in which it could potentially improve their lives. Zuckerberg was the driving force behind the brainstorming, mapping out ideas on a large dry-erase board in their dorm room.

Harvard Yard, a central location on the university campus.

The Facemash incident earned Zuckerberg a reputation as a programming prodigy on campus, attracting the attention of Harvard seniors Divya Narendra and Tyler and Cameron Winklevoss, identical twins and champion rowers. After reading about him in the *Harvard Crimson,* the three upperclassmen approached him about working on coding for a social-networking web site they were building and planned to call Harvard Connection. Zuckerberg agreed to help. "I had a hobby of just building these little projects," he said in the book *The Facebook Effect.* "Of course I wasn't fully committed to any of them." Indeed, though he worked intermittently writing code for Harvard Connection in fall 2003, by the time he returned to Harvard after winter break, he was immersed in a social networking project of his own. He avoided contact with the twins before revealing that he no longer had time to work on Harvard Connection in mid-January.

CAREER HIGHLIGHTS

Thefacebook

On February 4, 2004, Zuckerberg launched his latest Internet project, Thefacebook, from his Harvard dorm room at Kirkland House with his suitemates

Kirkland House at Harvard University, the dorm where Zuckerberg first created Facebook.

Hughes and Moskovitz and his fraternity brother, Eduardo Saverin. He had approached Saverin about contributing $1,000 in seed money to cover the cost of hosting the site he had registered, www.thefacebook.com, in exchange for 30% ownership of the site. He also charged Saverin, a member of Harvard's investment club, with assessing whether Thefacebook could become a successful business endeavor. The site was an instant phenomenon on campus from the moment it went live. Its homepage read: "Thefacebook is an online directory that connects people through social networks at college. We have opened up Thefacebook for popular consumption at Harvard University. You can use Thefacebook to: Search for people at your school; Find out who are in your classes; Look up your friends' friends; See a visualization of your social network." As Moskovitz recalled in the *New Yorker:* "When Mark finished the site, we told a couple of friends. And then one of them suggested putting it on the Kirkland House online mailing list, which was, like, 300 people. And, once they did that, several dozen people joined, and then they were telling people at the other houses. By the end of the night, we were, like, actively watching the registration process. Within 24 hours, we had somewhere between 1,200 and 1,500 registrants."

Although Thefacebook had similarities to other online networking sites like Friendster and MySpace, it was exclusively available to those with a Harvard.edu email address and required members to use their real names.

Perhaps most importantly, it included privacy controls, allowing users to determine who would be able to see their profiles, which included a photo and personal information such as relationship status, phone number, email address, current course load, political affiliation, clubs, and favorite books, movies, music, and quotes.

Within two weeks, the number of users at Harvard had skyrocketed to 4,300 and Zuckerberg was fielding requests to open it up to other schools. By March 2004, Thefacebook was available to students at Stanford, Columbia, and Yale universities. Costs, however, were mounting as more and more servers were required to handle traffic to the site. Both he and Saverin agreed to invest another $10,000 into the company, and Saverin, now the chief financial officer, began selling advertising space to generate revenue. The site boasted 150,000 users from 40 schools by the end of June.

California

Inspired by a lecture given by Microsoft founder Bill Gates, who, as Zuckerberg put it, "really encouraged all of us to take time off school to work on a project," he decided to rent a house for the summer in Palo Alto, California. He convinced Moskovitz to join him, while Hughes traveled to France for a study abroad program. Saverin, meanwhile, pursued an internship at a New York City investment bank and searched for potential advertisers. In Palo Alto, Zuckerberg got to know Sean Parker, co-founder of the controversial Internet file-sharing service Napster. Parker had connections in Silicon Valley and shared Zuckerberg's vision that Thefacebook had the potential to change the world. Zuckerberg invited Parker to live with his friends and him at "Casa Facebook." Parker became his adviser, hiring a lawyer to create a new legal structure for the company. Parker also began shopping for investors and introduced Zuckerberg to Peter Thiel, one of the founders of the online monetary transaction service Paypal. Thiel invested $500,000 in the project, which allowed Zuckerberg to hire a staff. "Mark was clearly a brilliant engineer with a great vision for his product," Thiel stated in *Newsweek*.

By the end of the summer of 2004, Zuckerberg had decided not to return to Harvard. He and Moskovitz were ready to launch the site on 70 new campuses in the fall, and Parker became CEO of the company. By November 2004 Thefacebook had one million registered members. At the time, Zuckerberg was 20 years old.

Legal Trouble

Parker's effort to restructure the company prompted an escalating dispute with Saverin, who disagreed with Zuckerberg about the role of advertising

Zuckerberg (right) and Facebook employee Matt Cohler at the Facebook office in Palo Alto, California, 2005.

on the site, among other issues. In the new corporate structure, Saverin would no longer be an employee, and his ownership stake would represent a decreasing percentage of the company as stock was issued to investors and new employees. Negotiations with Saverin were ongoing and led to a lawsuit, which was settled in 2009 and granted Saverin a reported five percent ownership stake.

In fall 2004, the Winklevoss twins and Narendra of the Harvard Connection web site (now rebranded as ConnectU) sued Zuckerberg in federal court for stealing their ideas and breaching an oral contract. They asked for control of the Facebook site and damages equal to the company's value. "I was a student who agreed to help a fellow student," Zuckerberg argued. "I did not agree to complete their project." He also contended that the two social networks were fundamentally different—Harvard Connection was intended as a dating site, while his emphasized networking. "[We] know we didn't take anything from them. There is really good documentation of this: our code base versus theirs," Zuckerberg maintained.

The Winklevoss twins and Narendra, on the other hand, claimed that he intentionally stalled so that the launch of Harvard Connection would be delayed and he could release his site first. They had emails in which Zuckerberg said he was busy with other projects and homework. "He said he was working for us; he led us on; he took unfair advantage of us," Tyler Winklevoss told the *New Yorker.* Zuckerberg denied wrongdoing. However, Jose Antonio Vargas of the *New Yorker* read the instant messages Zuckerberg wrote in 2003 and characterized them as "backstabbing, conniving, and insensitive." Zuckerberg acknowledged that he had matured in the intervening year. "If you're going to go on to build a service that is influential and that a lot of people rely on, then you need to be mature, right? I think I've grown and learned a lot."

The Winklevoss twins obtained a $65 million out-of-court settlement in 2008. They later sued for more, claiming that Facebook misled them about the value of the stock. The appeals court upheld the original settlement. Then, in April 2011, their lawyers filed paperwork in federal court asking for an investigation into Facebook's withholding of critical evidence, including the instant messages mentioned in the *New Yorker.* Facebook considers the case closed.

Growing Facebook

In 2005, Accel Partners—owned by entrepreneur Jim Breyer—invested $12.7 million for 13% of the company. Breyer recalled making the deal over dinner. "I ordered a nice pinot noir and Mark ordered a Sprite, telling me he was underage," he said in *Newsweek*. Zuckerberg moved business operations from an apartment to new offices near Stanford University and acquired the domain Facebook.com so the company could simplify its name to Facebook. He took over the position of CEO at the end of the summer of 2005. At that time, 85% of American college students were on Facebook, and the company was preparing to open up membership to high schools. In 2006 he entertained billion-dollar buyout offers from media giants Viacom and Yahoo!, but ultimately rejected them. As former Yahoo! CEO Terry Semel told the *New Yorker:* "I'd never met anyone … who would walk away from a billion dollars. But he said, 'It's not about the price. This is my baby, and I want to keep running it, I want to keep growing it.' I couldn't believe it." "I'm here to build something for the long term," Zuckerberg said. "Anything else is a distraction."

In September 2006 Zuckerberg introduced the News Feed feature, which sent automatic announcements of users' activities to everyone in their network. Members protested, arguing that the company was using information without permission. The release of News Feed became the biggest crisis the company had yet faced, prompting hundreds of online protest groups. Zuckerberg apologized, saying: "We really messed this one up. When we launched News Feed and Mini-Feed we were trying to provide you with a stream of information about your social world. Instead, we did a bad job of explaining what the new features were and an even worse job of giving you control of them." The company worked for three days to improve security and introduced privacy features that allow users to control the flow of information into News Feed.

Later that month Facebook opened membership to all users, promoting itself as a social utility that allows people to share information with friends, family, and coworkers through the "social graph, the digital mapping of people's real-world social connections." "We're not trying to help you make new friends online," Zuckerberg clarified. "We're just trying to help you digitally map out the relationships you already have." Within a week of launching open registration, Facebook reached 10 million users and was growing at a rate of 50,000 new users per day. By January 2007 it had 14 million members.

Zuckerberg's next big launch was the May 2007 introduction of Facebook Platform, which opened up the opportunity for outside developers to create applications to run inside the Facebook site. Programmers could now develop software—such as the popular games FarmVille and Mafia Wars—and integrate it into the Facebook infrastructure, making it fast, effective, and inexpensive for entrepreneurs to reach an audience with their ideas. The platform allows for users to choose only the applications that interest them, such as the game Scrabulous, which Zuckerberg claimed "got my grandparents on Facebook." Within 10 weeks, 2,500 new applications were launched, increasing to 6,000 applications by the end of 2007. Facebook was now a platform for new applications just as MS-DOS was for Bill Gates in the 1980s. In September 2007 Zuckerberg announced the formation of FbFund, which provides grants from $25,000 to $250,000 to developers with business plans built upon the Facebook platform.

Privacy Issues

In October 2007 Microsoft bought $240 million in Facebook stock, a 1.6% share of the company. At that time, Facebook was valued at $15 billion due to its expansive database of member information that would allow for targeted advertising. The next month Facebook announced plans to increase revenue through Facebook Ads and Facebook Beacon, a component that allows friends to see each other's purchases on advertiser web sites. The release of Beacon had unfortunate consequences. Girlfriends learned about surprise engagement rings, and holiday gifts were revealed to future recipients. Political group MoveOn.org led a widespread backlash against Beacon, buying Facebook ads that read "Is Facebook Invading Your Privacy?" Many in the media agreed that Facebook had violated privacy rights be-

A view of the casual atmosphere at Facebook headquarters, known for its relaxed work environment.

cause it did not ask for permission from members to share their purchases on partner sites with those in their network. "We made mistakes in communicating about it. We made mistakes in the user interface. We made mistakes in responding to it after it was out there," Zuckerberg admitted. Eventually Facebook redesigned Beacon as an opt-in system and created an option for users to disable the feature.

Beacon would not be Facebook's last privacy controversy, however. In late 2009 Facebook changed its privacy policies, making more user information viewable to the general public by default. Users were in an uproar, claiming the company violated the compact they made when they joined, since Facebook was built on the notion that personal information would be visible only to those whom the user accepted as friends. Moreover, the American Civil Liberties Union and the Electronic Privacy Information Center filed complaints, accusing the company of unfair and deceptive practices. Facebook's new privacy policy, they argued, endangered its users in a climate of identity theft, surveillance, and online predators. At first, Zuckerberg defended the policy. "People have really gotten comfortable not only sharing more information and different kinds, but more openly and with more people," he argued. "That social norm is just something that has evolved over time." Later, though, he admitted that the company "missed the mark," and Facebook released a simpler version of the privacy settings.

The Social Network

Zuckerberg's life is dramatized in the 2010 film *The Social Network,* written by Andrew Sorkin and directed by David Fincher. The movie, with Jesse Eisenberg as Zuckerberg and Andrew Garfield as Savarin, was based on Ben Mezrich's book *The Accidental Billionaires. The Social Network* reflects various perspectives on the moment Facebook was invented. It also depicts the lawsuits filed by co-founder Saverin, who claims that Zuckerberg betrayed him, and the Winklevoss twins, who contend that Facebook was their idea. The movie was a tremendous popular and critical success. Nominated for eight Academy Awards, including Best Picture, it won three awards. "*The Social Network* is the movie of the year," Peter Travers wrote in *Rolling Stone.* "But Fincher and Sorkin triumph by taking it further. Lacing their scathing wit with an aching sadness, they define the dark irony of the past decade. The final image of solitary Mark at his computer has to resonate for a generation of users … sitting in front of a glowing screen pretending not to be alone."

According to Zuckerberg, the film is fiction. He claims many of the details are wrong, especially his character's motivations. "I started Facebook to improve the world and make it a more transparent place," he said at a press conference. "This movie portrays me as someone who built Facebook so I could meet girls." In a statement reported in the *New York Times,* a Facebook spokesperson said, "They do a wonderful job of telling a good story. Of course, the reality probably wouldn't make for a very fun or interesting movie." Aaron Sorkin has said that he took artistic license with the screenplay but conducted thorough research to present accurate facts. However, he admitted in *New York* magazine, "I don't want my fidelity to be to the truth; I want it to be to storytelling. I feel like, had I met Mark, … I probably would have had an affection for him that I wouldn't have wanted to betray." As Lev Grossman said in *Time,* "This character bears almost no resemblance to the actual Mark Zuckerberg. The reality is much more complicated."

Facebook Today

"Facebook has merged with the social fabric of American life.… We have entered the Facebook age, and Mark Zuckerberg is the man who brought us here," Grossman said in *Time,* which named Zuckerberg the 2010 Person of the Year. *Time* credited him with connecting and mapping the relationships of over 500,000 people, designing a new system of exchanging information, and "changing how we all live our lives in ways that are innovative and even optimistic."

As CEO of Facebook, which has over 2,000 employees, Zuckerberg sets the overall direction and product strategy for the company. He also heads the

Scenes from the movie The Social Network, *with Jesse Eisenberg as Zuckerberg.*

design and development of the Facebook service and infrastructure. In Zuckerberg's view, Facebook's map of human relationships is "one of the strongest product elements that ever has existed." In March 2011, *Forbes* magazine estimated his net worth at $13.5 billion, making him the 19th richest American. Zuckerberg has pledged to give away one half of his personal wealth in his lifetime. In September 2010 he announced a $100 million gift to the long-troubled Newark Public Schools.

As of May 2011, Facebook boasted over 600 million user profiles. Put another way, one out of every 11 people in the world has a Facebook account, including nearly 50% of Americans; 70% of Facebook users, however, live outside of the United States, and the site offers translations into more than 70 languages. It has become the largest site on the Internet in terms of page views and time spent navigating it. In his quest to "make the world a more open place by helping people connect and share," Zuckerberg is fundamentally changing the way the world communicates and uses the World Wide Web. "I think he is arguably the most influential person of his generation," said David Kirkpatrick, author of *The Facebook Effect,* in the *Observer.* "It is difficult to think of anyone else the same age who has had remotely the same global impact."

HOME AND FAMILY

Zuckerberg lives in Palo Alto with his girlfriend, Priscilla Chan, a Chinese American from the Boston area. They met at a Harvard fraternity party during his sophomore year. "He was this nerdy guy who was just a little bit out there," she told the *New Yorker.* Chan is in medical school at the University of California, San Francisco, studying to be a pediatrician. She is a former elementary school science teacher. The pair is fond of board games like Settlers of Catan, walks in the park, bocce ball, and rowing. They also enjoy traveling abroad, having visited China and India together in 2010. In March 2011 they both updated their Facebook status from "single" to "in a relationship" after purchasing a puppy together, a Puli Hungarian Sheepdog named Beast. Beast has his own Facebook page with more than 100,000 fans.

HOBBIES AND OTHER INTERESTS

Zuckerberg reportedly works long hours, leaving little time for leisure. When he is not working, however, he can usually be found working out with a personal trainer, studying Mandarin Chinese, or reading Latin and ancient Greek. For Thanksgiving break, 2010, he took his family to the Wizarding World of Harry Potter in Orlando. On his Facebook profile page

Zuckerberg talking with Facebook employees, 2010.

he lists Orson Scott Card's science fiction novel *Ender's Game* as one he likes."But there are definitely books—like the *Aeneid*—that I enjoyed reading a lot more," he clarified. He has cited Green Day, Jay-Z, Taylor Swift, and Shakira as favorite musical artists, and he enjoys playing the guitar and quoting lines from the movie *Top Gun*. In addition, he is a fan of comedian Andy Samberg, who impersonates him on "Saturday Night Live." Zuckerberg had an opportunity to meet Samberg in January 2011 when he made a guest appearance on an episode of"Saturday Night Live"hosted by actor Jesse Eisenberg, who portrayed him in *The Social Network*. He also guest starred as himself on"The Simpsons"in October 2010, meeting the character Lisa Simpson at a trade show.

Despite his financial success,"Zuck," as his friends call him, maintains a humble lifestyle. He drives the moderately priced Acura TSX because it is "safe, comfortable, [and] not ostentatious."As many have pointed out, he prefers to dress comfortably, usually sporting a hoodie and Adidas flip-flops. The hoodie, in fact, has become such a signature for him that at a town hall meeting at Facebook headquarters in April 2011, President Obama introduced himself as"the guy who got Mark Zuckerberg to wear a jacket and tie."At the end of their exchange, Zuckerberg gave the president a Facebook hoodie, saying:"As a small token of our appreciation, in case, for some reason, you want to dress like me." Zuckerberg's favorite color is blue, primarily because he is red-green colorblind. "Blue is the richest color for me—I can see all of blue," he explained. His colorblindness influenced the design of the cornflower blue Facebook logo.

HONORS AND AWARDS

Achiever of the Year (*Success* Magazine): 2010
Person of the Year (*Time* Magazine): 2010

FURTHER READING

Books

The Facebook Effect: The Inside Story of the Company That Is Connecting the World, 2010

Periodicals

Chronicle of Higher Education, May 28, 2004, p.A29; June 18, 2004, p.A29
Current Biography Yearbook, 2008
Fast Company, May 2007, p.75; Nov. 2007, p.84; Mar. 2010, p.52; Feb. 2011, p.86
Financial Times, Dec. 4, 2010, p.14
Fortune, May 26, 2008, p.37; Mar. 2, 2009, p.48
Guardian, Jan. 4, 2011, p.23
Los Angeles Times, Oct. 7, 2007, p.M1
New York Times, Sep. 23, 2010, p.A27; Oct. 4, 2010, p.B1
New Yorker, May 15, 2006, p.50; Sep. 20, 2010, p.54
Time, Dec. 27, 2010-Jan. 3, 2011, pp.43, 44

Online Articles

http://www.theatlantic.com
(Atlantic, "How *The Social Network* Saved Mark Zuckerberg," Sep. 27, 2011)
http://www.ft.com
(Financial Times, "Interview: Mark Zuckerberg, Facebook Founder," Sep. 11, 2007;
"Man in the News: Mark Zuckerberg," Sep. 28, 2007)
http://topics.nytimes.com
(New York Times, "Mark Zuckerberg," multiple articles, various dates)
http://www.newyorker.com
(New Yorker, "The Face of Facebook," Sep. 20, 2010; "Zuckerberg the Philanthropist," Sep. 24, 2010)

http://www.newsweek.com
(Newsweek,"Facebook Grows Up," Aug. 20, 2007)
http://www.successmagazine.com
(Success,"The Facebook Age," Apr. 1, 2011)
http://www.telegraph.co.uk
(Telegraph,"600m People Can't Be Wrong about Facebook," Dec. 16, 2010)
http://content.usatoday.com/topics
(USA Today,"Mark Zuckerberg," multiple articles, various dates)
http://topics.wsj.com/index.html
(Wall Street Journal,"Mark Zuckerberg," multiple articles, various dates)

ADDRESS

Mark Zuckerberg, CEO
Facebook
1601 South California Avenue
Palo Alto, CA 94304

WORLD WIDE WEB SITE

http://www.facebook.com/markzuckerberg

Photo and Illustration Credits

Front Cover Photos: Angelina Jolie: Movie still: THE TOURIST Photo by Peter Mountain © 2010 Columbia Pictures/Sony Publicity. All Rights Reserved.; Charles Martinet (Mario): ar/Newscom; Aaron Rodgers: Tom Lynn/Milwaukee Journal Sentinel/MCT via Newscom; Mark Zuckerberg: AP Photo/Jeff Chiu.

Usain Bolt/Photos: Feng Li/Getty Images (p. 11); Andy Lyons/Getty Images (p. 14); Lisa Coniglio/Getty Images (p. 17); Sipa via AP Images (p. 19); Feng Li/Getty Images (p. 22).

Chris Bosh/Photos: Reuters/Hans Deryk/Landov (p. 27); AP Photo/Chuck Burton (p. 29); Kevin Kolczynski/Reuters/Landov (p. 32); Mike Cassese/Reuters/Landov (p. 35); AP Photo/Tom DiPace (p. 38); AP Photo/Larry W. Smith, pool (p. 40).

Robert Bullard/Photos: AP Photo/Ric Feld (p. 45); David Rae Morris/Bloomberg via Getty Images (p. 48); Book cover: DUMPING IN DIXIE: Race, Class, and Environmental Quality by Robert D. Bullard © 1990, 1994, 2000 Westview Press/Perseus Book Group (p. 50); AP Photo/Ric Feld (p. 53); Courtesy of Robert D. Bullard (p. 55).

Steven Chu/Photos: Lawrence Berkeley National Laboratory/Roy Kaltschmidt, Photographer (p. 59); Linda A. Cicero/Stanford News Service (p. 61); H. Mark Helfer/NIST (p. 65); AP Photo/Jonas Ekstromer (p. 68); Lawrence Berkeley National Laboratory (p. 70); U.S. Department of Energy (p. 72, top and middle); Official White House Photo by Pete Souza (p. 72, bottom).

Chris Colfer/Photos: Frank Micelotta/PictureGroup via AP Images (p. 77); Patrick Ecclesine/FOX (p. 80); Adam Rose/FOX (p. 82); Michael Yarish/FOX (p. 84).

Suzanne Collins/Photos: Cap Pryor/Scholastic (p. 87); Still from TV show: CLARISSA EXPLAINS IT ALL/Nickelodeon (p. 89); Book cover: GREGOR THE OVERLANDER (Book One) © 2003 Suzanne Collins. All rights reserved. Published by Scholastic Inc. Cover art © by Daniel Craig. Cover design by Steve Scott. (p. 91); Book cover: THE HUNGER GAMES © 2008 by Suzanne Collins. All rights reserved. Published by Scholastic Press, an imprint of Scholastic, Inc. Jacket art © 2008 by Tim O'Brien. Jacket design by Elizabeth B. Parisi & Phil Falco (p. 93); Book cover: MOCKINGJAY © 2010 by Suzanne Collins. All rights reserved. Published by Scholastic Press, an imprint of Scholastic, Inc. Jacket art by Tim O'Brien © 2010 Scholastic, Inc. Jacket design by Elizabeth B. Parisi (p. 97); Movie still: THE HUNGER GAMES/© Lions Gate Entertainment (p. 100).

Paula Creamer/Photos: Jonathan Ferrey/Getty Images (p. 105); Icon Sports Media 356/Icon SMI/Newscom (p. 109); AP Photo/Daytona Beach News-Journal/William Dunkley (p. 111); AP Photo/Mike Groll (p. 114).

Lucas Cruikshank/Photos: Mark Davis/PictureGroup via AP Images (p. 117); PRNewsFoto/ContentNext Media/Newscom (p. 119); Vivian Zink/Disney Channel via Getty Images (p. 122); Movie still: FRED: THE MOVIE © 2010 Lions Gate Home Entertainment (p. 124).

Jason Derülo/Photos: Angela Weiss/Getty Images (p. 127); Larry Marano/Getty Images (p. 130); CD cover: WHATCHA SAY © 2010 Beluga Heights/Warner Bros. (p. 133); PictureGroup/MTV (p. 135).

Nina Dobrev/Photos: AP Photo/Damian Dovarganes (p. 139); DVD cover: DEGRASSI: THE NEXT GENERATION (Season Eight) © 2010 Echo Bridge Home Entertainment. All rights reserved. (p. 142); Quantrell Colbert/The CW/Landov (p. 145, left and right); Andrew Eccles/Scripps Howard Photo Service/Newscom (p. 147).

Andy Goldsworthy/Photos: © Andy Goldsworthy/Courtesy Galerie Lelong, New York. Photo by Melanie Einzig/Courtesy, Museum of Jewish Heritage-A Living Memorial to the Holocaust (p. 151); © Julian Calder/CORBIS (p. 153); Iris & B. Gerald Cantor Center for Visual Arts at Stanford University. Courtesy of Andy Goldsworthy and Haines Gallery (p. 157); © Andy Goldsworthy/Courtesy Galerie Lelong, New York. Photo by Melanie Einzig/Courtesy, Museum of Jewish Heritage-A Living Memorial to the Holocaust (p. 159, top and bottom); Photo credit: Andy Goldsworthy, East Coast Cairn 2001. Collection Friends of the Neuberger Museum of Art, Purchase College, State University of New York. Museum purchase with funds from the Roy R. Neuberger Endowment Fund, the Klein Family Foundation, Sherry and Joel Mallin, Douglas F. Maxwell and other private donations. Photo credit: Jim Frank. © Andy Goldsworthy/Courtesy Galerie Lelong, New York. (p. 162); Book cover: ANDY GOLDSWORTHY: A COLLABORATION WITH NATURE. Published in 1990 by ABRAMS, an imprint of Harry N. Abrams, Inc. Jacket photograph by Andy Goldsworthy. © Andy Goldsworthy (photographs and text) and Cameron Books, 1990. (p. 164).

Jay-Z/Photos: PictureGroup/MTV (p. 169); CD cover: REASONABLE DOUBT © P 1996, 1998 Roc-A-Fella Records Inc. Manufactured and Distributed by Priority Records LLC. All Rights Reserved. (p. 171); CD cover: VOL. 2 - HARD KNOCK LIFE © 1998 Def Jam/Universal Music Group. All Rights Reserved. (p. 173); CD cover: THE BLUEPRINT © 2001 Def Jam/Universal Music Group. All Rights Reserved (p. 175); PRNewsFoto/Newscom (p. 178, left); UN Photo/Paulo Filgueiras (p. 178, right); Gary Hershorn/Reuters/Landov (p. 180); Anthony J. Causi/Splash News/Newscom (p. 182).

Angelina Jolie/Photos: SPE, Inc./Santiago Gonzalez Sanchez © 2010 Columbia Pictures/Sony. All Rights Reserved. (p. 187); Movie still/DVD: GEORGE WALLACE 2009 © Warner Home Video. All Rights Reserved. (p. 190, top); Movie still: HACKERS Photo by Mark Tillie/United Artists Pictures, Inc. (via Movie Goods) © 1995 All Rights Reserved. (p. 190, middle); Movie Still/DVD: GIRL, INTERRUPTED © 1999 Global Entertainment Production GmbH & Co. Movie KG. All Rights Reserved. Distributed by Columbia Pictures/Sony Home Entertainment (p. 190, bottom); Movie still: LARA CROFT: TOMB RAIDER © 2001 Paramount (via Movie Goods).

All Rights Reserved. (p. 192); UNHCR via Getty Images (p. 194); Movie still: KUNG FU PANDA © 2008 Dreamworks Animated (via Movie Goods) (p. 197); Movie still: THE TOURIST Photo by Peter Mountain © 2010 Columbia Pictures/Sony Publicity. All Rights Reserved. (p. 199); AP Photo/UNHCR/Aziz (p. 201).

Victoria Justice/Photos: Jen Lowery/Splash News/Newscom (p. 205); TV show/ Nickelodeon: ZOEY 101 Cast, Season 4. Photo: Andrew Eccles/Nickelodeon. ©2007 Viacom International, Inc. All Rights Reserved. (p. 208); Movie still: SPECTACULAR! 2009 Nickelodeon TV Movie. DVD distributed by Sony Pictures Home Entertainment (p. 210); TV show/Nickelodeon: VICTORIOUS Cast. Photo: Aaron Warkov/ Nickelodeon ©2009 Viacom International, Inc. All Rights Reserved. (p. 212).

Elena Kagan/Photos: Steve Petteway, Collection of the Supreme Court of the United States (p. 215); b09/b09/Zuma Press/Newscom (p. 217); UPI/University of Chicago Law School/Landov (p. 219); AP Photo/Elise Amendola, file (p. 221); AP Photo/ Dana Verkouteran (p. 225); Steve Petteway, Collection of the Supreme Court of the United States (p. 227, top and bottom).

Jeff Kinney/Photos: Photo by Julie Kinney/Courtesy, ABRAMS/Books for Young Readers and Amulet Books (p. 231); Courtesy, ABRAMS/Books for Young Readers and Amulet Books (p. 234); Book cover: DIARY OF A WIMPY KID by Jeff Kinney. Published 2007 by Amulet Books, an imprint of ABRAMS. Book design by Jeff Kinney. Cover design by Chad W. Beckerman and Jeff Kinney. Wimpy Kid text and illustrations copyright © 2007-2010 Wimpy Kid, Inc. DIARY OF A WIMPY KID®, WIMPY KID™, and the Greg Heffley design™ are trademarks of Wimpy Kid, Inc. All Rights Reserved. (p. 236); Drawings: Wimpy Kid text and illustrations copyright © 2007-2010 Wimpy Kid, Inc. DIARY OF A WIMPY KID®, WIMPY KID™, and the Greg Heffley design™ are trademarks of Wimpy Kid, Inc. All Rights Reserved. (p. 238, top and bottom, and p. 241); Movie still: DIARY OF A WIMPY KID. Photo: Rob McEwan © 2010 Twentieth Century Fox Film Corporation. All Rights Reserved. DIARY OF A WIMPY KID®, WIMPY KID™, and the Greg Heffley design™ are trademarks of Wimpy Kid, Inc. All Rights Reserved. (p. 243).

Lady Antebellum/Photos: © CMT, Krista Lee Photography (p. 247); Ethan Miller/Getty Images (p. 250); CD cover: LADY ANTEBELLUM © 2008 Capitol Records Nashville/EMI Music North America (p. 252); CD cover: NEED YOU NOW © 2009 Capitol Records Nashville/EMI Music North America. Photo credit: Miranda Penn Turin (p. 254); Photo credit: Miranda Penn Turin/EMI Music North America (p. 256).

Miranda Lambert/Photos: Lester Cohen/WireImage (p. 259); Photo courtesy of CMA (p. 262); CD cover: KEROSENE © 2005 Epic/Legacy/Sony Music (p. 265); CD cover: REVOLUTION © 2009 Columbia Nashville/Sony Music (p. 267).

Liu Xiaobo/Photos: Kyodo via AP Images (p. 271); Forrest M. Anderson/Getty Images (p. 276, top); AP/Jeff Widener (p. 276, bottom); AP Photo/Vincent Yu (p. 278); Kyodo via AP Images (p. 281); AP Photo/Heiko Junge, pool (p. 283); Ed Jones/AFP/Getty Images (p. 286).

Monica Lozano/Photos: La Opinion Photos/Newscom (p. 291); Los Angeles Daily News Negatives. Part of Department of Special Collections, Charles E. Young Research Library, University of California at Los Angeles, ID: uclalat_1387_b37_24570-

1 (p. 293); J. Emilio Flores/La Opinion/Newscom (p. 297); Aurelia Ventura/La Opinion/Newscom (p. 299); Larry Downing/Reuters/Landov (p. 301).

Jane Lubchenco/Photos: Courtesy, National Oceanic and Atmospheric Administration (NOAA) (p. 305); Courtesy, Oregon State University via NOAA (p. 308); Official White House Photo by Pete Souza (p. 311); Courtesy, National Oceanic and Atmospheric Administration (NOAA) (p. 313); Tami A. Heilemann/U.S. Department of the Interior (DOI) (p. 316).

Mike Lupica/Photos: Charles Eshelman/FilmMagic (p. 319); NY Daily News Archive via Getty Images (p. 322); John Atashian/ESPN (p. 324); Book cover: TRAVEL TEAM © 2004 Mike Lupica. All Rights Reserved. Published by Puffin Books (Penguin Group). Cover photo courtesy of PM Images/Getty Images. Cover design by Monica Benalcazar. (p. 326); Book cover: SHOOT OUT (A Comeback Kids Novel) © 2007 Mike Lupica. All Rights Reserved. Published by Puffin Books (Penguin Group). Cover photo © Marc Tauss, 2007. Cover design by Tony Sahara. (p. 330); AP Photo/Charles Sykes (p. 333).

Charles Martinet/Photos: Splash News/Newscom (p. 337); ar/Newscom (p. 340); Splash News/Newscom (p. 342); Video Game cover: SUPER MARIO BROS. Wii © 2010 Nintendo (p. 345).

Bridgit Mendler: Disney Channel/Randy Holmes (p. 349); Movie still/DVD: THE CLIQUE © 2008 Warner Home Video. All Rights Reserved. (p. 351); Eric McCandless/Disney Channel via Getty Images (p. 353); Disney Channel/Danny Feld (p. 356).

Lea Michele/Photos: CMB/Splash News/Newscom (p. 359); Poster: Copy from the original dated 1985-CMI. Designed, Printed, and Produced by Dewynters LTD, London. Reproduction, Movie Goods (p. 361); RAGTIME © Joan Marcus/Photofest (p. 363); DVD/TV show stills: GLEE: THE COMPLETE FIRST SEASON © 2009 Twentieth Century Fox. All Rights Reserved. (pp. 365, 367, and 368).

Janelle Monáe/Photos: © Warner Elektra Atlantic (p. 371); Michael Loccisano/ FilmMagic (p. 373); CD cover: METROPOLIS © 2008 BB/Bad Boy Records/Warner Elektra Atlantic (p. 375); CD cover: ARCHANDROID © 2010 BB/Bad Boy Records/ Warner Elektra Atlantic (p. 377); © Warner Elektra Atlantic (p. 380).

Melanie Oudin/Photos: Louis Lanzano/Landov (p. 383); Doug Benc/Getty Images (p. 385); Ian Walton/Getty Images (p. 388); AP Photo/Paul J. Bereswill (p. 391); AP Photo/Petr David Josek (p. 394).

Sarah Palin/Photos: PRNewsFoto/Independent Group Home Living Foundation/News com (p. 397); AP Photo/Heath Family (p. 399); Anchorage Daily News/MCT/Landov (p. 400); UPI/Landov (p. 402); AP Photo/Mat-Su Valley Frontiersman (p. 404); AP Photo/Chris Miller (p. 406); Brian Baer/MCT/Landov (p. 409); Sean Cockerham/ MCT/Landov (p. 411); Melina Mara/The Washington Post via Getty Images (p. 413).

Aaron Rodgers/Photos: Foto AP/Eric Gay (p. 417); Dilip Vishwanat/Sporting News/Icon SMI (p. 420); Joe Robbins/Getty Images (p. 422); AP Photo/LM Otero (p. 424); Rick Wood/MCT/Landov (p. 426); AP Photo/Tom DiPace (p. 428).

Laurie Santos/Photos: Photo by Lee Kibbie/Courtesy, Laurie Santos (p. 431); Courtesy, Laurie Santos (p. 433); Photo by Lee Kibbie/Courtesy, Laurie Santos (p. 435); Photo by Neha Mahajan/Courtesy, Laurie Santos (p. 438).

Ryan Sheckler/Photos: Mike Coppola/FilmMagic (p. 441); Jason Merritt/WireImage (p. 444); Kevin Novak/CSM/Landov (p. 446); TV still/DVD: LIFE OF RYAN: The Complete Series © 2009 MTV. All Rights Reserved. (p. 448); Bo Bridges/Getty Images (p. 450).

Esperanza Spalding/Photos: Photo by Sandrine Lee/Montuno Productions. Courtesy, Heads Up International Records/Concord Music Group (p. 455); Phil Farnsworth/ Splash News/Newscom (p. 457); Photo by Johann Sauty. Courtesy, Heads Up International Records/Concord Music Group (p. 460); CD cover: CHAMBER MUSIC SOCIETY © 2010 Heads Up International Records/Concord Music Group. Photo by Sandrine Lee/Montuno Productions (p. 463); Photo by Johann Sauty. Courtesy, Heads Up International Records/Concord Music Group (p. 465).

Mark Zuckerberg/Photos: AP Photo/Jeff Chiu (p. 467); © Prill Mediendesign & Fotografie via iStockphoto.com (p. 471); William B. Plowman/Getty Images (p. 472); Karen T. Borchers/MCT/Landov (p. 474); Gilles Mingasson/Getty Images (p. 477); Movie: THE SOCIAL NETWORK © Sony Pictures Publicity. Photo by Merrick Morton (p. 479, top, middle and bottom); AP Photo/Tony Avelar (p. 481).

Cumulative General Index

This cumulative index includes names, occupations, nationalities, and ethnic and minority origins that pertain to all individuals profiled in *Biography Today* since the debut of the series in 1992.

Places of Birth Index

The following index lists the places of birth for the individuals profiled in *Biography Today.* Places of birth are entered under state, province, and/or country.

Birthday Index

January		Year
1	Salinger, J.D.	1919
2	Asimov, Isaac	1920
	Cox, Lynne	1957
3	Dawson, Matel Jr.	1921
	Fuller, Millard	1935
	Manning, Eli	1981
	Tolkien, J.R.R.	1892
4	Naylor, Phyllis Reynolds	1933
	Runyan, Marla	1969
	Shula, Don	1930
5	Ocampo, Adriana C.	1955
6	Van Draanen, Wendelin	?
7	Hurston, Zora Neale	?1891
	Rodriguez, Eloy	1947
	Soriano, Alfonso	1978
8	Castellano, Torry (Donna C.)	1979
	Cooper, Floyd	1956
	Ford, Maya (Donna F.)	1979
	Hawking, Stephen W.	1942
	Spelman, Lucy	1963
9	Dobrev, Nina	1989
	Garcia, Sergio	1980
	Graves, Earl	1935
	McLean, A.J	1978
	Menchu, Rigoberta	1959
	Nixon, Richard	1913
10	Streeter, Tanya	1973
11	Leopold, Aldo	1887
12	Amanpour, Christiane	1958
	Bezos, Jeff	1964
	Capolino, Peter	1945
	Lasseter, John	?1957
	Limbaugh, Rush	1951
13	Bloom, Orlando	1977
	Burnside, Aubyn	1985
	Webb, Alan	1983
14	Bellamy, Carol	1942
	Lucid, Shannon	1943
15	Agosto, Ben	1982
	Brees, Drew	1979
	Teller, Edward	1908
	Werbach, Adam	1973
16	Aaliyah	1979
	Fossey, Dian	1932
	Hakim, Joy	1931
	Lipsyte, Robert	1938
	Pujols, Albert	1980
	Tarter, Jill	1944
17	Carrey, Jim	1962
	Cormier, Robert	1925
	Jones, James Earl	1931
	Lewis, Shari	?1934
	Obama, Michelle	1964
	Tartakovsky, Genndy	1970
	Wade, Dwyane	1982
18	Ali, Muhammad	1942
	Chavez, Julz	1962
	Messier, Mark	1961
19	Askins, Renee	1959
	Johnson, John	1918
20	Bourdon, Rob	1979
	DeMayo, Neda	1960
	Wright, Will	1960
21	Domingo, Placido	1941
	Nicklaus, Jack	1940
	Olajuwon, Hakeem	1963
22	Chavis, Benjamin	1948
	Orianthi	1985
	Ward, Lloyd D.	1949
23	Elion, Gertrude	1918
	Foudy, Julie	1971
	Thiessen, Tiffani-Amber	1974
24	Haddock, Doris (Granny D).	1910
25	Alley, Kirstie	1955
	Keys, Alicia	1981
26	Carter, Vince	1977
	Dudamel, Gustavo	1981
	Hale, Shannon	1974
	Morita, Akio	1921

January (continued)		**Year**
	Siskel, Gene	1946
	Tarbox, Katie	1982
27	Lester, Julius	1939
	Roberts, John Jr.	1955
	Teter, Hannah	1987
	Vasan, Nina	1984
28	Carter, Nick	1980
	Culpepper, Daunte	1977
	Fatone, Joey	1977
	Gretzky, Wayne	1961
	Wood, Elijah	1981
29	Abbey, Edward	1927
	Gilbert, Sara	1975
	Hasek, Dominik	1965
	Peet, Bill	1915
	Rosenberger, Grayson	1992
	Winfrey, Oprah	1954
30	Alexander, Lloyd	1924
	Cheney, Dick	1941
	Engelbart, Douglas	1925
	Horvath, Polly	1957
31	Collier, Bryan	1967
	Flannery, Sarah	1982
	Funk, Wally	1939
	Robinson, Jackie	1919
	Ryan, Nolan	1947
	Timberlake, Justin	1981

February		**Year**
1	Cabot, Meg	1967
	Hughes, Langston	1902
	Patton, Antwan	1975
	Spinelli, Jerry	1941
	Yeltsin, Boris	1931
2	Shakira	1977
3	Heimlich, Henry	1920
	Nixon, Joan Lowery	1927
	Rockwell, Norman	1894
	Sanborn, Ryne	1989
4	Parks, Rosa	1913
	Patterson, Carly	1988
5	Aaron, Hank	1934
6	Leakey, Mary	1913
	Reagan, Ronald	1911
	Rosa, Emily	1987
	Zmeskal, Kim	1976
7	Brooks, Garth	1962
	Kutcher, Ashton	1978
	Nash, Steve	1974
	Wang, An	1920
	Wilder, Laura Ingalls	1867
8	Allen, Will	1949
	Davis, Jeremy	1985
	Farrell, David	1977
	Grisham, John	1955
	Hamilton, Bethany	1990
9	Love, Susan	1948
	Whitson, Peggy	1960
10	Konigsburg, E.L.	1930
	Norman, Greg	1955
	Roberts, Emma	1991
11	Aniston, Jennifer	1969
	Brandy	1979
	Lautner, Taylor	1992
	Palin, Sarah	1964
	Rowland, Kelly	1981
	Shinoda, Mike	1977
	Yolen, Jane	1939
12	Blume, Judy	1938
	Kurzweil, Raymond	1948
	Small, David	1945
	Woodson, Jacqueline	?1964
13	GrandPré, Mary	1954
	Moss, Randy	1977
	Sleator, William	1945
14	Highmore, Freddie	1992
	McNair, Steve	1973
15	Groening, Matt	1954
	Jagr, Jaromir	1972
	Sones, Sonya	1952
	Spiegelman, Art	1948
	Van Dyken, Amy	1973
16	Cantore, Jim	1964
	Freeman, Cathy	1973
17	Anderson, Marian	1897
	Armstrong, Billie Joe	1972
	Fiasco, Lupe	1982
	Hargreaves, Alison	1962
	Jordan, Michael	1963
18	Kenyon, Cynthia	1954
	Morrison, Toni	1931
19	Justice, Victoria	1993
	Kinney, Jeff	1971
	McNutt, Marcia	1952
	Tan, Amy	1952
20	Adams, Ansel	1902
	Barkley, Charles	1963
	Cobain, Kurt	1967
	Crawford, Cindy	1966

June (continued) **Year**

Daly, Carson 1973
Warner, Kurt 1971
23 Clemons, Kortney 1980
Memmel, Chellsie 1988
Rudolph, Wilma 1940
Sotomayor, Sonia 1954
Thomas, Clarence 1948
Tomlinson, LaDainian 1979
24 Lasky, Kathryn 1944
Mulanovich, Sofia 1983
25 Carle, Eric 1929
Gibbs, Lois 1951
26 Ammann, Simon 1981
Harris, Bernard 1956
Jeter, Derek 1974
LeMond, Greg 1961
Vick, Michael 1980
Wilson, Gretchen 1973
27 Babbitt, Bruce 1938
Bell, Drake 1986
Dunbar, Paul Laurence 1872
Perot, H. Ross 1930
28 Elway, John 1960
Yunus, Muhammad 1940
29 Basich, Tina 1969
Jiménez, Francisco 1943
Kopp, Wendy 1967
30 Ballard, Robert 1942
Phelps, Michael 1985

July **Year**

1 Brower, David 1912
Calderone, Mary S. 1904
Diana, Princess of Wales 1961
Duke, David 1950
Elliott, Missy 1971
Lewis, Carl 1961
McCully, Emily Arnold 1939
Tharp, Twyla 1941
2 Bethe, Hans A. 1906
Branch, Michelle 1983
Fox, Vicente 1942
Gantos, Jack 1951
George, Jean Craighead 1919
Kadohata, Cynthia 1956
Lohan, Lindsay 1986
Lynch, Chris 1962
Marshall, Thurgood 1908
McGrath, Judy 1952
Petty, Richard 1937
Thomas, Dave 1932
Tisdale, Ashley 1985
3 Simmons, Ruth 1945
5 Haywood, Dave 1982
Watterson, Bill 1958
6 Bush, George W. 1946
Dalai Lama 1935
Dumitriu, Ioana 1976
7 Chagall, Marc 1887
Heinlein, Robert 1907
Kwan, Michelle 1980
Leslie, Lisa 1972
Otto, Sylke 1969
Sakic, Joe 1969
Stachowski, Richie 1985
8 Bush, Sophia 1982
Hardaway, Anfernee "Penny" 1971
Keith, Toby 1961
Kübler-Ross, Elisabeth 1926
MacArthur, Ellen 1976
Sealfon, Rebecca 1983
9 Farmer, Nancy 1941
Hanks, Tom 1956
Hassan II 1929
Krim, Mathilde 1926
Lee, Jeanette 1971
Rodriguez, Gloria 1948
Sacks, Oliver 1933
10 Ashe, Arthur 1943
Benson, Mildred 1905
Boulmerka, Hassiba 1969
11 Belbin, Tanith 1984
Cisneros, Henry 1947
Hrdy, Sarah Blaffer 1946
White, E.B. 1899
12 Bauer, Joan 1951
Cosby, Bill 1937
Johnson, Johanna 1983
Yamaguchi, Kristi 1972
13 Ford, Harrison 1942
Stewart, Patrick 1940
14 Taboo 1975
15 Aristide, Jean-Bertrand 1953
Ventura, Jesse 1951
16 Ferrell, Will 1967
Johnson, Jimmy 1943
Sanders, Barry 1968
17 An Na 1972
Stepanek, Mattie 1990

July (continued)

		Year
18	Bell, Kristen	1980
	Diesel, Vin	1967
	Glenn, John	1921
	Lemelson, Jerome	1923
	Mandela, Nelson	1918
19	Glennie, Evelyn	1965
	Kratt, Chris	1969
	Tarvin, Herbert	1985
20	Hillary, Sir Edmund	1919
	Santana, Carlos	1947
21	Catchings, Tamika	1979
	Chastain, Brandi	1968
	Hartnett, Josh	1978
	Lozano, Monica	1956
	Reno, Janet	1938
	Riley, Dawn	1964
	Stern, Isaac	1920
	Williams, Robin	1952
22	Calder, Alexander	1898
	Dole, Bob	1923
	Gomez, Selena	1992
	Hinton, S.E.	1948
	Johnson, Keyshawn	1972
23	Haile Selassie	1892
	Krauss, Alison	1971
	Williams, Michelle	1980
24	Abzug, Bella	1920
	Bonds, Barry	1964
	Irwin, Bindi	1998
	Krone, Julie	1963
	Lopez, Jennifer	1970
	Moss, Cynthia	1940
	Wilson, Mara	1987
25	Goldsworthy, Andy	1956
	Payton, Walter	1954
26	Berenstain, Jan	1923
	Clark, Kelly	1983
27	Dunlap, Alison	1969
	Kimball, Cheyenne	1990
	Rodriguez, Alex	1975
28	Babbitt, Natalie	1932
	Davis, Jim	1945
	Potter, Beatrix	1866
29	Burns, Ken	1953
	Creech, Sharon	1945
	Dole, Elizabeth Hanford	1936
	Hayes, Tyrone	1967
	Jennings, Peter	1938
	Morris, Wanya	1973
30	Allen, Tori	1988
	Hill, Anita	1956
	Moore, Henry	1898
	Norman, Christina	1963
	Schroeder, Pat	1940
31	Cronin, John	1950
	Kwolek, Stephanie	1923
	Radcliffe, Daniel	1989
	Reid Banks, Lynne	1929
	Rowling, J.K.	1965
	Weinke, Chris	1972

August

		Year
1	Brown, Ron	1941
	Coolio	1963
	Garcia, Jerry	1942
2	Asbaty, Diandra	1980
	Baldwin, James	1924
	Healy, Bernadine	1944
	Howe, James	1946
3	Brady, Tom	1977
	Roper, Dee Dee	?
	Savimbi, Jonas	1934
	Stewart, Martha	1941
4	Gordon, Jeff	1971
	Obama, Barack	1961
	Whitman, Meg	1956
5	Córdova, France	1947
	Creamer, Paula	1986
	Ewing, Patrick	1962
	Jackson, Shirley Ann	1946
6	Carter, Regina	?1963
	Cooney, Barbara	1917
	Robinson, David	1965
	Warhol, Andy	?1928
7	Byars, Betsy	1928
	Crosby, Sidney	1987
	Duchovny, David	1960
	Leakey, Louis	1903
	Villa-Komaroff, Lydia	1947
8	Boyd, Candy Dawson	1946
	Chasez, JC	1976
	Federer, Roger	1981
9	Anderson, Gillian	1968
	Holdsclaw, Chamique	1977
	Houston, Whitney	1963
	McKissack, Patricia C..	1944
	Sanders, Deion	1967
	Travers, P.L.	?1899
10	Hayden, Carla	1952

1992

Paula Abdul
Andre Agassi
Kirstie Alley
Terry Anderson
Roseanne Arnold
Isaac Asimov
James Baker
Charles Barkley
Larry Bird
Judy Blume
Berke Breathed
Garth Brooks
Barbara Bush
George Bush
Fidel Castro
Bill Clinton
Bill Cosby
Diana, Princess of Wales
Shannen Doherty
Elizabeth Dole
David Duke
Gloria Estefan
Mikhail Gorbachev
Steffi Graf
Wayne Gretzky
Matt Groening
Alex Haley
Hammer
Martin Handford
Stephen Hawking
Hulk Hogan
Saddam Hussein
Lee Iacocca
Bo Jackson
Mae Jemison
Peter Jennings
Steven Jobs
John Paul II
Magic Johnson
Michael Jordon
Jackie Joyner-Kersee
Spike Lee
Mario Lemieux
Madeleine L'Engle
Jay Leno
Yo-Yo Ma
Nelson Mandela
Wynton Marsalis
Thurgood Marshall
Ann Martin
Barbara McClintock
Emily Arnold McCully
Antonia Novello
Sandra Day O'Connor
Rosa Parks
Jane Pauley
H. Ross Perot
Luke Perry
Scottie Pippen
Colin Powell
Jason Priestley
Queen Latifah
Yitzhak Rabin
Sally Ride
Pete Rose
Nolan Ryan
H. Norman Schwarzkopf
Jerry Seinfeld
Dr. Seuss
Gloria Steinem
Clarence Thomas
Chris Van Allsburg
Cynthia Voigt
Bill Watterson
Robin Williams
Oprah Winfrey
Kristi Yamaguchi
Boris Yeltsin

1993

Maya Angelou
Arthur Ashe
Avi
Kathleen Battle
Candice Bergen
Boutros Boutros-Ghali
Chris Burke
Dana Carvey
Cesar Chavez
Henry Cisneros
Hillary Rodham Clinton
Jacques Cousteau
Cindy Crawford
Macaulay Culkin
Lois Duncan
Marian Wright Edelman
Cecil Fielder
Bill Gates
Sara Gilbert
Dizzy Gillespie
Al Gore
Cathy Guisewite
Jasmine Guy
Anita Hill
Ice-T
Darci Kistler
k.d. lang
Dan Marino
Rigoberta Menchu
Walter Dean Myers
Martina Navratilova
Phyllis Reynolds Naylor
Rudolf Nureyev
Shaquille O'Neal
Janet Reno
Jerry Rice
Mary Robinson
Winona Ryder
Jerry Spinelli
Denzel Washington
Keenen Ivory Wayans
Dave Winfield

1994

Tim Allen
Marian Anderson
Mario Andretti
Ned Andrews
Yasir Arafat
Bruce Babbitt
Mayim Bialik
Bonnie Blair
Ed Bradley
John Candy
Mary Chapin Carpenter
Benjamin Chavis
Connie Chung
Beverly Cleary
Kurt Cobain
F.W. de Klerk
Rita Dove
Linda Ellerbee
Sergei Fedorov
Zlata Filipovic
Daisy Fuentes
Ruth Bader Ginsburg
Whoopi Goldberg
Tonya Harding
Melissa Joan Hart
Geoff Hooper
Whitney Houston
Dan Jansen
Nancy Kerrigan
Alexi Lalas
Charlotte Lopez
Wilma Mankiller
Shannon Miller
Toni Morrison
Richard Nixon
Greg Norman
Severo Ochoa
River Phoenix
Elizabeth Pine
Jonas Salk
Richard Scarry
Emmitt Smith
Will Smith
Steven Spielberg
Patrick Stewart
R.L. Stine
Lewis Thomas
Barbara Walters
Charlie Ward
Steve Young
Kim Zmeskal

1995

Troy Aikman
Jean-Bertrand Aristide
Oksana Baiul
Halle Berry
Benazir Bhutto
Jonathan Brandis
Warren E. Burger
Ken Burns
Candace Cameron
Jimmy Carter
Agnes de Mille
Placido Domingo
Janet Evans
Patrick Ewing
Newt Gingrich
John Goodman
Amy Grant
Jesse Jackson
James Earl Jones
Julie Krone
David Letterman
Rush Limbaugh
Heather Locklear
Reba McEntire
Joe Montana
Cosmas Ndeti
Hakeem Olajuwon
Ashley Olsen
Mary Kate Olsen
Jennifer Parkinson
Linus Pauling
Itzhak Perlman
Cokie Roberts
Wilma Rudolph
Salt 'N' Pepa
Barry Sanders
William Shatner

Elizabeth George Speare
Dr. Benjamin Spock
Jonathan Taylor Thomas
Vicki Van Meter
Heather Whitestone
Pedro Zamora

1996

Aung San Suu Kyi
Boyz II Men
Brandy
Ron Brown
Mariah Carey
Jim Carrey
Larry Champagne III
Christo
Chelsea Clinton
Coolio
Bob Dole
David Duchovny
Debbi Fields
Chris Galeczka
Jerry Garcia
Jennie Garth
Wendy Guey
Tom Hanks
Alison Hargreaves
Sir Edmund Hillary
Judith Jamison
Barbara Jordan
Annie Leibovitz
Carl Lewis
Jim Lovell
Mickey Mantle
Lynn Margulis
Iqbal Masih
Mark Messier
Larisa Oleynik
Christopher Pike
David Robinson
Dennis Rodman
Selena
Monica Seles
Don Shula
Kerri Strug
Tiffani-Amber Thiessen
Dave Thomas
Jaleel White

1997

Madeleine Albright
Marcus Allen
Gillian Anderson
Rachel Blanchard
Zachery Ty Bryan
Adam Ezra Cohen
Claire Danes
Celine Dion
Jean Driscoll
Louis Farrakhan
Ella Fitzgerald
Harrison Ford
Bryant Gumbel
John Johnson
Michael Johnson
Maya Lin
George Lucas
John Madden
Bill Monroe
Alanis Morissette
Sam Morrison
Rosie O'Donnell
Muammar el-Qaddafi
Christopher Reeve
Pete Sampras
Pat Schroeder
Rebecca Sealfon
Tupac Shakur
Tabitha Soren
Herbert Tarvin
Merlin Tuttle
Mara Wilson

1998

Bella Abzug
Kofi Annan
Neve Campbell
Sean Combs (Puff Daddy)
Dalai Lama (Tenzin Gyatso)
Diana, Princess of Wales
Leonardo DiCaprio
Walter E. Diemer
Ruth Handler
Hanson
Livan Hernandez
Jewel
Jimmy Johnson
Tara Lipinski
Jody-Anne Maxwell
Dominique Moceanu
Alexandra Nechita
Brad Pitt
LeAnn Rimes
Emily Rosa
David Satcher
Betty Shabazz
Kordell Stewart
Shinichi Suzuki
Mother Teresa
Mike Vernon
Reggie White
Kate Winslet

1999

Ben Affleck
Jennifer Aniston
Maurice Ashley
Kobe Bryant
Bessie Delany
Sadie Delany
Sharon Draper
Sarah Michelle Gellar
John Glenn
Savion Glover
Jeff Gordon
David Hampton
Lauryn Hill
King Hussein
Lynn Johnston
Shari Lewis
Oseola McCarty
Mark McGwire
Slobodan Milosevic
Natalie Portman
J.K. Rowling
Frank Sinatra
Gene Siskel
Sammy Sosa
John Stanford
Natalia Toro
Shania Twain
Mitsuko Uchida
Jesse Ventura
Venus Williams

2000

Christina Aguilera
K.A. Applegate
Lance Armstrong
Backstreet Boys
Daisy Bates
Harry Blackmun
George W. Bush
Carson Daly
Ron Dayne
Henry Louis Gates, Jr.
Doris Haddock (Granny D)
Jennifer Love Hewitt
Chamique Holdsclaw
Katie Holmes
Charlayne Hunter-Gault
Johanna Johnson
Craig Kielburger
John Lasseter
Peyton Manning
Ricky Martin
John McCain
Walter Payton
Freddie Prinze Jr.
Viviana Risca
Briana Scurry
George Thampy
CeCe Winans

2001

Jessica Alba
Christiane Amanpour
Drew Barrymore
Jeff Bezos
Destiny's Child
Dale Earnhardt
Carly Fiorina
Aretha Franklin
Cathy Freeman
Tony Hawk
Faith Hill
Kim Dae-jung
Madeleine L'Engle
Mariangela Lisanti
Frankie Muniz
*N Sync
Ellen Ochoa
Jeff Probst
Julia Roberts
Carl T. Rowan
Britney Spears
Chris Tucker
Lloyd D. Ward
Alan Webb
Chris Weinke

2002

Aaliyah
Osama bin Laden
Mary J. Blige
Aubyn Burnside
Aaron Carter
Julz Chavez
Dick Cheney
Hilary Duff

Billy Gilman
Rudolph Giuliani
Brian Griese
Jennifer Lopez
Dave Mirra
Dineh Mohajer
Leanne Nakamura
Daniel Radcliffe
Condoleezza Rice
Marla Runyan
Ruth Simmons
Mattie Stepanek
J.R.R. Tolkien
Barry Watson
Tyrone Willingham
Elijah Wood

2003

Yolanda Adams
Olivia Bennett
Mildred Benson
Alexis Bledel
Barry Bonds
Vincent Brooks
Laura Bush
Amanda Bynes
Kelly Clarkson
Vin Diesel
Eminem
Michele Forman
Vicente Fox
Millard Fuller
Josh Hartnett
Dolores Huerta
Sarah Hughes
Enrique Iglesias
Jeanette Lee
John Lewis
Nicklas Lidstrom
Clint Mathis
Donovan McNabb
Nelly
Andy Roddick
Gwen Stefani
Emma Watson
Meg Whitman
Reese Witherspoon
Yao Ming

2004

Natalie Babbitt
David Beckham
Francie Berger
Tony Blair
Orlando Bloom
Kim Clijsters
Celia Cruz
Matel Dawson Jr.
The Donnas
Tim Duncan
Shirin Ebadi
Carla Hayden
Ashton Kutcher
Lisa Leslie
Linkin Park
Lindsay Lohan
Irene D. Long
John Mayer
Mandy Moore
Thich Nhat Hanh
OutKast
Raven
Ronald Reagan
Keanu Reeves
Ricardo Sanchez
Brian Urlacher
Alexa Vega
Michelle Wie
Will Wright

2005

Kristen Bell
Jack Black
Sergey Brin & Larry Page
Adam Brody
Chris Carrabba
Johnny Depp
Eve
Jennie Finch
James Forman
Wally Funk
Cornelia Funke
Bethany Hamilton
Anne Hathaway
Priest Holmes
T.D. Jakes
John Paul II
Toby Keith
Alison Krauss
Wangari Maathai
Karen Mitchell-Raptakis
Queen Noor
Violet Palmer
Gloria Rodriguez
Carlos Santana
Antonin Scalia
Curtis Schilling
Maria Sharapova
Ashlee Simpson
Donald Trump
Ben Wallace

2006

Carol Bellamy
Miri Ben-Ari
Black Eyed Peas
Bono
Kelsie Buckley
Dale Chihuly
Neda DeMayo
Dakota Fanning
Green Day
Freddie Highmore
Russel Honoré
Tim Howard
Cynthia Kadohata
Coretta Scott King
Rachel McAdams
Cesar Millan
Steve Nash
Nick Park
Rosa Parks
Danica Patrick
Jorge Ramos
Ben Roethlisberger
Lil' Romeo
Adam Sandler
Russell Simmons
Jamie Lynn Spears
Jon Stewart
Joss Stone
Hannah Teter
Brenda Villa
Tyler James Williams
Gretchen Wilson

2007

Shaun Alexander
Carmelo Anthony
Drake Bell
Chris Brown
Regina Carter
Kortney Clemons
Taylor Crabtree
Miley Cyrus
Aaron Dworkin
Fall Out Boy
Roger Federer
Will Ferrell
America Ferrera
June Foray
Sarah Blaffer Hrdy
Alicia Keys
Cheyenne Kimball
Keira Knightley
Wendy Kopp
Sofia Mulanovich
Barack Obama
Soledad O'Brien
Jamie Oliver
Skip Palenik
Nancy Pelosi
Jack Prelutsky
Ivan "Pudge" Rodriguez
Michael Sessions
Kate Spade
Sabriye Tenberken
Rob Thomas
Ashley Tisdale
Carrie Underwood
Muhammad Yunus

2008

Aly & AJ
Bill Bass
Greta Binford
Cory Booker
Sophia Bush
Majora Carter
Anderson Cooper
Zac Efron
Selena Gomez
Al Gore
Vanessa Hudgens
Jennifer Hudson
Zach Hunter
Bindi Irwin
Jonas Brothers
Lisa Ling
Eli Manning
Kimmie Meissner
Scott Niedermayer
Christina Norman
Masi Oka
Tyler Perry
Morgan Pressel
Rihanna
John Roberts Jr.
J. K. Rowling
James Stewart Jr.
Ichiro Suzuki
Karen P. Tandy
Marta Tienda
Justin Timberlake
Lee Wardlaw

2009

Elizabeth Alexander
Will Allen
Judy Baca
Joe Biden
Cynthia Breazeal
Michael Cera
Miranda Cosgrove
Lupe Fiasco
James Harrison
Jimmie Johnson
Heidi Klum
Lang Lang
Leona Lewis
Nastia Liukin
Demi Lovato
Jef Mallett
Warith Deen Mohammed
Walter Dean Myers
Michelle Obama
Omarion
Suze Orman
Kenny Ortega
Robert Pattinson
Chris Paul
Michael Phelps
Rachael Ray
Emma Roberts
Robin Roberts
Grayson Rosenberger
Dinara Safina
Gloria Gilbert Stoga
Taylor Swift
Shailene Woodley

2010

Beyoncé
Justin Bieber
Charles Bolden
Drew Brees
Ursula M. Burns
Robin Chase
Hillary Rodham Clinton
Gustavo Dudamel
Eran Egozy & Alex Rigopulos
Neil Gaiman
Tavi Gevinson
Hugh Jackman
Jesse James
LeBron James
Taylor Lautner
Chuck Liddell
Mary Mary
Christianne Meneses Jacobs
Melinda Merck
Stephenie Meyer
Orianthi
Alexander Ovechkin
Brad Paisley
Keke Palmer
Paramore
Candace Parker
David Protess
Albert Pujols
Zoë Saldana
Sonia Sotomayor
Caroll Spinney
Kristen Stewart

2011

Bolt, Usain
Bosh, Chris
Bullard, Robert
Chu, Steven
Colfer, Chris
Collins, Suzanne
Creamer, Paula
Cruikshank, Lucas
Derülo, Jason
Dobrev, Nina
Goldsworthy, Andy
Jay-Z
Jolie, Angelina
Justice, Victoria
Kagan, Elena
Kinney, Jeff
Lady Antebellum
Lambert, Miranda
Liu Xiaobo
Lozano, Monica
Lubchenco, Jane
Lupica, Mike
Martinet, Charles
Mendler, Bridgit
Michele, Lea
Monáe, Janelle
Oudin, Melanie
Palin, Sarah
Rodgers, Aaron
Santos, Laurie
Sheckler, Ryan
Spalding, Esperanza
Zuckerberg, Mark